GENERAL ALLENBY, THE CONQUEROR OF PALESTINE AND SYRIA

VIII.

THE LITERARY DIGEST
History of the World War

Compiled from Original and Contemporary Sources: American, British, French, German, and Others

BY

FRANCIS WHITING HALSEY

Author of "The Old New York Frontier," Editor of "Great Epochs in American History," "Seeing Europe with Famous Authors," "Balfour, Viviani, and Joffre, Their Speeches in America," etc.

IN TEN VOLUMES—ILLUSTRATED

VOLUME VIII

THE WAR AGAINST TURKEY IN THE CAUCASUS, EGYPT, PALESTINE, THE
DARDANELLES AND GALLIPOLI, ARABIA AND MESOPOTAMIA—
SERBIA'S TRAGIC DEFEAT, ROUMANIA OVERRUN AND
THE FINAL VICTORY OF THE ENTENTE
UNDER D'ESPEREY

August 1, 1914—October, 1918

FUNK & WAGNALLS COMPANY

NEW YORK AND LONDON

1919

CONTENTS—VOLUME EIGHT

IN THE EAST, NEAR EAST, AND SOUTH—*Continued*

PART V. THE WAR AGAINST TURKEY

CONTENTS—VOLUME EIGHT

PART VI. THE BALKANS AND GREECE IN THE WAR

ILLUSTRATIONS—VOLUME EIGHT

FULL PAGES

ILLUSTRATIONS—VOLUME EIGHT

TEXT ILLUSTRATIONS

ILLUSTRATIONS—VOLUME EIGHT

ILLUSTRATIONS—VOLUME EIGHT

MAPS

IN THE EAST, NEAR EAST AND SOUTH

Part V

THE WAR AGAINST TURKEY

WILLIAM II IN THE UNIFORM OF A TURKISH FIELD-MARSHAL

2

TURKEY AS GERMANY'S ALLY—THE BAGDAD RAILWAY AS GERMANY'S ROAD TO INDIA

HAD not the Turk dug his own grave and committed suicide?—this was the burden of most comments after Turkey forced the Allies to declare a state of war with her. For several years Turkey had been in extreme peril; the "Sick Man of Europe" had, so to say, been kept alive by his friends, the doctors, altho they deemed his malady incurable. Except for the protection Germany gave her, the political existence of Turkey in Europe probably would have ceased after the Balkan wars in 1913. For this reason the Turk had voted to stand or fall, according as the war resulted in favor of or against Germany. His entrance into the great conflict had long been foreseen. Some trained observers went much further—for example, Sir Harry Johnston, the traveler, statesman, and diplomat, who had declared at the beginning of the conflict that Constantinople was "the core of the war."

The plans of Germany for years had meant the creation of a confederation of European and West Asiatic States, starting at the North Sea and going to the Persian Gulf, and including within its boundaries Holland, Belgium, Denmark, Germany, Austria, the Balkans, Turkey, and Persia. Great overland roads from central and northern Europe to the Persian Gulf would thus have been controlled by Germany. As far east as Constantinople, the completed railways already existed. The completion of another line from Constantinople to Bagdad and the Gulf would not only have thrown open to European capital Asia Minor and the great plain of Mesopotamia, but would have furnished a commercial road to the East through which in time would flow a trade making the great confederation rich, and of this confederation Turkey would have been an integral and essential part. Adrianople, the key to the Balkans; Saloniki, the key to the Aegean; Constantinople, controlling the outlet of the Black Sea and the land approaches of Europe to the Tigris and Euphrates valleys—all these an alliance with the Turk would have given to Germany. The stronger the Turkish State became, the better organized and the larger its army and fleet and the greater its resources, the more useful it would have been to Germany, and the more thoroughly would it have insured the success of Pan-Germanism.

English and French control of Turkey through a long period had been fortuitous and artificial; it depended solely on a little group of men in Constantinople. German influence in Turkey, on the contrary, had acquired deep and fundamental roots in a large and significant part of the Turkish population, and had appealed to their highest impulses. Enlightened Turks honestly believed they saw in Pan-Germanism a democratic Turkey with constitutional self-government, a Turkey developing its own resources, gradually freeing itself from the fetters of European alliances and becoming strong enough to take its place in the Pan-Germanic chain of states. On the other hand, they saw in the defeat of Pan-Germanism political and national death, the annexation of Turkey by its enemies, and its subjection to the rule of the Infidel.

For more than a century Russia had been the hereditary enemy of Turkey. Russian aggression had swept away all ancient Turkish possessions east of the Pruth and north of the Black Sea, while Russia's support of the Serb and Bulgar had resulted in driving Turkish rule from the Danube to the Bosporus. Even there the Russian advance had halted rather than terminated, for Constantinople still remained the goal of Romanoff ambition. To plant the cross over Saint Sophia was the dream of Nicholas II in the twentieth century, as it had been that of Peter the Great in the eighteenth. Twice when Russia's soldiers were almost within sight of Constantinople, British intervention had prevented its capture. The Crimean War of 1854-56 and the arrival of British warships after the Treaty of San Stefano in 1878—these were the checks that had twice held back the Czar. But now the British were allied with the Russians, and so the chance that Great Britain, in her hour of triumph, would oppose Russia's ancient ambition was slight.

If Russia were the immediate enemy of Turkey, Great Britain and France had become only less definitely so. Formal British occupation of Egypt after the war began had already deprived the Turk of his finest province, and France, by acquiring Algeria, Tunis, and Morocco had further weakened Moslem power. To save Stamboul, to regain Egypt, Tunis, Algeria and Tripoli, to restore the ancient Mediterranean Empire of Mohammed, this had long been a vital part of the dream of every Turkish patriot. For the Turk, it was clear in 1914 that the final hour had come. If defeated, he must quit Europe and go back to his earlier home in Anatolia, lose Arabia, Syria, and the valley of the Euphrates, and surrender his half of Armenia. Even his primacy in the religious hierarchy of Islam might be lost.

It was not until Germany acquired a paramount position on the European continent that she heard "the East a'calling," and it was then her professors who led the way. Dr. Sorenger, a distinguished Orientalist, cited Mesopotamia, the richest land of ancient times, as a fit field for German colonization. Economists pointed out vast natural resources that only waited to be developed for German commerce and industry—corn and wine, mineral deposits, oil-fields extending to the Persian Gulf, and fertile plains which would yield all the cotton required for the German market.

Field-marshal von der Goltz was an early advocate of a forward German policy in Turkey—and was sent to Constantinople. To him the Golden Horn city seemed a bridge over which Germany could pass from Europe into Asia, there to find a field of adventure reaching to the Persian Gulf. Turkey became overrun with German manufacturers, engineers and capitalists. In 1888 the Deutsche Bank obtained the right to work a short railway from the Bosporus along the sea of Marmora—a right that originally had been given to an English company. To this was added an extension line to Angora, which, after the Emperor's first visit, was pushed on with energy, and soon developed into a German monopoly of railway enterprise in Asiatic Turkey. German trade increased by leaps and bounds. Imports and exports were multiplied four fold within a decade. At Constantinople

German influence became paramount. When other powers, and notably England, tried to curb Turkish misrule, Germany was ready to deprecate any interference with the sovereignty of the Sultan.

In the autumn of 1898 William II, accompanied by the Empress, made a visit to Turkey, followed by a progress through Palestine and Syria. The Emperor entered Jerusalem as a Knight Templar, and appeared at shrines of the Christian faith, as the protector of Christendom. At Damascus he proclaimed himself the protector of Pan-Islamism, and defined what was to be henceforth the position of Germany not merely toward Turkey, but toward Turkey and Islam. Germany publicly recognized the Sultan's title as Calif, and so endorsed the greatest of his ambitions while exploitation of the Ottoman Empire went on. Within the next twelve months a convention was signed between Dr. Siemens, director of the Deutsche Bank, and the Sublime Porte, conceding in principle to the German Anatolian Railway Company the right to be extended down to the Persian Gulf. A commission of German engineers, headed by the German Consul-General, and including a German military attaché at Constantinople, was sent out to report on the route, while a German cruiser visited the Persian Gulf in order to discover a suitable terminus.

The railways of European Turkey had already passed under control of the Deutsche Bank group. The new concession promised an early fulfilment of the great Pan-Germanic scheme, already known in Berlin as the B. B. B. (Berlin-Byzantium-Bagdad Railroad). Not the least of its features was a kilometric guaranty for the whole trunk line from Constantinople to the Persian Gulf, and its numerous feeders by which Germany would receive the profits from a long succession of lucrative financial operations. The final convention for the railway was signed, sealed and delivered in 1902. Excepting the Manchurian Railway concession, which Russia had secured some years previously from China, it was probably the most remarkable charter ever granted by one independent State to another.

Most writers on remote causes of the war in Europe have emphasized the Bagdad Railway concession. By this road

Constantinople would be connected, not only with the Gulf of Persia, but by a southern branch line, with Egypt. Originally it was believed in England that the enterprise was a private one, but more recently it had come to be regarded as distinctly a Prussian State undertaking. The meaning of the concession, in economic and military advantages to Germany, and its meaning to the future of Asiatic Turkey, and especially to the valley of the Euphrates,

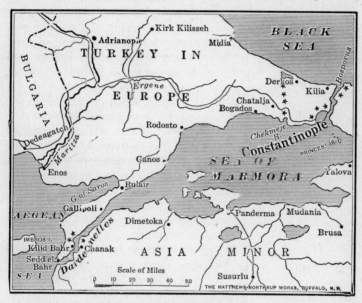

THE ENVIRONS OF CONSTANTINOPLE AND GALLIPOLI

if not to the Nile valley, was well understood in European capitals.

With the line completed, a bird's-eye view would have shown a railway from a point opposite Constantinople running across the Turkish Empire in Asia to the River Tigris, and thence southerly to the Persian Gulf, which is the back door to India. Back on the main line, a second line would have been seen branching from the first and pointing southward through Syria, parallel to the eastern coast of the Mediterranean and bringing up near the frontier of Egypt.

Looked at through English, French or Russian eyes, the concession was a grave menace. But to Germany it was a necessary prerequisite to Pan-Germanic expansion. The mileage of the road when completed was estimated at 1,300, of which 538 miles had been built in October, 1914, leaving 800 miles yet to be constructed.

German engineers, as long ago as 1875, had been authorized to build for the Turkish Government a short railroad from Haidar Pasha, opposite Constantinople, to Ismidt, which was dignified with the name of the "Anatolian Railway," Anatolia being practically synonymous with Asia Minor. Thirteen years after this a German company, whose "angel" was the Deutsche Bank, acquired the privilege of exploiting this line, and it was extended into northern Anatolia as far east as Angora, in the province of that name south of the Black Sea. Had this line been extended farther east, paralleling the Russian border, it would have proved of incalculable value to the Turks in their Caucasian campaign against Russia in the World War. In 1896 an extension from Ismidt was projected southeasterly to Konia in the Turkish province of Adana, which borders on the Mediterranean, a province which Mahemet Ali once said was worth more than all Egypt. Good cotton is now produced on the Cicilian plains. Twenty-three years after the building of the first section of the railway, or in 1898, when the German Kaiser visited Constantinople, he proclaimed himself Abdul's "only friend in Europe." Abdul then gave him a concession for the construction of the railway to connect Constantinople with the Persian Gulf by the way of Bagdad, which was turned over to a German syndicate. Such was the beginning of the Bagdad Railway proper, which was to become one of several indirect causes of a war-drama whose stage was to be three continents and half the population of the globe its direct or indirect participants.

The capital valuation of the road was fixt at 54,000,000 francs per section of 200 kilometers (about 130 miles). It was expected that, with branches, there would be twelve such sections. The total mileage afterward projected considerably exceeded this estimate. When the road was fully completed, the annual charge to the Turkish Government was expected to be 31,000,000 francs. About 100 miles in the interior lies Aleppo, the emporium of northern Syria, for centuries the receiving and distributing point for the export and import trade of Alexandretta, situated in the midst of a rich agricultural district and the center of manufactures of carpets and rugs, cotton and wool, silk and leather goods. The Bagdad road runs southeast from Konia through the Taurus Mountains, and connects with Aleppo. A branch line connects that city with Alexandretta, thus bringing the railway to the open sea. After the Aleppo connection the line turns northeast and crosses northern Syria. Bridging the Euphrates, it then runs almost directly east to the City of Mosul, on the Tigris, in Mesopotamia. Here, too, is a land where cotton can be produced. Three hundred miles south of Mosul is Bagdad, formerly the seat of the Saracenic califate, around which clusters much romance.

It was believed in November, 1916, that an important tunnel on this line, running through the Taurus range, had at last been completed. In piercing the Taurus range, one of the greatest obstacles in the path of the road was eliminated. It brought the Germans into nearer touch with Persia and Armenia through the already existing railhead at Nisibin and with Egypt through the Medina Railway, with branches at Aleppo. In the first year of the war Turkish motor-service had counteracted the handicap of a break in the line in the Taurus. From 15,000 to 20,000 Turkish peasants had been employed in completely rebuilding an old mountain road famous since the days of the Phenicians. Roads had also been laid or improved in other parts. There had been several gaps in the Bagdad Railway. The first was at the Taurus range, where the tunnel was roughly 20 miles long, and extended from Karapunar some 13 miles south of Bozanti (645 miles from Haidar Pasha) as far as Doirak. Between Nisibin and Jibbara, where it connected by rail with Bagdad, was another gap of some 250 miles.

In the completion of this railway the world was to witness the reopening of the bridge from Europe to Asia for Western control, through a great railway covering nearly 2,000 miles from a point opposite Constantinople. That project, well under way at the outbreak of the war, ranked in its historical background as one of the most momentous enterprises of our age—more momentous than the opening of the Suez or the Panama Canal. A railway from Constantinople to Bagdad under European control was a symptom of the dissolution of the Turkish Empire which had become

a mere shadow of its former self and a token of the invasion of the East by Western enterprise. Passing over a highway on which armies had marched from the earliest days of which any records have survived, it was a link connecting the present with the more distant past.

Turkey had for years been virtually a member of the Triple Alliance. If not a very active or effective partner, she had in her sympathies been much more real as an ally of Germany and Austria than had Italy, the third actual member of the Alliance. At times diplomatic difficulties arose, as from 1911 to 1912, when Turkey was at war with

GEN. LIMAN VON SANDERS
German commander of the Turkish Army during the war, who fled to Constantinople when General Allenby was advancing from Damascus to Aleppo

Italy, and again during the Young Turk Revolution of 1908, when Austria declared the annexation of Bosnia and Herzegovina, but with Germany herself, since the advent of William II to the throne, Turkey had maintained increasingly intimate relations. Bismarck might have said the Eastern question "was not worth the bones of a Pomeranian grenad'er," but in this domain, as in some others, Bismarck's politics had now been discarded by Prussia. In the time of Abdul Hamid, Germany had acquired political and commercial ascendency, and was advancing her trade interests and exploiting her mineral wealth. "Peaceful penetration" was her method. With the Turk ever pecuniarily embarrassed, she found many opportunities to strengthen her hold on this country. To build and own his railways, to be his banker, to drill his soldiers, to sell him Krupp guns, to dominate his diplomacy, were the objects pursued, in a hope that one day, either by some dramatic turn of events, or gradually and almost imperceptibly, the Sultan's scepter in Asia would pass from a feeble Oriental grasp into her own strong hands.

The drama to be unfolded during this Turkish phase of the great war promised to be of the most sensational kind, because the end of the Ottoman Empire might be in sight. What was more, its heirs and successors might be other great Moslem powers—Great Britain, Russia, France, and Italy. Thus the future promised to see the British in possession of Turkey's first capital, Mosul; the French in possession of their second capital, Konia; the Russians in possession of their third and last, Constantinople, and the Italians occupying Smyrna. Each power was already a Mohammedan empire in a real sense, but the greatest Moslem country in the world was the British Empire. Moslems in India were known to favor removing the Sheik ul Islam, or the head of the Mohammedan creed, from Constantinople to Delhi or Cairo, under British protection. The Head of the Church in India had volunteered as a private soldier in France, and later was serving with the Anglo-Indian army in Mesopotamia.

In August, 1914, when the war began, two German ships, the *Goeben* and the *Breslau,* were off the Algerian coast. The *Goeben* was the fastest armored vessel in the German fleet, displacing 22,640 tons, with a speed of 28 knots, and carrying an armament ten 11-inch, twelve 5.9 inch, and twelve 21-pounder guns. The *Breslau* was a fast, light cruiser, with about the same rate of speed, and a displacement of 4,478 tons. She was the vessel which several months before had been sent by Germany to Albanian waters in order to join the international squadron which was to keep the unfortunate Mpret, William of Wied, in countenance. Both ships had great coal capacity. The *Breslau* could cover 6,000 knots without taking in fresh fuel. Both were admirably suited to act as commerce-destroyers.

In August, 1914, they fired a few shots into the Algerian coast towns of Bona and Philippeville, but did little harm, and then turned northwest, with the object, apparently, of running to Gibraltar, but were headed off by British ships. On August 5 they appeared at Messina, where their captains and officers made their wills, and deposited with the German consul their valuables, including signed portraits of the Kaiser. Decks were then cleared for action, and with bands playing "Heil, dir im Siegerkranz," they sailed out—so at least it was recorded in German papers—under a blood-red sunset. Escaping from the British, and going at full speed

THE GERMAN CRUISER "GOEBEN"

eastward, they encountered, off Cape Matapan, a British cruiser, the *Gloucester*, a ship slightly larger than the *Breslau*, which attempted to engage them, and did damage the plates of the *Goeben* and the smoke-stack of the *Breslau*. The superior speed of the German boats by the end of the week carried them to the Dardanelles, and presently they reached Constantinople, where they passed into the hands of the Turkish Government, and thereby started that disquieting of the diplomatic relations of the Porte to the Great Powers which, before many weeks, produced war with Turkey.

When the *Goeben* and *Breslau* appeared at the mouth of the Dardanelles, it was the duty of Turkey, as a neutral

Power, to see that they either left within twenty-four hours, or disarmed and laid themselves up. But instead of doing that Turkey "bought" the vessels from Germany.

The most important thing the Turk did for Germany when it entered the war was to close the Black Sea, for then a few mines in the Dardanelles promptly put an end to Russian trade from the Black Sea and so dealt southern Russia a great blow commercially. Germany thus struck at England also, because a large part of the English food supply came through the Dardanelles and the Mediterranean, which had been one of England's chief reasons for maintaining control of that route. So important was this source of supply, that

THE GERMAN LIGHT CRUISER "BRESLAU"

After the *Breslau* was taken over by Turkey she received a Turkish name. In the last year of the war she was reported to have been sunk off the island of Imbros, in the Ægean Sea, but appears to have been saved eventually. The *Breslau* was of the same type as the commerce-raider *Emden*.

England now had considerable difficulty in replacing it. The Black Sea district also had supplies of oil of enormous value to England and France, now that extensive use of the automobile in warfare had made gasoline a commodity second in importance only to powder and food. If the Turkish Navy, augmented by German cruisers, could dispose of Russian ships in the Black Sea, the Turk could seize for Germany the Black Sea ports' supply of oil, a stroke of the utmost consequence. The closing of the Black Sea by the Turk, plus the closing of the Baltic by the German fleet, accomplished another important result—the absolute

IN THE EAST, NEAR EAST, AND SOUTH

isolation of Russia from contact with all parts of Europe, except her enemies—Germany, Austria and Turkey.[1]

[1] Principal Sources: Roland G. Usher in the *World's Work*, The *Times*, The *Evening Sun*, New York; The Calcutta *Englishman;* The *Wall Street Journal, The Review of Reviews,* New York; Morris Jastrow's "The War and the Bagdad Railway" (J. B. Lippincott Co.), The London *Times'* "History of the War."

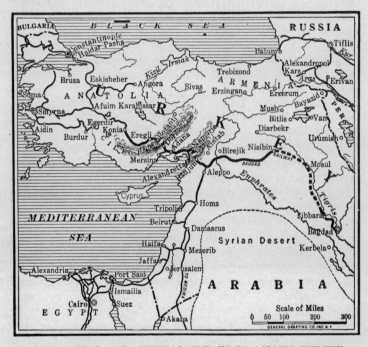

THE BAGDAD AND OTHER RAILWAYS IN ASIATIC TURKEY

Railways from Constantinople eastward into Anatolia for some 300 miles had existed for many years before the world heard of, or even thought of, a railroad to Bagdad. The latter enterprise was a result of the growth of German influence in Turkey, including an ambition to reach Mesopotamia and the Persian Gulf, beyond which lay a clear water route to India.

The Bagdad Railway extension, in one sense an extension of the Anatolian Railway, properly began at Konia and thence ran eastward to Adana, Aleppo, Nisibin, Mosul, Jabbara, and Bagdad. From Aleppo a connecting railroad had been built southward into Arabia, and there was a short branch line from Namurie on the main Bagdad line to the important fort of Alexandretta. The Bagdad line proper was not yet completed. Two tunnels through the mountains west of Aleppo, were understood not to have been in use until the second or third year of the war, and further east some considerable roadbed—perhaps 200 or even 300 miles—remained to be built between Nisibin, Mosul and Bagdad

14

II

EGYPT ATTACKED EAST AND WEST OF THE SUEZ
CANAL—WAR WITH THE SENUSSI AND IN
DARFU—EGYPT AND CYPRUS TAKEN
OVER BY GREAT BRITAIN

October 26, 1914—February 2, 1915

ON October 26, 2,000 armed Bedouins crossed the
Egyptian frontier and watered their camels at Mag-
dada wells, twenty miles beyond the Egyptian line. A
Turkish destroyer flotilla at the same time raided Odessa
and sank a Russian gunboat. British, French, and Russian
Ambassadors then asked for their passports. On November
5 Great Britain being definitely at war with Turkey, Anglo-
Egyptian posts were withdrawn from the Sinai Peninsula west
to the canal, Fort Nakhl was evacuated, and certain buildings and rock-wells which might be of service to an invading
force were blown in with dynamite. Save for the exchange
of a few shots between Bedouin scouts and Egyptian coast-
guard patrols no encounters took place till November 21,
when a coast-guard patrol composed of twenty Sudanese
camelmen was surprized while encamped east of Bir-en-
Nuss, and captured. Captain Chope, of the Bikanir Camel
Corps, pushing eastward to gain touch with the coast-
guards, found their camp empty. After an hour's ride
further east Captain Chope saw ahead of him twenty men
mounted on white camels, waving white flags. Thinking
they were the missing Egyptians he let them approach.
When they got within thirty yards the Bedouins raised their
rifles, only to be promptly shot down by the Bikanirs, who
similarly disposed of another party which attempted to
attack.

Captain Chope then advanced toward Katia, when suddenly 150 horsemen were observed trying to move round
his right flank, while a like number tried to turn his left.
He fell back fighting, hard prest by the mounted men, who
kept up a hot fire from the saddle but dared not close with

the Bikanirs, who fought the enemy off till they reached their supports. Only five of them escaped wounds. Captain Chope had a narrow escape, having had his water-bottle pierced and his sword hilt shivered by bullets. An Egyptian officer was killed, and ten of the Bikanir men, five other men being wounded. Of the Bedouins over fifty were killed and many wounded. Tactically the Bedouins had the best of the skirmish, but the moral effect of the resistance was such that the raiders fell back on Katia, and made no other forward movement to the canal for nearly six weeks.

In Egypt the immediate objective of Turkey and Germany was the Suez Canal, because to block this would be to interrupt the flow of commerce between England and India, cut off Indian soldiers sent to Europe to fight with the Allies, and, if Indian unrest culminated in a revolt, it would delay any British troops that might be sent east. For the Sultan there was in prospect the immediate gain incident to a possible reconquest of a province still nominally subject to him. Its Mohammedan population had long been reported disaffected, and it might welcome the Sultan. England would then have to send to Egypt troops that were needed in France and Belgium and her difficulties, already increased by a South African revolt, would be multiplied. The Germans might hope, when the Sultan proclaimed a "holy war," to cripple France in Algeria, Tunis, and Morocco, England in India as well as in Egypt, Russia in Europe—that is if the Mohammedan populations responded to her summons. On the other hand, since the Italian colony of Tripoli was bound to be affected, Germany ran the risk of bringing Italy into the war against her.

After these border encounters on the canal, Turkish troops were promptly sent forward by way of the Mecca railroad toward the Sinai peninsula and Suez. British warships quite as promptly appeared on these coasts and London announced that territorial garrisons had been sent to Egypt, that the Australian contingent would soon arrive, that the Egyptian troops remained loyal and that Egypt showed no immediate signs of revolt. Early in November a "holy war" was proclaimed against Russia, France, and England. The chief ecclesiastical dignitary of the Moslem

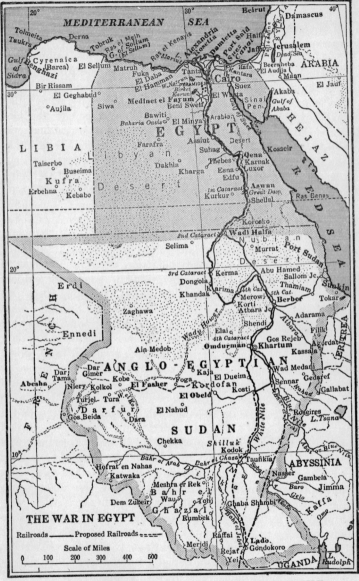

THE BATTLEGROUND EAST AND WEST OF THE NILE

After the fighting east of the Suez Canal, and while the British were making their way into Palestine, war was begun west of the Nile Delta in the Cyrenaica country by the Senussi, and later there occurred a short-lived rebellion in Darfur.

faith issued a statement to the faithful declaring that it was the duty of every Moslem to war against the enemies of Turkey. His Highness was to make a pilgrimage to Mecca immediately. It was expected that this announcement would result in serious trouble for England and Russia among their Moslem subjects, but it caused no disturbance. Correspondents saw no indication that it was effective anywhere outside the actual dominions of the Sultan. Neither in India, nor in Egypt was it "anything but a Platonic pronouncement." It had some effect, however, in northern Africa, with which France alone was concerned.

© AMERICAN PRESS ASSOCIATION.

AN EGYPTIAN CAMEL CORPS UNDER REVIEW

Two neutral nations, Italy and Spain, were alarmed more by it than any of the belligerent Allies. In England it was not even taken seriously.

The Calif is not an elected Pope, nor a "Lama sanctified by birth," but simply "the Moslem chief who holds the road to Mecca," and if the Sultan's army could not hold that road, he would cease automatically to be Calif. The Ottoman Empire might lose Constantinople and still "remain the first Power in the Moslem world," but if it lost Arabia it "would lose all claim to the veneration and obedience of Moslems." Britain would lose nothing, but would perhaps emerge the stronger with her Mohammedan dependencies extended. The Aga Kham, whose word in religious things was law to millions of Mohammedans in India and elsewhere, did not seem to favor the idea of a "holy war" made in Germany, for Germany. In his message he said:

"If Germany succeeds, which Heaven forbid, Turkey will become only a vassal of Germany, and the Kaiser's Resident will be the real ruler of Turkey, and will control the holy cities. No Islamic interest was threatened in this war, and our religion was not in peril, nor was Turkey in peril, for the British and Russian Empires and the French Republic had solemnly offered to guarantee Turkey all her territories in complete independence if she had remained at peace. Turkey was the trustee of Islam, and the whole world was content to let her hold our holy cities in her keeping. Now that Turkey has so disastrously shown herself a tool in German hands, she has not only ruined herself, but has lost her position of trustee of Islam and evil will overtake her."

Late in November an important step for Turkey was taken in the appointment of Field-marshal Kolmar von der Goltz, then Military Governor of Belgium, as active German councilor of the Sultan of Turkey. He was regarded as one of the greatest of German strategists. Despite his 71 years, he had been looked upon as likely to lead the German armies against the Russians. He was a native of East Prussia and had fought in the Franco-Prussian War and the Austrian campaign. Thirty years before he had gone out to reconstruct the Turkish army and remained at his work for thirteen years, being known as "Goltz Pasha." He created an army out of chaos. Turkey's defeats in the Balkans were not regarded by his apologists as discrediting Von der Goltz, as it was contended that without his training the Turkish army would have been much more seriously defeated.

When Turkey plunged into war, it was obvious that some change in the character of the British occupation of Egypt would have to be made, and so at once the Turkish suzerainty was declared ended and a British Protectorate proclaimed. The executive changes made were slight. All that Great Britain desired was to defend Egypt against attack and keep the internal administration running smoothly. Other questions could wait until peace were restored. There was a strong reason why the word "annexation" should not be used. While the Khedive, Abbas Hilmi, was formally deposed, his uncle, Prince Hussein, was placed on the throne in his stead, and the new ruler received the title of Sultan of Egypt in disregard of the designation "Khedive" which had been established by an Imperial Turkish firman. The selection was made in accordance with the Turkish law of succession, under which the throne passes to the eldest male member of the family, but which had not been observed in Egypt since 1866, when the succession was made hereditary, and that tradition had gone by the board. Prince Hussein's elevation was also based on the practical ground that of all his family he was "most worthy to occupy the position." Prince Hussein was described as a prudent and experienced man. Thus with scarcely a ripple, so far as the actual world could see, the Ottoman suzerainty in Egypt gave place to a British Protectorate. A proclamation announcing Great Britain's decision and explaining the cause was published, and the thunder of 101 guns laid the ghost of Turkish rule. Great Britain by this act felt that she had confirmed and regulated her position in the valley of the Nile. Until the Anglo-French agreement of 1904, her occupation had never been officially recognized by Europe. The agreement of 1904 involved recognition by France, and subsequently by other Powers, of Britain's predominant interests in Egypt, but it was "a self-denying ordinance," in that Great Britain bound herself not to make any change in the status of the country. Neither the Turkish adventure in 1906, nor the annexation of Bosnia and Herzegovina by Austria-Hungary, nor the proclamation of a French Protectorate over Morocco in 1911, induced Britain to alter the status of Turkey's vassal. It was not till the maintenance of the *status quo* had been rendered impossible by Turkey's attack on Great Britain and her Allies that the British Government took the one step, short of annexation, that she could take.

For thirty years the actual sovereign of Egypt, the Sultan of Turkey, had exercised no direct influence on the country. The nominal government was in the hands of his Vali, or

Viceroy, the Khidewi-Misr, or as more commonly called, the Khedive, who ruled through native ministers, each assisted by an English "adviser." In reality, the ruler of Egypt was the British Consul-General at Cairo, whose "advice" to the Khedive had the force of a command. The Protectorate in Egypt as now established followed the model established by France in Tunis and constituted a control "as real and complete as sovereignty in the technical sense of the word." The Allied Powers and neutral countries subsequently recognized and approved the change. Of more permanent meaning than any battles could have been was this proclamation of a British Protectorate. On the political side the step deprived Turkey of a shadowy sovereignty over some 12,000,000 people and definitely closed the rule of the Osmanli in Africa. As with Algeria in 1830, Tunis in 1881, Tripoli in 1911, so now with Egypt in 1914, was set up a milestone of Ottoman ruin in Africa. Morocco had never been a Turkish province, but by the proclamation of the French Protectorate in 1912 it became a Christian dependency, so that the last fraction of an independent Islam in Africa had vanished.

A triangle of sand-dune, rock, and mountain, its apex pointed due south, its sides marked to the east by the Akaba Gulf and the Turko-Egyptian frontier line delimited in 1906, to the west by the Gulf of Suez and Suez Canal, with the shore of the Mediterranean between Rafa and Port Said for its base—such are the outlines of the Sinai Peninsula. Geographically and orographically, it is divided into three zones—the zone of the Drift-sand, the Plateau, and the Mountain. Scattered about the region of the drift-sand are "islands" of firmer ground, outcroppings of rock, patches of hard gravel, small tracts where torrents, flowing from the plateau perhaps once in five or ten years, have deposited layers of mud and gravel. In the main it is a country of soft sand, sometimes blown by the wind into multitudinous dunes, where the way is easily lost, so like is each dune to its fellow. In the mountain-zone a small raiding party operated during this year's campaign, but was destroyed as soon as it had ventured out of the impassable labyrinth of peaks, gorges and cliffs that form the southern third of the peninsula. No army could operate therein; but it contains two of the few permanently inhabited settlements in the peninsula, the Monastery of Mount Sinai and the Tor quarantine-station for pilgrims returning from the Holy places by the Red Sea route. The population of the whole peninsula did not exceed 40,000 persons, a few settled inhabitants in and near El Arish, 400 or 500 Djebeliyeh Arabs, descendants probably of slaves or tenants of the Sinai monks in pre-Islamic times, who still lived around the monastery, and Bedouins of small and generally unimportant sects.

When the war broke out, the Turks had had three months in which to complete their mobilization. Difficulties of transport and lack of equipment, which was only gradually supplied from Austria and Germany, prevented them from taking an immediate offensive against Egypt. But by the end of November, and early in December, a large Turkish army had poured through the Cicilian Gates into the plain of Adana. The proclamation of a Holy War, however, had been coldly received by most Moslems in Syria. A few recruits were obtained in Beirut, Jaffa, Nablus, and other cities, but they failed, as a rule, to arouse enthusiasm among the educated classes and the peasantry.

By the middle of December the British garrison in Egypt had been brought up to a strength that would enable it to repel a more formidable attack than that which the Turks ultimately directed against the canal. It was composed of the "Anzacs," or Australian and New Zealand Army Corps,

AUSTRALIANS IN CAMP NEAR ONE OF THE PYRAMIDS

the East Lancashire Territorial Division with most of their divisional troops, a mounted brigade of yeomanry, and a strong Indian force, including a number of Imperial Service troops, mostly mounted, and many excellent regular battalions, of the strength of an army corps. The efficiency of the Anzacs improved rapidly. During the campaign on the canal few of its units were actually engaged; it was not till fighting occurred on the beaches of Gallipoli that it had a chance of displaying the spirited dash and wild valor of the colonial soldier.

Early in the New Year Arab bands which had been engaged at Biren-Nuss began to show themselves to the west of Katia. Meanwhile El Arish had been converted into an advanced base and large quantities of stores collected there; small bodies of Turks had come down to El Audja from Beersheba, and others had strengthened the force which had occupied Fort Nakhl. The Turkish transport was well organized. Each regiment had about 250 camels, the reserve transport being effected by shifts of 500 camels working over stages of as yet unknown length. The bulk of Turkey's main army left Hebron on January 11, and on January 19 a hydroplane located a force of about 8,000 men at Beersheba. On January 27 the Nakhl column made an attack on the Baluchistan and El Kubri posts, and was repulsed. Early on the following morning an attempt was made to rush the British outposts at El Kantara, but was repulsed by the Fourteenth Sikhs, who lost a native officer, and had about twenty other casualties. For the next three days there were constant skirmishes at long range between British outposts and the Turkish patrols, while warships sent occasional shells at the larger bodies which occasionally showed themselves, but took care to entrench just beyond the effective range of the shrapnel fired by British naval guns. More damage was probably done by airmen, who flew aeroplanes and hydroplanes over the advancing columns, now and again planting bombs among the men and camels. Several had narrow escapes. The Turks, marching rapidly and suffering from cold rather than from heat, brought their main body to the great pool at Er Rigm.

By the evening of February 1 Djemal Pasha had pre-

pared his plan of attack. The main force, composed of the
Twenty-fifth Division and all or part of the Twenty-third
Division, was brought to attack the canal, and if possible
force a passage between Serapeum and Tussum, while by
a feint attack its right wing held the British troops at the
Ismailia Ferry bridge-head. The northern column was to
attack El Kantara while showing itself at Ferdan to prevent the reinforcement of the other post. The southern column was ordered to make a demonstration at Kubri
near Suez, an order which it carried out very feebly. Early
on February 2 an Indian reconnoitering force of all arms
met the Turks about four miles east of the Ismailia Ferry.
A desultory engagement ensued, to which a violent sand-
storm put an end. After nightfall the main attacking force
pushed forward toward its destination. Between 25 and 30
galvanized-iron pontoon-boats, seven and a half meters in
length, which had been dragged in carts across the desert,
were hauled by hand toward the water, with one or two
rafts made of kerosene barrels in a wooden frame. All was
now ready for the attack.

The first warning of the approach was given by a sentry
of a mountain-battery, who heard voices in an unknown
tongue from across the water. The noise soon increased,
and from what could be heard and understood, it appeared
that Mudjah Ideen ("Holy Warriors"), mostly old Tripoli
fighters, were accompanying the pontoon-section and regulars. Loud exhortations, often in Arabic, of "Brothers, die
for the faith," and "we can die but once," betrayed also
the presence of enthusiastic irregulars. The Egyptian force
waited till the Turks began to push their boats into the
water. Then Maxims attached to the battery suddenly
spoke and warships on the canal and lake joined in the
fray. The Turks brought six batteries of field-guns into
action from the slopes west of Kataib-el-Kheil. Shells
admirably fused made fine practise at all visible targets.

Supported by artillery, Indian troops took the offensive.
The Serapeum garrison, which had stopt the enemy three-
quarters of a mile from their position, cleared its front, and
the Tussum garrison by a counter-attack drove the enemy
back. Two battalions of Anatolians were thrown into the

fight, but British artillery gave them no chance. By 3.30 in the afternoon a third of the enemy, with the exception of a force that lay hidden in bushy hollows on the east bank between the two posts, were in full retreat, leaving many dead, a large proportion of whom had been killed by shrapnel.

Meanwhile British warships had been in action. A salvo from a battleship woke up Ismailia early in the morning and crowds of soldiers and civilians climbed every available sandhill to see what had happened. A dramatic duel followed between Turkish guns and a warship. The Turks fired just over and then just short of 9,000 yards. The warships sent in a salvo of 6-inch shells. As the fighting ceased at the ferry it died down at El Kantara. There the Turks came to grief on wire-entanglements and another attempt to advance from the southeast was forced back by Indian troops. Late in the afternoon there was sniping from the east bank. Next morning it was renewed. Indian troops moving out to search the ground encountered several hundred of the enemy. A sharp fight followed in which all the Turks were killed, captured, or put to flight. Subsequent operations were confined to "rounding up" prisoners and to the capture of a considerable amount of military material left behind. So ended the battle of the Suez Canal. The British losses had been small, totaling about 111 killed and wounded. The Turks probably lost 2,000 men. Indian troops bore the brunt of the fighting and were well supported by British and French warships and by Egyptian troops. The Turks fought bravely and their artillery fired well if unluckily.

After the conquest of Serbia by the Teutonic forces in the late autumn of 1915 it was declared that another assault would now be made by Turkey on the Suez Canal—the "heel of Achilles" of the British Empire—but it was not until August, 1916, that an attack occurred. The same number of men—14,000—was given as the attacking Turkish force. Looked at from a distance, the attempt seemed as wild as the former attack had been. Again the Turkish force had to cross a pitiless desert, drag guns through the sand, suffer from terrible heat and from lack of water. The decisive battle was fought on August 7 and ended at sunset. Under a crescent moon, which faintly lighted up the desert and cast fantastic shadows over the broken, sandy country, the British pursued the beaten Turks. This second attempt suffered a more severe defeat than the other, despite German leadership and more scientific methods. More than 2,000 prisoners were taken, including several Germans. Machine-gun fire "cut down men like reaping corn," troops were scattered far and wide in the desert, not in orderly columns, but in small parties. The brunt of the fighting was borne by Anzac mounted troops, consisting of the Australian Light Horse and New Zealand Mounted Rifles, released from Gallipoli. These horsemen had been anxious to follow their comrades to France, but were retained in Egypt because they were ideal troops for work in that country. For more than a week before the battle they had had little rest, keeping in touch with the Turks, pushing back patrols, and reconnoitering in a country where the Turks largely outnumbered them. At midnight of the day before the battle the Turks, a division strong, had held a north and south line through the Katia Oasis, about seven miles long, with flanks thrown westward. From a little south of Romani to the Mediterranean coast were Scottish infantry, while the Anzacs were in front of them, and from an hour before daylight fought with steadiness and determination against a well-handled enemy in superior numbers.

The situation at midday was that the British securely held the line Muhamedie-Romani-Katia-Gannit, the latter a sand-dune nearly 300 feet high and an excellent observation

A BRITISH CAMEL CORPS DRILLING IN AN EGYPTIAN DESERT

post. From Gannit, for a mile to the west, was Wellington Ridge, an elevated stretch of bright yellow sand, which the Turks made attempts to reach. Two miles due south was Mount Meredith. Here and at Mount Royston, three miles west-northwest, the Turks got a footing in the afternoon. They had chosen what appeared to be the easiest path toward the canal, a broad, undulating, sandy plain flanked by sand-dunes. About 3 o'clock they made a fierce attack on Romani and Gannit, but the Light Horse and Scottish Territorials drove them back toward Abu Hamra. Meanwhile a Lancashire brigade, brought up by rail, left the train at a place within sound of heavy rifle-fire, and light-heartedly marched away to attack through ankle-deep sand. At 5 o'clock infantry began to attack from north to south, while Yeomanry moved over the sand-dunes working in touch with the infantry. Nothing could withstand the machine-gun fire. The Yeomanry and infantry drove the Turks off Mount Royston and the slopes of Wellington Ridge, and, after a brief delay, cleared Mount Meredith, collecting 1,000 prisoners during the advance, and scattering the remainder of the force over the face of the desert.

The defenses of the canal were evidently stronger than the Turks had expected. These had been strengthened at the time of an expected attack by Von der Goltz's forces and the army in Egypt had also been increased by additions to the Australian and New Zealand troops. The Turks must have found the defenders better able than they had expected to withstand the severe conditions of desert warfare. The movement, however, must have been well organized in order to have advanced so near the British lines. Had it succeeded, it would have been a severe blow to British prestige in the East. In its failure, the British remained secure in control of the canal, and were in position to menace the Ottoman power in Asia by furnishing more active support to the revolting Arabians.

The great military importance of Egypt to the British Empire was now made newly manifest. The country became at once a training-ground for Australasian, Indian, and British troops, a base for the Allied Mediterranean Expeditionary Force, and a center from which contingents

26

could rapidly be dispatched in several directions. While guarding the Suez Canal against attack and retaining a sufficient force to deal with any possible internal disturbance, the British were also able to detach Indian troops for service in France, Mesopotamia, and elsewhere. The greater part of the Australasian Army Corps and of the East Lancashire Territorial Division were to be employed in European Turkey. As each force left Egypt new troops arrived to take its place, to go through a course of training in great camps around Cairo or near the canal. Here also

FRENCH SOLDIERS NEAR ALEXANDRIA, EGYPT, FOR THE FIRST TIME SINCE NAPOLEON WENT THERE TO FIGHT THE BATTLE OF THE PYRAMIDS

had been received the great majority of the Allied wounded from the Dardanelles.

That the Turks would endeavor to invade Egypt from Syria had been foreseen from the moment when the Ottoman Empire was drawn into the war on the side of the Central Powers. An attack upon Egypt from the west—from the direction of Tripoli—was not, however, anticipated. Therefore surprize was felt near the end of 1915 when a considerable force of Arabs, Turks, and Berbers, under the leadership of Sidi Ahmed, head of the Senussi fraternity of Moslems, invaded western Egypt from Cyrenaica, and were joined by some thousands of Egyptian Bedouin. It was only after a campaign of about five months that the invaders were decisively beaten, and the danger to Egypt from that quarter rendered nearly negligible. The danger to Egypt from the Senussi movement had been serious— much more serious, in fact, than the Turkish attempts already made and to be made in 1916 from the Sinai Peninsula to cross the Suez Canal. General Sir John Maxwell, then commanding British forces in Egypt, said that throughout the summer and autumn of 1915 his principal cause of anxiety had been the possibility of trouble on the Western Frontier, for such trouble "might lead to serious religious and internal disorder." No danger of that kind arose in connection with the Suez Canal operations. But a jahad proclaimed by the Senussi sheikh might have met with a wide response in Egypt, for the order of which he was chief was the most powerful Mohammedan sect in Northeast Africa, and the only brotherhood exercising sovereign rights and possessing a disciplined armed force on a permanent war footing. Up to 1915 the Senussi had maintained friendly relations with Egypt, but the position was unsettled, because Sidi Ahmed for many years had fought hard to oppose the extension of French authority in the Central Sudan, and when the war in Europe broke out was conducting a campaign against the Italians in Cyrenaica.

Tripoli and Cyrenaica had become Italian possessions as the result of Italy's war with Turkey in 1911–12. The Turks, however, had never withdrawn the last of their troops from Cyrenaica, and these, aided by the Senussi, had continued in a somewhat desultory way the conflict with the Italians. At the end of 1914 the whole interior of Cyrenaica was held by the Senussi, and, as the western border of Egypt is conterminous with Cyrenaica, they had every facility needed for crossing the frontier, where, except along the Mediterranean and at the oasis of Siwa, were stationed no forces to oppose them. The Turks had never loyally attempted to carry out with Italy the provisions of the Treaty of Lausanne, which closed the Tripoli war. The invasion of western Egypt was thus a sequel to the campaign in Tripoli and Cyrenaica and was traceable to Turko-German influence.

Cyrenaica and Tripoli had formed separate governments under the Turks, and remained separate provinces under the Italians who, however, had taken Libya as a common name for Tripoli and Cyrenaica. Altho the two provinces have many characteristics in common, they are distinct entities separated as they are by the Gulf of Sidra. Tripoli adjoins

WOUNDED INDIAN SOLDIERS IN A HOSPITAL NEAR ALEXANDRIA

Tunisia; Cyrenaica adjoins Egypt. The strength of the force at the disposal of the Turks was conjectural; it probably was not less than 30,000 and consisted of a nucleus of Turkish troops, with Turkish, German, and Arab officers, the Muhafizia or Senussi regulars (a well-disciplined uniformed body of some 5,000) and a varying number of irregulars, every adult male in Cyrenaica being accustomed to arms. The troops were supplied with machine-guns, pom-poms, and a number of field-pieces. Starting from Bir, Warr and Msead, camps somewhat west of Sollum, they rapidly overran the country as far east as Daba. The first encounter between them and the British occurred on December 11, with sharp fights west and south of Matruh. When the eventual failure of Turkish efforts in western Egypt became certain, they succeeded in getting Ali Dinar, the Sultan of Darfur, to defy the Sudan Government, and an expedition against Darfur was sent out under Sir Reginald Wingate, who had to rely on his own resources, except for the help of a detachment of the Royal Flying Corps under Major Groves. All the rank and file engaged belonged to the Egyptian army, but the officers were British. In March a mixed force of all arms entered Darfu after slight opposition. In April, Abaid, a place 90 miles west of El Fasher, Ali Dinar's capital, was occupied and became the base for further operations. Many chiefs surrendered, and in a short time Darfur was at peace.

Since the first defeat of the Senussi, early in 1916, and the reoccupation of Sollum, little had been heard of Sayed Ahmed and his followers; but it was known that after they were driven across the Western Frontier they found their way in detachments to the Siwa Oasis, and there the Sheikh rallied them. Altho they no longer constituted a menace to lower Egypt, Sir Archibald Murray decided to send a force after them. During the winter a force, the strength and constitution of which was not divulged, was assembled under the direction, if not the executive command, of Major-General Sir Charles Dobell, the conqueror of the Kamerun. Nothing was made public about the concentration or movement of this force till February 9, 1917, when the main body of the Senussi had been located in a well-defended position south of Girba, and 15 miles west of Siwa. They were taken by surprize, but succeeded in holding their position till nightfall, when, after burning their tents and destroying their stores and ammunition, they fled toward Shiyata, 10 miles west of Girba, where the Sheikh had taken refuge when the battle began.

The Sheikh's intention apparently was to retreat into Tripoli and recover his communication with the sea, but the British commander anticipated his plans by sending a detachment to occupy the Munasib pass, when Sayed Ahmed turned back in a southeasterly direction and made, as was supposed, for Kuffra, which is 370 miles from Siwa, and the headquarters of the Senussi tribe. British troops entered Siwa on February 5. The Senussi lost 200 men killed and wounded, but no prisoners were taken and little if any war booty. British armored-cars were used in routing the enemy. Crews traveled 200 miles into the Libyan desert and fought a stubborn battle with a well-hidden enemy for twenty hours. Twenty-two men in cars remained one night 500 yards from a foe who outnumbered them 25 to 1. The Senussi were found hidden in a series of low hills. The cars had a hot reception but finally overcame the enemy who before daybreak retired. When dawn broke figures silhouetted against the sky showed them and their camels trekking westward a long way out of range and impossible to reach, owing to precipitous hillsides. Fully 200 Senussi soldiers were killed or wounded.

Brilliant work during the operations in Darfu of 1916 was done by British aviators. First they had to move south at short notice, by sea, rail, and desert track for hundreds of miles before they could reach the barren spot from which they were to operate against the Turks. On arrival they had further to face all the difficulties of flying under tropical conditions with an equipment not designed to meet such special circumstances, and in a country unknown to them and where maps were of little use. They became of great service in the operation. When the natives first saw the machines in the air they showed no astonishment, but they were surprized beyond expression when they saw men alight from them. One was heard to say: "The Government was always great, but now it is greater than ever." The intense heat that prevailed caused petrol cans to burst and evaporation was so great that a consignment of seven cases supposed to hold fifty-six gallons was found to contain only thirty-seven. Desert plants having sharp thorns punctured tires. With the thermometer registering 120 degrees in the shade it was hard work to get stores. Most of the transport was done with camels. For at least 150 miles it was impossible to carry stores except in camel-packs. As the tents for housing machines had required twenty-eight camels to carry them, the labor involved in transport may be imagined, especially as it was extremely difficult to find one's way in the country. In the morning, when camel transport-trains were on the move, airmen could pick up the exact line, but the camels had to be rested from 9 A.M. till 4 P.M. Flying was dangerous after midday because of heavy storms, of which no warning came.

Another feature of the war in Egypt that developed unique features was the battle of Romani, in 1916, when the Sinai had to be crossed with big guns and other war equipment during the heat of summer. The Turkish expedition engineered by German officers had laid plans for another advance from El Arish, ninety miles from the canal. About half this distance is a waterless desert and at this time of year the heat was intolerable. Moreover, it was impossible to march in sands when men sank to the ankle at every step. The only means of transporting troops and supplies was on camels, which was the method the Turks employed. Several hundred beasts were used. Progress was necessarily slow. Long before the Turks reached watered positions some miles in front of Romani, British were waiting for them. At midnight on August 3 the Turks began the attack, which ended in complete disaster for them on August 5.

Since 1878, under the terms of a convention between Great Britain and Turkey, Cyprus had been leased to and administered by the former. The island, which has an area of 3,584 square miles and a population of about 290,000, was now, in September, 1914, definitely annexed to the British Empire. An annual rent of £92,800 had been paid to Turkey since 1878, but that ceased with the annexation. Great Britain's proclamation turned back the pages of history to days when King Richard Cœur de Lion conquered this island from the Roman Emperor Izaac. King Richard sold it to the Templars, who had lost many of their knights and much wealth during Saladin's conquest of Latin Syria. Eventually the Templars found they could not pay the full price, and Cyprus went back to King Richard, who gave it to King Guy, the dispossest Lusignan King of Jerusalem, on condition that he pay the Templars a sum equivalent to that part of the purchase price which they had paid Richard and which Richard, having spent, could not repay. Thus Cyprus, the island of Aphrodite Anadyomene and of St. Barnabas, passed to the French House of Lusignan, under which it became an outpost of Latin civilization in the Levant and one of the most important trading centers of the Middle Ages. One of its rulers, a woman, unable to resist the Turks, finally made over the island to Venice. This was the celebrated Caterina Cornaro, a Venetian woman of rank, now

CAMELS LEAVING CAIRO BY RAIL FOR THE FRONT
They are standing in an open "box-car," each tied to the car with a rope

the widow and heir of the Cypriote king, James III. The year of the cession was 1489. With Venice in possession of the island we can understand why Shakespeare could place there a scene in "Othello." There came an end to Cypriote glories after the Venetians had starved the island of its revenues and dismantled its castles. The population in 1916, was put at 298,775, comprising Greeks, Turks, Armenians, Maromites, and a few Jews. The island has stamps and coins of its own.[2]

[2] Principal Sources: The London *Times'* "History of the War," The *Sun* (New York), The Calcutta *Englishman;* The *Evening Post, The Literary Digest, The Outlook,* The *Times,* New York; The *Daily Chronicle,* The *Standard,* London; a Petrograd statement issued by Reuter; The *Journal of Commerce,* The *Tribune,* New York; "Nelson's History of the War" by John Buchan, *The Fortnightly Review* (London), Associated Press dispatches.

III

THE OUTBREAK OF WAR IN THE CAUCASUS, AND THE ARMENIAN MASSACRES

November 19, 1914—October 15, 1915

IN the Caucasus and on the Armenian frontier reports chronicled early Russian victories and an advance toward Erzerum. That Armenia which had long suffered from the Kurds would welcome Christian armies seemed natural. Caucasia is a medley of races, tongues, and religions. Nowhere else in the world can one find in a similar area so many types, so many languages and dialects, or so many religions and sects, as in this Russian government where the troops of the Czar and those of the Crescent were now to resume their age-long combat. The cosmopolitanism of New York is provincial compared with the confusion of tongues and peoples in the Caucasus. Some seventy dialects, strange to the West, are spoken within its boundaries. Caucasia is a broad, rocky isthmus which, extending from the southeast corner of Europe to Asia, divides the Black and the Caspian Seas. Its area is about 180,000 square miles, or more than four times that of Ohio. It has good ports on the Black and Caspian Seas—Batum on the one, and Baku on the other. It is ground that has been fought over in all generations. Such names as Kars, Ardahan, and Bayazid ring familiar in the ears of students of history. The region has, in fact, been the cockpit of Asia Minor, the Belgium of the Middle East. Since Noah's ark rested on Mount Ararat it is doubtful whether the inhabitants of those mountains have ever enjoyed any long spell of peace.

The Russian attack on Turkey was opened with a dash equal to that which earlier in the war carried the Russian arms into the heart of East Prussia. One column covered forty-seven miles over difficult mountain tracks in two days, rushing into a fight with the Turks, who were not expecting so rapid an offensive, captured Diadin, and dispersed large forces of Kurds, taking their arms and supplies, and making a number of prisoners. The Russian advance was made along passes and river-beds in a mountainous, difficult, and dangerous country. This initial Russian success was regarded as a demonstration rather than an advance in force. Transcaucasia was to Russia a secondary theater of war. Her general policy was to act on the defensive during the winter months. The Turks, however, had no intention of remaining on the defensive, and at the end of November began an advance. Erzerum was Turkey's most important fortified place in Asia, and corresponded to Adrianople on her European frontier. The Russian concentration took place at Kars.

When the Turkish offensive began, the Turks pushed the Russians back toward Khorosan and held it during Christmas week. Meantime two Turkish corps were struggling through icy winds and deep snow at high altitudes in the mountains, and reached, but did not enter, Sarikamish on Christmas Day. The first army, coming from the valley of the Chorok, crossed a mountain pass 8,000 feet above sea, and bearing down upon Ardahan, drove out a Russian force of 4,000 men on January 1. On January 3 the Russians drove the Turks out of Ardahan. With two Turkish corps in retreat, a third, which was still fighting, was surrounded and wiped out. The only unbeaten Turkish corps could as yet do nothing, for it was engaged with the head of the Russian column and had made no progress for over a week. Iskan Pasha, and the whole of his staff, including the German officers, and the corps which he commanded, surrendered.

During a defense of Sarikamish from December 25 to December 28 the Russians had assumed the offensive until reinforcements arrived and saved the town. The Russians advanced by a forced march through deep snow, engaging the enemy in the evening about thirteen miles from the town. Ragged, hungry, half-frozen Turks rolled on in columns of defense. Machine-gun detachments allowed them to approach within 300 paces, and then mowed them down. New columns sprang up in their places, and the Russians then slowly retired eastward step by step. The enemy, realizing that every hour was precious if Sarikamish was to be taken, came on fighting in the darkness. Turkish columns hurled themselves on the slender Russian line, which had to fall back as the Turks fired standing. The Russians then resorted to the bayonet, and with ringing cheers charged the enemy in masses, inflicting slaughter. The Turks were finally driven back under pressure of weight of numbers, and forced to retreat two or three miles from Sarikamish. More Turkish artillery arrived at this juncture, but too late to claim the victory, as the Russian guns were then covering their infantry. Reinforcements poured in steadily. A protracted engagement culminated in a Russian victory.

The Russians had inflicted a terrible blow on the Turks. They overcame or destroyed something like 50,000 men, whom they trapt in fastnesses of the Caucasus range. Of two Turkish army corps, all that remained were a few hundred prisoners. The best corps in the Turkish army, normally stationed at Erzerum, had led in the invasion of Russian territory, supported by another army corps from Van. The Ninth Corps was surrounded and crusht by the fire of mountain-artillery, maxims, and rifles. The commander, Ished Pasha, as well as the division commanders, with a hundred other officers, were made prisoners. The artillery, maxims, ammunition and stores, all fell into Russian hands. Another Turkish corps, tho not annihilated, was hotly pursued by native hillmen. Such was the record of fighting in the Caucasian area up to the end of January. It left the Russians far on the road to Erzerum, where the Turks were hastily attempting a new concentration, while in the northwest fragments of two beaten corps had effected a junction and were attempting a fresh offensive.

Here in Russian Armenia, in the heart of the Caucasus battlefields, with thick, crumbling walls, and ragged foundations of ancient buildings, lies Ani, a sort of Armenian Pompeii, in a rolling, parched, upland country, now almost deserted, altho near the Alexandropol-Erivan railway. It is a little more than thirty miles south of Alexandropol, and some thirty-five miles from the Russo-Turkish boundary. Through a tortuous gorge, alongside the dead city, flows the Arpa Canal, a weird, bright-green stream. Ani was once a

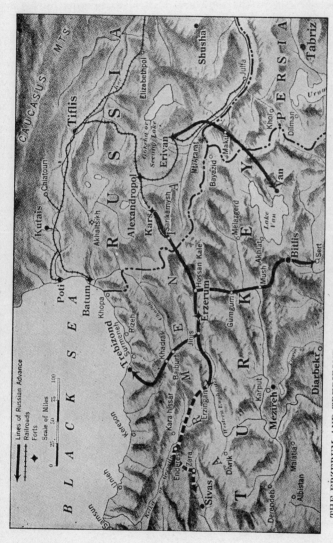

THE ERZERUM AND TREBIZOND TERRITORY OVER WHICH THE GRAND DUKE WAS TO CON-
DUCT HIS SUCCESSFUL CAMPAIGN IN THE WINTER OF 1915-1916—HIS
HEADQUARTERS AT TIFLIS

splendid capital, with a thousand and one churches—so says the legend—whose influence extended throughout the Caucasus and at one time reached into Europe, but all that now remains are an aged Armenian monk, who acts as director of excavations and a pleasant host of stray antiquarians and tourists, with a few Armenian peasants. Before the war these few were living in peaceful isolation among scant memorials of a nation's greatness. The monk's home was headquarters for the dead city, a one-storied, stone structure, near the cathedral, with a single large, bare, and rather dirty room in which on occasion guests were accommodated. Four beds made it a bedroom, and benches a dining-room.

Ani was a strong fortress in its ancient days. Powerful walls, with many towers, still stand on the surrounding plain, but in the centuries in which the city has been unpeopled they have much decayed. Back of the walls, in uneven, indiscriminate distribution, lie the remains of churches, palaces, and public buildings, almost without number, some heavy in the groundwork that suggests their old-time proportions, with other buildings of high masonry, amid which stands the cathedral, unbroken, a solitary, weather-torn edifice of red and brown. A thousand years ago—in 961—this city became the capital of the Bagratid kings of Armenia. Later it was captured by the Byzantium emperor and rose soon to be a wealthy and inviting city. Nearly twenty years later the Seljuk Turks carried fire and sword into it. Warlike Georgians took it five times between 1125 and 1209. Mongols overran it in 1239 and an earthquake, in 1319, completed the work of ruin. The great cathedral dates from 1010.

Here also in the southern Caucasus, near the meeting point of Persia, Russia, and Turkey, is the most treasured possession of the Armenian nation—the monastery and cathedral of Echmiadzin, the Holy See of Armenian Christians, the source of that strength which has held them together through centuries of persecution, warfare and massacre. Echmiadzin is the seat of the Catholicus, or primate, of the Gregorian Armenian Church. Nearly a thousand years have gone by since the fall of the last definite political state of the Armenians, but their church has held them in national consciousness and preserved in them distinguishing racial and social characteristics. The Church is more than religion to the Armenian; it is his patriotism, his hope for survival, and the banner under which he rallies for his people. Here runs the Russo-Turkish frontier, and many miles to the southeast lies Persia. About 3,000 feet above the sea, forty miles north of Ararat, and twelve miles west of Erivan, the capital of the Russian government, lies this Armenian Rome, surrounded by massive, gray-mud walls, which enclose monastery, cathedral, and academy. The buildings are arranged around a great quadrangle, in the center of which stands the cathedral of St. Gregory the Illuminator, a church of more ancient beginnings than Saint Sophia of Constantinople. It has served as a bulwark for Christianity against the barbarians of Asia since 302. Its fight has been long, severe, and heroic. Little is known of Echmiadzin among peoples of the West.

In the library of Echmiadzin are kept manuscripts of the Gospels dating from the ninth century. Monks maintain a type-foundry and a printing-press, and have accomplished great things for the education of their people and the development of Armenian literature. The academy is one of the first educational institutions of the Armenian world. Many of its pupils have done graduate work in German and Russian universities. Adherents of the Armenian church claim that it is the oldest established Christian church in the world, having been founded in the first part of the third century. It is probably the most national of all churches in the world. Only Armenians belong to it.

Mount Ararat, which has known hardly a moment's peace since Noah and his ark grounded upon its massive shoulder, forms at present a huge boundary mark between the Rueks and Russia. Ararat is the original home of the Haik people, the center of what has ever been the world's most troubled area. Tribes from Europe and Asia have fought each other here from the dawn of history. Survivors from many battles settled here, as neighbors, hating, despoiling, and massacring one another. Ararat, one of the most impressive of mountains, rises out of an immense plain sheer up to the clouds, with no neighboring peaks to soften its isolation and take away its majesty. Mount Everest in the Himalayas is set well within a massive, sky-touching range of mountains. Mount Blanc is merely one of several imposing peaks, but Ararat stands aloft, with only a background of sky and plain and a framework of little mountains, a splendid thing among mountains and without a peer.

There are two peaks, Great and Little. Great Ararat rises to a height of 17,000 feet above the sea; Little Ararat, where the boundaries of the Turkish Empire, Russia, and Persia meet, reaches 12,840 feet. The snowline here is very high—14,000 feet—but the dome of Great Ararat is covered with glittering fields of unbroken white. Pastures begin a little below the snowline. After the pastures runs a belt of for the most part sterile land. Purplish-blue is Ararat. It rests its feet in a plain of golden sands, splashed with vivid greens and reds, which shimmers like a Persian carpet. The Armenians hold that they were the first people who lived after the Flood, the immediate descendants of Noah, so to speak. The first village that Noah founded, after abandoning the ark, was Nakhitchevan—so the Armenians think—and his people were the first race of men who grew up after the Flood. The name Ararat means "high." The Persian name, Koh-i-Nuh, means "Noah's mountain." Noah's wife was buried near its base. Grapes are still grown at Ararat from vines believed by the natives to be direct descendants of vines planted by Noah. Ararat was first ascended in 1892 by a German named Parrot. The climb has been made by many tourists since, among them James, now Viscount Bryce, the noted British diplomat, who wrote a book about it.

Germany still controlled the Turkish fleet and Constantinople was commanded by its guns, but with these Russian advances the last temptation to Bulgaria to join Turkey seemed to have vanished. Roumania, meanwhile, seemed freed from any possible menace from Bulgaria. Russian troops being in Bukowina and advancing toward Transylvania, were a reminder that if Roumania would share in the spoils she must enter the battle-line. Turkish defeats in the Caucasus abolished, or seemed to abolish, the temptation for the Balkan States to join the Kaiser. It opened a way to Bulgaria, Roumania, and Greece to win easy laurels and new provinces. In addition it practically assured the British position in Egypt and the Near East. Thus had the first German adventures in the Holy War apparently came to naught. It was impossible not to feel sympathy for Turkish troops, fighting as they had always fought, and once more caught in the toils of European intrigues and persuaded to risk their existence. Apparently the gamble on the Golden Horn had reached the most desperate plight it had known in its long and checkered history. But this story had not yet all been told, because in the future lay British

CAMELS IN THE CAUCASUS CARRYING RUSSIAN MUNITIONS

failure at the Dardanelles and German success in the Balkans.

There was desperate fighting throughout the second week in January, which seems to have turned to the advantage of the Russians, who on the 14th almost annihilated with the bayonet the Fifty-second Turkish Regiment, with the exception of its commander, staff-officers, and the men who were made prisoners. The fortunes of the Turkish campaign in the Caucasus had become slender since the *Goeben* and *Breslau* failed to control communications in the Black Sea between Constantinople and Trebizond, and since the Turkish army around Erzerum had found itself cut off from reinforcements and supplies.

By April 8 the Turks were ousted from districts bordering on Batum and Kars, and the Russian offensive was continued in Turkish territory, on the right bank of the Chorokh, as well as on the front of the Tortum. Overcoming the difficulties in an extremely mountainous region, making their way along paths few and far between, frequently moving by ways that passed over almost inaccessible mountain-summits, and marching in deep snow, the Russian troops dislodged the Turks from strongly fortified positions, and by May 4 had taken possession of the Turkish territory between their old frontier and the rivers.

Russia had carried on a vigorous campaign in this territory over a front of about 400 miles, running in a diagonal line across mountains and plateau-valleys in Transcaucasia, Turkish Armenia, and Persian Kurdistan, from the Black Sea to the heart of northern Persia. Ever since October, 1914, her army had been drawing away several Turkish army corps and had held them up in the Erzerum region. Irregular bands of Kurds had endeavored to protect them from the Russians in the Black Sea region, while on the Turko-Persian borderland remnants of Halil Bey's army still operated against the Russian left. The Russians in this enterprise and the British Expeditionary Force to the Persian Gulf were thus becoming closely related, since for six months they had been drawing closer and closer together, the Russians going south, the British north, but with an inhospitable tract of the Kurdish highlands intervening, with the opportunities they gave for protracted guerrilla warfare.

On June 4 the Russians began an attack on certain Turkish positions that were accessible only with great difficulty. By a thrust in the Sevritchai valley they carried the first line of fortifications, and afterwards by a series of assaults extending over five days, stormed one position after another. Advancing by paths and tracks, transporting men and guns over mountain-summits reaching 10,000 feet in height, and frequently making attacks with the bayonet, they dislodged the Turks from positions they had previously organized, but which they had defended obstinately. On June 6 the Russians occupied Ardost, and on the following day Ide.

THE WAR AGAINST TURKEY

After a victory at Dilman the Russians had undertaken to scatter the Ottoman troops that were operating between Lake Van and Urmia. They began a general offensive with their left wing and moved in three directions, first on the north, from the Alaschkert and Kaidin valleys on Meliaschkert; secondly, from the northeast and the east, on Van; and, thirdly, from Tabriz on Urmia, with the object of carrying out an enveloping movement from the south side of Lake Urmia. The column that was marching south from the Alaschkert, by the valley of the Euphrates, began by bringing close pressure on a number of Kurdish regiments.

THE ANCIENT FORTRESS OF OTTY IN THE CAUCASUS

Cossacks charged the enemy who, being unable to withstand these onslaughts, fell back in a southerly direction. By a brilliant dash cavalry captured the town of Meliaschkert, in the Sanjak of Moush. On the same day another column occupied Pathnos, after which cavalry carried out a series of reconnoissances in various directions. The Turks then fell back to Kop, and the Russian troops encamped near Deril in front of the Turkish positions. On June 4, after another fight, the Russians captured the village of Adiljevaz, at the northwest extremity of Lake Van. Soon the whole region between the Alla Dagh mountain-chain and the northern shore of Lake Van, as well as part of the

Sandjak of Moush, with the town of Meliaschkert, were in Russian hands, having been evacuated by the Turks.

Simultaneously with the Meliaschkert offensive the Russians began a march on Van, in a northeasterly direction, by way of Karta and Aynch, and also from Dilman. The Turks, who occupied strong positions in the mountains south of Dilman, began a retreat toward the southwest, in the direction of Van, by way of Dizagaverska, with Russian troops close on their heels. The northern column having successfully taken the Tapariz Pass, assumed an offensive, prest the Turkish and Kurd advance guards, and on May 15, after two days' fighting, inflicted defeat on the enemy. Continuing its offensive this column, on May 19, captured the city of Van, where the population received the Russian troops with ceremony, and the notables presented the commander with the keys of the town. The Russians captured 25 pieces of fortress-artillery, over 100,000 pounds of powder, and a quantity of arms. By June 6 the Russians had secured the region of Van and a part of the Sanjak of Moush, had annihilated Khalil Bey's original corps, and had cleared of Turkish troops the region between Lakes Van and Urmia. On the right wing they occupied Turkish territory between the old frontier and the line of the rivers Chorekh and Tortum and the mountain-range of Chakhi Baba.

Lake Van is the Great Sea of the Armenian people, and easily the most striking physical feature of their high plateau. It is the largest lake in Asiatic Turkey, and roughly, marks one of the wildest borders of the Near East, a border to which the authority of Constantinople has seldom reached and to which the ordering endeavor of the Russian Cossack had not yet come. Near the borders of Persia and Russia, Van lies on the borders of Armenia and Kurdistan, a lake with an area of 1,400 square miles, its greatest length 80 miles and its greatest width 50 miles. The Euphrates and Tigris rivers rise in mountains near this lake.

The physical aspects of the country are as savage as is its history. Densely-wooded, massive mountains, succeeded by chill, bare, dark rocks, girt the lake. Much of the irregular shore-line is rugged and dangerous, while the forests behind form a "no man's land," where the hasty usages of race-feuds hold sway. The water of the lake is bitter and undrinkable, and, in the autumn and winter, its surface is swept by violent storms that make all navigation hazardous. It stands more than 5,000 feet above the sea level. Lake Van has been navigated from earliest times. For a short time in the ancient world it played a rôle as a highway for commerce. Before the outbreak of the World War it floated 90 sailing boats, of 20 and 25 tons burden, which were engaged mainly in the transport of wheat and firewood. The chief town of the region, near the eastern shore of the lake, is also called Van, and is a place of some 30,000 people, of the oil-and-water mixture of half Kurds and half Armenians.

To any one who remembered the rejoicings which welcomed the bloodless Turkish Revolution of 1908, the ensuing fraternization of Moslem and Christian, and the confidence that grew up of a better future for the Armenians, the story of new and systematic persecution of the Armenians beginning in the early summer of 1915 and extending over many weeks, was a bitter tale. Talaat Bey and his extremist allies shocked not only his allies but their German friends, attaining as they did an eminence for "frightfulness" to which the "Red Sultan" had never before soared. No massacre had taken place during the Turkish mobilization for war, or during the early stages of the campaign in the Caucasus. It was not till Enver Pasha's army invaded Russian territory and another Turkish force, composed in part of Kurdish irregulars, had invaded Azerbaijan, that massacres began in which Armenians were thrown over cliffs, women violated and abducted, children frequently Islamized. Many of the population, after suffering great privations, escaped into Russian territory. In the first outburst, according to Russian newspapers and American missionaries, over 2,000 were killed, under orders from Turkish consuls in northwest Persia, while Kurdish tribesmen committed gruesome atrocities near Bayezid, and began to raid Armenian villages near Van.

The later defeat of Sary Kamish by a Russian army, which included many Armenians, infuriated Enver. At this period the systematic massacre of 25,000 Armenians in the Bashkala district, of whom less than 10 per cent. were said to have escaped, appeared to have been ordered. In April Armenians in Van, who before the war had collected arms to defend themselves against the Kurds, were attacked by Kurds and Turkish gendarmes and in some places were massacred. In others they more than held their own, and finally captured the town of Van and took a bloody vengeance on their enemies. Early in May a Russo-Armenian army entered Van.

Turkish officers commanding in the provinces received orders in April and May authorizing them to deport all individuals or families whose presence might be regarded as politically or militarily dangerous. In the case of some of the Cilician Armenians, deportation began earlier. Talaat was believed to be the chief author of these crimes. ''I intend to prevent any talk of Armenian autonomy for fifty years,'' said he. Their disappearance ''would be no loss,'' he added. Eastern Anatolia, Cilicia, and the Anti-Taurus region were scenes of the worst cruelties. At Bitlis and Moush a large number, according to some accounts 12,000, many of them women, were shot or drowned. At Sivas, Kaisari, and Diarbekr many executions took place and several Armenian villages were wiped out. At Urfa the first massacre did not take place until in the third week of August, when it was witnessed by Allied women and children who afterward escaped from Syria. An English girl ten years of age saw an Armenian's brains blown out and the bodies of women and children burned with kerosene. Several smaller massacres followed the first outbreak.

The massacred Armenians had mostly given up their arms in accordance with advice from their clergy. At four widely separated places resistance was offered. At Shaban Karahissar, in northeast Anatolia, they took up arms, and were finally overwhelmed; some 4,000 were believed to have been killed or sold at this place. At Kharput, on hearing of the intention of the authorities to deport them, the Armenians rose on June 3, and for a week held the town. They were then overpowered by troops with artillery and were mostly killed. In Talaat Bey's methods massacre was followed by a crueler system of persecution than Abdul Hamid ever invented. The Red Sultan's abominations were seldom accompanied by the wholesale deportation of survivors; the violation and abduction of women and the conversion of children, tho sadly frequent in some places, were by no means general in the massacres of 1894–1896 when, as has been said, "the wild beast was allowed only to run amuck for twenty-four hours, and was then usually chained up." In Talaat Bey's campaign the preliminary massacre, which was sometimes omitted, was followed by the separation of able-bodied men from their women-folk. The former were drafted into labor-battalions or disappeared. Women, children, and old men were said to have been led into the desert south of the Euphrates and left there to starve.

ARMENIANS IN A TRENCH NEAR VAN DURING ITS SIEGE
BY THE TURKS

These Armenians were the survivors of a large number, the most of whom had been massacred. They had fled to the American Mission Compound and fortified it against further Turkish attacks

By late summer a series of frightful massacres by which some hundreds of thousands of Christians were affected had taken place. At Bitlis, in June, in an attempt at a general disarmament of Armenians, the authorities, without regard to age or condition, undertook to torture, and even to brand with red-hot irons, the bodies of notables, hoping thus to frighten the other people. Turks visited private homes and, under pretext of searching for arms, robbed them and dragged out women and girls. Kurds joined the Turkish assailants. Wholesale abductions of young women and of boys between 10 and 15 years of age were carried out with the object of converting them to Islam. Few Armenians escaped this Moslem barbarity. Refugees swore that on one occasion Turks tied together some fifty old men and threw them into the lake of Van. Men above seventy and lame, blind, or paralytic persons were stript of what few rags they wore as clothing. Many refugees walked at night in the darkness through mountains and hid behind rocks, so as not to be seen by wandering Moslems, and lived on grass roots which they could gather. Appalling massacres took place in the districts of Bitlis, Moush and Khinis (Erzerum). After a desperate attempt at self-defense in Vartemis, east of Moush, the Armenians were overwhelmed by large Turkish forces, and about 2,000 men and women of every age and condition who had taken refuge in the church of the village were burned to death amid indescribable horrors.

Toward the end of July the military situation of the Transcaucasian front had taken an unfortunate turn for the Russians. Apparently encouraged by Russian reverses in Poland, the Turks had sent large reinforcements, some 40,000 regular troops, to the Armenian front to begin a strong offensive, whereupon the Russians ordered a general withdrawal all along the front, even compelling the Armenian volunteers to evacuate the city of Van, which the latter had captured from the Turks in May and had held ever since. In consequence, about 250,000 Armenians who had taken refuge in Van were ordered to leave their homes and march over a distance of about 100 miles across the Russian frontiers. As there are no railways, nor even good roads in Turkish Armenia, all means of transport being

48

scanty and slow, thousands of sick women and children, exhausted by the sufferings of five months, found themselves unable to move. Hard prest by the advancing Turks who wished to cut off the line of retreat, Armenian volunteers fought several bloody rear-guard actions in order to hold back the Turks and secure the safety of 250,000 refugees.

A special correspondent [3] described the scenes as the most horrible he had ever witnessed. He saw people dying by the roadside owing to hunger and thirst or exhaustion, and mothers throwing away their children in order to lighten their burden. One hundred thousand of these refugees were

FIVE GENERATIONS OF ARMENIANS

quartered in and around Erivan. In spite of the fact that several Armenian societies and towns in Transcaucasia volunteered to take care of between 50 and 100 children each, there were about 3,500 boys and girls below 10, almost all orphans, who remained in Erivan awaiting attendance and care. By the end of October it was declared—apparently an exaggeration—that only 200,000 Armenians were left in Turkey, and that more than 1,000,000 had either been killed, enslaved, or exiled. It was feared that the residue might disappear before the end of the war. That

[3] Of the *Horizon*, an Armenian paper published in Tiflis.

the Turkish Government had doomed the hapless Armenian people to extermination many no longer doubted. With fire, sword and strangling knot, Turkish irregulars were carrying out a sentence that was pronounced in cold blood and declared that "the only way to get rid of the Armenian question is to get rid of the Armenians."

The extermination was carried out by massacre, deportation, and forced conversion to Islam. Throughout the whole of Armenia these methods prevailed. The Government released from prison criminals whom it had organized and enrolled. These criminals were put in charge of the Armenian convoys. There was no brutality they did not commit. An eyewitness, an Armenian taken prisoner at the Dardanelles, where he had been made to serve in the Turkish army, described the declaration of martial law at Zile as including the confiscation of all Armenian property. Women were tied to the tails of ox-carts and exposed to hunger and rough weather until they accepted conversion to Islam or death; mothers were bayoneted before the eyes of their children, and Armenian girls were distributed as chattels among civil and military officials. This Armenian had been compelled to assist in many massacres. On one occasion he was a member of a party of forty soldiers who superintended the death of 800 Armenians.

The Kurds who on the Persian border shared in these barbarities are a survival from ancient days when self-respecting men lived only, or, at least principally, by the sword. Wild tribes of them are still scattered through Asia Minor, where they thwart well-meant efforts to give the land the modern comforts of security through social organization. Altho they inherit a country once fabulously rich, that country has not been able to bring forth a sufficiency through all the years that the Kurds have practised their untamed housekeeping on its soil. The Kurd is a picturesque person. Whatever his numbers may be—and the census-takers of Turkey are indefinite—he is much more in evidence than are the Armenians and other people among whom he lives. It is from the Kurd that the traveler obtains his first impressions of Asia Minor, and in most cases he remains the predominate figure. He wears clothes of vivid

THE WAR AGAINST TURKEY

colors, the poorer ones among them wearing rags of the most forlorn sorts. He rides the best horse obtainable, is always armed, and bullies Armenians and travelers at the same time that his overlord, the Turk, bullies him.

Unable to get a complete mastery over the Kurds, the Turks have employed toward them an administrative policy of letting them alone, even when they massacre and rob Armenians and travelers. Both occupations are considered by them the exercise of a simple right. In his useful state the Kurd lives in hills where he herds sheep. In summer he is a pastoral tent-dweller, in winter he moves to the Mesopotamia plains, where he either lives in a tent or turns the owner out of a selected house and lives in that. His tent is of black, homespun goat's-hair; its furniture, mats, quilts and cooking tools. His children go naked and his women ragged. When by chance he builds a winter home, it consists of a hole in the ground with a flat roof of wattle and clay, air-tight, smoke-tight, light-tight, except that there are small smoke vents in the roof. The whole effect is that of a prairie-dog's dwelling.

Kurds are possest of a conscious superiority that gives them a certain nobility of bearing. A Kurdish chief is an impressive and, often, an affable individual, and Kurds occasionally attempt some of the arts of civilization. Officially, they are Mohammedans, but they reject the custom of veiling their women. They reverence fire and on the subject of religion are altogether liberal. Many are Kizilbashis, or heretic Moslems, and some few are Christians. Little feudal organizations give them their only claims to anything approximating nationality.

The Armenian massacres of 1915 were perpetrated under cover of the World War by "the gang who were in control of Turkey," as Lord Bryce called the Turkish Government. Germans at Berlin protested that stories of outrages at Trebizond and elsewhere were deliberate exaggerations, circulated for political effect, and an attempt was made to justify the Turks. Lord Bryce gave, in the British House of Lords, a heart-piercing account of the circumstances in which the Armenian people were being exterminated. Not since the days of Tamerlane had the world known such horrors. He computed that from May to October hundreds of thousands of Armenians, men, women, and children, had been slain in cold blood in Asia Minor. The Armenian nation, however, was not yet quite extinct; forlorn remnants had found refuge in the Caucasus; some had managed to reach Egypt; a few, ill-armed, half-starved bands were bravely defending themselves from would-be assassins in the mountains of Sassun and Cilicia. On behalf of these pathetic survivors of a fine race he made an appeal to neutral nations.

Americans were sick at heart over these awful disclosures. The severance of diplomatic relations with Turkey would have been justified but the United States Ambassador to Turkey could not be taken from his post without the abandonment of the Armenians and without peril to Americans who remained in Turkey. The Ambassador was Henry Morgenthau, whose efforts to procure some alleviation of the lot of the Armenians proved unsuccessful. Talaat and Bedri both turned deaf ears to all his pleadings. German and Austro-German residents in Turkey seem at first to have approved of the punishment of Armenian "traitors," but the methods of the Turkish extremists turned their stomachs and there were some Turkish protests against these abominations. Turks at Aintab, for example, refused to permit the exile of local Armenians. Rahmi Bey, the bold Vali of Smyrna, repeatedly protested to the Porte and refused to hand over suspected Armenians for trial. The Sheikh ul Islam salved his conscience by a tardy resignation, and Djahid and Djavid Beys uttered plaintive protests when it was too late.

What to do about the Armenian atrocities was a question that agitated many minds. The United States Government made informal representations to Turkey pointing out "the bad effect upon public opinion in the United States of the treatment of the Armenians," but, beyond this, nothing could be done. Lord Bryce said there was only one Power that could stop the Armenian atrocities and that was Germany. The German press, however, gave warning to the United States that "the Germans would not only not interfere with Turkish massacres of infidels, but that they would not

AN AMERICAN RELIEF-TRAIN ARRIVING IN ARMENIA

permit the United States to interfere.'' The *Frankfurter Zeitung* pointed out that the Armenian affair ''was no more America's business than the lynching of negroes was Germany's business.'' A writer in the *Vossische Zeitung* added that the Armenian question was ''a purely theoretical discussion about humanity.'' Germany ''had battles to fight at present in order to insure her very existence.''

Two years before an appalling tragedy such as this would have stirred protests from the whole world. In the summer of 1915 it occupied only a fraction of the attention of readers of the daily papers, who turned to it from the more striking details of some new great battle, not in Asia but in Europe. Terrible as was this new Turkish massacre, it failed to fire the public because a neutral nation, such as the United States, which had read and believed the reports of German atrocities in Belgium and northern France, could find no new words, and feel no new emotion, at beholding the Turk imitating Europeans in the task of exterminating a population. This terrible page of history was regarded as an echo and an extension of the incursion into Belgium fourteen months before.

In a strict sense, there was no Armenia. When used, the name refers in general to a region centering about Lake Van in Asiatic Turkey, and extending thence north and southwest. Armenia means a country whose bounds have continually changed with the fortunes of war. The greater part of the region lies within the Turkish Empire, and is called Kurdistan. It is inhabited by Turks, Armenians, Russians, Persians, Kurds, Circassians, Greeks, Nestorians, Yezidees, Syrians, and Jews.

The early history of the Armenians is so mixed with myth and legend that the truth is difficult to find. During the Assyrian and Median periods there was evidently a great organized monarchy, with a strong military power in the Lake Van basin. At times they were formidable enemies of the Medes. This country was well known to the Assyrians as early as the ninth century B.C. It was inhabited by four races—the Mairi, the Urard, the Minni, and the Hittites. These races appear to have maintained their independence until the time of Ashur-banipal, about 640 B.C., when the last king of that series succumbed to the Assyrian yoke. But in the time of Herodotus, a strange people had entered the land, bringing with them a new language, new names and customs, and a new religion. Herodotus believes they came from Phrygia, but their language and religion indicated Media. One thing was certain; the old Turanians had ceased to rule, and the Armenian race had come as a mixture of ruling Aryan tribes with primitive Turanian populations.[4]

[4] Principal Sources: The London *Times'* "History of the War, "Bulletins" of the National Geographic Society (New York), The *Morning Post* (London), *The Independent* (New York), The *Times* (London); The *Evening Sun, The Literary Digest,* New York; "The Encyclopedia of Missions."

THE ERZERUM, TREBIZOND AND ERZINGAN OPERATIONS

IV

A YEAR IN THE PERSIAN GULF AND ON THE TIGRIS—TOWNSHEND TAKES KUT-EL-AMARA, BUT FAILS AT CTESIPHON AND RETIRES TO KUT

November 1, 1914—December 30, 1915

ONE of the immediate effects of Turkey's becoming a combatant was to extend the war-area to the head of the Persian Gulf, where hostilities quickly began between the Turks and British and Indian troops. The British soon captured the port of Bassora, gained the delta of the Tigris and Euphrates, and drove remnants of the Turkish force northward toward Bagdad. These operations, which formed an entirely separate campaign, were of much political importance. They seemed at once to shatter Germany's dream of domination in the Middle East, where Bassora was to have been the terminus of the Bagdad Railway, Germany's great enterprise in the domain of world politics. As the fall of Bassora would deprive Germany of access to the seas in southern Asia, the political consequence of the campaign promised to surpass the military.

The question was often asked why, with so much on their hands elsewhere, the British diverted so large a force into Mesopotamia with the intention of occupying Bagdad. What was Bagdad to Great Britain? The answer was that Bagdad was on the high road to India. That fact gave the city strategical importance. If a line were drawn from Berlin through Vienna, Constantinople, and Bagdad to Karachi, it would be nearly straight. With this road completed from Haidar Pasha to Bagdad, a journey from London to Karachi, which takes fifteen days by the sea-route through the Suez Canal, would take only eight by a land-route through Bagdad. Thus the Bagdad railway would be a short cut to India. The British believed that the Germans installed at

Bagdad would convert it into a powerful offensive *point d'appui* for a descent into the Persian Gulf. So great a menace to the security of Britain's sea-route to India had to be opposed with all the available strength at her command. Bagdad, moreover, was not only on the highway to India, but was the gateway into Persia, where Great Britain and her Russian ally had long established economic interests, irreconcilable with the aims of German statesmen.

This war in Mesopotamia was an enterprise of the Indian Government, and in India alone for several months were details of it published. Modest as the campaign at first was, it had a strategical importance of the first order. It was of an old-fashioned campaign type which had become obsolete in Europe. In Mesopotamia there was no fixt line of trenches buttressed by impregnable flanks. The Turks had been skilful at taking up positions and digging themselves in, but once their front could be broken there would ensue a rout and a chance for effective use of cavalry. The land, however, was not without strategic difficulties. Floods, in February, 1915, created huge lagoons on both sides of the river, and as these shrank there remained isolated meres and large areas of swamp. Old irrigation-canals, often deep and wide, and running out from the river, complicated the problem of transport. At dawn the heat might be 110° Fahrenheit and in the afternoon well over 120°. Baked sands retained the heat so that night brought little coolness. Of shade there was none, a blinding glare being reflected from yellow earth and blue water. Many British soldiers yearned for trenches in the deep meadow-lands of Flanders. By the end of September, 1915, this campaign, which for months had been almost forgotten in Europe, assumed real importance in the eyes of Allied statesmen. Efforts, heretofore sporadic in this region, acquired a major value in the late autumn owing to the German menace to the Balkans. Here was a revelation of strategy which threatened India as well as the Near and Middle East.

The great battlefields in France and Russia and the diplomatic warfare for control of the Balkans had at the time completely overshadowed the Mesopotamian contest, which now was profoundly affecting a region of high importance—

a region which in time was destined again to support a civilization worthy of its resources and its fertility, and more than worthy of its political and economic traditions. The British campaign represented the consolidation of a colonial policy in that part of the world that had been in process of development for two decades. Germany had at one time hoped to obtain Koweit, which lies at the head of the Persian Gulf and has a magnificent harbor, as a terminus for her Bagdad railway, but Great Britain had forestalled her by treaty with Sheik Mobarek of Koweit, thus leaving Germany without an adequate port for her railway.

For many years Great Britain had had treaties with Arab chiefs on both sides of the Persian Gulf. The commerce of the gulf had been nearly all in British hands, the Indian rupee had ousted or displaced Turkish coinage, and the only post-offices in the gulf were under British Indian administration. Meanwhile, piracy had been checked as well as slavery. Great Britain, in fact, had policed the gulf. New lighthouses were being erected, the entire coast charted, and a more active commerce had been made possible when the war came. The battle of Bassora in November, 1914, seemed at the time to decide the destinies of Mesopotamia. The viceroy of India, Lord Hardinge, paid a visit to Koweit, decorated the ruling chief, secured the good will of the Arab tribes, and also visited Bassora. In both places American missionaries received acknowledgments for their aid to wounded during the war, with a donation from the viceroy in recognition of their services. The streets of Bassora, for the first time in the memory of man, were made clean.

The possible economic future of the Euphrates valley can be estimated from the fact that, in the days of Nineveh and Babylon there flourished in it a population estimated by Rawlinson to have reached forty millions; under modern Turkish misrule the population has been a little less than two millions. This decline has been attributed chiefly to tribal warfare, to the disappearance of the vast irrigation works of antiquity, and to a lack of all enterprise on the part of the government. Those familiar with the development of Egypt under British rule have believed that Mesopotamia, under some future Lord Cromer, could be made equal to at least one, if not two, Egypts in fertility, commerce, and the economic and political happiness of the people. When Sir William Willcocks, the engineer of the Assuan Dam, or some successor of his, shall have completed similar works on the Euphrates and Tigris, the same agricultural transformation which has come to Egypt may be looked forward to in Mesopotamia. One of the great oil deposits of the world is found at Mohammerah in this valley.

A LOG RAFT BEARING FREIGHT DOWN THE TIGRIS

Recorded human history begins in the Persian Gulf. The destinies of empires were formerly swayed from its lonely shores, and to a degree that has been too little understood in the modern world. In Turkish Asia, thirty days by caravan from Constantinople, and westward only fifty miles from the legendary Garden of Eden, man's birthplace, still stands the once splendid city of Bagdad, which for centuries was the capital of the Mohammedan world, and long the second city of importance in the Ottoman Empire. Bagdad lies on both sides of the Tigris, on the west bank the old town, with streets so narrow that it is often impossible for two donkeys to pass one another, on the east bank the new town, with Government offices, barracks, consulates, prisons and the Government army factory. From Bagdad, as far as the eye can reach, stretches the vast, flat, treeless, empty plain of Mesopotamia. The older houses are box-shaped, with flat roofs, almost windowless, and huddled together. Arabs spend sultry summer-nights on these roofs with tom-toms, flutes, water-pipes and dancing women. But the license, indolence, and insecurity of old Bagdad are gone. To-day the city is commercial in spirit. It has a large foreign trade, and is a distributing center for a spacious territory. Only fifty foreigners—British, German, Russian, Italian, and French—lived in Bagdad before the war began, twelve of whom were consuls.

Germany saw the value of the Persian Gulf and for ten years before the war began she had sought to establish her influence there. No other inland sea possesses so ancient and so strange a history, and none is so little known or visited. The narrow entrance to it lies in a corner of the Arabian Sea, where lees from southern oceans collect and strange marine monsters disport themselves. In approaching the entrance, a ship may either shape its course past the land-locked harbor of Maskat, set in the midst of volcanic heights, or coast along the desolate shores of Mekran, where dwell the Icthyophagi, or fish-eaters, as they did in the days of Alexander's retreat from Sind. The bay of Koweit is the finest harbor on the gulf. At the head of the gulf sands and mountains are replaced by green and smiling fields, with palm groves which, with desert and swampy lands beyond, form the delta of the Tigris and Euphrates. From the point where these rivers unite the stream flows through an alluvial land as flat as Holland. Some sixty miles above the river stands Bassora, the center of Turkish influence in the gulf.

Local issues have long unsettled the Persian Gulf. The Turks tried to dispute in various ways the predominant influence which the British exercised for perhaps three hun-

dred years. After the Turks entered into an understanding
with the Germans, their pressure against British interests
at Bassora steadily increased, so that the whole situation
gradually changed. It was not now Turks and Britons
alone who were at Bassora, but Germans too, and they were
seeking domination. in the gulf. The lure which lay before
them was the short road to India.

Dreams of controlling as administrators the fertile plains
of the lower Euphrates and Tigris, and making them once
more the granary of the world, must have been wonderfully
attractive to the Germans. In this rich country primeval
man found wheat growing wild. It was here that man first
evolved the art of cultivating the soil and making a wilderness into a garden. Paul Rohrbach, a German economist
and State official, whose eyes were long on Mesopotamia,
told the Germans that, as recently as the eighth century,
the land between these rivers produced ten million tons of
wheat annually, and supported six millions of people, while
now it maintains only one million. The objects of the Germans were economic, but they were also political. While
wishing to build a railway terminus in the gulf waters,
whatever flag the port should fly the place was meant by
them to be a German stronghold, with an army at its back,
under German influence, and to serve in future years as a
stepping-off place for India. The vital thing, however, was
first to reach the Persian Gulf. Whether it paid or not,
the Bagdad railway, on its economic side, was most praise-
worthy. Asia needed railways, and no part of that continent
was more in need of good ones than Asiatic Turkey. British
opposition to the railway had been based partly on improper methods of finance, but far more on a belief that
Germany's motive in promoting it was primarily political,
and meant to undermine British influence in the Middle
East and British paramountcy in the Persian Gulf.

After ten years of growth in German influence, the Ham-
burg-American Company entered the Persian Gulf in 1906,
and a line of steamers plying between Hamburg and all
principal gulf ports was started. The arrival of the first
German steamer was long remembered at each port in the
gulf, where it had entered with a band playing "Deutsch-

land über Alles," an air which some listening Britons at the time fondly assumed to be "God save the King." German trade thenceforth made steady progress at Bassora until the World War stopt it.

British claims to paramountcy in the Persian Gulf rested on a long sequence of events. The flag of England was flying in the Straits of Oman as long ago as when the Germans were engaged in the Thirty Years' War. England had shouldered burdens there before the *Mayflower* landed at Plymouth. Had England in the meantime lost her grip, piracy, slave-dealing raids and counter-raids, all the characteristics of barbarism, would probably have reappeared there. Having performed a work for civilization during three hundred years, England was aggrieved that Germany should challenge her presence and purposes. Great Britain regarded predominance in the gulf as an essential part of her defense of India. She believed the mere presence of another power, whether its port were fortified or unfortified, would have an unsettling effect on India. People in India could not be induced to believe that from such a port their country could be safeguarded. The fact that another flag was flying in a region where the British had been dominant for three hundred years, and supreme for more than a century, would persuade them that England's strength was declining. Such confidence as she inspired would be diminished. It was not for strategic reasons alone that Britain was compelled to maintain her position in the Persian Gulf. She had to think also of the moral effects on India.

A rupture of the relations between Great Britain and Turkey had been fully expected in 1914 by the small British community at Bassora. Many had left for Mohammerah, which is in Persia. A British warship of 1,070 tons had been lying off Mohammerah for some weeks, when people at Mohammerah noticed on October 31 that she was clearing for action. Then they knew a conflict was near. The Government of India, which had charge of operations in the gulf, had been fully forewarned, and some time earlier had strengthened their forces in the gulf. First came the taking of Fao, which was a very brief episode; two gunboats bombarding the Turkish fort and reducing it to silence in about an hour. A force of marines from a battleship which lay outside was then landed and the town occupied. The invasion of Chaldea had begun. With a position at Fao made good, a detachment of native infantry, under General Delamain, advanced thirty miles up the river, its banks lined with trees, largely dates, and behind them swamps and desert lands. Proceeding past the Abadan Oil Works and round the bend of the river, he anchored at Sanïyeh and debarked his brigade, which made an entrenched camp close to the river and awaited the arrival of reinforcements. At dawn on November 11 the British outposts were attacked

THE BRITISH OCCUPATION OF BASSORA

Bassora, near the head of the Persian Gulf, is the reputed place from which came Sinbad, the sailor

by a Turkish force, evidently from Bassora, but were quickly checked by Mahrattas. The enemy having established themselves in a village from which they could be dislodged only by considerable effort, the Punjabs made a counter-attack, supported by fire from a mountain-battery. The Turks were finally routed, the Turkish casualties amounting to about 80.

On November 21 came news that the Turks had evacuated Bassora, and that Arabs were looting the city. General Barrett pushed on at once. When in sight of Bassora he saw black clouds of smoke rising from the Turkish Customhouse, which had been fired. Ships had meanwhile arrived.

A quarter of an hour afterward the German flag on the imposing German Consulate was lowered, and the British naval ensign hoisted in its stead. When the British expedition made a formal entry into Bassora on November 23, a proclamation, stating the reasons for the occupation and the friendly intentions of the British Government was read in Arabic, the Union Jack hoisted in the presence of guards of honor and, as the troops presented arms, three cheers were given for the King and Emperor. Warships fired a salute of thirty-one guns.

Late in July, 1915, a British force, under Major-General G. F. Gorringe[5], attacked and captured in succession advanced Turkish positions, in face of a stubborn resistance. On the same day gunboats shelled Nasiriyeh on the Euphrates. During the night the Turks retreated toward the north, and British troops occupied the town. In the earlier part of the fight the British captured eleven guns, two machine-guns, and several hundred prisoners, while about 500 dead Turks were counted. British casualties were estimated at between 300 and 400. In forwarding his report, General Sir John Nixon stated that these operations, lasting for twenty days, and culminating in an attack on a series of entrenched positions, were carried out in a shade temperature of 113 degrees under most difficult and onerous conditions, the country being a network of marshes and canals. In June there were twenty-seven cases and nine deaths from enteric fever. Troops were supplied from Bombay with spine protectors and goggles, mosquito-nets and veils, ice, mineral waters, and fresh vegetables. Electric lights and fans were fitted up in buildings where possible.

In September the British won another battle in the retreat of the Turks toward Bagdad. One position carried by the British contained a long line of defenses extending astride the Tigris. At a point seven miles east of Kut, two brigades crossed the river from the right bank, and by a forced march reached the left wing of the Turkish position, carrying it by assault. The Turks had clung with great tenacity to their trenches, which, when finally reached, were found filled

[5] A cousin of Commander Gorringe, U.S.N., who brought from Egypt to New York the "Cleopatra's Needle" now in Central Park.

with corpses. A number of cannon, many rifles, several hundred prisoners and a quantity of ammunition were captured. General Nixon gave the British casualties as "under five hundred." Kut, or Kut-el-Amara, is ninety miles southeast of Bagdad, and two hundred and thirty miles northeast from the head of the Persian Gulf, on an elbow of the Tigris, which at this point runs east about fifty miles. It was on the morning of September 28 that the British moved forward to the final attack. The Turks resisted bravely; but after hard fighting and several counter-attacks their left was completely enveloped, and by two o'clock the whole northern end of the position was in British hands. A scorching wind, with dense clouds of dust, had swept the desert during the whole day; and the long fight in the heat, coming after the night march, had exhausted General Delemain's troops, who were suffering severely from thirst, the marsh water being undrinkable. He was therefore obliged to give them rest. Then he set them in motion again and prest on to complete the victory. His weary troops swept forward, and altho the Turks fought well, they were overthrown and routed. During the night the Turks evacuated all the trenches they still held, and their whole force fell back along the river. They had lost fourteen guns and 4,000 men, of whom over 1,000 were prisoners. The British loss in killed and wounded amounted to 1,233. Altho fought some distance below Kut, the battle was called the battle of Kut.

The British force comprised about 11,000 British-Indian troops and a few hundred British Territorials, who had been sent from Egypt after the Turkish pressure on the Suez Canal was relieved in December, 1914. The opposing army was made up of from 15,000 to 20,000 Turkish troops and Arab irregulars. Among them were a score or so of German officers. By October, when the British cavalry were in Kut-el-Amara, the town was found deserted, with the Turks in flight toward Bagdad by road and river. Along the river gunboats and steamers with an Indian brigade aboard, started in pursuit. An aeroplane dropt bombs on one of the Turkish steamers. The captured Turkish positions had shown that the trenches were constructed with remarkable thoroughness. They had communication, trenches extending for miles, and a system of contact mines.

Kut was occupied by General Townshend's troops on October 29. It was described by Sir Mark Sykes, who saw it at this time, as "a dirty, tumble-down, unsanitary little town," but with a minaret and decorated portals as perfect in design and line as the best work of ancient days. The town lies in a loop of the Tigris, about 340 miles from the sea, by the river route, and contains about 6,000 inhabitants, mostly Arabs. There is fertile ground about it, which might be greatly developed, but, except for its position at the northern end of the Shatt-el-Hai, it has no special importance, and it will owe its place in history solely to its connection with one of the outlying episodes of the World War. Under Nixon, Townshend was here in full command.

The floods that had spread over the valley of the Tigris had subsided in September. North and west of marshes which surrounded Kurna the country opened out into a valley of luxuriant pasture land, where herds of cattle and horses and flocks of sheep met the eye. Canals intersect the great Tigris Valley in all directions, while every now and then ruins bear record of some long past civilization. Encampments of wandering Bedouins were seen in the campaign dotted about here and there, and hordes of naked children played along the banks of canals. Before the war the Arabs used to vary the monotony of their peaceful lives by firing on trading steamers as they passed up and down these great waterways. In the summer of 1915, they had learned to treat with more respect the armed boats which plied there, but among the Expeditionary Force it was still an axiom in the art of preserving life that an Arab should never be allowed to approach too close.

An inspection of the position captured by the British showed that the Turkish defenses were designed and constructed with remarkable thoroughness and study of detail, and on the most approved principles. The communication trenches extended for miles. Ranges were marked by flags. Arrangements had been made for covering the retirement of troops, and for their embarkation. There was an elaborate system of observation and contact-mines, a number of which were exploded by British engineers without accident, but severe casualties were caused by mines. The field of fire was everywhere open and flat. Nur-ed-Din Pasha's forces consisted of six squadrons of cavalry, 26 guns, and the 38th infantry regiments, with some other formations, aggregating some four extra battalions, assisted by a considerable number of tribesmen.

GEN. SIR C. V. F. TOWNSHEND

The action at Kut, altho a victory, had not resulted in the complete rout of the Turks. After the first confusion of defeat, they had retired in fairly good order, covered by a strong rear-guard with infantry and guns; and by October 3 Townshend knew that they had halted and taken up a fresh entrenched position at Ctesiphon, across the Bagdad Road. All chance of riding into Bagdad at the heels of the rout was now over. The question had to be regarded from a fresh point of view. Townshend, pressing on in pursuit with part of his force, reached Azizieh, 30 miles from Ctesiphon by land, about 100 miles by river, and from there sent to Sir John Nixon, or his Chief of Staff, a telegram which seemed to show that under existing conditions he considered it dangerous and undesirable to march on Bagdad. Notwithstanding this, on November 11 his advanced troops—cavalry and a brigade of infantry—broke camp at Azizieh, and a few days later the whole of the force found itself on the march for Bagdad. It was still a small force for such an undertaking—perhaps 12,000 men all told. Why they moved forward was not made clear.

On November 24 a *communiqué* issued by the British India Office announced that on November 22 Townshend had reached Ctesiphon, eighteen miles from Bagdad and three or four miles east of the Tigris, where he found the Turks holding a position which he attacked, and after severe fighting captured, along with 800 prisoners and a quantity of arms and equipment, his losses being estimated at 2,000 killed and wounded. It was further stated that after bivouacking on the field of battle, the British force was "heavily counter-attacked" by the Turks on the night of the 23d, and that owing to want of water, the British troops had withdrawn to the Tigris. A second *communiqué* was published on the 27th, stating that Townshend's troops were in possession of the battlefield, and the Turks retiring on Dialah, ten miles above Ctesiphon, while the British wounded were being sent down the river. The number of prisoners, previously given as 800, was reported to be 1,300, and the number of British wounded as 2,500. A third *communiqué* was issued on the 30th, in which the enemy's strength at the battle of Ctesiphon was reported to have been four divisions, one of which was believed to have been completely wiped out.

Owing, however, to the approach of Turkish reinforcements, Townshend, having completed the removal of his wounded and prisoners, had withdrawn his troops to a position lower down the river. Further information was given in a fourth *communiqué*, published on December 4, when the British casualties were reported to be 4,567 and the Turkish prisoners 1,600, and the Turks were stated to be following up the British retreat. On the night of November 30 Townshend had fought a rear-guard action against greatly superior Turkish forces, his casualties being estimated at 150. He reported his troops as retiring in order, but he had been obliged to leave two river-boats behind, after destroying their engines. On December 7 the India Office reported that the British troops had retreated to Kut-el-Amara without further fighting, and on the 12th another *communiqué* announced that, after arrival at Kut-el-Amara, the British position was "heavily bombarded," and that the Turks made infantry-attacks, which were repulsed.

When Townshend reached Ctesiphon he found a much larger force opposed to him than he had anywhere previously encountered on the way up from Fao. Four Turkish divisions were brought into line as against one British division, which, however, had been reinforced by other troops. The Turks were probably not less than 20,000 strong. Outnumbered and attacked by fresh troops, Townshend eventually had to fall back on his reinforcements rather than wait for their arrival. The Turks were holding Bagdad in force, and he was 350 miles from his sea-base on the Shatt-el-Arab, and his troops had suffered severely in the Ctesiphon fighting. Depending on water-transport for feeding his troops, he had experienced great difficulty in getting up supplies owing to the river being at its lowest in September, rendering the passage of even small boats slow and precarious. Retreat was clearly necessary.

Unless the British could take and hold Bagdad, the expedition into Mesopotamia would have failed in the main object for which it was undertaken. Setting aside the prestige attaching to possession of the place, the strategic position of Bagdad, on the high road into Persia, was incontestably of such importance as to justify the effort to capture it before the Germans could come to the assistance of the Turks. If Bagdad was to be taken and fortified against attack, no time was to be lost in pouring reinforcements of British troops into Mesopotamia, for by the middle of 1916 the Bagdad Railway might be completed, when the strategical advantage enjoyed by Great Britain would pass out of her hands into those of the two Central Powers. A "severe check" had been administered to the Expeditionary Force, whose record till then had been one of unscarred success. There was now to be no early capture of Bagdad. It was a deep disappointment to the British Nation, already saddened by the gloom which hung over the Dardanelles.

Ctesiphon was a place of deep historic interest. It had been the capital of the Persian kingdom of the Chosroes; and thirteen hundred years before the date on which it first heard the sound of British guns it was the scene of memorable warfare between Moslems and Infidels. In the year 636 A.D., soon after the death of the Prophet, when the Arab tribes, swarming from their desert sands in all the ardor of a new-born faith, had boldly thrown down the gauntlet to the two great powers of the world, Rome and Persia. The host of Islam, marching from victory to victory, finally drove the Persians back to their capital on the Tigris. At that time Ctesiphon extended to both banks of the river, and included Seleucia, the former capital of the Alexandrian kings.

The Persians, taken by surprize, fled panic-stricken, and the whole city fell into the hands of the conquerors. The spoil was of priceless value—millions in coin, with countless vessels of gold and silver, and a great store of jewels and wealth of all kinds, including the regalia of the Persian Empire and the sword of the Chosroes. The Arab leader took up his residence in the royal palace, and the Great Hall was turned into a house of prayer for the worship of the god of Islam. A hundred years later, when the Khalif of the day had chosen Bagdad for the site of his future capital, he resolved to demolish the palace of the Chosroes to provide material for a new city. Much of it he overthrew and carried away, but not all. A noble arch, hard as iron, withstood the pickax, defying all efforts. On the river's left bank still stands that ancient monument, while all around it is a bare and sandy plain. This arch now was looking down, after twelve centuries had passed, upon a grim struggle in which British and Turks, backed by their Indian and Arab allies, contended for the mastery of Mesopotamia. From the British line at Lajj on the evening of November 21, it had been seen standing out against a blood-red sunset

A TURKISH GUNBOAT SUNK IN THE TIGRIS

sky; and in the morning the British soldier awoke from his sleep on the chilly moonlit plain to see it facing the sunrise, with the Turkish host gathered about it.

Townshend attacked the left of the enemy's position, and after a severe fight the front line of trenches was stormed. The Forty-fifth Turkish Division, which held them, was practically destroyed. It lost 1,300 prisoners, and the trenches were choked with dead. The attacking force then prest on, across the flat, bare desert, toward the second line, losing heavily from the artillery- and rifle-fire of the Turks. Nevertheless, advancing by short rushes they at last reached the line, and, fighting fiercely, carried a portion of the trenches, taking eight Turkish guns. After this the success of the British troops came to an end. Bringing up strong reinforcements of fresh men, the Turks made one counter-attack after another; the tide of the battle swayed backward and forward; the captured guns changed hands time after time; ammunition ran short, all the mules having been killed by shrapnel, and at last, as night fell, it was seen that the British could do no more. More Turkish reinforcements came up afterward, and during the afternoon large columns moved down to turn both of the British flanks, while bodies of cavalry began to threaten the rear. Faced by fresh troops greatly outnumbering his own, perhaps in the proportion of three or four to one, and encumbered by thousands of prisoners and wounded, the British commander recognized that another attack could not succeed. To remain where he was would be to incur the danger of being cut off from his base. Accordingly during the night of the 25th he withdrew to Lajj, where his boats and supplies had remained. The advance on Bagdad was over. The Arch of the Chosroes for the present proved the high-water mark of the British invasion.

It was necessary to withdraw down stream to a more secure locality until conditions might permit of a resumption of the offensive The place selected was Kut, which had already, to some extent, been supplied and prepared. There the retreating force might hope to be joined before many weeks had passed by reinforcements from below. Kut was far in the rear—120 miles by river, and 70 or more by road

—but the decision seemed sound. On November 27 the retreat began, and for about half the distance was not much molested. But the Turks had no intention of letting their enemy escape unscathed, or escape at all if they could help it. Their mounted troops were pushing down the river round the British flanks, and, as Townshend had foreseen, the Arabs of the neighboring country were hostile. The position was one to cause grave anxiety.

On December 3, the British force was "installed at Kut," and the retreat was at an end. Altho closely prest, Townshend had brought in with him 1,650 prisoners taken at Ctesiphon, and there had never been anything approaching a rout. Nevertheless, the losses of the force during the battle and retreat had been severe—4,567 men. Once the retreat was over, Townshend set to work to strengthen his position and prepare to stand a siege until relief should arrive from the south. Reinforcements for Mesopotamia were known to be coming from overseas. The siege of Kut now set in. On December 8 the enemy bombarded from three sides, and Nur-ed-Din called upon Townshend to surrender. On the 9th the Turks attacked the detachment on the right bank covering the bridge, and it was forced to retire. Then followed several days of continuous bombardment, varied by attacks which were beaten off with severe loss to the Turks. After this the enemy settled down to regular siege operations, and confined themselves to sapping and mining. Thus had ended an advance from which much had been hoped.

The attempt on Bagdad had failed, but the invaders were still in possession of a great tract of Turkish territory. Townshend's force had been far too small for the work expected of it. Had Bagdad now fallen, the whole Arab world might have sprung to arms against the despised Turk, Islam might have been divided, Syria provoked into revolt, and the road from Constantinople to Suez permanently closed. All this would have meant that the Turkish frontier would be thrown back upon the Taurus Mountains, that Mesopotamia would become a possession of the British Empire, an outpost of India, and that the German dream of an advance along the Bagdad railroad to the Gulf of Sinai and the Indian Ocean was destroyed. But the venture

THE BRITISH OPERATIONS IN
MESOPOTAMIA

Scale of Miles

0   25   50   75   100

Railroads:

THE MATTHEWS-NORTHRUP WORKS, BUFFALO, N.Y.

failed. The back door to the Turkish Empire seemed to have been slammed shut, soon after the front door at Gallipoli was bolted by German guns in the hands of the Turks.

Under peculiar conditions of hardship for British troops, the Mesopotamia campaign had been conducted. The climate, admittedly one of the worst in the world, took a heavy toll of British and Indian troops. The fruits of the first nine months of the campaign included the defeat of the Turks on three lines—the Tigris, the Euphrates, and on the Ahwax line—and the occupation of a large area of valuable country. The troops who opposed the British were in the main Turkish regulars. In these were included several Constantinople regiments who had been dispatched to the southern campaign before Constantinople was threatened by the Allies. The Turkish regulars were ably assisted by Arab and Kurd levies. Turkey, even in her most distant provinces, enforced universal military service. Another class who resisted the British were warlike Arab tribesmen. Throughout the campaign these tribesmen, who seemed to spring in thousands from nowhere and anywhere, played a three-cornered game, watching for their opportunity as the fortunes of the fight swung in the balance, and devoting their energies to harassing whichever side should waver. Altho the Turks had a primary claim on their services, it happened more than once that a Turkish defeat was changed to a disastrous rout by the actions of their treacherous allies.

Never was a campaign fought under such adverse conditions. Two important actions occurred on the supposed site of the Garden of Eden. Nothing has ever shaken a local Mesopotamian conviction that in Kurna, at the junction of the Tigris and the Euphrates, Mesopotamia possesses the original first home of civilized man. Units of the garrison who occupied its defenses during the torrid months of May and June, 1915, acquired new doubts of the authenticity of this tradition, but yielded to local opinion in so far as to apply such names as "Serpent's Corner," "Temptation Square," etc., to the more important thoroughfares. Mesopotamia is bitterly cold and damp in winter and intensely malarious and hot in summer. The heat adds enormously to the difficulties of operations. During the first half of the year in which operations took place, excessive floods inundated the country. An amphibious sort of warfare was the result, where soldiers of the British and Indian armies and sailors of the Royal Navy met one another half-way.

Bagdad lies on the natural line of communication between Persia and the West, and between the West and the Persian Gulf. Three caravan routes, one from Khorasan, another up the Euphrates into Syria, and a third leading up the Tigris into the Armenian plateau and to the Black Sea behind it, were the sources of Bagdad's trading strength in ancient times. To-day, its importance is almost wholly bound up in the potential wealth of its surrounding plains, watered by the Tigris and Euphrates, and in its dominating position on lines of communication between India, Persia, and the West. Bagdad, once "the Magnificent," was now a city in decay. The years that had rolled by since a Turkish over-lordship was first established had seen it sink slowly in importance as a mart for trade, as a station on the path of caravans from the East and West, and as the center of a land of abundant harvests.

The Tigris, on whose banks flourished the great city of Lagash and the Babylonian Empire more than three thousand years before the Christian Era, has to-day fallen to so lowly a state that even Turks and Arabs scorn to honor it. Almost contemptuously, they call it "the cheap cameleer," because it is used by natives on its upper reaches to bring down *kelleks* or rafts of wood from Diarbekr to Bagdad. At Bagdad inflated skins used as floats, are deflated and then transported back to the hill-country by caravan. On its turbid course through Mesopotamia the Tigris, which is traversed by small boats for a distance nearly four times as great as the navigable reaches of the Hudson, flows past ruins which have proved an almost inexhaustible mine of information for archeologists. Opposite Mosul, from which came our word "muslin," as applied to the fabric first imported into Europe from this town in the twelfth century, are the extensive remains of what was once Nineveh, a place still associated in the popular mind with the Biblical account of Jonah, the great fish, and the gourd.

Sixty miles below Nineveh, which was the last capital of

THE WAR AGAINST TURKEY

Assyria, is the little Arab village of Kal'at-Shergat, on the buried ruins of Ashur, the oldest great city of the Assyrian Empire. It was in honor of their good Ashur that the high-priests founded the city of the same name. These priestly builders and administrators were at first under the sovereignty of Babylonia, but when that empire fell into decay, they succeeded in establishing themselves as independent kings, founding a dynasty which held sway over this section of the world for centuries. The Tigris has two main sources in the Taurus Mountains, at an elevation of 5,000 feet. The head-waters of the western branch are only two or three miles from one of the sources of the Euphrates. After the two branches come together, the river flows in a southeasterly direction for 800 miles, until it unites with the Euphrates seventy miles above the Persian Gulf, and forms the Shatt-el-Arab.[6]

[6] Principal Sources: The London *Times'* "History of the War"; The *Times,* The *Journal of Commerce,* New York; The *Times* (London), *The Outlook* (New York), The Manchester *Guardian* (London), "Bulletins" of the National Geographic Society (New York), *The Fortnightly Review* (London), "Nelson's History of the War" by John Buchan.

THE DARDANELLES AND THE DISASTROUS ALLIED NAVAL ATTEMPT TO FORCE THEM, WHICH ALMOST SUCCEEDED

November 2, 1914—March 5, 1915

THE Turks were still in Europe, for they held the Dardanelles. Thus they controlled the southern door leading to Russia and divided the strength of the Allies. With the Dardanelles in an enemy's hands, Russia could not send to France and England her grain and goods in exchange for guns, ammunition, and other war-supplies. In the north her few open doors—Vladivostok and Archangel, when open—were already congested with incoming freight. At Archangel and Vladivostok she could receive locomotives, freight-cars, automobiles, cotton, shell, cannon, rifles, and barbed wire, but so heavily taxed were her facilities at these points that it was almost impossible to transport and discharge to steamers the foodstuffs she had to sell. Thus she could take, but she could not give for egress, as the Baltic was barred by the Germans, the Black Sea by the Turks. In the meantime, the ruble had fallen to a disastrous discount in London and elsewhere, because, as Russia could not export goods in exchange for the material she imported, she was expected to pay for goods in actual money. Russia owed money to everybody. As nobody owed Russia any money, the exchange value of Russian money greatly depreciated. A Russian oil company earned a dividend during the war, but was unable to pay dividends to its English shareholders because of the loss involved in converting Russian into English money. This situation would have been greatly altered if the entrance to Russia through the Black Sea had been open.

The magnitude of the economic gain to come to Russia from the opening of the Straits should not be obscured by the political and military considerations that prompted and sustained the effort. The enormous volume of Russia's Black Sea trade was not generally appreciated. Russia had exported by sea twice as much in volume, and two and one-half times as much in value, of merchandise as she exported by land. Of these exports, valued in 1913 at 1,520 millions of rubles, 557 millions were sent out through the Black Sea and the Sea of Azof. For nearly twenty years the economic growth of Russia, both in the products of its agriculture and the activity of its industries, had come from immense fertile plains, whose great rivers are her cheapest and most convenient highways and lead out to sea-borne commerce. Odessa was rapidly developing into another Hamburg, and, given the development of tributary railways, and canal-feeders for the great rivers, there was no longer question about the Black Sea littoral becoming the granary of Europe.

The war operations now to be undertaken in the Dardanelles inspired memories of momentous events in human history—of the fleets of historic Greece; of the legendary heroes of Greece; of ancient Troy; of Xerxes sitting on his throne above Nagara Point watching columns of Persian warriors, said to number 2,000,000 men, crossing the bridge of boats which Egyptian and Phenician engineers had built for him across the Hellespont, seven days and nights being consumed in the crossing; of Alexander of Macedon, leading his legions on to Arabia; of galleys bearing Byzantine and Saracenic soldiers; of the hosts that composed the Fourth Crusade, with its splendid purpose turned into an historic crime.

Here at the Dardanelles Europe and Asia met, and here still meet. The bold headlands which guard its entrance from the Ægean Sea are crowned on either side by two ponderous masses of medieval architecture, the Castles of Europe and Asia, or as they have been sometimes called, the Castles of Roumelia and Anatolia, massive stone walls, with crenelated towers and moated approaches rising squarely against the sky-line. Here is the setting of the story of Hero and Leander, one of the earliest of all love stories, which Kit Marlowe wove into passionate verse. It was this feat of Leander, in swimming the straits to gain the presence of the beautiful priestess of Sestos, that inspired Lord Byron nearly 3,000 years afterward to emulate his achievement.

With the development of the ancient world, the Dardanelles are inexplicably entwined. This corner of Asia Minor, known of old as the Troas, and later as the Troad, contains the site of Troy within which was waged the famous ten-year siege. Archeologists in the last century actually uncovered the precise location of the city that owned the rule of Priam, and to which the stolen Helen was taken by Paris. The site of Troy lies near the present Turkish village of Hissarlik. Far beneath it are the crumbling remains that represent seven of its vanished communities. Here, where British marines and French bluejackets in the spring of 1915 were landing in whaleboats, Agamemnon's flimsy galleys, in the tenth or twelfth century before Christ, beached their keels and discharged their companies of spearmen and archers in order to assault "the topless towers of Ilium." By a curious circumstance, one of the British ships which in 1915 bombarded the fort on the Asiatic shore, sending shots so far inland as to reach the reputed tomb of Achilles, bore the name of *Agamemnon*. Where now modern ordnance was hurling messengers of destruction, Homer's heroes waged their spectacular, single-handed combats, with admiring armies grouped around to watch them.

From the siege of Troy to the impersonal battle of 1915 was a far cry, yet the old walls of Troy must have brought some sort of inspiration to the soldiers who were fighting in their shadows, whether soldiers of the Allies or of the Turks. The Trojan walls of thirty centuries ago are still in evidence—the actual walls that defied the onslaughts of Agamemnon and Menelaus, of Ajax, Nestor, Diomedes, Ulysses, and Achilles, only to fall at last by the stratagem of the wooden horse. They provided the stage for an insignificant little drama compared with the modern one, but a drama that was made big with human interest became so divinely recorded that the world has not since produced its equal. If we take the "Iliad" literally, men then fought for an ideal; the Homeric warfare was a beautiful pastime, from which emerged a happy few who were rewarded with immortality in song

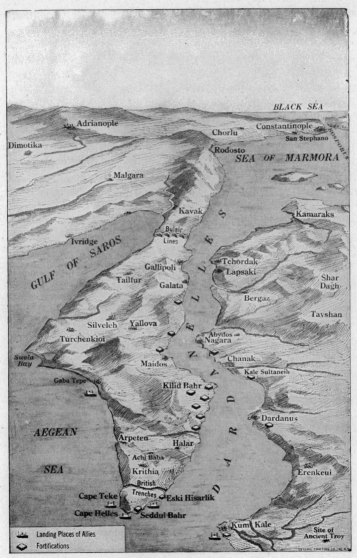

Landing Places of Allies
Fortifications

GALLIPOLI, THE DARDANELLES, AND THE SEA OF MARMORA

It was no mere coincidence that, after the lapse of more than thirty centuries, a new war should again have come around in these waters, that a new *Agamemnon*—a ship now instead of a man—should sail the same sea from which the king of Mycenæ landed his army; that blood should flow among hills and valleys in full sight of Troy, and even of the banks of the Scamander. Turks and Germans were fighting in 1915 for the same object as Trojans and Lycians in the twelfth century B.C. The aim of both alike was to keep the ships of southern and western Europe from having commerce with the Black Sea. The Black Sea or Euxine trade is now, just as it was then, one of the essential needs of western Europe: Those who could stop or control it have always been in a commanding position. The tolls which they could derive from it in one form or another were, however, so abundant that an actual stopping of the passage would have been to them economically suicidal. It was possible for the king of Troy to close the Hellespont (the ancient name of the Dardanelles) to ships when he chose to do so. As he was rich, he did not venture permanently to block the way. His plan was, by preventing ships of the west from sailing up the straits, to force other ships to bring their wares down from the north and east and then to barter with the west under the walls of his fortress, a method of procedure which became the source to him of great wealth and power, and a power that became intolerable to the enterprising Greeks, just as it had long been intolerable to modern western countries, that all the world should be cut off by Turkey from the rich granaries of Russia and the Danubian plains. The Greeks of 1000 B.C., as the Allies of 1915 A.D., fought in order that this waterway should not be closed against the economic needs of a great and masterful race lying west.

The Dardanelles cut off Europe from Asia along a course from southwest to northwest. They are only 45 miles long, and vary in width from one to five miles. The average depth of the water is 180 feet. On the European side the shores are steep and barren; on the Asiatic they have long slopes, are fertile and, for the most part, are clothed with beautiful forests. The Dardanelles were first fortified by two castles, one on either shore, by Mohammed II. in 1462.

These forts have often been remodeled. During the last century, with Turkish power and initiative on the wane, the modernization of the fortifications was secured, now under French, now under English, now under German, prodding just as the interests of one or the other nation centered in the Golden Horn.

The expedition of the western Allies to the Dardanelles in the early months of 1915 was criticized because it diverted strength from Flanders and the north of France, where Sir John French needed every man, gun, and shell he could get. Concentration, said the critics, not dispersion, should be the guiding principle in all strategical combinations. The Allies had for their task first of all to drive the Germans out of Belgium and the north of France. When they had done this, it would be time enough to think about driving the Turks out of Europe.

Critics who talked and wrote thus misconceived the conditions under which the Allies were waging this war, and undervalued the advantage which sea supremacy conferred. The primary purpose in seizing Constantinople was, not to expel the Turks from Europe, tho that would incidentally follow, but to open up communications with Russia, facilitate the intervention of neutral states, and establish a fresh base for operations against Austria-Hungary. It was easier to attack Austria from the south than to attack Germany from the west or from the east. If the Allies could reach Vienna by the valley of the Danube, the effect would be to divert German troops for the defense of Germany's southern frontier, and by so doing relieve the pressure on Belgium.

As soon as war broke out between the Allies and Turkey in the autumn of 1914, a joint Franco-British squadron established an effective blockade of the Dardanelles. On November 2 the squadron bombarded at long range the forts at the entrance to the Dardanelles, in order to ascertain the range and to test their defenses. The reconnaissance being inconclusive was not prest. On December 13 Lieutenant-Commander Holbrook navigated a British submarine beneath the mine-field in the Straits and succeeded in torpedoing in the Sea of Marmora the old, but still useful, Turkish battleship, the *Messudiveh*, and for this feat received the Victoria Cross. Holbrook's submarine, the *B*-11, was not fitted with the latest appliances, as she dated from 1905, and her submerged displacement was only 313 tons, as compared with 800 tons in the *E* class. Her length was 135 feet, diameter 13½ feet, surface speed 13 knots, submerged speed 9 knots, and armament two torpedo tubes. Considering her comparatively small size, the work she did showed that the older classes were still effective, and might do better work in narrow waters than bigger boats.

The *B*-11 had for some time been attached to the Medi-

TURKISH BATTLESHIP "MESSUDIVEH" SUNK IN THE
DARDANELLES BY A BRITISH SUBMARINE

terranean fleet. Lieutenant-Commander Holbrook had been appointed to command her on December 30, 1913. Five successive rows of mines in the Dardanelles were passed under by the *B*-11, all being anchored. It was an act of extreme hardihood to dive under these mines, because at any moment the submarine might have fouled an anchor chain, or entangled her screw, or drawn one or more mines into contact with her hull as she went ahead. No one withheld admiration for the daring Holbrook displayed. But daring was not the only quality required. There was endurance as well. So long as the submarine could use her periscope, she could direct her course by observation, but she had to remain submerged for long periods. A handful of officers and men, perhaps twenty altogether, had to be submerged for a

FRENCH WARSHIPS SUNK IN THE EASTERN MEDITERRANEAN

The upper ship, the *Bouvet*, was sunk in the Dardanelles operation; the middle one, the *Léon Gambetta*, by an Austrian submarine; the lower one, the *Suffern*, by a submarine off Beirut

period of nine hours in narrow quarters, in parts of which a man could not stand upright. During a large part of that time they were as good as blind, owing to the necessity of withdrawing the periscope.

The *Messudiveh* was built in the Thames in 1874, but reconstructed at Genoa in 1901, when she received water-tube boilers and engines of 11,000 horse-power. Her displacement was 9,120 tons. She carried two 9.2 inch, twelve 6 inch and fourteen 3 inch guns, and twelve of lesser caliber. For her size she had a large anti-torpedo armament, but this availed nothing against *B*-11; nor did the pursuit of the torpedo-boats which followed the sudden raid. Another British submarine, *B*-9, entered the Straits next day, but was detected before she had gone far. Altho observation mines were exploded all around her, she made good her escape. A month, later the French submarine *Saphir* was less fortunate. While traversing the Straits, she struck the bottom near Nagara Point, came to the surface in a disabled condition, and was destroyed by shore batteries.

During January 1915, a decision was reached by the Allies to attack the Dardanelles in real earnest. The watching warships had been increased in numbers, and by February a powerful fleet was assembled, including the then newest British super-dreadnought, the *Queen Elizabeth*. The islands of Tenedos and Lemnos, near the entrance to the Dardanelles, were occupied. The bay of Mudros, in the latter island, became the principal base for the operations which followed. On February 17 the *Triumph*, accompanied by several destroyers, began their naval operations against the Dardanelles. The destroyers made dashes to within a thousand yards of the batteries guarding the entrance, but the Turks did not fire. Then the *Albion* bombarded a battery between Cape Hellas and Point Texel (which the bluejackets had rechristened "Tickle Point"), and the *Triumph* at 7,700 yards opened a slow indirect fire with ten-inch guns. The *Queen Elizabeth*, which bluejackets called "Big Lizzie," a super-dreadnought just out from the hands of the builders, followed with 15-inch shells. Still the Turks failed to reply. The *Ark Royal*, a water-plane ship, reported that Battery 50 was undiscoverable; that trenches and barbed wire had been set up and could be seen on shore, and there were troops at the top of the cliffs, but the Turks still refrained from responding. The *Triumph* reconnoitred along the shore and then opened fire with 7.5-inch guns on trenches and field-works. A naval chaplain wrote:

"You can not imagine a sight more majestic than the one we saw as we went back in the evening to join the fleet. The French ships were firing furiously against the Asiatic forts and the *Vengeance* and the *Cornwallis* were steaming up and down firing salvoes at Fort 3, which was a tough nut to crack. Imagine a glorious

SUNDAY SERVICE ON BOARD THE "QUEEN ELIZABETH"
OFF GALLIPOLI

sunset flaming across the sky behind the ships and the constant blazing of the salvoes shooting out over the smooth water. The high barren hills and the absence of everything to distract the eye from the great ships and their thundering guns made the bombardment a scene of grim, unforgettable impressiveness."

Bad weather now set in on February 19, and lasted until the 25th, which obliged the fleet to confine its activities to patroling. On February 25 the *Triumph* discovered Battery 50 and pounded it to pieces. That day three runs into the straits were made. The *Vengeance* and *Cornwallis* went first, the French warships *Gaulois* and *Bouvet* next, and then the *Albion* and *Triumph*. When the ships had steamed up 3,000 yards (less than two miles), they hove to under a tornado of Turkish shells that lasted three-quarters of an hour. Some of the shots fell short, and some fell beyond, the ships. Bricks and masses of earth, heaps of stone cannon-balls, which had been lying in the fort probably for a hundred years or more, were thrown into the air. When night came on the Turks set fire to the ruins of forts and barracks. Then bad weather started in again and brought the operations to a standstill.

On the 26th, as the only Turkish defenses left at the entrance were a few howitzers and field-guns, French and English mine-sweepers passed into the Straits. By March 1 all the defenses up to, but not including, the Narrows were believed to have been reduced. Then the *Albion* and *Triumph*, ordered to make a run to a fort on the Asiatic side, passed under heavy fire, the ships being deluged with shots falling all around them. Two Turkish shells fell on the *Triumph's* quarter-deck and one bruised the armor-belt. Of two that pierced her, one burst in the captain's cabin and destroyed the furniture. Another fell near the gun-room. In the evening men who had landed blew up and dismounted what guns were left in the batteries. An observer [7] of this storming, who was stationed on the heights of Mount Ilios, said of it:

"The sight was most magnificent. At first the fleet was ranged in a semi-circle some miles out to sea from the entrance to the Straits. It afforded an inspiring spectacle as it came along and took up positions. The picture became most awe-inspiring when the guns began to boom. The bombardment at first was slow, shells from the various ships screaming through the air at the rate of about one every two minutes. Their practise was excellent, and with strong glasses I could see huge masses of earth and stonework thrown high up into the air. The din, even at a distance, was terrific, and when the largest ship, with the biggest guns in the world, joined in the martial chorus the air was rent with the ear-splitting noise.

[7] Writing in The *Daily Mail* (London).

THE WAR AGAINST TURKEY

"The Turkish batteries, however, were not to be drawn, and, seeing this, the British Admiral sent one British ship and one French ship close inshore toward the Sidd-ul-Bahr Forts. It was a pretty sight to see the two battleships swing rapidly away toward the Northern Cape, spitting fire and smoke as they rode. They. obscured the pure atmosphere with clouds of smoke from their funnels and guns, yet through all I could see that they were getting home with the shots they fired as they went.

"In they sped, right under the guns of the shore-batteries, which could no longer resist the temptation to see what they could do. Puffs of white smoke dotted the landscape on the far shore, and dull booms echoed over the placid waters. Round the ships fountains of water sprang high up into the air. The enemy had been drawn, but their marksmanship obviously was very bad.

"Out came the two ships again, ineffectively pursued by shells from the Turkish batteries. As they retired they still continued to make excellent practise, and their parting shots were quite as good as their first. The position of the enemy's batteries had been covered as a result of this work, and soon the Turkish guns were under a hail of the most deadly shells warfare has ever known. From a distance, which must have been ten miles at least, monstrous projectiles dealing destruction and death were poured in upon the forts guarding the entrance, and each appeared to create a frightful inferno where it landed. The people gathered on all high points to see the awe-inspiring spectacle, the wonder of which struck them with utter amazement."

Extreme caution was necessary in using the attacking battleships, as the number of mines in the Straits was enormous. The Turks used not only anchored mines, but floating mines, which swirled round in uncertain fashion at the mouth of the Straits. Some of these mines were picked up outside as far away as Tenedos Island. The larger Turkish batteries were skilfully hidden, and it became necessary to knock out each gun individually. Seaplanes were busy during the bombardment on March 5, in order to discern the effect of indirect fire and to locate concealed positions. They had to fly very low, and thus were often in danger. Seaplane No. 172 was hit no fewer than 28 times; and Seaplane 7 eight times. One day a seaplane became unstable and dived nose forward into the sea. Both officers were injured.

87

Admiral de Robeck, who had taken command of the Allied squadrons, decided to deliver another naval attack unsupported by land forces. Shortly before noon on the following day, March 18, three successive squadrons entered the Straits and steamed toward the Narrows, bombarding vigorously. Three British battleships, the *Queen Elizabeth*, *Lord Nelson* and *Agamemnon*, with the battle cruiser *Inflexible*, mounting between them eight 15-in., sixteen 12-in., twenty 9¼-in., and ten 6-in. guns, bombarded the west and east sides of the Narrows, while the battleship *Prince George*, armed with four 12-in. and twelve 6-in. guns, engaged at Kephez Point, which is about three miles outside the Narrows. These ships did not get within decisive range of the forts which they were attacking, for when the French squadron of four battleships, the *Suffern*, *Gaulois*, *Charlemagne*, and *Bouvet*, moved up the Straits, soon after noon, to engage the forts at closer range, the forts replied so savagely as to indicate that the first bombardment had not been effective. Subsequently the fire of the ten battleships inside the Straits silenced these forts.

Admiral de Robeck followed up this initial success by sending into the Straits six battleships, the *Vengeance*, *Irresistible*, *Albion*, *Ocean*, *Swiftsure*, and *Majestic*, their combined armament being twenty 12-in. and four 10-in. guns. They were to relieve the six ships which had been engaged during the forenoon. It was on this occasion that the *Bouvet* was blown up by a mine north of Erenkoi, and sank in less than three minutes with all hands on board. Later on during the same day the *Irresistible* and the *Ocean* were also sunk, after having been struck by mines; but their crews were saved. In spite of these casualties, the remaining British ships continued in action till it was too dark to see their targets, when they withdrew, but without having completely subdued the fire of the shore-batteries.

The ships sent into the Dardanelles never had a chance of accomplishing their purpose. Owing to the narrow waters in which they were operating and the heights on shore, they were unable to get within decisive range of the forts without exposing themselves, not only to the risk of floating mines, but to being attacked individually by the

© UNDERWOOD & UNDERWOOD. N. Y.   THE ALLIED FLEET AT THE ENTRANCE TO THE DARDANELLES

VIII.

concentrated fire of shore-batteries. A battleship is a big target, and her only chance to avoid being hit is to keep in motion, as ships did during the bombardment of Alexandria, when, after advancing to within decisive range, they circled round and round in front of the forts all the time they were firing. While the ships bombarded the Dardanelles forts, they in turn were bombarded by mobile guns and heavy field-howitzers from concealed positions outside fixt batteries. The damage done to the ships was, for the most part, due to the field-pieces, which were moved about as circumstances required. While the ships could keep out of the effective range of fixt forts, they could not get away from mobile howitzer-batteries, which, favored by the configuration of the ground on both sides of the Straits, were able to fire at the ships without the latter being able to fire back at them. Herein lay the difficulty of the operations as long as they were confined to a naval action, a difficulty which was increased by danger from floating mines and from torpedo-stations on the shore. A German artillery officer who wrote an account of the battle claimed that the three Allied battleships were sunk by the fire of guns situated close to Chanak. He said the fire of the forts was first concentrated on the *Bouvet,* and, when she was sank, was diverted to the *Irresistible* and subsequently to the *Ocean,* causing both to share the fate of the French battleship. Admiral de Robeck's report stated that the three ships were sunk after striking floating mines.

It was now clearly seen that, before again sending ships against the Dardanelles, it would be necessary to land a force of men in the Gulf of Xeros, to seize the lines of Bulair, and to subjugate the Gallipoli Peninsula. So there was nothing to do but to wait for the arrival of land forces. Operations for the next five weeks were accordingly confined to mine sweeping and occasional bombardments of forts in the Narrows. Attempts at long-range bombardment had not prospered. The majority of the batteries at the Narrows were still effective. Neither indirect nor direct fire from the biggest guns afloat had really put them out of action for any length of time. Thus the high hopes created by the initiation of the naval operations were greatly diminished.

Even the destruction of batteries at Kum Kale and Sedd-el-Bahr, the two points forming the outer entrance, had not achieved the full purpose of the assailants. Turkish troops had afterward crept forward and entrenched themselves near the ruins, so that they had to be shelled once more. It was evident that the Dardanelles could never be forced by long-range fire, and it was still more evident that an army was needed to carry through the operation.

If the moral effect on the Balkan States and Italy of the opening of an attack on the Dardanelles had been great, it was impossible to exaggerate the counter-effect on them of this disaster. Greece settled back placidly to await a more promising time for casting in her lot with the Allies; Bulgarian soldiers once more began to invade Macedonia and threaten Serbia with a war on two fronts; German officers in Constantinople—Von der Goltz, notably—issued statements proclaiming that the forts of the Dardanelles were impregnable; the Sultan, himself, invited war-correspondents to visit him that he might express to them his confidence in his forts. Not even the appearance of a Russian fleet at the Bosporus served to counterbalance the confidence of the Turks. For the time being, sea-power had met with a considerable reverse. But if the loss in warships was heavy, it was not vital. The French and British ships actually sunk were old, had become mere platforms for heavy guns, and were of little value in the battle-line; but for these losses, such as they were, there had been no corresponding military advantage.

When a coming Allied attempt on the forts of the Dardanelles became known in Constantinople, in January, 1915, Henry Morgenthau [7a] says it was reported that the Allies had assembled "a fleet of forty warships," and a belief generally prevailed "that such an attempt would succeed." Even Baron von Wangenheim, the German Ambassador, "shared this belief," and so "in a modified form" did Field Marshal von der Goltz, "who probably knew as much about the Dardanelles defenses as any other man, as he had for years been Turkey's military instructor." On all sides "there were evidences of the fear and panic that had

[7a] "Ambassador Morgenthau's Story" (Doubleday, Page & Co.).

THREE OF THE BRITISH WARSHIPS THAT STORMED THE
DARDANELLES FORTS

The upper ship is the *Irresistible*, which was sunk; the middle one the
Inflexible, which was hit and set on fire; the lower one the *Ocean*, which
was sunk

stricken not only the populace but the official classes."
Wangenheim, making little attempt to conceal his appre-
hensions, had set on foot preparations to send his wife to
Berlin, and had invited Mrs. Morgenthau to accompany
her, "so that she, too, could be removed from the danger
zone." Wangenheim even showed a fear, which was then
the prevailing one, "that a successful bombardment would
lead to fires and massacres in Constantinople, as well as in
the rest of Turkey."

Mr. Morgenthau remarks that it "all seems so strange
now that this conviction should have been uppermost in
the minds of everybody then"—that the success of the
Allied fleets against the Dardanelles was thought to be inevitable and that the capture of Constantinople "was a
matter of only a few days." Among the wild rumors afloat
was one that seventeen transports had arrived at the strait
loaded with troops; another was that the warships had
already fired 800 shots and had leveled all the hills at the
strait. Had the Allies been able to capture the city, Mr.
Morgenthau says, the ruling powers had made their plans
for the event. They had intended to do to that great capital
"precisely what the Russians had done to Moscow when
Napoleon appeared before it." "They will never capture
an existing city," some of them told Mr. Morgenthau, "only
a heap of ashes."

This, he says, was no idle threat. He was told that cans
of petroleum had been actually stored in police stations and
other places, "ready to fire the town at a moment's notice,
"which, as Constantinople was largely built of wood, would
have been no very difficult task. The plans even aimed at
Saint Sophia, which had been marked for dynamiting. Early
in March the exodus from the capital had begun, Turkish
women and children being moved into the interior; all
banks compelled to send their gold into Asia Minor; the
archives of the Sublime Porte carried to Aski-Shehr; while
practically all the ambassadors and their suites, as well as
most of the government officials, "had made their preparations to leave." At the station stood trains which were to
take the Sultan, the Government and the ambassadors to
Asia Minor. These trains "had steam up, ready to move

at a minute's notice." We were all awaiting "the triumphant arrival of the Allied fleet." Enver Pasha was the man who had demonstrated "the vulnerability of the British fleet." When on March 18 the fleet made its greatest attack on the strait, the attack "proved disastrous to the Allies," the outcome being the sinking of the *Bouvet, Ocean,* and *Irresistible* and the serious crippling of four other vessels. Even then most people "still believed that the Allied fleets would succeed in forcing their way through." The only question was whether the Entente "was ready to sacrifice the necessary number of ships." Then the fleet went away and for days the Turks "anxiously waited for the fleet to return." It never came back.

Had the ships returned, "what would have happened?" asks Mr. Morgenthau. He answers by saying "the one overwhelming fact was that the fortifications were very short of ammunition"; that they "had almost reached the limit of their resisting power" when the British fleet passed out on the afternoon of the 18th. Once these defenses could have been made helpless, the problem of the Allied fleet would have been a simple one, the only bar to their progress being a mine-field, but the Allied fleet had plenty of mine-sweepers, which could have made a channel in a few hours, and once having silenced the outer straits, "there was nothing to bar the passage to Constantinople, except the German and Turkish warships." The *Goeben* was the only first-class fighting ship in either fleet, and would not have lasted long against the *Queen Elizabeth.* As for Constantinople, the populace and the best elements among the Turks, far from opposing the arrival of the Allied fleet, "would have welcomed it with joy." The Turks themselves were "praying that the British and French would take their city," for this "would have relieved them of the controlling gang, emancipated them from the hated Germans, brought about peace, and ended their mission." [8]

[8] Principal Sources: *The Fortnightly Review* (London) ; The *Evening Post,* The *Sun,* "Bulletins" of the National Geographic Society, New York ; Walter Leaf in *The Quarterly Review* (London), *The Literary Digest* (New York) ; The *Times,* The *Morning Post,* The *Daily Mail,* The *Daily News,* London ; Reuter's News Agency, The *Daily Chronicle* (London), The Cologne *Gazette,* The *Journal of Commerce* (New York), The *Standard* (London), The London *Times*' "History of the War."

VI

THE UNSUCCESSFUL LAND OPERATIONS AT GALLI-POLI, AND THE EVACUATION—ACHI BABA. SARI BAIR AND ANAFARTA

April 25, 1915—January 10, 1916

IN the weeks which elapsed between the great naval attack on March 18 and the first landing of troops on April 25, field defenses on the Peninsula had been prepared

with feverish haste by the Turks under German supervision. British troops had expected open fighting, and so believed they could carry Achi Baba (Tree Hill) by nightfall on the first day. Instead of this, they found themselves in contact with what proved to be a tremendous fortress, in which all natural advantages had been utilized to the utmost. The Turks held the heights and the British were on the lower ridges. It was like the position at the Shipka Pass, in 1877, when the Russians held the summit for six months and were never dislodged.

© ELLIOTT & FRY.

GEN. SIR IAN HAMILTON

The Turks on Gallipoli had their hands comparatively free. It might almost be said that there was no limit to the number of men whom they had available for use on the Peninsula. Nearly 800,000 had been mobilized at the outbreak of war, and of these 600,000 had been armed. For all practical purposes, at the time the Allies landed on the Peninsula at the end of April, they were potentially in contact with the bulk of the strength of the Turkish Army.

Not all the Turkish troops were there, but they were "within call." The Allies were thus matching 120,000 men against a military reservoir containing perhaps half a million. Under these conditions the man at home—the tax-payer who was ready to spend the last penny that the world might win the great fight for free government, free institutions and the right of the people to be governed according to their lights—was wondering why, instead of landing in the Gulf of Saros and following the course of the Maritza River for water, the British army had been sent to put its head into the lion's mouth at the entrance of the Dardanelles.

General Sir Ian Hamilton, who commanded the British troops, then just over 62 years old, had been soldiering all his life. He had been born in the Mediterranean, on the island of Corfu, within a short voyage of the scene of this most desperate undertaking. No soldier of high rank in the British army had seen so many varieties of warfare, or had enjoyed so many opportunities of studying at first hand operations on a grand scale in the struggle that now ensued. What came to be known as the battle of the Landing was in certain respects unlike any other battle ever known. Hamilton found himself in an extraordinary position. He had not planned the campaign, was without intimate knowledge of the scene, and had to undertake a task for which the number of available troops had been prescribed by others. The hills of the Gallipoli Peninsula really formed a natural fortress defending the Dardanelles. From the southern point a rocky plateau more than 600 feet high extended inland for five miles. Its highest ridge runs up to a summit known as Pasha Dagh. These hills form a salient, having its point toward the Gulf of Saros, the sides curving back to the Dardanelles above and below Kilid Bahr. To the north the high ground is broken into by a pass, through which a rough track runs from Krithia to the town of Maidos, on the channel opposite Nagara in the Narrows. To an invader, coming from the West and aiming at Maidos, the Pasha Dagh is not the only obstacle. West of it and south of Krithia rises the bold peak of Achi Baba, nearly 600 feet high, which sends out rocky spurs on both sides to the Dardanelles and the Gulf of Saros, and forms a barrier from sea to sea across the narrow western point of the Peninsula.

Hamilton found on arrival that while a force of troops had been assembled at the Peninsula, it was practically impotent, owing to the transports having been wrongly laden, a mistake for which he was in no sense responsible. Twenty-four hours after he arrived he had the mortification of witnessing a great naval attack accompanied by the loss of three Allied battleships. Because of the improper loading of the transports, he saw himself compelled to remove his troops to Egypt in order that the transports might be laden afresh, altho every day's delay enabled the Turks still further to improve their defenses.

The gathering-place of warships and troops was in the harbor and town of Mudros, on the island of Lemnos, which now became packed with men and ships, both British and French. Besides British soldiers there were Frenchmen in blue tunics and red trousers, Chasseurs d'Afrique with exquisite Arab horses, Senegalese Infantry, black as one's hat, with little tents, 8 feet long by 4 feet wide, and 2 feet high, in the middle of which six men slept. These tents were made in six pieces and were buttoned together, two on either side, and one at either end. The officers were Frenchmen, fine, sunburnt, big men; some dark-haired from the south, some quite fair. Ordinary French soldiers were in khaki. The Australians were big men, loose-limbed and big-jawed, riding carelessly, rough-coated, ugly horses. Here also were Territorials, Marines, Artillery, Flying Corps, Sappers, Army Service Corps, and all sorts of Greek soldiers and sailors, and women wearing the yashmak.

Wooden shops, run by Greeks who sold fruit, candy, post-cards, sponges, canned goods, whisky, brandy and beer sprang up in all directions at Mudros. Mules staggered about under heavy loads of fodder and supplies. There were ammunition carts, Red Cross wagons, and small boys crying "Pennie! Signor, pennie!" Out in the bay were battle-ships, cruisers, destroyers, transport supply ships, colliers, hospital ships, Greek trading schooners by the score, huge flat barges laden with fodder, and everywhere little puffing French patrol boats and larger British ones.

TURKISH BARBED-WIRE ON TOP OF A GALLIPOLI CLIFF

BRITISH FORCES LANDING IN GALLIPOLI

From this narrow beach the British had to surmount the steep hillsides
before they could attack the Truks, who were strongly fortified on top

The debarkations began on April 25. There were three of these: the Australian and New Zealand Army Corps, which landed on the shore north of Gabe Tepe—that is, about ten miles above the southern end of the Peninsula on the Ægean side; the troops from India on the extreme point south, and the French Division on the Asiatic side of the Straits in the neighborhood of Kum Kale. Altho the landing at all three points was successfully accomplished, the losses of the Allies were very heavy, owing to the nature of the shore combined with the elaborate defense which the Turks had constructed under the direction of German engineers, and the skill with which the defense was organized.

The advanced guard of the Gaba Tepe force was disembarked from three battleships, troops being sent ashore in the shall boats towed by pinnaces, followed by seven destroyers and a number of transports containing the rest of the force with guns and equipment. The landing took place north of Gaba Tepe, where only thirty or forty yards of beach intervened between the sea and the high cliffs which rise precipitously from the shore. The Turks were entrenched on the beach under the cliff, and opened fire on the boats just as they reached the shore, but were dislodged with the bayonet from their first position, as also from a second one on the cliff, which was stormed by the Australian covering parties, who then advanced inland in order to drive the Turks away from the coast, and enable the transports to land the rest of the troops and supplies in safety. The Turks being reinforced, counter-attacked the Australians in such numbers that they had to retire to the crest of the cliff, where they entrenched themselves against further attacks. Through the night Turks, led by German officers, continued their attacks with great determination, but with help from the fire of the ships their offensive was broken. By the night of the 26th, Colonial troops had dug themselves securely into their positions on the lower slopes of the Sari Bair ridgeway northwest of the Bokhali Valley. While the Turks renewed their attacks with the help of a reinforcement of field-guns, they could make no impression on the Australians and New Zealanders, who held a semi-circular line of trenches on the cliff covering the descent to the beach.

The Twentieth Division of the southern force landed simultaneously with the northern force. Under the same conditions, warships covered the debarkation with fire from their guns. Landings were effected on five different beaches. At places the troops gained a footing on land without much difficulty, but in and around Sedd-el-Bahr the Turks were so strongly entrenched that, after going on shore in two places, the landing parties had to withdraw till forces landed under Cape Helles, made a flank attack on the Sedd-el-Bahr position and drove the Turks out of their entrenchments. By the evening of the 27th, the Twentieth Division, after hard fighting, established itself across the whole of the Peninsula. The French landed on the same day at Kum Kale, not for the purpose of operating on the Asiatic shore of the Straits, but as a feint, made with the object of diverting attention from the British debarkation on the opposite shore. After the landing had been accomplished, and Kum Kale occupied, the French crossed over to the Gallipoli Peninsula and joined the British.

In the interior, which is a mass of tortuous hills and ravines, with here and there commanding points which dominate the surrounding country, is Achi Baba, which rises 730 feet above the sea and commands the road from Sedd-el-Bahr through Krithia to Maidos, as well as the Suandere Valley on the north. Before the Allied troops could pass the hill had to be stormed. It was here that the guns of the fleet came in with help afterward. The hill afforded a good target from the sea. Achi Baba is just six miles from the lower point of the Peninsula and midway between the Straits and the sea. From it two arms extend in a slight semi-circle reaching to the shore line on both sides. The mountain itself has a particularly forbidding aspect. One writer described it as most resembling an old Chinese idol, with great round stupid-looking head and two short, thickset shoulders, two long arms stretching out on either side as if barring the way to some forbidden inner temple. Between these arms lies the plain across which the Allies had to charge with the utmost heroism in their efforts to storm the mountain.

IN THE EAST, NEAR EAST, AND SOUTH

At the northeastern end of the Peninsula lies the city of Gallipoli, toward which the Allies were expected to make their way. It guards the Peninsula where it joins the mainland, and is near an elbow formed by the Dardanelles and the Sea of Marmora. It is the last inner defense of the Dardanelles, powerfully fortified, defensive works in modern style having been begun there in 1878, when the Russians threatened to take possession of Constantinople. At irregular intervals the work of strengthening it had been carried on. Gallipoli is not comparable in strength to the world's great fortresses, yet with modern batteries and extensive outworks it was made to form a proper complement to the other fastnesses of the Straits. It was the first land in Europe that the Ottomans gained in the 15th century. To-day the town itself is anything but beautiful. The streets are narrow and dirty. Most houses are wooden structures, in decay and untidy, with few buildings of any architectural interest. It has leaden-domed bazaars that appeal to westerners and a few uncared for relics of the Eastern Empire and Greek times,

RUPERT BROOKE

The English poet who died during the Gallipoli campaign. Brooke lies buried on the Island of Lemnos

but these are in a state of neglect and decay. It has two good harbors, both improved. One serves as the principal roadstead of the Turkish fleet. Gallipoli is 132 miles from Constantinople, and lies south of Adrianople. Here the Dardanelles are about two miles wide. Until the Turkish occupation Gallipoli seemed destined as a well-placed port, on one side of Nature's natural avenue of water trade, to become one of the greatest commercial cities in the Near East, but through centuries of Turkish rule it had slept an almost dreamless sleep.

The story of the landing of troops on the Peninsula was

told in much impressive detail by Ellis Ashmead-Bartlett. He described how "every round of ammunition, all water and all supplies had to be landed on a narrow beach, and then carried up pathless hills, valleys and bluffs, several hundred feet high, to the firing-line." The whole mass of troops, "concentrated on a very small area, and unable to reply," were exposed to a relentless and incessant shrapnel-fire, which swept every yard of the ground, altho fortunately a great deal of it was badly aimed, or burst too high. On going ashore, through a fire of burning shrapnel, you landed on a beach thirty yards wide between the water and a cliff which rises steeply for some hundred feet, to find there regiments waiting to move to the trenches, fatigue-parties unloading boats and lighters, others making great pyramids of canned foods and biscuits, others bringing water, of which a supply had been found on shore. Trains of mules were dragging field-guns into position; Indians were in charge of mountain-guns, and dressing-stations where the wounded were hastily tended before being sent to the ships. Other fatigue-parties were laying telegraph and telephone wires, and still others carrying supplies up the cliffs.

Mr. Ashmead-Bartlett said the problems in Southern Gallipoli were different from those which the Australians sucessfully solved further north. Here cliffs rise from fifty to one hundred feet from the water's edge, with little or no foreshore, jagged rocks making landings in some places impossible. There were at intervals stretches of beach. Five of these were selected for the disembarkation of troops, each under the covering fire of warships. Once men had climbed the low cliffs at any of these points, they found themselves on an open, grassy plateau, which stretched inland about two miles until the ground became more hilly and broken, near the village of Marethia, and the slopes of the dominating heights of Achi Baba. It was hoped by the Allies that the trenches would be rendered untenable by fire from the ships' guns, but the expectations failed to be realized.

A desperate struggle raged all day for what Mr. Ashmead-Bartlett called "W Beach," and the adjoining hills between

Cape Tekeh and Cape Helles. The landing parties had to
land on a wide expanse of sand, enfiladed by hills, and to
force their way up a semi-circular valley inland. Everywhere
the Turks had made trenches, protected by barbed wire
and held in force, while their snipers, hidden in broken
ground, covered every yard of the foreshore with a deadly
fusillade. The place was described as a death-trap. At
dawn, for three-quarters of an hour, it was swept by a tremendous fire from covering ships, which it was hoped would
effectively destroy the barbed wire on the foreshore.

Just at daylight troops were taken ashore from the
cruiser *Euryalus* in eight tows. All were exposed to a
heavy fire when approaching the shore. The tows which
made for the cliffs to the right reached the beach, and immediately scaled the cliffs and obtained a footing on the
crest right under the Turkish trenches, but here they were
held up and could advance no further. Troops literally
clung to the edge of the cliff on both sides of the beach.
The tows on the left, which had made for the shelter of
Cape Tekeh, finally got ashore and hung on in the same
manner. Other boats found themselves confronted by a
solid edge of uncut barbed wire and exposed to a terrible
cross-fire from concealed pom-poms, Maxims, trenches, and
snipers. In the cliff were holes in which Maxims were concealed, rendering them perfectly immune from shell-fire
from ships. Almost all who landed in the center were shot
down. Afterward another regiment landed, swept up the
valley and cleared the Turks off the sky-line, when it became possible to clear the wounded from the beach, cut the
barbed wire, and start landing stores and ammunition.
On the following day, more troops debarked on W Beach,
and the whole line, joining up with troops on X Beach,
was able to move forward and get astride the Peninsula.
Everywhere was found a scene of destruction and desolation
—trenches knocked into shapeless heaps by shell-fire, abandoned kits, broken rifles, and wire.

Running back from a fort was a perfect net-work of
trenches and barbed wire, running round a semi-circular
valley overlooking the beach and finally joining up with
the old castle and fort of Sedd-el-Bahr on the farther side.

THE "RIVER CLYDE" BEACHED AT GALLIPOLI

Loaded with British troops, this antiquated ship was driven ashore in order to effect a landing on a coast where the water was shallow. As the device recalled the "wooden-horse" story in Homer's "Iliad," the *River Clyde* became known as the "Ship of Troy." This landing place was hardly more than ten miles distant from the actual site of Troy

The Turks had mounted pom-poms on the Cape Helles side, and had snipers concealed everywhere. On the right was the old castle fronting the Straits, but now sadly battered by shells, yet still presenting a solid mass of masonry in which sharpshooters and Maxims could lie concealed. Just east of the castle were remains of the great battery which had been silenced by guns on February 19 and 25. Twelve-inch guns were finally demolished by a landing party of marines and bluejackets.

Behind the fort and castle lay the remains of the village of Sedd-el-Bahr, in which there was not a house left standing, for all had been destroyed by repeated bombardments of castle and fort. Nevertheless the ruins and gardens provided cover for the enemy's sharpshooters, from which to snipe the foreshore. Behind the remains of the village the ground rises to a height known as Hill 141, on which Turks had constructed a maze of trenches and barbed wire, and from which they could dominate the beach at point-blank range. The foreshore and valley leading inland were likewise protected by trenches and wire. The whole position was indeed one of the most formidable which troops ever attempted to take under normal conditions. Remembering that these troops had to be landed in boats and rowed ashore without cover, the feat becomes almost inexplicable.

The landing on V Beach will remain memorable, because of the novel experiment of running a liner—the *River Clyde*—full of troops deliberately ashore and thus allowing them to approach close in under cover without being exposed—a sort of application of the "wooden-horse" strategy of the Greeks at the seige of Troy. A great many lives were saved by the cover which steel sides afforded to hundreds of soldiers crammed between the side decks. Great doors were cut in the ship's sides, to allow a rapid debarkation, and wooden gangways were slung from ropes gradually down from these doors, so that men could pass down on both sides in single file and either jump into the water, if it was not too deep, or on to the lighters which were towed in with her. Her bridge was made a citadel with steel plates, and twelve Maxims, also protected by improvised casements and manned by the Maxim section of the Naval Division, were placed in

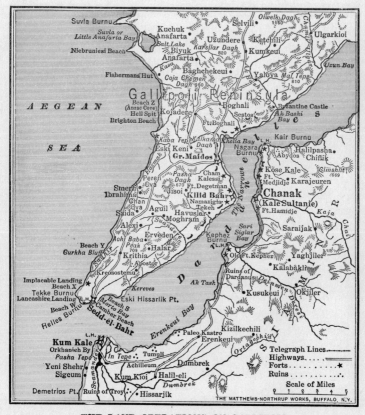

Map labels (Aegean Sea region, Gallipoli Peninsula):

Suvla Burnu · Suvla or Little Anafarta Bay · Niebruniesi Beach · Kuchuk Anafarta · Salt Lake · Biyuk Anafarta · Kasa · Coja Chemen Dagh 950 · Fishermans Hut · Uzundere · Karslar Dagh 820 · Selvili · Ollwek Dagh 1100 · Ketchili · Kumkeui · Baghchekeui · Ulgarkioi · Uzun Bay · Yalova Nal Tepe ·

Gallipoli Peninsula

AEGEAN · SEA · Beach Z (Anzac Cove) · Hell Spit · Brighton Beach · Kojadere · Boghali · PuBoghali · Sestos · Byzantine Castle · Ak Bashi Bay

Kaba Tepe · Kilkana Dagh · Khelia Bay · Nagara Burnu · Kair Burnu · Eski Keni · Gr. Maidos · Cham Kalessi · Abydos · Halilpasha · Chiflik · Köse Kale · Gimshlit 669 · Ft. Medjidje · Karajeuren · Pereu Ova · Pasha Dagh 670 · Ft. Degetman · Killd Bahr · Namazigia · Kekeh · Chanak (Kale Sultanie) · Ft. Hamidje · Kaja Chai · Smeru · Ibrahima · Chan · Oya · Aguil · Moghram · Havuslar · Sari Siglar Bay · Saraijak · Suida · Alexi · Achi Baba Peak 709 · Erveden · Halar · Kephez Burnu · L.H. · Old Ft. Kephez · Yaghjiler · Kalabakli · Beach Y · Gurkha Bluff · Krithia · Apostor · Kreosostemu · Ruins of Dardanus · Okjiler · Kusukeui · Implacable Landing · Beach X · Tekke Burnu · Lancashire Landing · Beach W · Helles Burnu · Kereves · Eski Hissarlik Pt. · Ak Tash · Beach S · Morto Bay · Camber Beach · Sedd-el-Bahr · Erenkeui Bay · Kizilkechili · Erenkeui · Paleo Kastro · L.H. · Kum Kale · Orkhanieh By · Pasha Tepe · Yeni Shehr · Sigeum · In Tepe · Tumuli · Achilleum · Dumbrek · Halil-eli · Dumbrek · Demetrios Pt. · Ruins of Troy · Hissarjik · Kum Kioi

Telegraph Lines · Highways · Forts · Ruins · Scale of Miles · 0 1 2 3 4 5

THE MATTHEWS-NORTHRUP WORKS, BUFFALO, N.Y.

THE LAND OPERATIONS ON GALLIPOLI

The various beaches where British and Australian troops made landings on the west coast of the peninsula, are indicated as "Beach W," "Beach X," etc., running north to "Beach Z" where the Anzacs (that is, Australians, New Zealanders, etc.) landed. Points where some of the severest fighting took place, after the cliff on the shore had been surmounted, were Krithia, Achi Baba, Gaba Tepe, and Anafarta. In the earlier operations with ships the Dardanelles were penetrated almost through the Narrows. Many have since believed that the French and British ships might have forced their way through to the Sea of Marmora, had they held on a few days longer, Turkish ammunition being about exhausted. The question then would have been, could Constantinople have been taken without a long siege?

her bows and lower bridge to sweep the shore when the troops debarked.

Over two thousand men were aboard the *River Clyde,* when at dawn, after a rapid bombardment from the battle-ship *Albion,* she slowly steamed toward shore, preceded by eight tows of steam-pinnaces and boats, that were to land the covering party. Those in the boats suffered terribly from rifle-fire, machine-guns, and the four pom-poms which swept the foreshore. Along the front of the beach was a bank of sand about four or five feet high. The survivors and the wounded crawled behind this, which gave them cover from the leaden storm. Meanwhile, the *River Clyde* had gone ashore further east than had been intended, bow-on, close to a reef of rock. The water was too deep to allow of men leaping from her and wading, but this contingency had been foreseen, and a steam-hopper was brought up and also run ashore to provide a gangway from the wooden gang-ways on either side. But this being not sufficient, it was necessary to drag a lighter to the far side of the hopper before the troops on board could attempt to debark. During this time the *River Clyde* was subjected to a tornado of rifle, Maxim, and pom-pom fire, the bullets rattling against her sides like hail-stones. The troops on board knew it meant almost certain destruction to leave her, yet at the call of their officers about two hundred dashed down the gang-way to the starboard side and attempted to reach the reef. Some were shot on the gangway; others were killed as they reached the hopper; others on the reef, and many of the survivors no sooner reached the beach than they fell. A few only survived, and lay under the shelter of the bank. Annihilation for the whole force was promised now if any further attempt to debark was made.

The battleships *Cornwallis, Albion* and *Queen Elizabeth* opened a furious bombardment on Sedd-el-Bahr, the hills be-hind and on the Turkish trenches, endeavoring to silence the pom-poms. Throughout the entire day, the *River Clyde* lay with two thousand of her men packed like sardines between her decks, and with officers crowded on her protected bridge. Bullets rattled against her steel-plates, but could not pene-trate them, while the sharpshooters on shore picked off every one who dared to show his head. Turks on the Asiatic shore endeavored to destroy the *River Clyde* by howitzer fire, but this was kept under by the covering warships in the Straits. Nevertheless, she was pierced by four big shells, all of which, fortunately, failed to explode. One way and other, about 1,000 men had left the *River Clyde,* and nearly half had been killed, wounded, or drowned. Most of the remainder were lying huddled under the sandy shelter on the beach, many with wounds. More than 1,000 were still cooped up on the collier, unable to land. The Turkish fire had grown in intensity, until it was almost certain death to pass down the gangway. After a time Maxim-guns held off the Turks and about 8 P.M. the whole of the thousand men still on board came out and quietly walked down the gangway without a casualty. Not a shot was fired against them.

Beach W had meanwhile been the scene of wonderful exploits. Sir Ian Hamilton said that "so strong were the defenses that the Turks may well have considered them impregnable." It was his firm conviction that "no finer feat of arms had ever been achieved by the British soldier or any other soldier than the storming of these trenches from open boats on the morning of April 25." The beach was practically in a bay enclosed by hills, and the way out of it led through a narrow gully. The Turks had fully expected a landing at this point, and had prepared for it. They had laid both land-mines and sea-mines, and on the edge of the sea had constructed broad wire-entanglements along the whole length of the beach. Heights overlooking the beach were covered with entrenchments, to which the gully gave sheltered access. Machine-guns were concealed in holes in cliffs and trained on the hedge of barbed wire.

Once the assailants emerged from the cup-like bay, they were instantly exposed to fire from two strong infantry redoubts near Hill 138, protected by wire-entanglements 20 feet broad. The fire swept a bare, open zone which had to be crossed in attacking the Turks. From these redoubts another strong wire-entanglement had been carried to the edge of the cliff, thus making communication between W Beach and the adjacent beach impossible until the redoubts were taken. Add to these defenses a host of snipers concealed behind sand-dunes and tufts of grass, and it was not surprizing that the Turks firmly believed W Beach able to resist any attack. The Turkish position had one weakness in rocks at the two ends of the bay which gave just a small foothold. From these rocks it was possible partially to enfilade the defenses. To this fact the success eventually achieved against heavy odds was in great measure due.

In the afternoon companies of troops landed on W Beach, advanced along the shore, and captured Turkish trenches on the hill overlooking V Beach, and also two pom-poms, but they were forced to retire at night. When it was sufficiently dark a fresh attempt to debark was made, and, strange to say, almost the entire force got ashore without the Turks firing a shot. On landing the troops were not pushed straight up the valley in front, but eastward, to get the shelter of the cliffs under the castle of Sedd-el-Bahr. At eleven o'clock the enemy was alarmed, and again opened a furious fusilade, sweeping the whole beach, but the Allies lay down under cover and suffered small loss. About eleven next morning began a final attack on the Turkish trenches. The losses were severe, but at noon the position was taken and the Turks fled. After these unparalleled exertions, V Beach was cleared, and the way paved for a further advance inland.

When the *River Clyde* had been run ashore at the landing beach immediately west of Sedd-el-Bahr, it seemed up to the last moment that the landing was to be made without opposition, but the moment the first boat touched sand the storm broke. A tornado of fire swept over the beach. The Dublin Fusileers and the Naval boat-crews suffered exceedingly heavy losses in the boats. Those who landed and crossed the strip of sand managed to gain some cover, but none of the boats was able to get off again. All were absolutely destroyed by Turkish fire on the beach. The situation was probably saved by machine-guns on the *River Clyde*, which managed to keep down the Turkish fire.

The ruins of Sedd-el-Bahr, as Ashmead-Bartlett describes them, presented an amazing spectacle. The castle, forts, and villages were a jumble of crusht masonry. Guns in the forts were smashed into huge pieces of steel, and had been thrown by the force of the explosions several yards from their mountings. Great piles of unused ammunition were piled up beside them. The old towers of the castle were partly standing, altho riddled by huge shells. The barracks at the back had been gutted by shells and flames. In the village beyond it was difficult to follow the lines of streets, as houses, orchards, and gardens seemed thrown into a great pot together. Everywhere the ground was scattered with débris—fragmentts of shell, scattered graves, knapsacks, great-coats, broken rifles, twisted bayonets, soldiers' caps and helmets, and tattered heaps of uniforms and clothes. Not a living soul was left in the village, except stray soldiers sight-seeing, and a horde of starving cats prowling among the ruins of their former homes. Interiors and roofs of houses had fallen in and lay mixed up with furniture, bedding, fire-grates, and cooking untensils. It was a scene of complete desolation. Beyond the village you could follow the line of the last attack, which ended in the capture of the Turkish trenches on Hill 141, by the graves, the barbed wire, and the extraordinary mazes of trenches which twisted and turned in all directions, many having disappeared altogether under the rain of shells from the ships. So ran Mr. Ashmead-Bartlett's thrilling narrative of which an outline has been given here.

Immense work was accomplished by the warships during these operations. The whole responsibility for landing the troops, and keeping up supplies of food and ammunition was left to them, and in addition the responsibility of protecting the flanks of the combined armies and keeping down the enemy's artillery-fire. All troops, animals, guns, wagons, stores, ammunition, and a thousand other things had to be taken from the hundred transports lying off the Straits, which arrived from Egypt full and left empty for a fresh cargo at all hours of the day and night, and conveyed in trawlers or lighters to two narrow beaches, neither of which was more than 200 yards in width. Cliffs prohibited landing anything at any other point. Naval commanders, lieutenants, and midshipmen in charge of this work developed an efficiency which astounded even expert theorists.

Piers were built out into deep water, so that the largest lighters could come alongside, with cut roads along the cliffs to increase the area of debarkation. A hundred devices were hit upon to lessen labor and increase efficiency, including systems of lighting which enabled the work to go on uninterruptedly night and day, for even when the day's work was over, and the last lighter had discharged her cargo, streams of wounded were walking or being carried down to the beaches, where they were embarked on empty barges and dispatched for transportation to hospital ships. The whole work of this landing meant perfection in organization. How it was managed will ever remain somewhat of a mystery. Perhaps such a task was never before attempted by an army and navy—even when the landing had been completed. The Turks on the Asiatic shore shelled the beach almost every day. Warships were continually engaged in trying to locate guns and knock them out, or force them to change position. On one beach the sight of the "ship of Troy," as the *River Clyde* came to be called, seemed to excite peculiar indignation. The Turks fired round after round at her, while the work of debarkation went on uninterruptedly.

, The ultimate objective was to obtain possession of Achi Baba. But before this could be attempted it was necessary to obtain possession of the two great arms of that somber mountain which stretch out, one to the Gulf of Saros and the other to the Dardanelles. From a hill above the beach a perfect view was obtained of the entire battlefield. It was from this observation-post that Ashmead-Bartlett saw and then described scenes which occurred, culminating in a tremendous combined infantry assault on the enemy's whole line on the evening of May 8. From this hill Achi Baba was distant exactly six miles to the northeast. The battle had lasted for two days without cessation, when it was continued next day with greater violence.

The ships opened up a bombardment of the right arm of Achi Baba, Krithia, and the ground behind them. When this had lasted for half an hour, infantry on the left center advanced to the attack, and again began another furious outburst of rifle- and machine-gun fire which showed that the Turks were still holding trenches with determination. Throughout this fighting in broken ground on slopes leading up to Krithia, a plain stretching below looked as if some annual maneuvers were taking place. Across the whole successive lines of khaki figures were pressing over green fields and through farms and orchards toward the firing-line. The enemy's shrapnel burst over them, but inflicted small damage, owing to the open formations. When each successive line reached the fire-zone, it doubled across open ground, resting in vacated trenches, and then passing on to the next. The whole plain seemed alive with these khaki-clad infantry. They were the New Zealand Brigade, who had moved up for the final assault, and, on their left, the Australian Brigade, who passed on the left of the Krithia Road for a like purpose.

Weeks of effort produced practically no alteration in the position of the Anzac lines at Gaba Tepe. On the other hand, the Turks pursued a course of action which had for its object the reduction of the conflict to one of siege operations, after the manner of the struggle in France. They attained their object, but at a heavy cost. The Germans and Turks, realizing the impossibility of driving the Allies off the Peninsula by infantry attacks, spasmodic night-attacks, and heavy shelling, put forth their best endeavors to dig, blast and bomb their enemies back into the sea. The fact that they did not accomplish their object with their greatly superior forces, and more commanding tactical position was because they were meeting troops of greater bravery, endurance and resource than themselves.

There was terrible carnage among the Turks during their supreme effort on May 19. The sight of seemingly endless masses of them advancing might well have shaken the nerves of already severely tried troops, but British machine-guns and artillery mowed them down in hundreds. Still the advancing wall swept on as if the ranks would never waste their strength. Not till the wave was at point-blank range from nimble trigger-fingers did it break and speed itself among barbed-wire entanglements. Some of the Turks were shot when in the act of jumping into the Allied trenches, so that their corpses lay with heads and arms hanging over the parapets. Allied fire gradually dominated the ground, and Turks who turned to fly were mowed down before they could run a dozen yards. The Germans sent supports and reserves forward in droves. It was sickening to observe the slaughter the Allied fire made among the massed battalions as they issued from concealing into open spaces. Turks scrambled over piles of dead bodies, but in an instant a company would be enveloped in the smoke of a shrapnel salvo. When the air cleared that company would be stretched, or writhing, on the ground, with another company approaching, and ready to share its predecessor's fate. It

TURKISH INFANTRY

became a question, not of the success or otherwise of the attack, but of how many Turks the British could kill. The wastage of life continued long after the failure of the assault had become apparent. A green patch became a shambles. On a few acres the burial party, working during the armistice which followed, counted no fewer than 4,000 Turkish and German dead. The Allied losses were perhaps not a tenth as many.

On May 22 the actual presence of submarines in the neighborhood of the Dardanelles was proved beyond a doubt. At 1.30 P.M. on that day a periscope was sighted. Mr. Ashmead-Bartlett, six months afterward, declared that the true history of the voyage of the German submarines from the English Channel and their arrival off the Dardanelles would, when written, make one of the most fascinating stories of the war. He could not help admiring the enterprise their commanders showed, and especially the skill with which they had organized their depots of oil. Judging from what English submarine boats had already accomplished in the Sea of Marmora and in the harbor of Constantinople, he believed, however, that, if they had had opportunities equal to those of the Germans, they would have accomplished far more.

The Allied fleet at the mouth of the Dardanelles had been confident and happy until the third week in May when vague rumors came that hostile submarines had passed Gibraltar, followed by other rumors that one had been seen off Malta, another had passed the Doro Channel and then been sighted again off Cape Matapan. One fine day the pride of the British fleet at the Dardanelles, the *Queen Elizabeth,* faded mysteriously away before all observers' eyes bound for some unknown destination. Men mourned her departure, but realized that some necessity unknown to them existed. Other vessels of the fleet, all of good fighting capacity, then were discerned to be visible on the horizon less and less, or off shore for short periods only and then they would fade away, bound apparently for distant ports. The admiral was seen to transfer from time to time four large flags to smaller and less valuable ships, and then the larger one which he had left would disappear. In the course of two months Ashmead-Bartlett himself lived on six different floating homes, which as to size and importance went gradually down in scale. When the submarine menace finally assumed definite and concrete shape, no ships of great fighting value, altho there were many that bore historic names, remained off the coast of Gallipoli. The smaller ships that remained now took up the work of the others as if nothing had happened. It was from the deck of the *Swiftsure* that Ashmead-Bartlett saw the *Triumph* go down, struck by a torpedo from a submarine.

After the *Triumph* was sunk the whole of the available

THREE BRITISH SHIPS THAT SERVED IN THE
DARDANELLES OPERATIONS

The ship at the top of the picture is the *Queen Elizabeth* ("Big Bessie,"
sailors called her), a superdreadnought. The one in the center is the
Queen Mary, which was afterward sunk in the Jutland battle, a shell piercing her thin-armored plating and causing her magazine to explode, so that
she went down "in a smother of smoke and flame." The one at the bottom
is the *Majestic,* which was sunk off Gallipoli by a torpedo

British destroyer craft started on a hunt after the submarines which were said to be making their way south from Gaba Tepe toward Cape Helles. The Admiral transferred his flag to the twenty-year-old *Majestic* which was now the only battleship left off Cape Helles, and the oldest British man-of-war at the Dardanelles. Thus the veteran of the fleet, after twenty years of service all over the world, found herself once more a flagship. Destroyers kept up an unceasing chase of the hostile craft which were sighted more than once beneath the surface, but they were at too great a depth to be rammed. On May 26 the *Majestic* was at her old anchorage off Cape Helles. Ashmead-Bartlett was on board. At 6.40 next morning, when sleeping on deck, he was aroused by men rushing by when some one of them trod on, or stumbled against his chest. This woke him and he called out, "What's the matter?" to which a voice replied: "There's a torpedo coming." He had just time to scramble to his feet when there came "a dull, heavy explosion about fifteen feet forward of the shelter-deck, on the port side. His narrative proceeds:

"The old *Majestic* immediately gave a jerk over toward port, and remained with a heavy list. Then there came a sound as if the contents of every pantry in the world had fallen at the same moment. You could tell at once she had been mortally wounded, and you felt instinctively she would not long stay afloat. Later the *Majestic* rolled right over to port, and so the old flagship disappeared forever, except for a small piece of her ram, which remained above water, as her bows were lying on a shallow sand-bank. As she turned over and sank, a sailor ran the whole length of her keel and finally sat astride the ram, where he was subsequently taken off without even getting a wetting. Some of those still clinging to the ship were dragged down by the fatal nets before they could get clear; others were probably killed inside by the explosion. Nevertheless, the loss of life was small, numbering only fifty."

On June 4 a general assault was begun on the Turkish trenches in front of Achi Baba, preceded by a bombardment. For an hour the fire of every British and French gun on the peninsula poured shells of various calibers into Turkish trenches. Battleships and a large destroyer off the northern coast battered the enemy's right, while a French warship in the entrance to the Dardanelles dropt heavy projectiles on the left of the Turkish position. British 18-pounders and French "75's" kept up a rain of shells on the parapets of the enemy's trenches. At times the whole line was obliterated behind a billowy curtain of creamy smoke. In Krithia a tower which had withstood a score of minor bombardments came toppling down, and fire broke out in the village. For an hour the air was rent with terrific crashes, one blending into another, and alive with shrieks and whistles of projectiles as they sailed overhead toward the enemy's lines.

Punctually at 12 the order to go forward was given, and men in the first line of trenches leapt out, parties of bomb-throwers accompanying them, and dashed across the intervening hundred yards to the Turkish trenches. The first line was to occupy and clear the first trench. The second was to pass over the first and capture the second. The second had thus considerably farther to go than the first, the lines of trenches being about 500 yards apart. A third was to advance after the others, fill up the gaps, and press home the attack. The second did not advance until a quarter of an hour after the first started.

The enemy, who had made no effective reply to the bombardment, immediately began to pour shrapnel on the troops rushing to the assault. The troops went forward with the capture of the first trench, being the work of a few minutes. The Turks, dazed and deafened by the avalanche of shell-fire which had been bursting around them for an hour, fired a shot or two upward from the trenches and then fled along the communication trenches to the rear trenches. A large number who were found dead and wounded in the trenches seemed to have fallen victims to the shell-fire. The second line, dashing forward under hot fire from the Turkish rear trenches, captured the second line, and the Turks being fairly on the run for the moment, British troops followed up their advantage wherever they could, which was chiefly in the center, where the resistance was weakest. They captured line after line of trenches.

At noon armored turret motor-cars using improvised paths

leading from Sedd-el-Bahr and Cape Helles to Krithia passed into something like roads, dashed up to the firing-line, four on each road, timing their attack to coincide with that of the first line. Crossing the British trenches on bridges, they went on jolting and rocking over pitfalls in the ground and so up to the Turkish trenches. Here the cars opened fire with Maxims on Turks fleeing from the first trenches to the rear. Soon bullets began to fall against the armored sides of the çars, and shells to fall around them. Being unable to advance further, the cars withdrew, shells falling between them as they drove back along the roads. One car was hit and the top of its turret knocked off, but nobody was killed. The total loss was a few men wounded. All the cars came back, only two being damaged.

The quick success of the Allied center had carried their line 600 to 1,000 yards forward. On the flank the Turks were much more strongly posted, and a desperate struggle began. On the right the French, stopt by the formidable barrier of the Kereves Dere gully, were unable to make similar progress. The Royal Naval Division dashed forward with the rest of the British line, but found itself unable to maintain the ground won, because it would have meant a gap between them and the French. The situation here tended more and more to resemble that in eastern France. The enemy had an ideal defensive position—a narrow peninsula traversed by ranges of hills or small mountains, every inch of which could be entrenched to advantage—with one flank safe from attack by sea and both incapable of being turned by land, as they reached down to the water's edge.

Achi Baba, the barrier in front, altho far less rugged and steep than the ridge on which the Australians established themselves, proved no less difficult to assault. The Australian ridge was like Majuba Hill,[8a] so steep that men climbing it would often be out of reach of others who were firing down from the crest. Achi Baba, on the other hand, was a series of smooth slopes, terraced at intervals, and much

[8a] A hill in South Africa, stormed by the British in the Boer War of 1880-81.

the same to mount as the glacis of an old-fashioned fort. Turkey was an enemy less fertile in resource than the Germans; less well equipped; less rigorous in attack; but she had advantages which the Germans could no longer claim. She had an ideal defensive position—a narrow peninsula traversed by ranges of high hills or small mountains, every inch of which could be entrenched to advantage.

Lack of progress by the Allies in the Dardanelles in April and May had produced a cheerful frame of mind in the Turkish capital. Constantinople papers were crying victory and seemed to regard the war as virtually over. They pointed satirically to the series of defeats which were to be inflicted by the Allies on Germanic arms as soon as the spring campaign began, and recalled Kitchener's famous prophecy that the war would "begin in May." Taking this for a text under the title of "The First Fruits of May," the Constantinople *Ikdam* said:

"As soon as the weather opened up, England was to send to France millions of troops; then with her Allies they would take up position against the Germans and make violent attacks on them; within two weeks, or three at the most, they would cut through the line of battle of the Germans; Alsace-Lorraine on the one side and Belgium on the other should be entirely freed; the Germans would receive such terrible blows that before June they would be suing for peace, for they would be beaten by land and by sea. At the same time the Russians would be well on their way toward Berlin. As for Austria-Hungary, that country would be cut to pieces by June; and because of the advance of the Russians toward Vienna, the Hungarians would secede and try to form a little State under the protection of Russia. Transylvania and Bukowina would also secede; Serbia would have occupied Bosnia and Herzegovnia; in short, the name of Austria-Hungary would have been wiped off the map. As regards Turkey, the Allies were to be in Constantinople before May, and the armies of Russia were to have made great progress in Anatolia.

"The first-fruits that spring has ripened are as sweet and pleasant to us as they are bitter and poisonous to them—so poisonous that they are carrying them off to death. In the west the Allies are being beaten; they are retreating, leaving prisoners, cannon and ammunition behind them. On the sea the German submarines and in the air the German Zeppelins are constantly striking blows at the English. On the Eastern Front, whether in the East Prussia region, in Poland, or in Galicia, the victories that are being gained are terribly shaking the Russians, especially do the Galician victories seem to be decisive. As for ourselves, by the grace of God, our heroic defenders have succeeded in inflicting terrible blows on the enemy in the Gallipoli Peninsula. Each day of spring that passes brings our enemies discouraging defeats."

All reports from the Dardanelles in those spring and summer days brought out with startling clearness the formidable nature of the Allied undertaking. The mountainous country which lay ahead of them was to be compared only with an immensely strong fortress, that could be taken only by storm. Some estimates of the losses of the Turks named 70,000. British losses, naval and military, up to the end of May were stated by Mr. Asquith in the House of Commons at 38,636. Nevertheless the battle of the fourth of June ended in substantial progress. The British and French line across the peninsula from the Ægean to the Dardanelles had been confronted by rising ground culminating in the center with the flat summit of Achi Baba, 800 feet high. On either side the ground falls away to the sea in ravines and dry watercourses, which the Turks had had time to make almost impregnable. The Allies had to storm an immensely strong fortress the advanced works of which, by an amazing feat of arms, they already held, but the glacis of which had to be crossed before they could move forward to the assault upon Achi Baba and beyond to the final assault upon the walls of the fortress.

Further up the coast the Australians and New Zealanders had made a lodgment on one of the strongest advance-works of the Kilid Bahr Plateau. As seen from the northwest, they threatened the communications of the fortress and were drawing against them a large part of the garrison. This was composed of the flower of the Turkish army. These troops were fighting with gallantry; with desperation, indeed, because they realized that when the bastion of Achi Baba fell the occupation of the Kilid Bahr Plateau would become a mere question of time, and that when Kilid Bahr

TURKISH TROOPS RESTING IN GALLIPOLI

fell the doom of Constantinople was at hand. The gain of a score of yards in the Gallipoli Peninsula fairly represented for the purposes of comparison a gain of 500 yards in the western theater of war. Therefore, to find its importance the gain of 500 yards on June 4 had to be named with Neuve Chapelle. Minor actions, generally inconclusive, followed for many days.

On June 21 it was determined to straighten the line on the extreme right. At 1.30 A.M. the preliminary bombardment began. The dawn had come clear, but soon a curtain of silver, through which gleamed the ghost of the rising sun, hung over the Kereves Dere, formed by the smoke of bursting shells. Slowly as the sun climbed up, the curtain became more substantial, then seemed to droop and sweep along hollows with a vanishing mist. During a respite the blue smoke of bivouac fires came tranquilly into the still air and the bombardment began again with greater fierceness than before. The 75's drummed unceasingly, while the reverberations of the 125's and the howitzers shook the observation-post. Over the Kereves Dere and beyond, on the sloping shoulders of Achi Baba, the curtain became a pall. As the sun climbed higher and higher all that first mirage of beauty disappeared. There was nothing but the monstrous shapes of bursting shells and ghosts of smoke along the Turkish lines.

All through that morning the cannonade went on. By noon the French on the left stormed and captured all the Turkish trenches of the first two lines. Even the Haricot Redoubt, with its entanglements and maze of communicating trenches was in French hands. But on the right, the First Division, after reaching their objective, were counter-attacked so effectively that they fell back only to advance once more to take trenches, and again to be driven out. There were still five hours of daylight for this battle on the year's longest day, with British guns and howitzers. At half-past five it seemed as if every gun on earth were pouring shells on the Turkish lines. At six o'clock there was a temporary shortage of ammunition in a Turkish trench but the Turks fought with stones, sticks, and fists. A battalion, hurrying up to reinforce the trench, was caught on open ground by drumming 75's and melted away. Six hundred yards of Turkish trenches were taken.

The smoke of the shells, which at dawn had been ethereal, almost translucent, was now at the sunset, turbid and sinister, yet the sunset was splendid, flaming in crimson streamers over Imbros, tinting the east with rosy reflections, and turning the peaks of Asia to sapphire. This possest peculiar significance for the longest day of the year, crowning as it did those five hours of daylight that, for the French, were fraught with achievement. Slowly the color faded out, and, minute by minute, the flashes of the guns became more distant; the smoke was merged in the gathering dusk, and over the more distant Turkish lines bursts of shrapnel came out like stars against the brief twilight.

The Turkish casualties were believed to be about 7,000. One trench, 200 yards long and 10 feet deep, was brimming over with dead. French officers who had fought in the west said that, as a fighting unit, one Turk was worth two Germans. With his back to the wall the Turk was magnificent. The French casualties were few, considering what a day it had been, what enemy was being attacked, and how much had been gained. The profile of Achi Baba seemed now to write itself less stolidly against the sky.

On June 28 Sir Ian Hamilton ordered the attack continued, his intention being to threaten Krithia by advancing his left wing west and east of the Saghir Dere ravine, which runs nearly parallel to the Ægean coast, about a mile inland. The battle opened with a combined artillery bombardment by French and British guns, assisted by the fire of the *Talbot*, *Scorpion*, and *Wolverine*. The bombardment was longer and more effective than that on June 4, the wire entanglements in front of the Turkish trenches being completely destroyed, and the trenches themselves so shattered that when the men of the Indian and Twenty-ninth Divisions rushed forward to attack they had a comparatively easy task. West of Saghir Dere, where the Turkish trenches had been exposed to the naval gun-fire, the Indians captured three lines of trenches, with little opposition, many of the Turkish soldiers being found buried in the débris, while those who remained were taken prisoners. East of the ravine the Royal Scots made a fine attack, capturing two lines of trenches. Meanwhile the Gurkhas, pressing along the Saghir Dere, captured a commanding knoll directly west of Krithia, the final result of the day's fighting being a gain of 1,000 yards, while the left wing was thrown forward so as to face east instead of north.

The net result of the fighting on June 28 was a gain of a mile along the coast, the capture of four lines of Turkish trenches, about 200 prisoners, three mountain-guns, and an immense quantity of small arms, ammunition, and many rifles, the total gain being a right angled triangle, each side of which was about a mile long. This, at the time, was the most successful engagement fought on the peninsula, and became newly important when judged by its effect on the morale of the Allied troops. The success was mainly due to changes made in tactics and to an enormous improvement in the support given by the artillery.

The battle of the Gully Ravine, as it came to be known, was a classical example of sectional attack, the kind which alone leads to decisive results in modern warfare; that is to say, there was no general advance along the whole line. A section was selected and every available gun concentrated on the works to be assaulted, which were battered to pieces or completely smothered by high-explosive shells, while the wire in front was cut to pieces by twenty minutes' concentrated shrapnel-fire. Thus, when the Allied infantry were let loose, they were able to walk into some of the works without opposition. The Turks who were not dead were running away or surrendering.

The captured trenches presented an extraordinary appearance. They were smashed by high-explosive shells and littered with dead and débris of all descriptions; the stench was unbearable; the entanglements had been cut to shreds in places by shrapnel. The Allies captured hundreds of rifles and thousands of rounds of small-arms ammunition. Every rifle taken was as good as a prisoner or a dead Turk, because the Turks had only a limited number, and in one engagement there were troops in the front line armed only with Martinis. The prisoners captured were mixed, coming from all parts of the Turkish Empire, while most of the officers were young and inexperienced, with only a few months' service behind them.

Years from now, when the surviving veterans of this campaign in Gallipoli shall gather round some festive board in London or Paris, in Australia or New Zealand, holding an annual celebration to commemorate the final Allied success in the war, the name which will recall to them the most somber memories may be the Gully Ravine. Someone described it as "a devil of a place," and that description was not inaccurate. Steaming along the western coast of Gallipoli you would not have suspected its existence. It varied in depth, in width, and in security as you passed along its course. After leaving the seashore it took a general direction toward Krithia and twisted and turned in a remarkable manner. At one point you could walk in security behind a bluff, while at another you caught a stream of bullets from Turkish trenches. The Ravine lay between overhanging craggy hills, which were in places 200 feet high, and covered with a thick green shrub, varied by patches of yellow, sandy soil, which seemed common to the whole of the southern end of Gallipoli. Except for the war, soldiers would have stopt to admire the beauty of the scene, which resembled the Scottish Highlands in its rugged grandeur.

The heat in summer was almost unbearable because no sea breezes penetrated the depths of the peninsula, and the sun beat down on the war-worn road with pitiless severity. But there was plenty of good water for men and horses, parched by sun and sand. Springs, carefully guarded against pollution, were known and beloved by every thirsty soldier. Some of them, flowing from interior hills, entered the valley in a tiny, trickling stream, clear as crystal and icy cold. Crowds of perspiring, dusty, thirsty men would wait indefinite periods in a long queue, each with his water-bottle in hand, for the privilege of obtaining a draught from one of these springs, more valued in Gallipoli than the choicest brand of champagne would have been in London or Paris. Along the road in every spot sheltered by overhanging cliffs could be found hundreds of weary men from the trenches who had flung themselves down to snatch a few hours' sleep. There they would lie unconscious of, and indifferent to, shells bursting overhead and the stream of stray bullets "sizzling" along. A man would drop and be immediately carried to the dressing-station, but no one took the smallest notice, for prolonged experience had the effect of making nearly all indifferent or fatalists. In the ravine one constantly came upon lonely graves, each with a cross and a name, marking the last resting-place of some soldier fallen in one of the early engagements, or who was buried just where he fell.

All the way up that gully which only twenty-four hours before had been in Turkish possession, had become a litter of the débris of the camp. Scattered bodies half protruding from the ground, hastily dug graves, hundreds of rifles and bayonets, some broken, but the majority intact; thousands upon thousands of rounds of ammunition, entrenching tools, loaves of bread, soldiers' packs, Turkish letters, a Mullah's prayer-stool (a souvenir eagerly sought), an overcoat and kits, blankets, and old sacks, cooking utensils, and firewood, left just where the enemy had abandoned them when the Allied infantry broke through at the bayonet's point. Great fires were burning at intervals. They were avoided by all, and gave forth a horrid, sickly stench. On these the Turkish dead, who had been hastily collected, were being burnt, for it was all important to get the dead out of the way as quickly as possible in so hot a climate.

On July 6 some of the heaviest fighting that had occurred on the peninsula resulted in a swing forward of the southern line for something over 3,000 feet and the infliction of severe losses on the Turks. British estimates placed the Turko-German casualties at 7,000 killed and from 14,000 to 15,000 wounded. The whole army in the southern part of the peninsula was engaged. The Australians and New Zealanders further north also took part. The success marked an indefinite stage in the initial work of throwing forces around Achi Baba, which the Allies had now begun to believe one of the strongest fortresses in the world. French and British machine-guns were rushed to the front, until a perfect wall of guns was in position. Suddenly the stillness was broken by a tremendous burst of shells from Turkish guns, and shrapnel poured down on the French front. The men were safely in positions in dugouts and little loss resulted. The battered *Goeben* was at work again, and pounded the Allied right with 11-inch shells, many of which, however, did not burst.

The hail of shells lasted an hour and a half and was the severest bombardment to which the Allied lines had been subjected during the struggle on the peninsula. No sooner had the heavy fire ceased than great solid masses of Turks leapt to the attack. On they came, the silence unbroken, save for their shouts, until they reached a point within sixty or seventy yards of the French position, when from well-placed machine-guns a devastating fire burst from the trenches, and rifles joined in, 20,000 of them, the big guns flaring and casting a lurid light over the scene. They reached the barbed-wire entanglements only to find that their artillery had been ineffective in attempting to demolish them. The slaughter here was terrible. At three points the enemy managed to swarm into the French trenches and even to turn some of the French weapons on the defending troops, but the second French line hurled itself instantly on the foe who, being badly supported, fled. Into the struggling, fleeing masses Maxims poured streaks of death, mowing the enemy down in heaps. Meanwhile, the naval division had been sustaining a portion of the attack and turned its machine-guns on the wreck of the attacking force. They held searchlights firmly fixt on the Turks and thus provided a ghastly target for guns and rifles. Soon the field presented an appalling spectacle Soldiers who fought in some of the fiercest fights in France and Flanders, and who had been through the terrible experience provided by the landing of Allied forces on the peninsula, said they sickened at the sight which lay before their eyes when the dim glow of morning was spread over the scene.

Bodies were lying four and five deep on the ground. Fallen men lay strewn on the barbed-wire entanglements, while many of the enemy's dead still stood erect, propt up against masses of their stricken comrades. Further and further, amid yells and groans mixed with shouts and the whistling of officers, the battered and beaten rabble retreated, followed by relentless death. The sight was so

terrible that many could not fire guns or rifles. This especially affected those in charge of machine-guns. At last the
poor remnant of the Turkish attacking force was sheltered in
trenches in front of Achi Baba's slopes. The opposition was
feeble. The first line of attackers easily carried the first line
of the Turkish position. Then the second line swept on, and
after a stubborn struggle the Turks were in headlong retreat. The British for the next two hours, in new positions,
were subjected to a bombardment of between 7,000 and
8,000 shells. When this died down, the Turks attempted to
recover the lost ground. No fewer than seven times did they
hurl themselves against new lines. On every occasion they
were driven back.

By July 14 the Allied line had made a further advance
against Turkish trenches to the right of the Achi Baba
nullah. This success was achieved after desperate fighting.
During the previous three months the Turks had constructed
a network of trenches and small redoubts, protected by
barbed wire and connected by saps and communicating
trenches. But they had been made to realize that no infantry could withstand tremendous bombardments, with
high-explosive shells concentrated on a small section of the
defense and, therefore, withdrew most of their men down
the communicating trenches while the bombardment lasted,
and so the Allied infantry were able to occupy two or three
lines with small loss. The majority of the Allied casualties
occurred in holding the trenches after they were won, for
the enemy, knowing the ground and the plan of their
trenches, attacked them with bombs through the saps, and
so the fighting took place at close quarters.

Parties of men would get too far forward and frequently
be lost for hours, while it was no uncommon occurrence for
men to gain possession of an advanced trench while the
Turks were still holding sections of those behind. Thus, after
each advance it took a long time to straighten out and consolidate a captured position. Many men had to be sacrificed, so many shells fired, and so many grenades used for
every hundred yards of ground occupied. It was bludgeon-
work, brutal and unattractive, and giving little or no scope
for skill in tactics or strategy. In front of Achi Baba the

WOUNDED BRITISH TROOPS FROM GALLIPOLI LANDING IN EGYPT

127

situation was the same as before Ypres, or Souchez. Victories could not be won in a day any more than they could in France, for sections of the enemy's line had first to be pounded to pulp, then stormed, and finally held against counter-attacks.

While a warship bombarded the observation-station on the top of Achi Baba with 12-inch guns, regiments of a brigade leapt from trenches and surged forward toward the redoubt and trenches. The whole scene "resembled some picture from the Inferno, for guns, shelling the works behind, made a great background of earth and smoke." Again Mr. Ashmead-Bartlett said the attack "resembled a gigantic steaming caldron, into whose thick vapors the gallant brigade poured without once hesitating or looking back." Individuals soon became swallowed up in mist, and all one could see were "black dots rushing about or jumping into trenches with bayonets flashing in the shrouded sun amid a continuous roar of musketry, which showed the Turks were resisting valiantly." But when the smoke lifted the Allies were seen to be in possession of the trenches. For nearly three hours this fighting continued on the right, hidden partly from view, and no one knowing exactly what was happening. The attack on the left was successful, being conducted with skill and dash. The infantry swept over everything in their front, bayoneting Turks who did not succeed in escaping down the saps. The infantry swept forward in small parties, often in twos and threes, in spite of shells and heavy rifle-fire. The Turks seemed demoralized by this final charge, and fled a long way back to the foot of Achi Baba, pursued by shells.

While a new landing was being successfully carried out early in August in Anafarta Bay, the Australian and New Zealand Corps at Anzac became engaged in a desperate struggle to obtain possession of the main ridge running northeast from the Anzac position. No troops were ever called upon to make an advance over more difficult and broken country. After the close of the battle of August 6 to 10, the greatest that had been fought on the Gallipoli peninsula, both armies were engaged in consolidating new positions, taking stock of gains and losses, replenishing am-

ANZAC COVE, FROM WHICH A LARGE FORCE WAS WITHDRAWN

VIII.   The troops at Anzac Cove were Australians and New Zealanders.   The narrow shore and steep hillside are characteristic of the country in which the British had to operate against the Turks

munition and munitions, and sorting out and reorganizing divisions, brigades, and battalions which, of necessity, had become intermingled in that rugged, mountainous country. In the fighting on the ground over which Australian and New Zealand army corps advanced in desperate efforts, extending over four consecutive days, to reach the crest of Sari Bair, the commanding ridge overlooking the Dardanelles, which gives access to the highest peak of all, the sinister heights of Koja Chemen, which was torn asunder by a giant ravine, the New Zealand infantry, the Gurkas, and other battalions almost reached their objective. A battalion of Gurkas actually got onto the crest of the plateau. At the same moment the Turks counter-attacked in great force, and then these gallant men from the hills of India were driven back.

But the survivors had obtained a view, and gave a description of, the promised land which lay beneath them. Below were the waters of the Dardanelles. These men looked down on the Narrows and on Kilid Bahr. Along the roads they had watched Turkish transports streaming southward and motor-cars dashing to and fro. It was a bitter disappointment to them to relinquish the crest when it seemed almost within their grasp, after so many months. The Anzac Corps had accomplished a feat of arms in climbing these heights almost without a parallel, but they were handicapped by the failure of a corps to make good its position on the Anafarta hills further north, and thus check the enemy's shell-fire. When details of these operations are collected they will form one of the most fascinating pages of the war. It was a combat of giants in a giant country.

At dawn on the 10th the Turks, reinforced, made a desperate assault on the Allied lines from Hill Q and Chunuk Bair. They hurled themselves on two regiments, who, after desperate resistance, were driven from their position by artillery-fire and sheer weight of numbers further down the slopes of Chunuk Bair. Following up their success, the Turks charged over the crest to gain a great gully. But they had reckoned without the Allied artillery and ships' guns. Four successive lines of infantry in close formation were plainly visible to all the warships and to all batteries on land. The Turks were caught in a trap. The momentum of their charge down hill prevented them from recoiling in time, and they were swept away by hundreds in a storm of high explosives, shrapnel, and common shell from ships' guns, howitzers, and field-pieces. As huge shells from the ships exploded, huge chunks of soil were thrown into the air, amid which human bodies were seen hurled aloft and then dashed to earth or down deep ravines. Even this artillery-fire might not have checked the Turkish advance had it not been assisted by the concentrated fire of ten machine-guns at short range. For half an hour they maintained a rapid fire until the guns smoked with heat.

Thus closed for the time being amid blood-stained hills the fiercest battle since Inkermann. But Inkermann was over in a few hours, whereas Englishmen, Scotsmen, Australians, New Zealanders, Gurkas, Sikhs, and Maoris kept up this terrible combat with the Turks for four consecutive days and nights, amid hills, dongas, and ravines nine hundred feet above the sea, to which point all water-rations and ammunition had to be borne along trails that existed only on maps, and down which every man who fell wounded had to be borne in the almost tropical heat of August in the Mediterranean. The result extended the Anzac position. The Allies no longer had a confined, stifled feeling of being too many men crowded into a restricted area.

The first attempt to seize the hills round Anafarta having broken down, it required time to sort and reorganize the units. It was not until August 21 that the army was in a position to make a frontal attack on the Turks in this quarter. For the bombardment which was to precede the attack the battleships moved in closer to shore, supported by cruisers and several monitors. Exactly at 3 P.M. on August 21 the first gun was fired. For half an hour was witnessed another of those terrible bombardments which had become commonplaces on that bloody soil. The battleships and cruisers concentrated on Hills 70 and 112, supported by field-guns and heavy howitzers. Once again the enemy's trenches appeared to be swallowed up in clouds of earth and smoke, but the Turks showed no sign, and not a man left his position. While this bombardment lasted the enemy's guns replied furiously, concentrating their fire chiefly on and behind Chocolate Hill, which was wreathed in bursting shrapnel. Very soon the shells set fire to the brush and shrub, which, fanned by a breeze, burnt furiously, spreading with amazing rapidity, and at times blotting out positions in clouds of rolling smoke and flame.

The Battle of the Landing succeeded in its initial object, because the landing was effected, but it failed in its later objects, which were to effect a junction between the Anzac and the southern contingents, to take Krithia and Achi Baba, and to advance upon Maidos and the Narrows. The primary cause of the failure was that the Allies delivered their attack in insufficient force; the second, that the forces available were unduly dispersed. Behind these lay a third, lack of accurate topographical knowledge of a peninsula which had been for centuries an object of deep interest to ardent soldiers, and especially to British soldiers. To these causes may be added the complete elimination of the element of surprize, due to the original Allied decision to rely on naval strength alone.

When in October it was announced that General Hamilton had been called home "to report," and that General Sir C. C. Monro had been appointed to succeed him, rumor was rife that the expedition itself was about to be recalled. Official reports showed that British casualties in the land operations up to October 9 had amounted to 96,889 men. The estimates placed French losses at nearly the same figure. For the seven months from the date of the landing of troops this campaign had cost the Allies nearly a thousand men a day, and to this was to be added the naval losses, including the battleships *Irresistible, Ocean, Bouvet, Majestic,* and *Triumph.* The operations were apparently no nearer success than they had been months before.

Every advantage of terrain was held by the Turks. The Anafarta region was compared to half of a huge saucer which had been broken, the line of breakage being formed by the shore of the Ægean Sea, and the bottom and rim being in the hands of the Allies and Turks. Until August 16, when the Turks retook Kiretch Tepe, the position of the Allies had been better, as they were masters of at least a part of the Anafarta region, but this advantage was lost on that day. The Allies thereafter held themselves in the Anafarta region solely by virtue of an immense artillery-fire superiority, supported by some forty warships, cruisers, and torpedo boats. Military observers attributed the failure in the Dardanelles rather to delay in beginning the attack, to mismanagement at the War Office, and to the natural difficulties of the task rather than to any shortcomings of General Hamilton.

General Monro was a striking instance of the emergence of Scottish leadership during the months the war had been in progress. At the outbreak he was merely an officer of a territorial force. He was now entrusted with the most difficult and dangerous task ever undertaken by British arms. Monro belonged to a definite type; sturdy-framed and strong-jawed, and looked every inch a soldier. All the characteristics of first-rate generalship were his—instant judgment, unlimited receptiveness to ideas, imperturbability, unflinching courage, and the dual capacity of winning popularity among his officers and men and inspiring confidence. He was comparatively young for such high command, being only 55 years of age. In August, 1914, he had gone out to France in command of the Second Division of the London Territorials. Before the battle of Mons-Charleroi he assumed command of the Second Regular Division. After the retreat of the Marne and the fighting in the Aisne, he was mentioned in dispatches, made a Knight Commander of the Bath, and given command of an army corps.

Would the British now undertake to withdraw their troops from Gallipoli? It was foreseen to be an operation of great delicacy and peril. Moltke once said he could see a dozen ways for invading England, but not one for getting away. The effect on the whole political and strategic situation of an Allied withdrawal from Gallipoli would obviously be grave. It would be plainly to acknowledge defeat, and it would have released a triumphant Turkish army for operations elsewhere. The apparent way out of a bad situation was to keep the Gallipoli army where it was, to strengthen it if necessary, and to keep "nibbling" at the

Turks, attacking them in force sometimes, and so holding them where they were, even if little progress was made against them. Meanwhile, Russia and Roumania might suddenly change the whole aspect of things.

The announcement made on December 20 of the British withdrawal from Gallipoli overshadowed all other war news. The shock was hardly broken by the fact that the withdrawal had been for weeks a matter of widespread discussion, or ever since Lord Ribblesdale's speech in Parliament, in which he declared that withdrawal had been recommended

THE BRITISH WARSHIP "GOLIATH" SUNK IN THE DARDANELLES

by "a high military authority." Thus ended an enterprise on which the highest Allied hopes had been built and which, if it had succeeded, might have turned the tide of the war. British troops continued for a time longer to occupy the tip of the peninsula at Sedd-ul-Bahr, which commanded the entrance to the Straits, and where many British have declared that a new Gibraltar will one day arise. The position here was protected by a double line of ships. At the beginning of August the British on Gallipoli had come near to their greatest victory in the war, and had suffered their greatest defeat. While a battle was in the balance, a detachment from Anzac had reached the top of Sari Bair, the dominating hill in the neighborhood, and for a few minutes had seen below them the whole of the Dardanelles Narrows. This was one of the supreme moments of the war.

"A tragic blunder" was the term used by the London *Daily News* to describe the ill-fated attempt to force the Dardanelles. The "blunder," if not tragic, was certainly costly, for the British alone suffered 112,921 casualties, including the death of 1,609 officers and 23,670 men. Only a tiny foothold had been obtained by the Allies. After nearly a year's operations they believed the expedition was hopeless, and so withdrew every man from the peninsula. In essence the expedition was an attempt, first, to liberate Russia from her blockade; secondly, to force Turkey to conclude a separate peace; and thirdly, to influence the Balkan neutrals. The whole scene of things changed when King Ferdinand of Bulgaria decided to throw in his lot with the Central Empires.

The withdrawal was a frank, if belated, recognition of the failure of a great campaign and the frustration of a great hope. The one event of the war with which the retirement could be compared was the defeat of the German armies at the Marne. The German rush on Paris, like the Allied attack on the Dardanelles, was an attempt to win the war by a single great stroke. If the Allies had forced the Dardanelles and entered Constantinople the Balkan nations would then have united against Austria at a moment when the Russians were at the crest of their power, and the Hapsburg resistance would have collapsed. But the Germans had been more quick to recognize failure and to seek a remedy than the Allies. When the Germans failed around Paris they tried for Calais. When they failed there, they gave up their offensive in the west and turned to Russia and the Balkans. The Allies now suffered in prestige just as Germany suffered at the Marne. But this war was not to be decided by prestige. It had resolved itself into a bitter, grinding test of ultimate resources. The Allied failure against Constantinople, like the German failure against Paris, testified to the fact that in this war there were no short-cuts to victory.

THE WAR AGAINST TURKEY

Every man, every animal, every baggage-cart, and all but six guns, intentionally left behind to fire till the last minute and then be destroyed, now embarked from Suvla and Anzac under the nose of the unsuspecting Turk. Whatever the fruits of the Dardanelles campaign may be adjudged to be, it will always stand out in military records for two things—the gallantry of the first landings and the skilfulness of the evacuation. In the evacuation masses of men and material were brought down in a short space of time to Anzac and Suvla. The few stores remaining were set on fire, chiefly bully-beef, biscuits, and rice. They were a small proportion of the supplies which had been kept there. Next,

© AMERICAN PRESS ASSOCIATION.

BRITISH BURNING THEIR STORES ON LEAVING SUVLA BAY

the breakwaters which had been built of old hulks were smashed by shell-fire from the ships at short range. The decision to leave Suvla and Anzac had been reached after long deliberation. The final word in an operation of this magnitude came from London, and it was given there on Kitchener's return from the Dardanelles.

Tennyson immortalized the heroic blunder at Balaklava, but what living poet was competent to sing the waste of human life at Suvla Bay? When the roll was called after the Light Brigade's return from the "jaws of death" it was found that 247 men had fallen on the field of battle. At Suvla Bay the loss to the British was 12,000. Whole brigades were shot to pieces, an army division was decimated and regiments were left without a single officer in command. Here was war's havoc on a titanic scale, and it was equally deadly to the Turks, whose losses were enormous. It was a staggering price to pay for "two pieces of ground, small and worthless as they seemed, but worth, according to the ethics of war, 10,000 lives" to the victor. "Some one had blundered" again, and with a genius for blundering without a parallel. No reinforcements came to sustain the advantage gained by this and subsequent attacks by the British; and the Turks, their ammunition spent and their last hope of resistance gone, reaped the fruits of the sacrifice. But if the poets should fail, General Hamilton's report would remain the prose epic of the fiasco in the Dardanelles. History has no more moving tale than that story of bravery in war baffled by incompetence. The crowning act of British "muddling along" was embalmed forever in the official report of a general who missed by a hair's breadth a great height of fame.

By January 10 the remaining positions held by the Allies on Gallipoli were abandoned, with the wounding of only one man among the British and French. All the guns and howitzers were taken away, with the exception of seventeen wornout guns, which were blown up before leaving. News of the final evacuation of the peninsula had then been expected for several days by observers of the Near Eastern campaign. The retirement of the troops from Anzac and Suvla Bay three weeks before had left no strategic advantage in a retention of the peninsula. The evacuation, in point of pure technical skill and soldierly resolution, ranked with the retirement of the Allies from Mons and the withdrawal of Russia from the Vistula.

Just as across the ribbon of the Dardanelles, on the green plain of Troy, the most famous of old world wars had been fought, so now the European shores had been made classic ground of arms. If the banks of the Scamander had seen men striving desperately with fate, so had the slopes of Achi Baba and the beaches of Helles. Had the fashion endured of linking the strife of mankind with the gods, strange myths would have sprung from the rescue of the British troops in the teeth of winter gales and uncertain seas! It would have been rumored, as at Troy, that Poseidon had done battle for his children.

The news of the withdrawal, at first received in France and Britain with incredulity, speedily changed into relief. The gallantry of the April landings, the long struggle for Krithia, the Australasian attack on Sari Bair had gone for nothing. Great Britain had spilled blood like water to win a mile or two of land, and now had to relinquish it. Fifty thousand Allied graves with rude crosses passed for a few years under the sway of the Crescent. Having failed, Great Britain escaped the worst costs of failure. She brought off three army corps to be refitted and reorganized for use in other lands.[9]

[9] Principal Sources: In the main, a condensation of accounts printed in London and other papers, written by Ellis Ashmead-Bartlett, an official eyewitness and war correspondent; in part compiled from *The Fortnightly Review* (London); "Bulletins" of the National Geographic Society, *The Literary Digest*, The *Times*, New York; The *Daily News*, The *Standard*, The Manchester *Guardian*, London; The *Evening Post*, The *World* syndicated articles by G. Ward Price (New York); The London *Times'* "History of the War," "Nelson's History of the War" by John Buchan.

VII

THE FALL OF ERZERUM, TREBIZOND, AND ERZINGAN UNDER THE GRAND DUKE NICHOLAS, AND THE DEATH OF VON DER GOLTZ

February 15, 1916—June 26, 1916

WITH the great Russian defeats in Poland and the retreat of the Russian army from Kovno and Vilna in the early autumn of 1915, the Grand Duke Nicholas had relinquished his European command and gone to the Caucasus, the Czar himself taking command against the Germans and Austrians. This change to outside observers implied censure, if not degradation, for the Grand Duke. His astounding successes early in the war, first in overrunning East Prussia, then taking Lemberg and capturing the fortress of Przemysl, later his penetration of the Carpathians to points beyond their crests, and two successive repulses of German drives into Russian Poland where the drives had reached almost to the gates of Warsaw, seemed to have availed him little in the face of his subsequent loss of nearly the whole of Galicia, of practically all of Russian Poland, and of a considerable strip of Russia itself. That his failure was due, not to his want of skill as a commander, so much as to an extraordinary shortage of effective guns and ammunition, in consequence of Russian inability to manufacture or forward them, apparently had not saved him from disgrace. To the Caucasus he went, almost as if into banishment, but only to achieve, five months later, a greater victory than he had won at Lemberg or at Przemysl; in fact, one of the most spectacular Allied victories thus far in the war—the conquest of Erzerum.

The whole country of the Caucasus is one of extraordinary difficulties for military operations. Switzerland and its mountains could be dropt into that region stretching down from the plains of Russia into Asia Minor and Persia without producing any remarkable variation in its rugged outline. Elburz and Ararat would still tower unchallenged over Mount Blanc and the Matterhorn. Ever since Ivan took Astrakhan, and Peter took Azof, the heart of Russia had been set on acquiring this mighty barrier stretching between two great inland seas and closing to Russia the gates leading south. To obtain possession even of the north ranges, Russia, as General Kuropatkin pointed out ten years before this war, had fought two wars with Turkey, only to find at the last that the south was guarded against her "not only by the Turks but by the Germans."

The traveler who would reach Erzerum has a choice of three more or less arduous routes. He might embark from Odessa on a Black Sea coaster and follow the northern shore of Anatolia, where a great plateau breaks down in forested steeps, with scarcely a creek or bay to vary the line, till he reached Trebizond, the walled city to which the Ten Thousand Greeks under Xenophon struggled through the Armenian hills. Thence a good road runs inland to Erzerum, crossing three passes, one of them 8,000 feet high, the distance from port to fortress 200 miles, with a week of fine weather needed for the journey. Or the traveler might cover a thousand miles by the Bagdad railway line to Ras-el-Ain, in the Euphrates valley, whence he would have 250 miles of hill-roads through the Armenian Taurus before he reached the city. Again he might go by rail to Angora, two days' journey from the Bosporus, and after that move eastward by road through the great wheatlands of Anatolia, where dwells the flower of the Turkish peasantry and the main strength of the Sultan's armies, past the rich city of Sivas, till the Euphrates valley had been reached at Ersingan and the real highlands begin.

Erzerum lies well among the mountains, a true frontier-fortress, guarding the road from Russia to the fruitful vales of the ancient Lycus and Halys, the heart of Asiatic Turkey. It stands on a pocket of flat ground, 6,000 feet above the sea. South and north and northeast rise lofty mountains through which roads to Moush and Trebizond make their way over high and difficult passes. Southwest is the vale of the western Euphrates; east are ranges of hills forming the watershed between the Euphrates and the Araxes. Erzerum is one of the highest placed of cities, and frequently snowbound for six months, in its hollow surrounded by high mountain peaks. Many writers have exhausted their powers in descriptions of the sublimity of the situation. This great fortress, seemingly untakable in winter and believed to be impregnable in summer, ''by far the most important strategical position'' in Asia Minor, reorganized and strengthened by Posselt Pasha, with an outer breastwork of forts on the eastern hill and with an armament, it was claimed, of over four hundred modern Krupp guns, not to speak of mountain-guns, was taken by the Russians, led by General Yudenitch, in the depth of a terrible winter, and within four weeks after the opening of the Grand Duke's projected campaign.

The strength of Erzerum against an army from the east lay entirely in its horseshoe of hills called Deve Boyun, the ''neck of the camel.'' Its weakness lay in the fact that it was a fort pushed into the borderland beyond the area of good communications, so that it could not speedily be munitioned or reinforced from a base. The nearest available railroad in the south was at Angora, 440 miles as the crow flies, and the way from Angora to Sivas traversed 200 miles of hilly country. Thence a rough road 230 miles long ran to Erzingan, and from Erzingan one had to cover a road of seventy-five miles to reach Erzerum. Assuming that convoys covered on an average twenty miles a day, two days by rail and twenty-five by road lay between the fortress and the Bosporus; so that, allowing for inevitable delays, thirty days was the minimum time for supplies to travel from that Turkish base.

While it could not be said that the fall of this fortress was a complete surprize, few had really expected it. That the Russians were conducting an aggressive campaign in the Caucasus was known, and now and then in newspapers items were printed about it. But nothing like a master-stroke was looked for—especially in winter when the snow around Erzerum might be several feet deep and the cold 40 degrees below zero. It was as far back as the beginning of September, 1915, that events had led to the transformation of

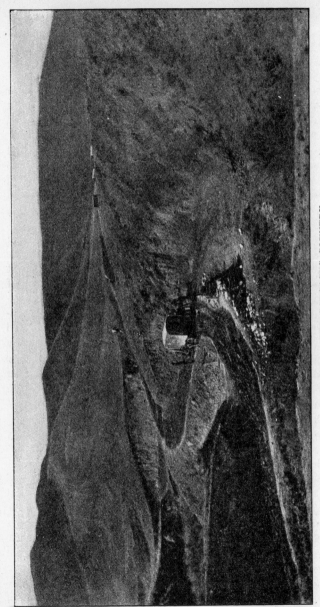

A ROAD IN THE CAUCASUS COUNTRY

This road illustrates some of the difficulties of the military operations involved in taking Erzerum

the Transcaucasian campaign, with the Czar's decree that he had himself taken over the supreme command of the sea and land forces of the empire, with General Alexeieff as his chief of staff, and that he had issued a rescript to the Grand Duke Nicholas, appointing him to command in the Caucasus. About that time—on September 28—the British army on the Tigris, having defeated the Turks at Kut-el-Amara, was advancing on Bagdad, and to facilitate this advance and relieve Turkish pressure increased Russian activity was being displayed in Persian territory. South of Van the Turks attacked from the Persian side on December 1 but were driven in disorder out of two fortified positions, while ten days later another Persian force carried the Sultan Bulak Pass and again opened the road to Hamadan, a body of Turkish and German mercenaries being routed with great loss. The Russians next took the Persian towns of Hamadan and Sultanabad, eighty miles to the southeast, on the road to Ispahan, intercepting the telegraph wire connecting the German headquarters at Teheran and the Turkish troops in Mesopotamia. By the end of February General Baratoff had reached Kermanshah, 100 miles southwest of Hamadan in the direction of Bagdad.

The British advance on the Tigris, however, had in the meantime received an unwelcome check at Ctesiphon when Townshend, almost in sight of Bagdad, late in November, was compelled to fall back on Kut. At the same time Serbia was being overrun by Teutons and Bulgarians, and the Anglo-French soon evacuated the Gallipoli peninsula, which released a large Turkish army, composed of the flower of the Ottoman troops, some of whom were sent to strengthen the army in Armenia. Mid-winter had now come. Even in the best of times six or seven weeks would be required to get the first of these Turkish reinforcements to the front. In these circumstances the Grand Duke decided to strike at once for Armenia. The evacuation of Gallipoli took place on January 9, 1916. The march on Erzerum began on the 16th. Kiamil Pasha, who was in command of the Turkish army, appears to have been completely taken by surprize by the suddenness and vigor of General Yudenitch's advance.

The forward move spread over a front extending from

Lake Tortum on the north to a point near Malazgert, just north of Lake Van. Before the Turks were well aware that the campaign had begun, Yudenitch had advanced twenty miles and struck against their main central position at Koprukeui, where the road from Kars to Erzerum crosses the Aras River. The result was a striking victory, which soon developed into a rout for the Turks, who fled, leaving behind them guns, munitions, and supplies. This was on January 19. On the 20th the victors were already at Hassan Kale, ten miles farther on the road to Erzerum, and only thirty miles distant from that "impregnable bastion" of

RUSSIANS WITH TURKISH FLAGS TAKEN AT ERZERUM

Asia Minor. On the 29th Yudenitch was before Erzerum with a force equipped only with mountain- and field-guns, in a country swept by constant snowstorms and with a temperature liable to reach 40 degrees below zero. Such daring movements might have been regarded as insane under ordinary circumstances but Yudenitch sent back to his base for howitzers and heavy guns, and moved his headquarters into the fighting-line. On the 15th the inner ring of forts was stormed, and on the 16th Erzerum itself was captured, the Turks in their retirement going west or south as they could find an opening to escape from Russian guns.

Yudenitch's victory was so sudden that the Grand Duke Nicholas, whose labors at headquarters had been invaluable, had not time in which to come up and be present at the final triumph. He received the great news at Tiflis, where he was enthusiastically acclaimed by the people in the palace square. It was compensation to him, for the disheartening retreats of the previous year. It appeared after the victory that, in the third week of January, a violent and unexpected thrust against the Turkish center had resulted in the Turks being disorganized and dislodged from strong positions extending east of Erzerum, from Lake Tortumghel to the River Chariason; that is to say, along a front of over sixty miles, and that the army was withdrawing in the direction of Erzerum. At several points this retreat had assumed the nature of a panic-stricken flight, in which several Turkish units were almost annihilated. The Russians had advanced across heights which towered above the clouds, and had dug trenches in deep snow during severe storms. The Russians then pushed steadily on toward Erzerum and before the end of the month were within thirty miles of the fortress and by the middle of February, as already told, had captured it.

This success was achieved as a counter-offensive to a Turkish attempt late in November to envelop a wing of the Russian army. Great things had been expected at that moment by the Germans who planned the Turkish movement, Field-marshal von der Goltz being, it was understood, in virtual command. Three army corps were concentrated at Erzerum, with the Russians in some strength at Kars, which is about eighty miles from Erzerum. Kars has railroad connection northwesterly with Tiflis, the old Georgian capital, and southwesterly with a point near the Turkish frontier. The German Staff had planned the enveloping of the Russian army at Kars. Bringing up reinforcements from Bagdad and Trebizond, the commander had 150,000 men at his disposal. To cope with this force the Russians had 100,000. Under German leadership the Turkish plan was to hold the Russians on the Kars-Erzerum road and, with columns marching to the left over the mountains, to turn the Russian right at Kars and then work round its rear. Meanwhile, a Turkish force at Trebizond was to

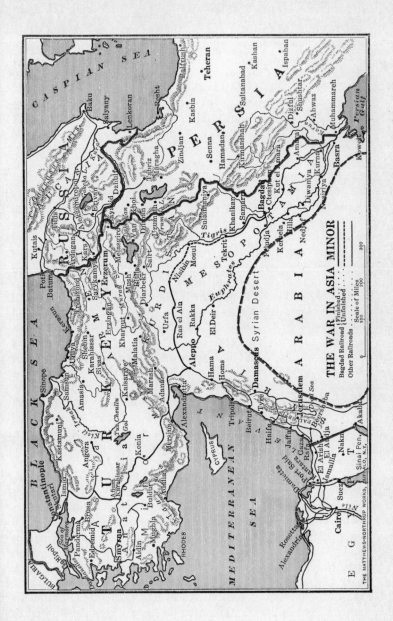

THE WAR IN ASIA MINOR

Bagdad Railroad { Finished ....
                 { Unfinished ......

Other Railroads ....

Scale of Miles
100   200   300

THE MATTHEWS-NORTHRUP WORKS, BUFFALO, N.Y.

traverse a mountain-pass 8,000 feet high, capture Ardahan, which lies north of Kars, and cut the railroad to Tiflis. The Turks in this movement succeeded in driving a force of 4,000 Russians out of Ardahan, and threw them back on Khorasan, toward Erzerum, seized the Saganuk heights above the railroad terminus of Sarikamish and made an effort to cut the railroad on the north.

But at this point the Russians rallied and beat back the Turkish Tenth Corps, ousted the First Corps from Ardahan, and surrounded the Ninth, which had occupied Sarikamish. At Kara-Urgan followed a week's fierce fighting, the Russians routing the Turks during a storm in which the snow fell ceaselessly. After driving the Turks out of Ardahan, they cut their communications with Trebizond. It was an old-fashioned campaign with incidental trench-fighting. The Russians were at first inferior in numbers, but were able later to bring down by rail from Tiflis reinforcements that had been spared from the Eastern Front in Europe. The Turkish enveloping movement was thus defeated, but the Turks, reinforced and with the aid of one of the ablest of German generals, Von der Goltz, had succeeded in blocking the road to Erzerum for weeks.

At this point the Grand Duke Nicholas took over the command in the Caucasus, and soon redeemed his reputation by investing and taking Erzerum. It became clear now that he had been sent to the Caucasus, not as punishment, but to undertake another job—at least that was how the change now appeared to the Entente world. The capture was accomplished by methods in which Russia had by this time been well drilled by the Germans. The attack was a typical Teutonic operation, as much so as the great "drives" of Hindenburg. It left nothing to improvisation, strategem, and maneuvering, but built up success out of elements that could be handled beforehand—efficient transportation, ample supplies of munitions, superior forces and a prearranged plan of advance. The Grand Duke's victory was the victory of railroad facilities, of ammunition supplies, of stronger regiments, of better planned lines of advance and of greater speed and method in movements. The points of Russian concentration were Batum on the Black Sea, Tiflis on the railroad from the Black to the Caspian Sea, and Baku on the Caspian. Here the Grand Duke assembled and trained his men and accumulated supplies. When ready, he moved forward from the frontier of Kars, which is within fifty miles of the Turkish border, taking the road that leads from Kars to Erzerum, the only passable road in the whole district. The Russians probably numbered eight army corps, roughly 300,000 men, to whom the Turks opposed perhaps two-thirds of that number. In an incredibly short time the Russians reached the defenses of Erzerum, which consisted of a ring of eleven fortresses that required garrisons of about 60,000. Nine of the forts had been constructed within a few years under the direction of German military engineers, and were armed with modern Krupp guns. Yet in five days after the fall of the first fort, the others had dropt into the Grand Duke's hands.

Military history received here another example of the truth, first illustrated on a great scale by Alexander of Macedon, that good generalship in leading courageous and trained troops can overthrow any odds. To the Grand Duke with his chief of staff, General Yanuskevich, belonged the plans of the Caucasus campaign, the execution of which was entrusted to General Yudenitch, who had held the Caucasus command ever since Russia took the field in Asia. In the attack on Erzerum the military odds were against Russia. Forty years before she had spent the best part of a year in efforts to capture the outer line of its defenses. Those defenses now had the advantage which German technical science and modern weapons could give them. Chobon Dede fort stood 8,500 feet above the sea-level, and none of the forts was under 6,000 feet altitude. All were taken with the bayonet.

The wiping out of this Turkish base promised to disrupt the whole Caucasus campaign of the Turks, since Erzerum not only served as a base for operations in the Caucasus but for others in Mesopotamia. Its fall left no strongly fortified point between Erzerum and Sivas, about 230 miles to the west, and brought once more to men's minds consideration of an eventual attack from the Allies on Constantinople from the east. Its capture had the immediate effect of making more secure the Russian positions along the Black Sea coast, while the possibility of a successful Russian thrust in aid of the British Expeditionary Force in Mesopotamia increased. Przemysl yielded a larger number of prisoners—120,000 odd—but in all other respects the cap-

A RUSSIAN CHURCH AT ST. STEFANO BLOWN UP BY THE TURKS IN THE WORLD WAR

At St. Stefano, which is near Constantinople, was negotiated the famous treaty bearing that name between Russia and Turkey in 1878, which was afterward torn up and the Treaty of Berlin substituted in its place. It was through the Treaty of Berlin that Austria acquired her hold on Bosnia and Herzegovina, ending in their annexation in 1908, and followed in 1914 by the assassination of the Austrian Archduke

ture of Erzerum stood out as a more fruitful and brilliant military achievement. Przemysl was virtually starved out, having been isolated for several months. Its fall did not make it any easier for the Grand Duke Nicholas to push his armies across the Carpathian barrier into Hungary. Nor did it forestall the German-Austro-Hungarian offensive which, two months later, swept back the Russians far beyond the San, cleared Poland of them and forced a partial evacuation of the Baltic provinces. The fall of Erzerum, however, opened up wide strategic and political vistas, Erzerum being the key to the Turkish defense of her Caucasus front. Kars used to be that key, but Kars, taken by the Russians in the war of 1877-78, remained Russian under the terms of the Treaty of Berlin. Erzerum thereafter was converted into Turkey's main military base on the northeastern frontier. Its loss meant that Trebizond, on the Black Sea, would be difficult to hold, the more so as the Black Sea itself was under Russian control; while to the south, in the Lake Van region, the Turkish position was outflanked, and Turkish access to Persia from that direction would be speedily cut off. The loss of Erzerum also weakened Turkey on her Mesopotamia front, where her prospects had been bright. Bagdad might now have to be evacuated, provided British pressure up the Tigris could be renewed with fresh troops.

The Grand Duke's success showed Russia's recuperative powers. A successful offensive had been conducted in the Caucasus, simultaneously with vigorous assaults against the Austro-Germans on Russia's southwestern front and a vigorous defensive in the direction of Dvinsk and Riga. The successful stroke at Erzerum was bound to be felt elsewhere. It meant a relaxation of Turkish pressure on the Tigris and in Thrace, a dissipation of the Turkish threat against Egypt, a shifting of the balance around Saloniki, and that the ambitious plan of a joint attack upon Turkey from the rear, the British coming north along the Tigris, the Russians coming south through Armenia, was once more making headway. Students of the art of war expected soon to see a Russian advance in Asia Minor to the west, and possibly in two directions, westward toward Trebizond on the Black Sea, southward to Diarbekr on the Tigris and within striking distance of the projected Bagdad railway. Trebizond and Diarbekr are about 150 miles from Erzerum. The occupation of a large slice of Armenia was thus imminent. But not until Erzingan had been passed, and the plain of Sivas reached, could a blow be struck at the true heart of Asiatic Turkey. In any such advance the flanks had first to be pushed forward; Trebizond to be taken, and Russia to be in possession of the Armenian Taurus and roads from the south.

On March 7 the important position of Rizeh, only forty miles east of Trebizond, was captured, a detached force having been able to cross the mountain pass between the Chorok valley and Rizeh and thus join hands with the Russian coastal force. The combined forces then took up a westward advance, and soon the Turks were thrown back across the Kalopotamos, which brought the Russians within little more than thirty miles of Trebizond. The doom of Turkey's chief Black Sea port now seemed sealed. Preparations for the evacuation of the civil population were hastily undertaken, altho a month was to pass before the actual fall. A British entry into Bagdad, coming on top of recent events in Armenia, Egypt, and Arabia, would at this time have turned the scale and so shortened the war in its Eastern developments, but Kut instead fell to the Turks at the end of April. After this the Turko-German régime in Constantinople received a fresh lease of life.

Along the coast the Turks were soon sending forward all the reinforcements that could reach Trebizond by road, with a view to stopping the Russian advance, which was now only thirty miles to the east. At the same time an almost as desperate attempt was made to reinforce and revictual the city from the sea. With the mystery as to the condition and whereabouts of the ships *Goeben* and *Breslau* still unsolved, the Russians could not claim absolute mastery of the Black Sea. One of the exciting incidents of these eventful days was the sudden reappearance of the *Breslau*, acting as convoy to a number of Turkish transports and grainships destined for Trebizond. The Turks claimed to have sunk two Russian transports, and endeavored to bombard the Russian positions on the coast, but the Russians were able to sink or burn a considerable number of Turkish vessels and to compel the *Breslau* to retire. Turkey's endeavor to stop the Russian coastal advance on land was thus made as ineffective as her efforts had been at sea. Taken between two fires Turkish resistance broke down as it had done at Erzerum; it collapsed with startling suddenness. Some of the Turkish troops, it was said, never came into action at all, bewildered as they were by simultaneous attacks from the east, west and the sea. Before the evening of the 12th the Russians were in full pursuit along the Gumushkhane road. The Trebizond garrison having departed, the Russians were received at the outskirts of the city by a deputation of citizens headed by the American and Greek consuls.

In the third week of April Trebizond fell. Quantities of supplies, including armored motor-cars, big guns and aeroplanes sent from Germany were captured. Trebizond was far less strongly fortified than Erzerum, but, after the fall of Erzerum, a good deal had been done to strengthen it on the land side. The importance of its fall lay in the fact that the rest of the Russian front in Asia had been waiting for its occurrence, so that, with their right flank made secure the whole Russian force could now be swung forward, using Erzerum as a pivot. Russian strategy aimed at keeping all Turkish forces, brought from Constantinople for the defense of Trebizond, occupied over the widest possible front, so that, while armies were making a successful advance in the Kara Dere region, and bringing up reinforcements by land and sea, the Turks were assailed by continuous attacks in the southeast, in the region of Erzingan and Baihurt.

The fall of Trebizond caused rejoicings in all Allied countries, since it was believed that it would involve the loss by the Turks of Erzingan, Kharput, and Diarbekr, and with the fall of these towns would come a complete isolation of the Turkish armies in Mesopotamia. The Turks had now lost the second of their two principal fortified points in Asia Minor. They would in the future have to depend solely on improvised defenses and the natural difficulties of the country, if they were to prevent a westward sweep of Russia's Caucasian armies. As Trebizond had never before surrendered to a Russian army, altho it was threatened from Baiburt in 1829, the moral effect of the victory promised to be enormous. Optimistic Russian observers were soon speculating on the possibility of a successful campaign against Constantinople from the west. Russia's new conquest was in a way more striking and inspiring than that of Erzerum. That great fortress, grim and forbidding on its snow-clad heights, was a symbol of forfeited power; but Trebizond, apart from its importance as a port and a mart, presented a scene of Mediterranean beauty and luxuriance. Nowhere else is the dawn of day more essentially "rosy-fingered." The scene is to-day the same as the one that brought tears to the eyes of Xenophon and his Ten Thousand followers, or that which inspired the Roman Emperor Hadrian at his first view of shore and sea. Trebizond is much older than Rome. It was already an ancient place when Xenophon and his men reached it in 401 B.C., after the long retreat from Cunaxa. The place is still shown at the mouth of the Pyxitis where he pitched his camp, rested for thirty days and celebrated the Olympic games. Long afterward Trebizond was a Roman colony. Hadrian is claimed as the builder of the harbor.

This triumph. was unhappily followed within ten days by the news—inevitable and long expected—of the surrender of General Townshend and his gallant little force at Kut-el-Amara, which rendered futile all the chivalrous efforts that had been made, alike by the extreme left wing of the army of the Grand Duke and by General Barstoff's force in Persia —not indeed to approach or to capture Bagdad, but to relieve the pressure on Kut and the Tigris valley by threatening some part of the Turkish communications, and creating a diversion on their flank. But Kut, having fallen, and the Bagdad enterprise being at an end, for the time being, there was no further object in an extreme lengthening of the Russian lines, either on the Persian frontier or south of the Van district. At this time, however, the Russian movement across the Persian frontier to Rowenduz against the Turkish flank had taken place, Rowenduz being eighty miles north of Mosul, and 200 miles north of Bagdad. The Russian forces, in spite of repeated attacks from Kurds and regulars, were everywhere successful. The Persian movement had been, on the whole, a profitable achievement, altho the Russians had been halted. In the Hamadan-Kermanshah district they gradually fell back in readiness for the counter-stroke that was sure to come.

The Russian position was a peculiar one, and by no means entirely satisfactory, depending, as it did, on command of the Black Sea, and not on land communications in the direction of Erzerum. The only road along the coast was controlled from the sea, and Russian command of the Black Sea was not altogether complete, as there were still several Turko-German submarines unaccounted for, not to speak of the *Goeben* and the *Breslau*. The Russian fleet, in forwarding Russian supplies and preventing the passage of Turkish supplies, had to patrol over 2,000 miles of coast line. But it could bombard Turkish camps, disperse bodies of troops, and effect important armed landings absolutely essential to the capture of Trebizond. With command of the sea not unchallenged, however, and with a good portion of the road between Erzerum and Trebizond in the hands of the Turks, the situation could not be regarded with complete complacency.[10]

In the midst of these events Baron Kolmar von der Goltz, Field-marshal and Commander-in-chief of the First Turkish Army, died at Turkish headquarters. The cause was stated to be spotted fever, but there were rumors of assassination. Von der Goltz, one of Germany's greatest strategists, was at the time of his death seventy-two years old. He had seen extensive military service, having fought in the Austrian campaign of 1866 and been on the staff of Prince Frederick Charles in the Franco-Prussian War. In 1883 he was sent to Turkey to reconstruct the Turkish army, and remained there thirteen years. In August, 1914, he was appointed Military Governor of the occupied part of Belgium, but in November was relieved of that command and sent to Constantinople, where he was appointed Military Commandant and Acting Minister of War. He was instrumental in forming the strong defense made by Turkey on the Gallipoli Peninsula, and had frequently predicted that the Allied

[10] The London *Times*' "History of the War."

FIELD-MARSHAL VON DER GOLTZ

Von der Goltz commanded in Belgium immediately after the Germans left
for France in 1914, but was soon sent to Turkey, where he formerly had
a large part in the reconstruction of the Turkish army. He died somewhat
suddenly in Asiatic Turkey during the war. He was one of the oldest
Generals in the German service, being over 70 when the war began

fleet would not be able to force a passage of the Dardanelles.
Dispatches had since reported him as engaged in operations
in Asiatic Turkey. Before the fall of Erzerum he was said
to be bottled up in that Turkish stronghold with 80,000
Turks.

The mastery of eastern Asia Minor virtually passed to
the Russians with the capture of Trebizond, which was the
gateway to Armenia and the geographical outlet for the
trade of western Persia. The significance of the capture lay
as much in the manner in which it was accomplished as in
the fact itself. The fall came as a direct result of the battle

SOME OF THE DEFENSES OF TREBIZOND

of April 14, on the Kara Dere, fifteen miles to the east. It
was clear that the Turks were badly beaten and were unable
to rally. The part played by the Russian fleet appears to
have been noteworthy. Russian supremacy in the Black Sea
was so near being established as to mean the loss of sea
transport for the Turks. Men and supplies would have to
be forwarded from Constantinople over hundreds of miles
of country destitute of railroads, while Russian armies would
be fed from the sea. To grasp the full value of Russia's
achievements, it needed to be recalled that Erzerum had
fallen five days before the German attack on Verdun began,
and that Trebizond fell when the Verdun attack seemed

to have failed. The Germans had won in France 100 square miles of territory, and the Russians in Turkey between 10,000 and 15,000 square miles. Even when allowing for differences in value between ground in France and ground in Asia Minor, the result remained striking. A peculiarity of the German mind was revealed, however, in a comment made by an eminent German-American, a man who was a genius in his profession, that the fall of Erzerum was "a joke."

Altho the Russians were still a long way from their main objective, which was Constantinople, no theater of the war was filled with greater possibilities. Russia was driving at Constantinople from a back door. It was in some sense not strictly necessary for Russia to reach Constantinople in order to achieve her object. Where the Mediterranean extends deep into Asia Minor and along the Holy Land, a line drawn from the Gulf of Alexandria to the Black Sea is only 300 miles long. If the Russians could reach this line, driving the Turks before them, they would have matters very much in their own hands. There was no defensive position the Turks could take along this line that could not be outflanked from the sea. Starting with the capture of Erzerum, the Russian campaign in Turkey had steadily grown in extent and importance.

Trebizond was a prize carrying with it the commercial mastery of the whole southern Black Sea coast. More coveted than Erzerum or Kermanshah, since it lies on the sea and advantageously near the old border of the Russian Caucasus, it was worth a war in itself. Its value as a means to further operations in war exceeded any intrinsic value it possest. From now on it would be possible to ship Russian supplies to troops in northern Asia Minor by direct route from Odessa to Trebizond. The Russian frontier was thus brought a full week nearer its ultimate base. A week was saved in the transmission of the cumbrous freight that follows an army, and this might mean as much as 100 per cent. in real fighting efficiency. Trebizond, in the course of a few weeks, would be serving as a new base on Turkish soil. Karahissar, Erzingan, Kharput and Diarbeker, forming a trio of inland cities running from north to south in the path of the Russians, were all within about 200 miles of

Trebizond and each seemed likely to fall under the battering of Russian shell brought down from Trebizond.

In the region of Ashkala in the direction of Erzingan, the Turks, after the fall of Trebizond, assembled large forces and took the offensive. After a furious battle, which lasted the whole day, they succeeded in forcing back the Russian advanced posts in places, but were compelled to cease their offensive owing to severe losses. Obstinate fighting continued until, on June 1, the Russians admitted they had withdrawn from Mamakhatun in face of simultaneous attacks and a threatened outflanking movement. The Turks had conducted a somewhat spasmodic offensive at various points. At Trebizond, toward the end of May, a series of attacks began without leading to any marked result. The Russians countered by an attack in the direction of Gumushkhane, which dislodged their opponents from a well-organized position on the northern slopes of the coast.

The Entente Allies at this time were on the eve of the great Anglo-French advance on the Somme. Desperate and almost continuous attacks were being made on Verdun. The Austrians were advancing in the Trentino; Bagdad and the Dardanelles had ended in failure; nothing was being done at Saloniki; there was Turkish pressure along the Armenian front; in Persia General Barstoff had been compelled to fall back, and Lord Kitchener had been lost on his way to Archangel. The first definite news of the advance of General Yudenitch came on July 12, altho the new movement itself appears to have begun on the 2d of the month. The great advance was soon in full swing and promised to be swift and as irresistible as that on Erzerum and Trebizond.

On June 26 Yudenitch entered Erzingan. The town was practically undamaged. As it was the headquarters of an army corps, with extensive barracks and military factories, the booty was very considerable. In three weeks Yudenitch had carried the Russian front forward seventy miles and had added two or three thousand square miles to his conquests. At Erzingan the advance was made over the scene of the most horrible of Armenian massacres. Erzingan, in fact, acted as the clearing-house of the victims who were being driven west, as Trebizond did of those driven north—

a clearing-house leading to death. The extraordinary feature of the fall of Erzingan was that the bulk of the Turkish forces based, on that town did not retire westward toward Sivas, as was expected. Instead they swept southeastward toward Lake Van, in the hope of falling upon the Russian left flank, or of cutting the line of communications; and eventually portions of these Turkish troops penetrated far into Persia.

This victory brought the Russians eighty miles further on the road, seven hundred-odd miles long, between Erzerum and Constantinople. They had now a less mountainous country to traverse. Sivas, their next objective, was 150 miles further on. Then further on would come Angora, the first station on the railroad to the Dardanelles. From here they had about two hundred miles of not too mountainous country to traverse before reaching their goal. Meanwhile their parallel campaign along the Black Sea had to go on, because, until Angora was reached there was no east and west railroad, and armies had to be provisioned by water from Batum. It was plain that an expedition moving southward from Erzingan could threaten Adana, a Mediterranean port, on the Bagdad railroad, and so could cut off European from Asiatic Turkey. Bagdad and Mesopotamia would then fall like ripe plums without more fighting.[11]

[11] Principal Sources : The *Sun, The World,* New York ; The London *Times'* "History of the War" ; The *Times,* The *Tribune,* The *Evening Post,* New York ; Associated Press dispatches, the *Encyclopedia Britannica;* The *Wall Street Journal* (New York) ; The *Morning Post,* The *Daily Chronicle,* London ; The *Journal of Commerce* (New York), "Nelson's History of the War" by John Buchan, *The Fortnightly Review* (London).

VIII

TOWNSHEND'S SURRENDER AT KUT-EL-AMARA— KERMANSHAH AND THE RUSSO-BRITISH JUNCTION ON THE TIGRIS

April 30, 1916—August 8, 1916

WHEN at the end of September, 1915, the Turkish defense at Kut-el-Amara was broken by the British, and the British began an advance on Bagdad, only to be checked at Ctesiphon and forced back to Kut, General Townshend was in a position in which many British generals had found themselves since the days of Elizabeth. He commanded little more than a single division, was outnumbered by potential Turkish levies and was well over three hundred miles from his sea-base. Townshend had a river for his sole communication, assisted by armed vessels, but that river was full of shallows and mud-banks more formidable than the cataracts of the Nile. All around him lay a country ill-suited for operations by white troops—a sparsely-watered desert and reeking marshes, baked by the hottest of Asian suns, and brooded over by those manifold diseases which heat and desert-soil engender. The local tribes were either treacherous or openly hostile, and might at any moment strike at his long, straggling connections with the coast, That a little British army, wearied with ten months of incessant fighting, should have advanced to conquer a great province belonging to a still powerful empire might well seem one of the rashest of enterprises.

The conquest of Bagdad at that time would have given great political advantages—if it could have been achieved. Its fall would have been a make-weight to German domination at Constantinople. It would have cut at their nodal point the principal routes of German communications with Persia and the Indian frontier. This success would not, however, have been final. There would have remained the great caravan routes of the northern Shammar desert, which followed the projected line of the Bagdad railway to Mosul, and went thence to Rowandiz on the Persian frontier. Full success in the British objective demanded control of the whole of northern Mesopotamia. Such a control might have been won, but it required an adequate force—at least two army corps fully equipped, and not one weary division. When the same task fell into Maude's hands after Townshend had become a prisoner of Turkey, success was achieved because Maude had ample supplies of men and equipment.

At the end of September, 1915, the advance on the Somme in western Europe had reached its limit with no decision. The Balkan affair had gone from bad to worse, with Serbia about to be isolated, Bulgaria entering the field on Germany's side, and Mackensen's guns beginning to sound on the Danube. British diplomacy, justly or unjustly, had suffered a serious loss of credit. Looking round the globe for something to restore British prestige, the eyes of soldiers and statesmen naturally fell on Mesopotamia. The expedition there had been up to date a brilliant success, with no mistakes. Miracles had been performed with a handful of troops. Kut-el-Amara and Nasiriyeh, however, were names not familiar to Europe, while Bagdad was known to all the world. If the old city of the Califs could fall to British arms there would be a resounding success wherewith to balance failure in the Ægean.

In October Turkey had in the field as many men as the British Empire. She was fighting nominally in four theaters of war—in Transcaucasia, on the Egyptian frontier, in Gallipoli, and in Mesopotamia. But of her four theaters, three were virtually in a state of stagnation. Probably not more than 150,000 had been mobilized along the Asiatic Russian frontier. Nothing was being done on the Egyptian border. The enemy in Gallipoli had shot his bolt. In Mesopotamia alone was there any urgent question of a needed defense. It was therefore open to Turkey, given a little time and some assistance from Germany in the way of supplies, to deploy on the Tigris little short of a quarter of a million men. To meet this possibility, Sir John Nixon had an Anglo-Indian division and an extra brigade—all told, perhaps, 15,000 bayonets. White troops formed one-third of the force. The remainder were Indian troops, including a number of Punjabs, Mahrattas, Rajputs, Gurkhas, and four regiments of cavalry. The accompanying flotilla was composed of every conceivable type of boat, from ancient Admiralty sloops to Burma paddle-steamers, river-boats, motor-launches, and flat-bottomed native punts of the Delta. The whole British force was battle-worn and weary. Large numbers had contracted ailments and diseases. All were jaded from an incessant struggle during a hot summer. To cheer them they had had, however, a record of unbroken success. Wherever and in whatever numbers they had met the enemy, they had beaten him. Little did they dream of the grim fate soon to overtake them.

In Mesopotamia, as in the Nearer East, the British found themselves confronted with the results of German foresight and organization, the Turkish army being now a very different organization from what it had been in the Balkan Wars, in numbers, efficiency, and armament. German officers, known to be engaged in its reorganization and expansion, had produced this marked improvement, and the results probably transcended any anticipations that the Allies had formed of them. Turkey, despite heavy losses, had been able to detach troops to Bulgaria and to send considerable reinforcements to the Tigris, beside maintaining a force of some kind against the British on the Syrian frontier. When contrasted with her defeat in the Balkan wars, her performance was remarkable

The British expedition had had to contend with exceptional difficulties. From April to October, the heat on the Tigris is excessive, and the rate of invaliding had been unusually high. The line of communication from the Persian Gulf to Ctesiphon is 350 miles in a direct line, and traversed a country peopled by hostile and predatory tribes. It absorbed large forces in its defense, thus diminishing the numbers effective for fighting at the front. The Turks had had their forces augmented by large numbers of tribesmen, who, if not very efficient, had their uses so long as things went favorably. The Turks also had the advantage of possessing ample sources of intelligence, while the British commanders were either ignorant of the enemy's strength and movements, or were liable to be deceived by false information. The one advantage enjoyed by the British was possession of facilities for the transport of troops and supplies by sea and river from Bombay and Karachi to the front, and for the co-operation of gunboats. The objects of the expedition were in the main political, the maintenance of British prestige in the East, which the Germans had been making every possible endeavor to undermine. This was cited as justification for an enterprise which could promise no decisive military results.

Aylmer's [11a] advance up the Tigris to join Townshend at Kut-el-Amara met with stubborn resistance. Townshend was entrenched there in a loop in the Tigris, and seemed to have a good defensive position, protected, as he was, on three sides by the river, and open only to attack on the north. Aylmer left Ali Gherbi on January 6, 1916, with his relief force, and on the 7th came into touch with the Turks, who were in position on both sides of the Tigris, two or three miles below Sheikh Saad, and were composed of three divisions, under command of Nair-el-Din. A battle took place on the 8th, resulting in the retreat of the Turks to Orah, twenty-five miles down the river from Kut-el-Amara. Heavy rains prevented pursuit of them, and Aylmer halted on the 10th at Sheikh Saad, partly on account of the weather, partly to get his wounded away. The Turks meanwhile had fallen back to the Essin position, from which Townshend had driven them in September.

Finding that Aylmer was not following him, Nair-el-Din went forward again to Orah, where he took up what was described as the "Wade. position." There he was attacked by Aylmer on the 13th, and driven back to his entrenchments at Essin, six miles down the river from Kut, but owing to the continuation of bad weather, which lasted till the 8th, there was again no pursuit. Aylmer had fought two pitched battles, and won them both. Bad weather coming when it

[11a] When Aylmer's name emerged with the day's war news many wondered if he might not be related to Rose Aylmer, that early sweetheart of Walter Savage Landor's, who died early in India, and in memory of whom Landor wrote his best-remembered lines, beginning "Ah, what awaits the sceptred race."

did was unfortunate, as it prevented the general from reaping the full fruits of his victories, and gave time to the Turks to strengthen their defenses.

During the week that preceded the surrender of Townshend on April 30, such news as came to Europe from Mesopotamia had indicated that he might soon be relieved. On April 5, a victory on the Tigris twenty miles below Kut-el-Amara was reported by General Lake, who had succeeded Aylmer in command of the British forces. A Turkish

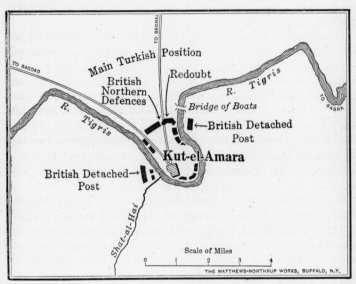

KUT-EL-AMARA
The British line of defenses when besieged by the Turks

entrenched position at Umm-el-Henna had been attacked and carried, and Lake had reported that operations were proceeding satisfactorily. The capture of Umm-el-Henna was the most important news from that theater received in weeks, and was regarded as giving promise of early relief for Townshend's force now under siege in Kut-el-Amara. Umm-el-Henna lies at an important bend in the river, and was believed to be the last serious barrier to Townshend's relief. Two or three less strong positions had, however, first to be overcome. Next to the Dardanelles expedition, the operation in Mesopotamia was the subject on which the British Government was most severely criticized; not only on account of the breakdown in its hospital arrangements, but on the question of responsibility for making an advance with insufficient forces.

Five days later the British attacked a Turkish position at Sannayyat, on the Tigris just below Kut-el-Amara, but failed to break through the lines. The check was due to floods, which were rapidly extending and seriously hampering British movements. The relieving force consisted of two divisions: one under General Gorringe, who was in chief command on the left bank of the Tigris, and the other under General Keary, who was on the right bank. The Sannayyat position extended about two miles on either bank of the river, the left bank resting on the Suwekie Marsh, and the right on nameless marshy ground stretching for twelve miles between Orak and Essin. Had Gorringe succeeded in driving the Turks from Sannayyat, there was another strong Turkish position at Essin, both flanks of which were protected by water defenses, which he had to overcome before he could reach Kut-el-Amara. Gorringe had had great experience in river warfare; he was with Kitchener in the advance to Khartum. In view of rising floods, further attempts to advance up the Tigris had now to be put off.

On April 15, the British troops on the Tigris, including those of the beleaguered garrison at Kut, did not number more than three, or at most four, divisions. Water transports were their sole means for bringing up supplies. The Turks were better off, being within easy distance of Bagdad, which had been turned into a large supply depot, and was constantly replenished from Constantinople. It was believed that they had at least six divisions in position on the Tigris, the British troops being thus outnumbered two to one. The Turks, moreover, were standing on the defensive, while the British were attacking in order to raise a siege.

On April 30 it was made known that Townshend's army in Kut had surrendered, after a resistance protracted for 143 days, and conducted with gallantry and fortitude.

Townshend was compelled to this step by exhaustion of supplies. The force under him consisted of 2,970 British troops, of all ranks, and some 6,000 Indian troops and their followers. The surrender had been expected after the failure of Gorringe and Keary to break through at Sannayyat, and after an unsuccessful attempt to send to the blockaded army provisions by steamers. Townshend's last messages to London from Kut were received by wireless on the morning of April 29, when he reported: "Have destroyed my guns, and most of my munitions are being destroyed; and officers have gone to General Khalil, who is at Madug, to say am ready to surrender. I must have some food here, and can not hold on any more. Khalil has been told to-day and a deputation of officers has gone on a launch to bring some food from Julnar." In his next message he said: "I have just hoisted the white flag over Kut fort and town, and the guards will be taken over by a Turkish regiment, which is approaching. I shall shortly destroy wireless. The troops go at 2 P.M. to camp near Shamran." On the same day the Turkish general, Khalil, received the British *parlementaires*. He was anxious, he said, that the garrison should be well rationed, and that Townshend especially, for whom he exprest admiration, should receive every possible comfort after the privations he had endured. He welcomed the request for food, and regretted that the supplies at his command were not more plentiful. The Pasha said he contemplated no reprisals. He could give no pledge, but he did not intend to hang or persecute any one.

Kut had held out to the verge of starvation. From April 16 the garrison had been reduced to a four-ounce ration

WOUNDED MEN FROM THE TIGRIS LEAVING FOR INDIA

of flour daily, with a ration of horse-flesh. During the first month of the siege men were fighting for their lives, only afraid that ammunition would give out before the relieving column could reach them. The relieving force, advancing from Algharbi in the first week of January, believed that Townshend was near the end of his resources, and the urgency of his case made it necessary to press on. As soon as the British advanced from Aligharbi the enemy relaxed his hold on Townshend, and there was no longer any danger that the ammunition would run short; but the check at Oran made longer resistance a question of supplies. The location of Kut-el-Amara on a peninsula extending into the Tigris River made it impossible to send supplies by air, as there was no landing place for aeroplanes. The forces which attempted to relieve Townshend had met with almost continuous misfortunes. Several times rising waters made further progress impossible, the Turkish position at Sannayyat being surrounded by water. The British once actually attacked Turkish positions after wading through mud and water waist deep, but, while meeting with some success, failure at other points made their sacrifices futile.

The British public never lost faith in Townshend, even after he was forced to capitulate, and regarded his campaign, despite its sorry end, as a brilliant one. The surrender was one of the few instances of the war in which an entire fighting unit had laid down its arms. Kut-el-Amara was nothing but a small collection of ramshackle mudhouses on somewhat raised ground. Behind the river front were a mosque and a collection of one- or two-storied houses. When it became evident that Townshend could not fight his way out, thirty thousand Indian troops and two Anglo-Indian divisions, which had been fighting in France, had been transported to the head of the Persian Gulf, making with the remnants of Townshend's main expedition, a relief force of 90,000 men, but General Aylmer's march up the river was turned to a retreat after the first dash. Floods came to increase his troubles, due to lack of equipment, until his position become almost as precarious as Townshend's was at Ctesiphon. Like him, Aylmer retreated.

Townshend, at the time of his surrender, was heir presumptive to the Marquisate of Townshend, but soon after the surrender a child was born to the existing Marquis, who before had been childless. Townshend was a great-great-grandson of George Townshend, who fought with distinction at Quebec in 1759, when Wolfe died in the arms of victory. He was 54 years of age, was married to the Countess Louise Cahen d'Anvers of France, and had served in the Nile expedition. His surrender was generally regarded as a blow to British prestige in the East, but it was clear that for a few thousand men to have attempted to penetrate four hundred miles into an enemy's country, with no support on either flank, and with only a shallow and uncertain river to connect them with a base of supplies, was a reckless undertaking. Nevertheless, he seemed at one time near success. The story of Townshend's siege, whenever it comes to be told, promises to form a thrilling chapter in British annals. The beleaguered garrison ran short of provisions and medicine, were weakened by disease and incessantly beset by superior numbers of Turks and Arabs. The narrow circumference of their camp afforded no landing place for aeroplanes, which, when they attempted to soar low enough to drop bags of flour, were liable to be brought down by fire.

When Townshend found he could no longer hold out, he offered to surrender his artillery and his money, over $5,000,000, on condition that his troops be allowed to retire down the river with military honors. The Turkish commander, Khalil Pasha, refused, and then Townshend surrendered, but was allowed to retain his sword. Turkish estimates of the British casualties on the Tigris were 20,000 for March and April. Most of the losses were suffered by forces under Gorringe and Keary in their last desperate attempts to rescue the Townsend expedition twenty miles away. Townshend was first bottled up three months after the fall of Grodno, in the autumn of 1915, during the great German invasion of Russia; one month after the Bulgarians captured Nish; a few days after the pro-German uprising in Persia, and a fortnight before the British evacuation of Gallipoli. Since then the face of the war map had changed. The recovery of the Russians under Brusiloff in a splendid but ultimately futile offensive, the collapse of the Turkish defense in Armenia, the end of uprisings in Persia, the maintenance of a Franco-British force under Sarrail in Chalcidice, the Austrian reverses before Czernowitz, and the repulse of the German attack at Verdun had swung the scales of fortune adversely to the Teutonic cause.

In most of their military operations the British had suffered from lack of preparedness, or from underestimating the force to be met or task to be performed. But notwithstanding this, British prestige had not commonly been affected by early defeats in the field—at least this had not been the case when it concerned the alien races whom the British governed. More than one British expeditionary force had been destroyed in Afghanistan, but ultimately Lord Roberts was able to march to Candahar. The Boers repeatedly defeated the British, and under humiliating conditions, but the British flag now floats over Pretoria, and Boers fought under it in this World War. The Zulus wiped out a British regiment at Isandula, but the British for a generation have governed Zululand with only a handful of white policemen. The New Zealanders were not subdued in the field, but by the diplomacy of Sir George Grey. Egyptians saw Gordon sacrificed and Hicks Pasha's army wiped out in the Sudan, but they fought shoulder to shoulder with the British during Kitchener's march to Khartum. India has seen the British defeated, but these defeats did not affect the prestige of the British Raj. Macaulay pointed out that Warren Hastings endangered British rule in India, not by his military reverses, but by his departures from uprightness in government, which was the real basis of British prestige. The British have won few battles, but they have not lost wars in recent times, or as some one has said, they never in war win but one battle—the last one.

Kut was a military disaster which could neither be exaggerated on the one hand, nor minimized on the other. The surrender, no matter for what reason, of five British generals, 240 British and 270 Indian officers, and 9,000 men, combatants and non-combatants, could not take place without striking a blow at British military prestige. The British could comfort themselves with knowledge that their troops were overwhelmingly outnumbered, but, while this exonerated Townshend and his men from any blame for failure, it did not remove responsibility from those who, without counting the cost, had placed them in an impossible position.

A report published in July, 1917, ascribed England's failure at Kut-el-Amara to lack of proper preparation and foresight, and proved, what had been suspected all along, that the Indian Government, which was responsible for the Mesopotamian expedition, originally had no adequate conception of the task with which it was faced. It failed to realize the difference between an enterprise directed against uncivilized Afghan tribes, and one against well-drilled Turkish soldiers organized by German military genius. There was lack of ammunition and medical supplies, and, above all, of transportation facilities for the relieving forces. Bitter experience finally taught the Government of India how to go about its task, with the result that Bagdad later fell into British hands.

Near the end of February some Persian troops concentrated in the region of Kermanshah, with the help of German and Turkish sappers, occupied and fortified two mountain passes, the Budsurks and the Sakahe. The Russians, after dislodging them from Bidsurks, and occupying Sakahe, pursued them and took Kermanshah, which lies 280 miles southwest of Teheran. Trade routes from Bagdad, Ispahan, Hamadan and Suleimaniyah all meet at Kermanshah and make it an important center. Built on rising ground, and connected with hills to the south, it has ancient walls, three or four miles in circumference, but now in ruins with the moat encumbered with débris. Kermanshah is in reality an open town in spite of five gates and numerous loop-holed towers that flank the ruined walls. Many Americans first learned its name from the rugs for which it and its neighborhood are famous. Rug manufacture, however, is almost a lost industry in Kermanshah itself. Rugs and carpets exported through its custom house come mostly from other parts of Persia. They are merely shipped by way of Kermanshah as a distributing center. Here was clearly seen a Russian attempt to effect a junction between their Caucasian army and the British then in sore straits on the Tigris. Aylmer's relief column, which had been pushing up the Tigris to relieve the beleaguered British under Townshend at Kut-el-Amara, late in February had opened a heavy artillery attack on the Turkish positions.

About a fortnight after the fall of Erzerum, the Russian army operating in Persia advanced seventy-five miles west of Kermanshah to Karind, on its way to Bagdad. Karind, like Kermanshah, is on the River Dijala, a tributary of the Tigris. From Karind this river runs northwest for fifty miles and then dips to the southwest for thirty miles to the frontier. For about seventy miles, broadening as it goes, it flows through Mesopotamia and joins the Tigris fifteen miles below Bagdad. This advance promised soon to flank the Turkish army opposing the British; indeed, the occupation of Bagdad by the combined Anglo-Russian armies seemed in prospect of early realization. The progress made in Persia had been little noticed, but it was hardly less important than the progress Russia had made in Armenia. Hamadan, a recognized center of pro-German agitation, had been taken before the Russians advanced against Kermanshah. When the main army captured Bitlis, it was only forty miles from the eastern Tigris and 125 miles from Missibin on the Bagdad Railway.

The Russian advance in Asia Minor, radiating along three main lines from Erzerum toward Trebizond, Sivas, and Bitlis, was meeting with success in all three directions. There had been no serious Turkish resistance since the fall of Erzerum. Baratoff, having occupied Karind on March 12, called a halt for two months in order to secure his flanks and reconstruct the road from Hamadan, which in some places was nothing more than a mule-track. In the first week in May he resumed his march, and on the 5th attacked and defeated the Turks in a position which they had strongly entrenched at Sermil, seven miles from Karind. Without giving the enemy time to rally, he advanced to Kasr-i-Shirlin on the 9th. This brought him within a day's march of Khanikin.

Thus, the campaign in the Caucasus which the Grand Duke Nicholas had launched in January, was now being carried on along a front extending for 700 miles or more from Trebizond to Kut-el-Amara. The front, however, was not continuously occupied, owing to the mountainous nature of the country. There were many localities in which movements by bodies of troops were impracticable. In this respect, the conditions in Armenia were different from those on the Western and Eastern Fronts in Europe, where rival armies faced one another across an unknown line of entrenchments, and where at Verdun more than twelve weeks had passed away since the opening attack, the Germans being as yet no nearer the fortress than on February 25, when they reached the Douaumont plateau, in their first offensive movement. By April 12 the Russian force in Persia having traversed the mountain district separating it from the Turko-Persian frontier, and driven the Turks upon their strongly fortified base at Khanikin, stood at the threshold of Mesopotamia, 110 miles northeast of Bagdad. Mosul, which before had scarcely been considered in the war, now became a chief center of interest. for one of the Grand Duke's armies there sat astride a main caravan route in the Tigris valley, and had cut an important line of communication with Bagdad.

Russian forces rapidly closed in on the ancient fortified town of Jaziret-ibn-Omar, which lies on an island in the Tigris, less than 130 miles southeast of Diarbekr, and about eighty miles northwest of Mosul. This movement, taken with the advance of Russian forces toward Mosul, brought pressure on the rear of the Turkish armies in Mesopotamia and placed between 100,000 and 125,000 men in jeopardy. The advance meant the cutting of the line of the Bagdad Railroad, and this meant not only disaster to Turkey, but the overthrow of one of the great German schemes of empire, in which the scattered Ottoman Empire was to have been braced together by German railways and German ports, its varied races to acquire consistency and Turkey to be employed as an instrument against England in Egypt and India—the only instrument by which British power could have been effectively curbed and controlled. Great Britain could be attacked and mortally wounded by land from Europe only in one part, and that was in Egypt.

Townshend's surrender at Kut-el-Amara, instead of causing the Russians to abandon, or change, their plans for invading Mesopotamia, appeared rather to inspire them with fresh incentives. They soon made conspicuous progress along the difficult roads of the Persian mountain-province, which borders Mesopotamia, and drove the Turks from another series of positions far to the westward, and close to their own frontier. The main threat upon Mesopotamia, however, lay not in this isolated Persian expedition, which was far removed from Russia's other Caucasian armies, but in concerted Russian efforts to drive the Turks southward from Mush in the direction of Diarbekr. This was the shorter route for reaching the Bagdad Railway, possession of which by the Russians would have been equivalent to a Turkish renunciation of Mesopotamia.

The Russians now partly achieved one of their main objectives in Asiatic Turkey—the joining of hands with their British allies fighting against the Turks on the Tigris. Without preliminary announcements, and apparently quite unexpectedly, a force of Russian cavalry, "after a bold and adventurous ride," formed a junction with the British General Gorringe on the right bank of the Tigris in the region of Kut-el-Amara, where only a few weeks before a British force under General Townshend, after a long siege, had been forced to capitulate to the Turks. How this junction of the Russians with the British on the Tigris was effected remained long unknown. The supposition was that it represented the work of a detachment from the Russian army which was threatening Khanikin, about 120 miles to the north. The sudden appearance of the Russians with General Gorringe raised the question whether the Russians already had not cut the Bagdad railway at Mosul.

To reach the British forces on the Tigris, Cossack cavalry would have had to ride about 200 miles across rough country from Russia's furthest south in the mountains west of Kermanshah. That was a difficult ride, but it could have been completed in four or five days. Infantry in this war had sometimes covered close to thirty miles a day. The strength of the force that reached General Gorringe was presumably not large, but it might be effective enough for reconnaissance work and skirmishing operations against Turkish line of communications. Like the arrival of the Russians in France, the primary purpose of this dramatic coup was not strategic. It was intended to serve notice on the Central Powers of that unity of Allied purpose which Premier Viviani had reasserted and specifically imprest upon the Turkish Government and the populations of Central Asia, and to show that the defeat of Kut-el-Amara had not checked the Allied advance against Bagdad and the Mesopotamian provinces. Simultaneous pressure against the Turks from the Caucasus, from Persia, and from the Persian Gulf made the defensive task of the Ottoman army highly difficult. It compelled a thinning of the line along a front of seven hundred miles, and left the initiative in the hands of the Allies. The Cossack officers were invited to Bassora to meet General Lake, where by order of the King of Great Britain they were decorated with the Military Cross.

The ride across that wild country into Mesopotamia was a daring achievement, an extreme test of hardiness, mobility, and resource. The route took the Cossacks across a mountainous region, which had been a familiar landmark to the British for months, but it was rough and precipitous, and the path often difficult even for mules. Some of the passes were over 8,000 feet high. The Cossacks met with no actual opposition during the whole journey, other than a few stray shots at long range. For transport they had less than one pack animal for ten men. These animals carried ammunition, cooking-pots, and a tent. Otherwise, beyond a few simple necessaries, Cossacks had no kit except what they stood in, and lived on the country, purchasing barley, flour, rice and sheep from the villagers. Fodder and fuel were always obtainable. They had only one surgeon provided with medical wallets, but none of the Cossacks fell sick. Their last march was one of thirty miles, during which five of their horses died of thirst or exhaustion on the parched desert. They reached the British camp after night-fall. After a dinner given in their honor, they indulged in singing and dancing, and did not turn in till one o'clock in the morning. The ride of the Cossacks, establishing direct contact between the Russian force in Persia and the British force on the Tigris, imprest tribesmen on both sides of the frontier.

Meanwhile the Russian column, advancing westward on Mosul, the ancient Nineveh, was attacked late in May by

Turks on a ten-mile front extending from Rewanduz to Dergala. On the previous day a mixed force of Turks and Kurds had attacked the southern Russian line at Serdasht. Both attacks proved ineffective. The Turkish forces which were thus attempting to stay the Russian progress toward Bagdad and Mosul were not new arrivals, but Mesopotamian commands released by the capitulation at Kut. Owing to railway connections, the Turks could still draw upon the central resources of the Ottoman Empire for a prolonged resistance, and thereby strengthen the defense of Bagdad. The loss of Mosul would inevitably have meant the loss of Bagdad. The Turko-Germans hoped to break through the Russian left center and take up a threatening position on the flank and rear of the Bitlis and Mush forces. The scene of fighting was only forty odd miles southwest of Erzerum, and about the same distance northwest of Mush. The country was all mountains, cut by gorges and occasional river valleys. The roads were mostly goat-tracks. This development indicated a definite strategic plan in reply to the Russian push southward from Trebizond, and these mountain-barriers were the last natural obstacles to a Russian march on Constantinople. Once they could be forced, there lay only a broad expanse of level plain of the richest soil in Asia Minor. Here was the route eastward and westward that had been followed by great world-conquerors of antiquity from the time of Greek and Roman domination to Tamerlane.

The Turks, in June, taking the offensive at three points, temporarily checked the Russian advance. All their attacks were finally repulsed, except one at Mamakhatum, 50 miles west of Erzerum, which was evacuated by the Russians. Here the fighting was over a front of about twenty miles. Attempts by the Turks, who had been reinforced by Austrians and Germans, to press back the Russians near Bairburt and Diarbekr, failed. Again in August the Turks made gains. On August 8 they captured the Armenian towns of Bitlis and Mush, and carried on obstinate fighting in the regions of Mush, Bitlis, Vanskou, Rmijsk, Semesk, Hkermanghan and Khanazan. In time they were forced to evacuate Bitlis and their attempt to encircle the left flank of the Russian Caucasian army received a crushing blow. Three weeks later the Russian forces reoccupied Mush.

Turkish forces in June made raids into Persia. The fall of Kut had released Turkish troops, and some of these had been diverted to the Persian frontier. By the beginning of June, they had driven the Russians from the neighborhood of Khanikin and Kasr-i-Shirin, and by July 1 had retake Kermanshah. News that the Grand Duke was advancing into Armenia did not check their movements. Farther north a Russian force near the frontier town of Rowanduz was driven back in the last week of July in the direction of Lake Urmia. In this area a great deal of obscure fighting developed. The main Turkish invading force did not pause long at Kermanshah, but soon captured Hamadan, which, by the most direct route, is 200 miles from Teheran. These checks to the Russians in Asia foreshadowed the disaster which ultimately was to overtake the splendid offensive which Brusiloff had seemed about to carry out with success on the frontier of Galicia and Bukowina. But they were followed in good time by the advance up the Tigris of the British under Maude and the capture of Bagdad.[12]

[12] Principal Sources: The *Times* (New York), The *Times* (London), The *Journal of Commerce* (New York), The *Fortnightly Review* (London), The *Evening Post, The Independent,* The *Evening Sun,* "Bulletins" of the National Geographic Society, The *Wall Street Journal,* The *World,* New York; "Nelson's History of the War" by John Buchan.

IX

REVOLT IN ARABIA AND THE NEW KINGDOM OF HEDJAZ SET UP

June 23, 1916—July 12, 1917

REPORTS reached London on June 23, 1916, of a serious uprisings against the Turks in the Hedjaz part of Arabia. Rebels had displaced them in the Holy City of Mekka, as well as at Jidda, the chief seaport of the country, while Taif, sixty-five miles southeast of Mekka, had proclaimed its independence of Ottoman rule. The rising had been preceded by a similar insurrection at Karbela, about forty-five miles southwest of Bagdad in Mesopotamia, also a sacred city containing the tomb of Hussein, a grandson of Mohammed. Hussein-ibn-Ali, the Grand Sherif of Mekka, was the most powerful prince of western and central Arabia. He, rather than the Turks, was the real ruler of Mekka. Along with his able sons, he exercised a unique authority, due to temporal possessions and the religious prestige that came from having sprung from the blood of the Koreish.

As the hereditary Keeper of the Holy Places, he had been the natural leader in a movement for Arab independence. As head of one of the two principal families in the Hedjaz, and of the tribe of the Prophet, he held a position resembling that of a feudal lord or a Highland chieftain. His tribesmen and dependents held property all over the Hedjaz, and acted as his deputies in the administration of ancient Arabic law. His office was temporal—that of Emir (Prince) of Mekka—but as custodian of the Holy Places he was looked upon as a religous leader, and in his action had the full support of the Ulema of Mekka. His personal qualifications added to his authority. A man somewhat past middle life, of good presence, known as a sagacious and prudent prince, strictly orthodox and yet free from fanaticism, he had a receptive mind and an appreciation of the material advantages of Western civilization. His sons, or the elder among them, had traveled extensively, were of keen intelligence, and already were known as capable leaders of men. One of them attended the Peace Conference and made an excellent impression on Europeans.

Difficulties had to be overcome before Hussein could take his decisive step. Turkish troops garrisoning the country numbered 20,000, and were highly disciplined, well equipped, and strong in artillery. Altho the Arabs could put double that number of men in the field, they had little military discipline, lacked material, and had scarcely any artillery, but they had the advantage of great mobility and an intimate knowledge of the country, the most of which was a barren, fairly level plateau, separated from the Red Sea coast strip by a rugged mountain range. Fully 700 miles in length and nowhere more than 200 miles wide, the Hedjaz, with an area somewhat larger than that of Great Britain, had only five towns of any size, and a total population scarcely exceeding 300,000, the majority of whom were Bedouins. The proclamation of independence was made at Mekka on June 5. The townsmen sided with the Sherif, but the Turkish garrison rejected his summons to surrender, and opened fire with their artillery on the Great Mosque. It was not until June 13 that the resistance of the Turks was completely overcome in the town, altho Turkish soldiers in one or two small forts outside the walls held out till the middle of July. The total captures of the Sherif were 950 unwounded and 150 wounded men, 28 officers, four guns, and large stores of munitions.

The immediate causes of the revolt, which extended beyond the Hedjaz, were both racial and religious. Secular hostility between Arab and Turk was notorious. While the Turk hated and distrusted the Arab, and had despoiled him of his finest lands, nowhere and at no time had Ottoman rule in Arabia been accepted by the Arab, who looked with disdain on a race intellectually and in many other respects his inferior. The Arabs in Arabia had succeeded in retaining a large measure of independence. After the conquest of Egypt in 1517 by Selim the Grim, who had already made himself master of Damascus and Jerusalem, the Emir of Mekka acknowledged him both as Calif and lord of the Hedjaz. Since that time the Emirs, or Sherifs, of Mekka, altho virtually independent, had been nominally Ottoman vassals. In recent times the Turks had maintained a precarious authority, chiefly by control of the seaports and heavy subsidies to Arab princes and tribes. The troops stationed in the country were only a garrison, whose authority extended no further than the range of their guns. The Hedjaz had always been a drain on the Turkish treasury, but it was a question of prestige for the Turks to hold the Holy Cities of Islam. To be "the Servant of the Cities of Mekka, Medina and El Kuda (Jerusalem)" was one of the most prized of their titles. The Sultan Abdul Hamid, by his Pan-Islamic policy, had kept the support of the Sherif of Mekka, and by building the railway from Damascus to Medina had appreciably increased Ottoman power in Western Arabia. Begun in 1901, the section of the line from Damascus to Ma'an (285 miles) was completed in 1904, and Medina, 820 miles from Damascus, was reached in 1908. Built to a considerable extent with money obtained from the Faithful, on the ground that it made easy pilgrimage to the Holy Cities, the railway enabled the Turks to tighten their hold on the Hedjaz and the provinces south of it, Asir and Yemen. Thus when Turkey joined in the World War in October, 1914, her position in Western Arabia was fairly strong.

The summer of 1916 appears to have been chosen for the revolt because the success at that time of the Grand Duke Nicholas in Armenia had weakened Turkish military power throughout Arabia. Great Britain, being in control of India, the greatest Moslem empire, had been interested in the movement. Since the early days of the war, she had endeavored to maintain an attitude of the highest respect for the Mohammedan religion, and a proclamation had been issued declaring that the holy places of Arabia, including the Shrine of Mesopotamia and the port of Jidda, would be "immune from attack or molestations by British military forces as long as there was no interference with pilgrims from India." The uprising was in a sense an outcome of a

Pan-Arab movement, which aimed at the ejection of the
Turks from the Arabian Peninsula, and the formation of a
great confederation of Arab tribes. It had a twofold character.
In addition to its political side, it was probably stimulated
by resentment among Mohammedans of the German domination of Turkey. While Turkey remained free and independent most races professing the Mohammedan faith had
been content with Turkey's guardianship of the Holy

THE EMIR FAISAL, SON OF THE KING OF HEDJAZ

The Emir arrived in England on December 10, 1918, to present the respects
of his father to King George. In the war he had led troops through three
successful campaigns. He is seen wearing a long black "abba," or cloak,
and the national head-cloth of Damascus silk with golden head-rope of
Mecca manufacture. From London he went to Paris, to attend the Peace
Conference

Places; they looked up to her as the last great Mohammedan State, a revered survival of days when the sword of Islam won widespread domination in three continents. But German control of Constantinople they thought meant in the end German control of the Holy Cities, and when the road from Berlin to Constantinople was reopened after Serbia was overrun in the autumn of 1915, Turkish independence came to an end. Many Mohammedans began then to feel that Turkey had forfeited her right to control Mekka and Medina, and the pilgrimages of pious Mussulmans to those sacred spots.

The rising was only the last of a series of Arab rebellions against Turkish rule. For nine years adjacent provinces had been centers of an insurrectionary movement under Said Idris, while the Yemen had periodically rebelled ever since the Turks first invaded it in 1870. Turkish control, in fact, had never been firmly established over the great tribes of Central Arabia, where the important cities of Riadh and Hail maintained independence. In 1913 Ibu Sand drove Turkish forces out of El Hasa, in Eastern Arabia, on the borders of the Persian Gulf. The revolt in the Hedjaz was the final episode in a long series of events which had been set in motion before the great war began. The so-called Pan-Arab movement had gained impetus since 1913. It aimed at the abolition of Turkish misrule, oppression and maltaxation, at the ejection of Turks from the Arabian Peninsula, and the formation of a confederation of Arab tribes. Arabia, never truly conquered by the Turks, had remained the real stronghold of the aristocracy of the Moslem world. More than a century before the great war, the Arabs had driven the Turks not only from the Holy Places, but from all Arabia, and even from Berbela, a Mesopotamian city. Never had the Arab wholly bowed to the Osmanli, and now that the Osmanli had fallen under the spell of the unbeliever, in yielding to German supremacy, it was logical that the conservative theologians of the Peninsula should assert themselves and precipitate a revolt.

Abdul Hamid built the Hedjaz railroad to Medina because he foresaw that the time might come when the Arabs would seize the Holy Cities, and he wanted facilities for sending troops southward. Since the Turkish Revolution of 1904, the conspirators who acquired control of Turkey had practically abjured Islam, making it certain that the Orthodox Moslems of Arabia, of whom the Grand Sherif was the principal representative, would eventually thrust the Turks out of Mekka. And so, when in the autumn of 1916 Turkey practically ceased to exist, when Enver Pasha and his colleagues almost transferred their country to Germany, making Prussian officers the real possessors of Turkish authority, the end was near.

Politically, the Sherif of Mekka as representing the old Emirs of Mekka, gave the Bedouins such laws as they could be made to accept. Two patrician families, however, had contested the office. By setting one against the other, the Sultan of Turkey had sustained with their varying fortune his hold on Arabia. While his position was bettered by the Ledjaz railroad and its strategic value, nothing had made his position in Arabia other than precarious. The Young Turks, with a genius for blundering, had sacrificed many soldiers in vain attempts to enlarge, or maintain, occupation of certain parts of the peninsula, but for eight years had steadily lost territory, and now Hedjaz was about to be lost.

Arabians, always ripe for insurrection, found in the plight of Turkey and the Russian successes in Armenia, sufficient motives for a revolt. Exactly what the Sultan, who then had little left to lose, would lose by this revolt, was hard to estimate, because the value of guardianship of the Holy Cities, a privilege that had passed from one chief Mohammedan State to another, had much diminished in modern times. No great Mohammedan State now survived, and the myth of a religious solidarity of Islam had been exploded, the Sultan's religious headship being a fiction more tolerated than believed in. At the same time, the spiritual focus of the Moslem world was Mekka. The innermost shrine of the place contains the Kaaba, a great sacred black stone, toward which every son of Islam turned when he offered his devotion, but Turkish troops had been indiscreet enough to bombard this "symbol of the unity of God."

The Sherif, after declaring his independence, divided his forces—horsemen, camelry, and foot—into four parties: one

remained at Mekka, another was sent north under the Emir
Faisal towards Medina, a third, under the Emir Abdulla,
went south to Taif, and a fourth, under the Emir Zeid,
westward to Jidda. For the success of the enterprise it was
essential that the Sherif should become not only master of
Mekka, but of the means of access to it, namely Jidda, and
the forty to fifty miles of country which lay between it
and Mekka. The conquest of the rest of the country might
follow more at leisure. Ability to receive and safeguard
pilgrims to Mekka would be the test of his claim to independent authority. The revolt spread like wildfire. The
Emir Nuri Shalan, who had already refused to support
Djema, joined the Grand Sherif, and presently the Said
Idrissi of Asir took up arms, and captured the Red Sea port
of Kunfidah, 150 miles south of Mekka. On July 27, Yambo,
the port of Medina, fell. In Medina itself Turkish troops
were closely besieged, while the fires of revolt spread northward among the Arabs all the way to Damascus. Constantinople could not sit still under a blow which threatened the
little religious prestige that remained to her, and so Turkish
troops were hurried south, forces destined for another invasion of Egypt being diverted to the new theater of war.

At the beginning of operations the Emir Faisal laid siege
to Medina, and his horsemen, riding across the desert, tore
up a considerable section of the railway near El Ala, 150
miles north of the city, an action which delayed the arrival
of Turkish reinforcements from Damascus. In August the
Turks made a great sally, and a pitched battle was fought
in the plain south of Medina. In this encounter Faisal's
casualties were about 500, those of the Turks were estimated
at over 2,000. The Turks retreated to the city, where they
perpetrated every species of barbarity upon inhabitants who
favored the Sherif's cause, many being hanged or crucified.
The Emir Faisal was unable to follow up his advantage, and
for months there was little alteration in the military situation. The first phase of the campaign was ended. Before
operations were actively renewed the Arab forces were reorganized and turned into a disciplined permanent army.
In September, Taif, the Turkish headquarters, and with its
vali and commander-in-chief, Ghaleb Pasha, surrendered,

and by the end of the year Ottoman authority in the Hedjaz had ceased to include more than a strip of territory bordering the railway leading from Medina to Eastern Palestine and Damascus.

In November, 1916, the Grand Sherif took the title of King of the Hedjaz, and early in 1917 sent an army northward, where it gained a series of notable successes between Akabah, at the head of the gulf and the Red Sea, at Ma'an, on the southern border of Syria, and in places on the Hedjaz railway between Medina and Damascus. Earlier in the war, from the time when they first appeared on the frontiers of Sinai, Mekkan forces had constituted a friendly army on the right of the Egyptian Expeditionary Force, and the British, from August, 1917, onward, had given them help by conducting air-raids on Ma'an, which was then in Turkish possession.

The formation of the Kingdom of Hedjaz, with the Grand Sherif as its King, followed by its recognition by all the Entente Powers, had a twofold importance. From the political point of view, it meant the resurrection of an Arab State and the independence of the Arab Nation after centuries of subordination to the Turks. From the religious point of view, it possibly meant a new orientation for 200,-000,000 souls professing the Islamic faith. In Hedjaz was the birthplace of Islam. Its population had not been ascertained, but it was estimated at 1,500,000, of whom 250,000 were city-dwellers, while the rest led a nomadic life. The Sherif was about sixty-two years old, of medium size, white-bearded, with a white round face, large eyes, and a big head. He was well educated and knew, besides the Arabic language, Turkish and Persian, both of which he spoke and wrote. He also spoke English, French and Russian, all of which he had studied in Constantinople. He was the first Sherif to have so wide a knowledge of foreign languages. Thus a new State that the war developed was seen in the Kingdom of Arabia.

When the victorious Sherif proclaimed himself King, the boundaries of the kingdom were not defined. Great Britain expected eventually to have as much to do with fixing them as the Arabs themselves. To detach Arabia from its shadowy allegiance to the Ottoman Empire and to bring it within the sphere of British influence had long been a part of England's political program in the Near East. With the Russians standing sponsor for a restored Armenia on the north, and the British for a revival of ancient Arabia in the south, the hold of the Turks was becoming as insecure in Asia as it was in Europe. The area of the peninsula of Arabia was about 1,200,000 square miles; but most of it was desert and half of it unexplored. The portion over which Turkey claimed lordship was the Red Sea coast country of Hedjaz, Yemen, etc., embracing Mekka, Medina, Jidda, the Holy Places, and the trading-ports—a tract with an area about twice that of the British Isles and a population of 1,000,000. The rest of Arabia was either waste or coastwise country toward the Indian Ocean and Persian Gulf, where British influence was paramount and the ruling chiefs were friendly.

Farther away, on the Edom border, was the forest of Hish, the principal source whence the fuel consumed by locomotives on this section of the Hedjaz Railway was obtained. A narrow gage railway connected the forest with the main line at Anaise station. It was to conquer this valuable region that the Emir Faisal set the Northern Hedjaz Army in motion in the early days of January, 1918. Strong parties were detached to keep the Turks at Ma'an in check, and General Allenby, who was then advancing to the north of Palestine, assisted with three air-raids on the town, in which barracks, supply depots and railway buildings were bombed. The Emir Faisal quickly followed up his advantage. Two days later (January 28) another of his columns prest north between El Kerak and the Dead Sea and reached the shores of that remarkable lake—the lowest point in the earth's surface, 1,292 feet below the sea level. They attacked and captured El Mezra, seized an armed launch and several dhows, captured large stores of grain and took 60 prisoners. The remnant of the Turkish force, some 40 men, fled to Kerak.

Now firmly established east of the Dead Sea, Faisal rested and reorganized his troops for the next phase, the advance on Kerek itself. Occupying a hill 3,000 feet high, with strong defenses, and only 20 miles from El Kutrani Station on the Hedjaz Railway, and thus capable of being quickly reinforced, the attack upon it required careful preparation. The operations were indirectly helped by Allenby's campaign. Jericho had fallen on February 21, and in March Allenby, crossing the Jordan, raided the Hedjaz Railway at

THE FLAG OF THE NEW KINGDOM OF HEDJAZ

Amman, 55 miles east-north-east of El Kerak. Allenby's raid gave the Emir Faisal his opportunity; he was further aided by units of the Royal Flying Corps and the Australian Flying Corps, which, on March 19, bombed El Kutrani. The raid was primarily intended to assist Allenby's own trans-Jordan advance, which began three days later, but it served a double purpose. The raiders were met by enemy aeroplanes, one of which was shot down. Two of the British machines were forced to descend by anti-aircraft fire, and were burned by their occupants. Two pilots and an observer were made prisoners by the Turks. Despite this mishap, the raid, Allenby stated, was effective, 470 bombs having been dropt on the station-buildings and on railway-trains, direct hits being observed. The result was that El Kerak, left to its own resources, was abandoned by the Turks almost without a struggle.

Leaving a contingent to mask Ma'an, the Arabs, shortly after the surrender of Jerusalem to Allenby, prest northward and in a brilliant campaign between January and April, 1918, conquered the fertile region south and east of the Dead Sea, El Kerak, the capital, being captured on April 7. Repeated and daring raids on the Hedjaz Railway were marked features of Arab operations, some of these raids being made as far north as the neighborhood of Damascus. Nevertheless the Arabs were unable for a long while to effect a permanent occupation of any part of the lines. The Turks, with German help, had shown great energy in repairing the damage done, and were able by means of the railway to send reinforcements to Ma'an and Medina, so that those places were able to hold out.

In two years of warfare, besides clearing the Turks entirely from southern and central Hedjaz, and from 300 miles of the Red Sea Coast, the Mekkans had killed, captured or immobilized fully 40,000 Turkish troops, the majority belonging to the finest regiments in the Ottoman Army. The loss was a great moral blow to the authority of the Osmanli Sultan in the eyes of almost all Moslems. As careful guardians of the interests of their Moslem subjects, all the Allied Powers continued to look with sympathy upon the Arab movement and to aid it from Palestine. It was the settled policy of Great Britain—a policy which had the support of France and Italy—that the "Sacred Lands" of Mekka and Medina should be under Moslem rule, and when it became apparent that Turkey was ceasing to represent Islam they were prepared to welcome the transfer of the Hedjaz to a native prince. As soon as his capture of

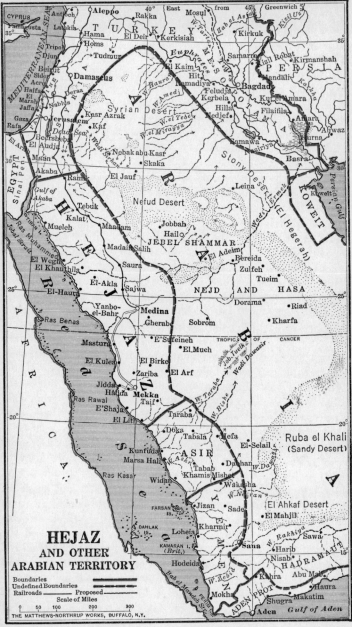

HEJAZ
AND OTHER
ARABIAN TERRITORY

Boundaries
Undefined Boundaries
Railroads ———————— Proposed
Scale of Miles
0 50 100   200   300

THE MATTHEWS-NORTHRUP WORKS, BUFFALO, N.Y.

Mekka and Jidda showed that the Emir Hussein possest real authority he received the moral and, as far as could be, the material support of the Allies. No countries were more intimately concerned, both politically and economically, in the fortunes of the Hedjaz than Egypt and the Sudan, inasmuch as the Red Sea little more than separated them.

The success of the Sherif reacted favorably on the African shores of that sea, and, coming about the same time as the overthrow of Ali Dinar in Darfur, and the Senussi Sheikh, in northwestern Egypt on the border of Tripoli, it had a salutary effect on the small but dangerous pro-Turkish party in Egypt. So long as Turkey held the opposite shores of the Red Sea, England's watch and ward, on land and sea, along the Egyptian and Sudan coast, had been an arduous business; but with a friendly State in possession of the Arabian Coast, that business was distinctly lightened.

There being every sign of a settled and independent condition, official recognition of the new State by the Allies was not long delayed. A month after the Grand Sherif assumed the title of King of the Hedjaz, his title was definitely recognized by Great Britain, France and Italy. British and French cruisers were sent to Jidda to congratulate the new sovereign, who went down to Jidda with his principal ministers to meet them. "The greatest of Arab princes," as the commander of the French cruiser hailed him, visited all the warships in turn. "I am happy," he said, "to visit the brave and heroic Allies, who have proved their virtues to the world, and who merit all respect and honor." This visit of Allied warships was more than a ceremony; it was outward evidence of the support the Allies were prepared to give a great Moslem prince in his efforts to liberate the Arab world from Ottoman tyranny.

Medina was surrendered to King Hussein of Hedjaz January 15, 1919, under the terms of the armistice of 1918 with Turkey. It was the last Turkish stronghold in Asia to complete the compliance of the Ottomans with the armistice terms. It also marked the end of the rule of the Sultan over the most sacred shrines of Islam. Of still more importance to the Moslem world, was the fact that the tomb of the Prophet had been saved from desecration. Medina was held in reverence next to Mekka, the true believer considering his hadj incomplete without a pilgrimage to the spot where the Prophet died and was buried. For more than three years Medina had been closed to pilgrims. With the small force at his command, King Hussein had been unable to overcome strongly entrenched Turkish forces which held defenses of the town. The most that he could do was to cut the line of communication which the Hedjaz Railroad afforded, and to imperil the position of the Turks. Aggressive action was halted by a threat from the Turkish commander that he would make his final stand at the tomb, that he would fortify it and the mosque of which it was a part, with artillery, and that rather than surrender he would destroy the shrine and then take his own life. This intelligence, which was quickly spread throughout Islam, caused the situation to be watched with intense interest. Had he carried out this threat, the Turkish commander would have ended all Turkish leadership in the Mohammedan world; but, at the same time, according to his own reasoning, he would have caused unpleasant complications for Allied nations having large Moslem populations. This was the explanation of an official statement that "it was incumbent upon King Hussein to secure the capitulation of Medina by arrangement and not by assault." [13]

[13] Principal Sources: The London *Times'* "History of the War," "Nelson's History of the War" by John Buchan; *The Literary Digest,* The *Times,* The *Sun,* New York; The *Times* (London), Associated Press and Reuter dispatches.

X

BAGDAD FALLS TO THE BRITISH UNDER GENERAL
MAUDE AND FURTHER ADVANCES ARE MADE

December 13, 1916—April 29, 1918

DURING the months that followed the disaster to Townshend at Kut-el-Amara, new supplies of men and ammunition had been collected and in January, 1917, the British
resumed the offensive. Northeast of Kut their troops drove
the Turks from a strip of land on the right bank of the
river until they obtained control of a trench-section on a
front of 2,500 yards, and advanced to a depth of 1,100
yards. Meanwhile the right bank of the river had been cleared
of Turks below Kut. Southwest of the town further progress was made. Constantinople, however, said that east of
Kut the British had launched three attacks, but that none
of them had been successful. Thus, while a German thrust
in the Champagne, a British advance on the Ancre, and
British success in Mesopotamia, were signs by mid-February
of the approach of grand-scale operations, it was only around
Kut that there rose the possibility of something like a
decision.

The Tigris at Kut flows from west to east, but makes a
sharp turn to the south and back to the north forming a
narrow peninsula within which, on the left, or northern
bank of the river, lies the town. The locality might be
compared to Manhattan Island as enveloped by the Hudson
and East Rivers; in a way those streams correspond with
the course of the Tigris around Kut. Before the end of
the month Kut had fallen to the British and thus atoned
for the long struggle which Townshend had made there in
1916. General Sir Stanley Maude, destined to conquer
Bagdad and then to meet a melancholy fate, had started for
Kut and Bagdad with 120,000 men on December 13, 1916, and
now two months later the Turks were in flight. The

fighting was of an open character, with the British forces disposed on a wide front. Having lost their trenches, and having no time to dig new ones after the fall of Kut, the Turks were soon driven twenty-four miles beyond Kut, altho fighting rear-guard actions. Bagdad was only ninety miles away.

Maude's victories became important, not only as dealing a blow at Germany's Bagdad ambitions, on which she had intended to lean heavily in peace negotiations, but as decreasing the available German forces on any given front in Europe. From Kut to Bagdad was less than half the distance which the British army had already covered in Mesopotamia from its base at Bassora. A swift advance upon Bagdad was expected, and this was what followed. The British were now much stronger in numbers, equipment, and leadership than the hazardous expedition which in 1916 had tried to take Bagdad. But in fairness to that expedition, it was to be said that everywhere in the war the forerunner among the Allies had made mistakes by which his successor was to profit. The mistake made on the Tigris of leaving open an undefended line of communication had not again been repeated. Altho important in itself as evidence of British determination and recuperative powers, this renewed thrust against Bagdad brought into the foreground once more the probable defeat of that Berlin to Bagdad dream which Germany had been inclined to regard as virtually realized. A southern terminus for the great nerve-line of Middle-Europe became now no longer an assured fact. Nor was the partnership of Turkey in that scheme likely to be established when one British army was in Mesopotamia, when Russians were in Armenia, and another British army was on the frontiers of Palestine.

Other factors in the situation were now more favorable to the Allies than when the British were hemmed in at Kut in 1916. The Turkish forces that threatened the Suez Canal had been driven back. The Kingdom of Hadjaz had been established in Arabia. A considerable force of Arabs had been armed by the French and British in their war against the Turks. The army of the Grand Duke Nicholas, now holding a strong position in Armenia, had been increased and was better equipped than ever before to force a way southward to the Bagdad lines and cut off the Mesopotamian Valley from the Turkish Capital. It was foreseen that a Russian line from the Caucasus to Alexandretta on the Mediterranean might eventually enable the Russians to open up a way from the east to Constantinople.

On March 2, what was left of Turkey's army in retreat had covered half the distance from Kut to Bagdad. Eight days later the British were in Bagdad. The day before by a surprize they had effected a crossing of the Diala and the Tigris, and driven the Turks back to within three miles of the city, the Turks for two days offering considerable resistance. Owing to the intensified submarine warfare that Germany had carried on since February 1, hardly anything more welcome than this progress could have come to the British public. Great Britain was beginning to feel the effects of the war in a reduced food supply, besides being thrown into a state of depression by revelations made in an official Dardanelles report, censuring the administration for that ill-starred expedition. On the night of March 8, the British established a footing on the north bank of the Diala, and on the 9th and 10th the troops on the right bank of the Tigris, in spite of dust and storms, drove the Turks back on Bagdad. At the same time troops on the Diala thrust them back, and the city was entered on a Sunday morning. Maude, in these operations, had made a march of 110 miles in fifteen days, during which the Tigris was crossed three times, and the march made over a country destitute of supplies.

The British fought their way to the walls of Bagdad on both banks. General Cobbe's force occupied the Bagdad railway station and adjoining parts of the city on the right bank, while General Marshall entered the part lying on the left bank. There was no display, nothing in the nature of a triumphal entry, but as the victorious troops, dirty and unshaven, tramped between palm groves and orange gardens, crowds of Bagdad people came out to meet them— Persians, Arabs, Armenians, Chaldeans, and Christians of divers sects and races, who lined the streets, balconies and roofs, hurrahing and clapping their hands. Groups of school-children danced in front, shouting and cheering, and the women of the city turned out in holiday attire. The gunboat flotilla, meanwhile, with mine-sweepers ahead, proceeded up the river, Maude and his Staff going with the flotilla and arriving at the citadel soon after the troops.

So fell Bagdad, the immediate base of Turkish warfare in Persia and Mesopotamia, and one of the most famous cities in the East. No romance could be stranger. Bagdad, which lies only sixty miles from the ruins of ancient Babylon, with memories reaching back to Harun-al-Rashid, now resounded to the footsteps of British soldiers, and Mosul, opposite which lay all that remained of Nineveh, "the great city," once mistress of the world, was at their mercy. Above the remains of an ancient tower that had formerly been one of the temples of Babylonia was a "wireless" station that had been installed there since the beginning of the war—a tower which tradition associated with the famous Tower of Babel.

When the British proceeded to consolidate their positions, their first act was to destroy all German wireless installations, which had been completed at enormous cost, and comprised one of the most powerful installations in their system. It had direct communication with Berlin, and possibly the earliest definite information that Bagdad was in British hands had arrived in Berlin by this route. Various measures, political and military, were then taken in hand to establish order, reassure the population and guard against mischief on the part of the beaten Turkish forces. For a fortnight before the fall, the Turks had systematically plundered the inhabitants. Large sums of money had been extorted from them, and everything of value that was portable had been carried off. "The Turks have taken everything," a Jewish Rabbi said, "even the pigeons on the Mosques are getting thin."

When the last train steamed out of the Bagdad railway station at two o'clock on the morning of March 11, the Kurds and other rabble of the slums had swarmed out to loot the wealthier quarters. For seven hours shops and houses were gutted in all directions, and even the Turkish hospital was not spared. The robbers looted shops, and took bedding, medicine and drugs, letting in their friends to share in the spoils. British troops arrived in time to save patients from being turned out of their beds. Summary steps were taken to put an end to this general orgy of looting, and soon the city was in order. Shops began to open again, the trading classes here, as elsewhere, showing confidence in British administration. Jews, Arabs, Armenians—such of the Armenians as had escaped from recent massacres—all alike seemed glad to be rid of the Turks, who had never been for them anything more than a horde of foreign oppressors.

Meanwhile General Maude, in his capacity as "political chief," issued to the people of the Bagdad Province a proclamation assuring them of the goodwill of the British Government and its Allies, and of their desire for the prosperity of the country. The British advance had covered more ground in a short period than almost any other movement of the war. It was assisted materially by defections of native tribes from Turkish rule, a result mainly of the action of the Grand Sherif of Mekka in declaring Arabia's independence. Various Bedouin tribes had put aside old enmities and become united. Peace, for example, was made between the Emir Arab ar Rowleh near Damascus, and the Emir of the Anzeh tribes near Aleppo, who had helped to assemble a troop of horsemen to fight the Turks after being supplied with drill-masters, presumably British, who had effected the organization of an Arab fighting unit possest of arms and ammunition of the latest type. The importance of this union of tribes lay in the fact that, all told, Arab tribes numbered not fewer than 4,000,000 souls.

The British cavalry which hung on the flanks of the Turkish army on the Tigris, and chased it to Bagdad, was almost exclusively Indian. The infantry included Indian units which had already fought in France, Gallipoli, and Egypt. This Tigris expedition was part of a comprehensive Entente plan against Asiatic Turkey. From Egypt British troops under Sir Archibald Murray were then approaching Jerusalem. In the Bitlis region the Russians were renewing their activities south of the Caucasus. On the Persian frontier the Russians who retired beyond Hamadan after the surrender of Townshend at Kut, were again starting out for

Kermanshah and Mesopotamia. Junction of the Russians with General Maude would form an Entente line of over 1,000 miles, broken only by mountains and reaching from Bassora, at the head of the Persian Gulf, to Trebizond on the Black Sea.

Germany's dream of world dominance received a severe setback at Bagdad. Here in the Near East she had aimed at an economic control which would have supplied her with the raw materials she had formerly imported from outside countries. Already she had acquired many Turkish concessions for exploiting and monopolizing nearly everything between the Dardanelles, the Tigris, and the Persian border. Some of the earth's most fertile soil lies in this region, as the ancient cities of Nineveh and Babylon bear witness. Bagdad itself, centuries before Christ, had a population of 2,000,000. Modern engineering projects had been started to restore Mesopotamian fields to their former productivity, the success of which would have meant for Germany a plentiful supply of wheat and other grains, fruit, vegetables, cotton, wool, and livestock. There is a rich oil territory northwest of Bagdad which was being connected with the city by branch railroads. Copper, silver, coal, cement, and other minerals were under German concessions, and not only the "Cedars of Lebanon," but other forest products which Germany needed, had practically passed under her control.

By the fall of Bagdad the Persian Gulf became free to the world. as policed by Great Britain. Had that control been wrested from Great Britain a naval base could have been established there by Germany, and connected with the Bagdad railway, so that a military line would have been opened from the Baltic to the Persian Gulf, as a standing threat to India and the Suez Canal, while the southern extension of the road through Syria would have threatened the western end of the canal and laid Egypt open to attack. Success here would in fact have meant a three-fold increase in the German Empire's population, and put the world at the Kaiser's feet. But the British had now made secure for themselves the eastern terminus of the road and were asking whether this had been the irony of fate or the hand of providence.

THE ENTRY OF GENERAL MAUDE'S ARMY INTO BAGDAD

193

Underlying the military was the political meaning of this new turn in the war. Mohammedans tho they were, the Arabs had never reconciled themselves to the supremacy of the Turks. The traditions of the great days of the Prophet and his successors who carried the Green Banner from Bagdad to the Loire in France still survived. The decline of Islam had been for the Arabs a consequence of Turkish supremacy. For many years there had been growing restlessness among them. Syria, which is Arab by population, was on the verge of a revolt when the Young Turks overthrew Abdul Hamid. It was long a Syrian dream to create an autonomous Syria. Away to the south, about Mekka, interminable Arab revolts had occurred, and now the last of these had driven the Turk out of the Holy City, had deprived him of the possession of the center of Islam, which was one of his chief claims to power. A succession of events— the failure of the Turkish expedition against Egypt, the fall of Bagdad, the invasion of Palestine—had combined to shake Turkish power. Then events, joined to the great misery and suffering that the war had brought to Syria and Mesopotamia, had created a sufficient basis for a revolt of the whole Arab population, from the Amanus Mountains to the Yemen, and from the Mediterranean to the Tigris. Its coming was regarded as one of the most probable consequences of the fall of Bagdad. To expel the Turk from Islam by separating him from Mekka, to restore the Arab to the place he once occupied, to confine the Turk to Asia Minor by erecting a French protectorate in Syria, a Russian province in Armenia and a British colony in Mesopotamia, with an extension of Egyptian territory to Palestine, or by the creation of an independent Holy Land—these had been conceptions of the Entente Allies, their answer in fact to the German success in capturing the Turk and the machinery of Islam.

If Saloniki was the side door of the Central Powers, Bagdad was its back door—and Bagdad had been broken open. Its great distance from London was a handicap, but an army could be provisioned and reinforced in Bagdad from Egypt and India without meeting the full strength of submarine menace that had so hampered Balkan operations.

Belgium, as providing a better route to the Atlantic, and Serbia, a vestibule leading to the East, had been the chief German war objectives. But failure before Paris and Calais had dimmed Germany's hope of keeping Belgium, and she turned for comfort to an Eastern empire that she believed she had securely won, and that was worth winning. Once a tunnel could be built under the Bosporus and the Bagdad railway pushed to Bassora, a man would be able to go from Hamburg without change of cars to a deep-water port off the Persian Gulf, where a Hamburg steamship line had actually been established before the war began. Thus travelers would have passed a dozen fine cities, or the routes that led to them, rich agricultural lands in Asia Minor, a Mesopotamia needing only irrigation to be once more a garden, and the gates to Persia and India. In the cold winter days of 1916-17, lacking food and coal, isolated from the world and sorrowing over dead, Germans had drawn comfort from their dreams of "a place in the sun" beyond the Mediterranean. Those dreams had now had a rude awakening. How the Turk was to get back Bagdad, or even to avoid further reverses, was a problem Berlin sought vainly to solve. Meantime the world took note that, for the time being at least, Berlin's war-cry had been reversed in Entente hands so that it read, not Berlin to Bagdad, but "Bagdad to Berlin."

The next objective of the British was Mosul, some two hundred miles farther up the Tigris. Here was the present eastern terminal of the railway from Constantinople to Bagdad, the part leading beyond Mosul down to Bagdad not having yet been built. Mosul was the center toward which further advances were now being made from three directions: First was the British army under General Maude advancing northward from Bagdad; secondly, the Russians advancing from Persia westward from the direction of Hamadan; and, third, other Russians, presumably under the Grand Duke Nicholas, advancing southward from Lake Van and Armenia. The distances were great, but that a junction could be made between these forces, and that they could then move westward toward Constantinople, was not beyond the bounds of probability. Such a movement, once under way, would threaten Constantinople from the rear. All indications were that the Turks were no longer receiving such assistance and overseeing from Germany as they had at Gallipoli and the Straits.

General Maude's expedition was curiously parallel to Kitchener's march to Khartum. For years the British efforts to reconquer the Sudan had failed, and at least one insufficiently equipped Egyptian expeditionary force had been destroyed. In óne of the best and most economically managed campaigns of its kind, Kitchener had reconquered the Sudan and left the Mahdists no chance to "come back." Maude's army was doing now what Kitchener did then, and what the unlucky Townshend undertook to do in the first advance on Bagdad. The occupation of Bagdad was accepted in Germany as "an undeniable success for the British, especially as they had also succeeded in driving the Turks from the Sinai Peninsula." The event was to be regretted, but it "had not the least influence on the decision of the war, Mesopotamia being a secondary theater of operations."

By March 14, British and Russian forces were nearing a point north of Bagdad, where it seemed possible for them eventually to effect a junction. On both fronts the Turks were hastily retiring. By March 18 the retreat of the Turks had been turned to a rout. General Maude had dislodged them from a strong position on the Tigris, and scattered remnants of three divisions were in flight toward Samara, over a distance of twenty miles. Coincident with this victory came news of Russian successes against the Turks on both the Persian and Armenian fronts. The Russians had come within ten miles of the Mesopotamian border at three points west and northwest of Kermanshah. Three important villages had fallen to them, and they had driven an entire Turkish column, with two battalions of infantry, six guns and three squadrons of cavalry, into the trackless mountains west of Kanijaran. On the Armenian front the Grand Duke's forces had captured Van, an important town on the eastern shores of Lake Van, and thus opened the way for an advance southeastward toward the British and other Russian armies.

THE WAR AGAINST TURKEY

The junction of British and Russian forces along the Diala River, northeast of Bagdad, signalized what was perhaps the most successful co-ordinated military operation the Allies had shown since the beginning of the war. When the British delivered the final blow at Kut-el-Amara, the Russians were in the neighborhood of Hamadan, and immediately took advantage of the Turkish defeat on the Tigris. The Russian advance from Hamadan to Khanikin covered nearly 250 miles in six weeks, a remarkable rate of progress considering the nature of the country through which the march lay. The territory won from the Turks by this advance and the parallel Russian movement further north in the mountains south of Lake Urumia, represented a gain of more than 25,000 square miles. The Anglo-Russian alinement along the Diala River recalled something of the precision of the Mackensen-Hindenburg advance into Russia two years before. The next step was to be a move upon Mosul, some 200 miles north of Bagdad. With the Allies established at that point the whole Turkish campaign in Armenia would be affected, and an Allied line would have been established from the Black Sea to the Persian Gulf, cutting off a vast Turkish area. By this junction the situation of the Turkish forces was rendered doubly critical. For weeks the move had been foreseen. It was brilliantly executed in spite of great difficulties arising from the character of the country. Ever since Maude's army captured Bagdad, the British had been steadily crowding the retreating Turks northward along the Tigris and Diala rivers, while the Russians rapidly moved westward from Hamadan and Kermanshah in Persia. Another Russian force threatened the Turkish communications with their base at Mosul. The breakdown of Turkey, hard prest as it was in Mesopotamia and Armenia, promised to leave Bulgaria little choice but to seek the best terms possible on her own account.

Disasters for the Turks on two fronts were officially reported on April 20. In Mesopotamia, seventy miles north of Bagdad, Maude had routed the Eighteenth Ottoman Army Corps and had taken more than 1,200 prisoners. In Palestine, before Gaza, the forces of General Dobell, assisted by warships operating from the coast two miles away, had cleared the Turkish forward trenches on a front of six and a half miles, and were advancing on the city. Maude's victory was the result of a flanking movement, in which he drove the Turks back from the Diala triangle after a brilliant night march across the desert from the right bank of the Tigris. He had now crossed the Adhem, another tributary of the Tigris. Apparently there was little to stop a Russo-British march on Mosul. Before a dash of British Indian troops the Turks had been utterly routed. General Maude on April 24 surprized an Ottoman division on the Shatt-el-Adhem and drove them ten miles further north, with heavy losses in prisoners and transport. His victory resulted in the capture of 687 prisoners and 17 guns, besides much valuable booty. In two days of fighting before Iztabilat, Maude took, besides the prisoners, a 5.9 gun, 14 Krupp guns, 2 machine-guns, 1,240 rifles, hundreds of handgrenades, 200 rounds of artillery ammunition, 540,000 rounds of rifle-ammunition, four limbers, 240 trucks, 16 engines, and much other material. Constantinople declared that the Turks "withdrew according to plan." The Turks, on April 13, sustained another defeat, when the British won by outgeneraling them. They made a strategic retreat, drawing the Turks after them, and followed this by a night march which enabled them to fall on the Turks from the flank, and put them to rout, inflicting upon them a loss of 200 killed and 700 wounded.

Samara, which fell in this fighting, had been for a brief period of forty years a rival of Bagdad. The Samara of to-day is almost swallowed up within the site of the ancient and famous city of Old Samara, or Samarra. It is connected with the right bank of the river by a bridge of boats. The ruins of the older city stretch along the left bank for a distance of nearly twenty miles. Among the crumbling monuments of its departed glory are the chief mosque, the Halviyeh minaret and two palaces built by the ninth century califs. One of the royal residences was erected by Motawakil at a cost of two million dinars ($4,500,000), the money being extorted from minor officials of the realm who had abused their power to amass great wealth. Samara is now a town of perhaps 2,500 inhabitants, with a few khans and shops on the opposite bank of the river. Eight califs ruled from Samara between 836 and 876, and of these five suffered violent deaths.

A battle in Mesopotamia on September 27, which resulted in the capture by the British of the village of Ramadi, was one of those illuminating incidents of the war which had come unfrequently. It demonstrated that, in spite of the development of trench-warfare, the old idea of strategy,

BRITISH RECLAIMING SWAMP-LAND IN MESOPOTAMIA

based on surprize made possible by great mobility, had not been abandoned. In fact the entire Mesopotamian campaign of the British had been, in its essential elements, strategical rather than tactical. This distinction was seen when the Mesopotamian situation was compared with that which existed on the Western Front. In the latter case strategy, as the term has always been understood, had no longer a place; the very existence of permanent trenches was anathema to the term. The success of the British, while based on elements of skilful leadership, was due entirely to the tactics employed—the unprecedented use of artillery in overwhelming quantities. But in Mesopotamia it was a war of movement. The mechanical superiority of one combatant over the other was not marked. The advantage in numbers, if on either side, rested with the Turks. And yet the year 1917 had been for the Turks an unending series of disasters. The answer was found in the skill of the British leader, in the excellence of General Maude's strategy.

The Turks had concentrated at the village of Ramadi a large store of supplies, both food and military, preparatory to moving down the Euphrates, following the south bank, with the idea of cutting in behind the British who, after the capture of Bagdad, had moved north up the Tigris to Samara, and had at the same time spread out southward as far as the northern bank of the Euphrates. By following the south bank of the river eastward, the Turks, if successful in their surprize-movement, would have been thrown to the rear of the British forces, and so threatened their lines of communication. As General Maude had a complement of airplanes for observation purposes, he undoubtedly discovered that a concentration was being made and guessed accurately its object. He moved forward, following directly up the southern bank, and his infantry seized a group of low heights about four miles east of the town. He then did exactly the same thing that Lee did at Chancellorsville when he detached a heavy column, under Jackson, from the main body and sent it forward over the road to fall on Hooker's flank. The British column which was detached left the river, maneuvered to the south of the Turkish position and thereby reached its flank, at the same time that a cavalry column, having greater mobility, reached to the west of the Ramadi position and occupied the low ridge which forms the eastern boundary of the little valley of Amih. The Turks were then surrounded.

The British force moved in two columns on the night of September 27, and at dawn attacked Mushaid Ridge, a low line of dunes running north and south from the Euphrates to the Habbaniyah Canal. By morning the dam of the canal had fallen into their hands and was rendered passable for all arms. As the Turks had evacuated the main crest of the ridge, the right column was withdrawn and swinging around to the west behind the left column became the left wing of the force. The British front, three and a half miles in breadth, now lay between the Habbaniyah Canal on the right and the Azizyah Canal on the left at a point nine miles from the Euphrates. Cavalry made a wide, sweeping movement across the desert around the right flank of the Turks and were soon established astride the Aleppo Road on a regular line of hills run-ning to the river at right angles, within five miles of Ramadie. By this move the Turks were cornered. They had no bridge behind them, and were cut off from all reinforcements or sup-plies. Their only chance was to make determined counter-attacks and break through. Meanwhile infantry was clos-ing in. One column attacked Ramadie Ridge on the right, while the other worked around to Aziziyah Ridge, on the left.

© INTERNATIONAL FILM SERVICE, N. Y.

GEN. SIR STANLEY MAUDE

General Maude had demon-strated that this was not every-where and necessarily a war of trenches and of pounding. The world had last heard of him early in the summer going up the Tigris while the Turks were throwing guns into the river in a mad rush to get away. Then the heat descended on Mesopotamia, putting an end to fighting as effectually as snows and rains did for four successive winters in France. When Maude found the Turks moving to cut his communications he turned their trap into one for themselves. There was not a particle of pounding in his method. He suddenly seized a commanding ridge when the Turks were not expecting it. By the time they were aroused their main position was being attacked on the southeast, while cavalry assailed them from the west. By nightfall the Turks were penned in, with the Euphrates on the north, British infantry and artillery on the east and south, and cavalry on the west. The surrounding army attacked from all sides with such fury that the Turks surrendered in thousands, including their general and his staff. This was a victory of strategy, dash, and determination, the old-fashioned kind of fighting, but it was won in Maude's own way. His accomplishment had had no precedent on the side of the Allies. Then suddenly the death of Maude at fifty-three was announced in official dispatches that reached London on November 10. At the outset of the war he was a colonel on the General Staff with a record achieved in the South-African War. He had served on various British fronts in the World War, and on August 28, 1916, was placed in command of the Mesopotamian army.

The circumstances of Maude's death, as stated in the House of Commons by Lloyd George several months afterward, in asking for a grant of £25,000 to Maude's widow, were that he had been invited to a native ceremonial, after his advance beyond Bagdad, in going to which he had warned the men who accompanied him against drinking the water, because of the existence of cholera in the country. At this ceremony, however, a cup of water formed an essential part of the proceedings and one was offered to Maude, who, out of respect for the natives whose guest he was, drank it. The cup contained the fatal cholera germ, and Maude died soon afterward.

The British campaign in Mesopotamia by April, 1918, had taken a rather surprizing turn. British forces advanced northward from Bagdad and east of the Tigris to within striking distance of Mosul. Several weeks before another expedition had been reported on the Euphrates—after defeating a considerable Turkish army—and apparently was advancing toward Aleppo, the junction of the Syrian and Bagdad railroads. It seemed then as if the English objectives were to cut off Mosul, on the one hand, and the whole of Syria, on the other, from communication with Constantinople by one and the same blow. Nobody at the time had imagined that the British had enough troops in Mesopotamia to strike simultaneously at Aleppo and Mosul. But this was what they were doing, and doing successfully. In that event, German-Turkish threats of a counter-effort either in Mesopotamia or Syria seemed mere pretext. Twelve additional field-guns were captured on April 29, when the total of prisoners reached 1,800.[14]

[14] Principal Sources: The "Military Expert" of The *Times,* The *Evening Post,* The *Sun,* New York; The London *Times'* "History of the War," "Nelson's History of the War" by John Buchan; The *World,* The *Times,* "Bulletins" of the National Geographic Society, New York.

ARMENIANS ESCAPING FROM A RAILROAD TRAIN ON WHICH THEY WERE DESTINED TO MEET THEIR DEATH

THE CONQUEST OF PALESTINE AND ALL OF SYRIA, FOLLOWED BY A TURKISH DÉBÂCLE

January, 1917—October 26, 1918

EARLY in the war Turkish forces had twice reached the Suez Canal, and so threatened British control of the shortest route to India, but it was not until January, 1917, that all Turkish menace to the canal was removed, as the result of a series of British victories which cleared the Turks out of the Sinai peninsula and carried a counter-attack into Palestine. Further south, the Red Sea coast of Arabia had meanwhile been lost to the Turks and the independent Kingdom of Hedjaz had been set up. Since leaving the Suez Canal one hundred miles of waterless desert had been traversed by the British by January, 1917. In the autumn of 1916 they had pushed a railway line from Kantara across the desert. This was one of the memorable achievements of the British campaign.

Warfare in this country had been much like warfare in the old Sudan campaign of thirty years before, the condition being that before each new move could be made, large quantities of supplies had to be collected at an advanced base. After an action was fought and the front cleared a pause would ensue until a railway could be carried forward and a new reserve of supplies accumulated. The task proved harder in the Sinai Peninsula than it was in the Sudan, because in the peninsula there was no river. After the Katia basin had been left behind, water was almost non-existent. Supplies of it had first to be brought by rail in tank-trucks and then a pipe-line had to be laid. The work entailed was arduous. Camel transports had to help to bridge gaps between the rail-head and the front.

Lands here fought over already, or soon to furnish battle-fields, had for twenty-six hundred years been a cockpit of war. Sometimes a conqueror from the north like Nebuchadnezzar, or from the south like Ali Bey, or Napoleon, or Mehemet Ali, had met an enemy in Egypt or Syria, and the decisive fight had occurred in Palestine. Ashkelon, Gaza, Rafa, El Arish, are famous in all history as battle names. Up and down that strip of seaward levels marched the great armies of Egypt and Assyria, while Jews looked fearfully on them from barren hills. In the Philistian plain Sennacherib smote Egyptian hosts in the days of King Hezekiah, only to see his army melt away under the stroke of the "Angel of the Lord." At Rafa, Esarhaddon defeated Pharaoh, and added Egypt and Ethiopia to his kingdom. On the same plain Scythian hordes were bought off with blackmail by Psammetichus. At Armageddon, Josiah was vanished by Pharaoh Necho, who in turn was routed by Nebuchadnezzar. At Gaza the first Ptolemy was beaten by the young Demetrius, and at Rafa a century later, Ptolemy the Fourth shattered the Seleucid army. Twenty years later came the siege of Gaza by Antiochus the Third, and then the land had rested until 614 A.D., when the last great Sassanid, Chosroes II, swept down on Egypt. Leaping across five hundred years the eyes of the world were again centered on Ashkelon, when Godfrey of Bouillon,[15] the crusading King of Jerusalem, defeated the Egyptians, and a century and a half later, after being for long a Frankish stronghold, it fell to the Mameluke Sultan after a battle at Gaza. In this gateway of ancient feuds it had now fallen to Turkey's lot to cross swords fatally with the British.

Palestine as a battle-ground might have been called the Belgium of the ancient and medieval world. From the dawn of history only two other regions could compare with it as a theater for the clash of peoples and conquerors—the lower Rhine and the plains of northern Italy. The lower Rhine rivaled Palestine in its thick-strewn names of great battlefields; northern Italy, in the names of great commanders who fought in its territory. Among renowned names in military history Palestine could claim all but

---

[15] Bouillon, the place from which Godfrey derived his title as a duke, is now a small town in the Belgian part of Luxemburg.

Hannibal and Cæsar and possibly Genghis Khan. All the others—Rameses, Alexander the Great, Pompey, Abu Bekr, Judas Maccabeus, Omar, Tamurlane and Napoleon—had fought on its soil. The parallel with Flanders ran much closer than with northern Italy, for Palestine, like Belgium, had been less an object of desire in itself than as a bridge between contending empires. What Belgium had been to Germans, British, and French, Palestine had been to the great monarchies of the Nile, Euphrates, and Tigris. The test of battle had usually taken place around Gaza, when it was Egypt that stood on the defensive, or one hundred miles further north, when the attack came from above. Between the heights of Gilboa and Tabor, near the shores of Galilee and Mount Carmel, lies the plain of Esdraelon (or Jezreel, or Armageddon), which is the Ramillies, the Fleurus, the Waterloo, the Po Quadrilateral, the Sedan, of the ancient world. Esdraelon had witnessed the victories of Thotmes over Hittites, of Gideon over Midianites, of Philistines over Saul and his sons, of a second Pharaoh over Josiah, King of Judah, and of Napoleon's Marshal, Kléber, over the Turks.

Soldiers in French and Flemish trenches had been inclined to look upon the Egyptian campaign as a realization of the war of movement that soldiers in the great war had longed for, but it was less the movement of cavalry riding for an objective than the slow process of engineers daily completing a small section of line in sun-baked sand. Hundreds of miles of water-piping were laid, with filters capable of supplying 1,500,000 gallons of water daily; reservoirs were installed, tons of stone being transported from distant quarries. In due course Kantara was transformed from a small canal village into an important railway and water-terminus, with wharves, cranes, and a railway ferry. A desert, till then almost destitute of human habitation, now showed successive marks of the British advance to firmly entrenched positions protected by hundreds of miles of barbed wire, standing camps where troops found shelter in comfortable huts, tanks, and reservoirs, railway-stations and sidings, aerodromes, signal-stations and wireless installations. These activities subdued the desert and made it habitable, with adequate lines of communication between the advancing troops and their ever-receding bases.

When, from time to time, the British were ready to strike, the Turks often were not there to meet them. On the night of December 19, 1916, it was found that they had evacuated positions they had elaborately fortified. On the night of the 20th Australian and New Zealand mounted troops, supported by camel corps, marched twenty miles, and reached El Arish at sunrise only to find that the Turkish garrison of 1,600 men had fallen back upon Magdhaba. A frontier town, which for two years had been in Turkish hands, was thus restored to Egypt. Mine-sweeping operations were begun in the roadstead, and a pier was built. By the 24th supply-ships from Port Said began to unload stores in the harbor which the British had won as a necessary advance base for major operations. A flying column found the Turks at Magdhaba, twenty miles to the south-southwest, in a strong position on both banks of the Wadi-el-Arish. Here followed a perfect little action in which, by four o'clock, after a bayonet-charge by a light-horse regiment, the place was won, the British casualties being twelve officers and 134 others killed and wounded. More than 1,200 prisoners were taken besides four mountain-guns, one machine-gun and over a thousand rifles. On January 9, Rafa had fallen, New Zealanders taking the main redoubt. When the action lasting ten hours was over, a relieving enemy column, from Shellal, was driven back, the British casualties being 487, and the enemy losing 1,600, besides unwounded prisoners, six machine-guns, four mountain-guns and a quantity of transport. The two actions of Magdhaba and Rafa showed the perfect cooperation of all arms of the service in battles of the old type, where mobility and tactical boldness carried the day. The result was the clearing of the Sinai desert of all Turkish troops. Operations back in the interior, conducted by small flying-columns of cavalry and camelry, kept pace with the greater movement. The British were now beyond the desert, on the edge of a habitable country, the next objective the Gaza-Beersheba line which was the gateway to Syria.

From Beersheba, the terminus of the trunk line north-

ward through Syria, to Aleppo on the Bagdad line was four
hundred miles. From this trunk line ran four branch lines
to the Levantine coast—at Tripolis, Beirut, Haifa, and Jaffa.
From Damascus the road ran in a southeasterly direction to
Medina. With the British advance on the Tigris, combined
with this advance into Syria, the Asiatic Empire of the
Turk appeared as if it had never been quite so imperiled
as now. The British in moving on toward Jerusalem had before them besides Damascus, Aleppo, their ultimate objective,
for it was the gateway leading from the west to Bagdad. If
Aleppo could be taken, the main supply-line of the Turkish
armies in the Near East would be taken. But before reaching either Damascus or Aleppo the British had to take
Jerusalem. High enthusiasm was aroused over this prospect. The ancient capital of Palestine, the city of the Holy
Sepulcher, was last held by the English in the time of
Richard Cœur de Lion. The menace was directed first
against the railroad from the port of Jaffa. Thirty-five
miles east of Jerusalem ran the Damascus-Medina railroad,
which fed Palestine, and the southern part of which was
already in possession of the Arabs. With Jaffa as a base, the
British would be able to assemble a force which, moving
north, could cut out the Damascus railway. British possession of both Jerusalem and Jaffa promised to solve a
serious problem for American missionaries. For many
weeks the United States ships *Des Moines* and *Cæsar* had
been waiting at Alexandria for assurances permitting them
to take to Syrian ports food and supplies desperately needed
in the interior, but had been put off by Teutonic diplomacy.
The hope now lay in an expulsion of the Turks by British
arms.

Late in March the British defeated a Turkish army of
20,000 men, capturing 900, including a general and the entire
divisional staff of the Fifty-third Turkish Division, and advanced fifteen miles along the coast, from Rafa to Wadi
Ghuzzeh, a river five miles south of Gaza—Gaza being
twenty miles north of the Egyptian-Syrian boundary. As
Gaza is almost directly west of Hebron, this brought the
British front to a straight line across nearly the entire
breadth of Palestine between the Mediterranean and the

Dead Sea. The army near Gaza undertook to construct a railway to facilitate operations in the interior.

The British success seemed as decisive as their victory at Kut-el-Amara on the Tigris, but doubtful if General Murray could follow up as rapidly as Maude had done at Kut. The latter had the Tigris and his gun-boats to harass the retreating Turks, while in Palestine the British had to follow a road along the coast, an ancient and historic highway now largely a desert road, unless a British fleet could cooperate with the army. The coast-road here runs so close to the Mediterranean as to lie under the fire of a moderate-sized naval gun. The immediate objective of the British was the Palestine ports as well as Jerusalem, rather than a drive through the desert against the Damascus-Mekka railway. The campaign as a whole coordinated itself with the fighting in Mesopotamia and Armenia, uniform pressure being exerted on Turkish armies from both directions.

The construction by the British of railways as incidents in such advances revealed the elaborate preparation necessary for victory even in such comparatively small operations. As the British had been carrying a railway into Palestine all the way from the Suez Canal, so Maude had built a railway from Bassora to Kut, and was engaged in extending it to Bagdad. In addition, Maude had constructed virtually a new channel for the Tigris, and created new harbor works at Bassora. Herein lay some future profit for the world out of the wreck and wastefulness of war. Railways, harbors, roads, and bridges built for military purposes, would remain to serve the interests of peace. Just as Poland, whatever might be her destiny, would profit by the roads which the Germans had built for their advance on Warsaw, so Palestine, whomever it was to call master, would have her railway into Egypt, and Mesopotamia would have hers to the Persian Gulf.

Gaza—Samson's Gaza—lies forty-eight miles southwest of Jerusalem. In the Book of Judges it is recorded how Samson, escaping from Gaza, "took the doors of the gate of the city, and the two posts, and went away with them, bar and all, and put them on his shoulders and carried them up to the top of an hill that is before Hebron." Thus, once more the war in the East put an old and sacred city again on the map, giving a military importance to historic localities of which little more had been left in modern memories than a name and a tradition. The Dardanelles expedition had reanimated the plain of Troy. Mekka and Medina, the old shrines of Moslem pilgrims, had become modern strategic points. Bagdad, city of the Calif, came again into chronicles of great deeds. The campaign of Xenophon's "Ten Thousand," after twenty centuries, had acquired a new parallel at Trebizond. A battle for mastery in Mesopotamia and Asia Minor was fought in the "Garden of Eden." Much that happened read like chapters from Rawlinson. While the Western Front had been a great theater of war since the time of Cæsar, it was the Far Eastern Front—the Holy Land and the Tigris and Euphrates—that revived the oldest of war's romances. That the cradle of the human race should have become in our century a great battle-ground, stirred romantic recollections as no other of the war's campaigns could do.

The British, in the third week of March, surprised the enemy on a foggy dawn when he could have known nothing of danger unless a German airman soaring in the filmy clouds on the previous evening had detected columns of dust arising from the western fringe of the great plain of Gaza. The fog delayed the opening and development of the attack till 10 o'clock and time was the essense of the day's work, as Turkish reinforcements were within fifteen miles. The position was separated from the sea by two miles of golden sand-hills with trenches that ran southwest and then bent toward the east, the position consisting of two main hills, one north of the other, with a sand-hill between. The southern hill was a perfect labyrinth of deeply cut trenches and redoubts, skilfully selected, but with no barbed-wire framework to disclose a position of formidable strength. There were seven Turkish infantry battalions, the artillery mostly served by Austrian gunners. When the western skies became aglow with an exceptionally beautiful sunset, the vast plain was seen to be alive with troops. Long lines trailed across the plain, lifting low clouds of dust. Equally long serpentine lines of cavalry raised higher clouds, while

© PRESS ILLUSTRATING SERVICE.

JERUSALEM FROM THE MOUNT OF OLIVES

artillery ammunition columns laboriously made their own paths. Slower and never ending supply-trains made other paths. Camels, bearing troops and war-material, wound their way over the plain long after the crescent moon had ceased to cast its light across the country.

The country fought over was otherwise difficult, intersected as it was by ravines and nullahs, big cracks in the ground, and the precipitous banks of the Wadi Ghuzzeh, which had to be crossed in an enveloping cavalry movement, its bed soft and sandy, its banks often forty feet high. Anzac mounted troops and British Yeomanry, with horse-artillery batteries, got across in the dark, after having cut down its banks and built ramps for guns. Gaza lay visible in the background with its red-roofed and white-walled houses, enclosed by lemon- and olive-groves. Towering above all was the minaret of the mosque, formerly the Church of St. John, founded by Knights Templars in the twelfth century, and taken from them by Saladin. One could also see Ali Muntar, the high mound up which Samson carried the gates. The artillery operations provided an inspiring sight when bursts of shrapnel smudged the cerulean blue and high-explosive shells raised clouds of dust with vast quantities of earth from enemy entrenchments. Here in the fourth week of April British forces defeated the Turks.,

Gaza was one of five great cities of the Philistines, having risen to commercial importance from its situation at the junction of trade-routes between Egypt and Babylonia, Elath and Arabia. The Philistines were a powerful warlike people, their soldiers equipped with copper helmets, coats of mail, javelins, and long lances, each man thus accoutered being accompanied into battle by a shield-bearer. After the Israelites conquered it, Gaza became a prey to Assyrians, Babylonians, and Persians, and resisted the Greeks under Alexander the Great for several months. More than two centuries later it was destroyed by Alexander Jannæus, a Jewish king. Subsequently a new Gaza, some distance to the south of the old city, was built and presented by the Emperor Augustus to King Herod. Upon the latter's death it became a part of the Roman province of Syria. Crusaders under Baldwin II tried to revive its former state, but without success. Twenty years after their erection here of a military stronghold Saladin plundered the town. Napoleon captured it in 1799. El Muntar ("the watch tower") is thought to be the eminence to which the strong man of Israel "took the doors of the gate of the city, and the two posts, and went away with them, bar and all." It was in Gaza that the final tragic chapter in Samson's life was enacted. "And Samson said: 'Let me die with the Philistines,'" so runs the Biblical account. "And he bowed him-

A VIEW OF HEBRON, IN PALESTINE, SOUTH OF JERUSALEM

self with all his might; and the house fell upon the lords, and upon all the people that were therein. So the dead which he slew at his death were more than they which he slew in his life." Gaza is to-day a city of some 40,000 inhabitants.

Late in October, Beersheba was captured by the British under General Allenby, who had succeeded to the command and was to fill the world with his fame for great martial deeds before the end of 1918. Beersheba, twenty-seven miles southeast of Gaza, was of strategic importance, lying as it did on the railway which, beginning near the Sinai frontier, ran north about fifteen miles from the coast and forty miles west of the Damascus-Medina line, to which it was parallel. Beersheba means "the well of oath," a name due to a covenant made there between Abraham and Abimelech. In the Old Testament it is frequently used to describe an extent of country, or the length of a journey, as "from Dan to Beersheba." Its capture was the first sign of activity that had come out of Palestine in months. The British under Murray had been checked after their advance had been going forward. Under Allenby the place was now taken in a brilliant night-charge in which the British surprized and overwhelmed the Turks. Infantry and Australian horsemen shared in the victory. Cavalry movements had to be carried out at night, because of the great clouds of dust that they raised, which in daylight would have disclosed their presence to the enemy. Infantry first tore down wire-entanglements. Then, just as the moon rose over the Judean hills, cavalry with fixt bayonets charged against strongly held trenches, overwhelmed the Turks and galloped into the town, infantry facing the northern, western, and southwestern defenses. The entrenchments were elaborate, skilfully chosen, and heavily protected by wire and guns.

What in the spring were fertile, rolling downs, had become sun-parched deserts, the slightest movement raising dust. Only a few trees and cactus-hedges between the sea and the gaunt hills relieved the picture. In these surroundings Allenby effected a surprize which the Turks had considered impossible, the place being deemed by them impregnable. Some of the horsemen had ridden thirty miles before they got into action. The taking of the Telelsaba foothills, three miles east of the town, was a difficult operation as the hills presented a redoubt of great strength and were almost unapproachable because of steep banks running along the river. In Beersheba everywhere was evidence that the Turks had been taken by surprize. They had blown up a railway engine and burned the engine-house. Warehouses full of corn were, however, almost intact, altho attempts had been made to fire them. Fifteen guns were captured and prisoners to the number of 444 included 26 officers.

THE WAR AGAINST TURKEY

By November 7 Allenby had advanced to within thirty-three miles of Jerusalem. Pushing northward along one of the caravan routes he had taken Khuwellfeh. Further west Gaza fell before troops advancing up the Mediterranean coast. The British had first attacked Turkish lines defending Gaza on November 1. They captured the first line defenses on a front of 5,000 yards and took 296 prisoners and five machine-guns. Three counter-attacks were driven off before the town fell. The British campaign at last was developing into ultimate success. The plan was practically the same as that of the previous year, wh'ch had met with failure because of Murray's check at Gaza. Two columns were now advancing simultaneously northward, one on the inland route by way of Beersheba, the other along the coast, by way of Gaza. The coast enterprise had back of it the railroad through the Sinai peninsula and a pipe-line that carried an adequate water-supply, and in addition it had the support of a British fleet. By November 9 the Turkish army in Palestine was retreating to the north. British airplanes were following up and bombing retiring Turks. Ashkelon was taken, ships from the British and French navies cooperating with British land forces. By November 16 Allenby's forces were three miles south of Jaffa, on the railroad that connects Jaffa with Jerusalem and about twenty-two miles northwest of the Holy City. Two days later Jaffa was taken, the Turks offering no opposition.

Altho the British force in Mesopotamia, after the death of Maude, had temporarily ceased its offensive, Allenby in Palestine continued his forward course. Jerusalem was practically surrounded by November 25 and its evacuation by the Turks was expected to follow soon. German influence in Syria, directed by Falkenhayn and Sanders, and Turkish influence throughout Asia Minor, was now in the balance, and if Jerusalem fell, would receive a staggering blow. The British in Mesopotamia and Palestine were widely separated, and, to the casual observer had little in common, but there was a close and distinct relation between them. Turkish resistance, wherever the British operated, was crumbling. Turks were showing complete inability to offer sustained and effective resistance. Should the British

215

take Jerusalem, with its advantages of terrain and rail-communication with the sea, there was strong possibility of their being able to move northward soon.

By December 10, Jerusalem was in the hands of the British. It capitulated to Allenby's force of British, French, and Italian troops, after it had been entirely surrounded. With its fall was swept away all that remained of the dream of Germans and Turks of driving southward through Palestine to capture the Suez Canal and invade Egypt. Since the taking of Jaffa and the gradual closing in on Jerusalem, the fall of the city had been anticipated. It was not lack of Allied strength that prevented its capture earlier. Allenby's desire was to carry out a plan of enveloping it and forcing its capitulation, since a frontal attack would have endangered numerous sacred places inside the city and its environs. Its capture marked the end, with two brief interludes, of more than 1,200 years of possession by Mohammedans. The last Christian ruler of Jerusalem was the German Emperor, Frederick II, whose short-lived domination lasted only from 1229 to 1244. Its fall was virtually assured after the British took Jaffa.

When Bagdad fell one of the historic centers of Moslem domination passed out of the hands of the receding Turks, but Bagdad was only a political capital. Turkish hold on it affronted no precious religious sense of the Moslem world. But Christian and Jew alike had long been impatient at the thought of alien and infidel occupation of the Holy Land— the land of Gethsemane and the Mount of Olives, the heritage of the house of David. The Western nations had shed their blood freely in the Middle Ages to recover its Christian sanctuaries. They did recover them for a time from the Saracens, but the crusading spirit died away and the military difficulties were found insuperable. Its fall in 1917 had little military significance. Indecisive from a military point of view, its loss, with its garrison, was, however, an unmistakable sign of Turkish collapse. All the world thus interpreted it. By Mohammedan, Christian, and Jew alike the passing of Turkish control was accepted as final and irrevocable.

Here in Jerusalem one political readjustment due

THE MAYOR OF JERUSALEM WAITING OUTSIDE THE CITY TO
SURRENDER TO GENERAL ALLENBY

to war was fully accomplished. The world was right in assuming that, whatever else happened, Turkish rule in Jerusalem was at an end. After seven centuries a new crusade had been crowned with victory. Ottoman dominion over the city had lasted all those centuries and now ended without so much as a stone of the city being scratched or an inch of soil destroyed. In none of her previous seventeen captures had Jerusalem escaped in war so absolutely unscathed. It was to the glory of British arms that the most venerated place of the Christian world came unharmed through the ordeal of battle. No British gun was sighted within a considerable distance of its walls, altho Turkish artillery fired from positions close to the city, including the Mount of Olives. Of British fire the inhabitants could make out nothing except the distant rumble of guns as carried by the wind. For a fortnight English, Irish, Welsh, Australians, and New Zealanders had looked on Jerusalem from distant hilltops.

The official entry was a ceremony worthy of the occasion. In the place from which the Savior's teaching of peace on earth and good will toward men was spread throughout the world, there was no pageantry of arms, no display of the pomp and circumstance of an army victorious in war. Allenby and his small staff, with less than 150 troops, became the center of a quiet ceremonial in which martial law was proclaimed and a meeting of city notables and heads of religious bodies was held. No thunderous salutes acclaimed the victory; no flags were hoisted; no enemy flag was hauled down; no soldiers shouted in triumph—just a short military procession took place in the Mount Zion quarter, 200 yards from the walls, a purely military act with a minimum of military display. No bells in the ancient belfries rang; no *Te Deums* were sung; no preacher came forth to point a moral to the multitude. It was not necessary for a parade of troops to tell the people that a new system of government had come in backed by military strength. The earlier fighting on the hills and in deep-cut valleys near the Holy City had been proof of that.

At high noon the commander-in-chief's official entry through a picturesque throng took place. From the outskirts of Jerusalem the Jaffa road was crowded with somber-clad youths of all nationalities, including Armenians and Greeks, who stood side by side with Moslems drest in the bright raiment of the East. Many Moslems joined in expressions of welcome. On flat roofs and balconies were gathered many of the population, but in streets with their cosmopolitan crowds, one saw the real demonstration. Allenby entered on foot after having been first met by the Mayor and Military Governor with a guard of honor outside the Jaffa Gate. On the right of the gate were men from English, Scottish, Irish, and Welsh counties, with fifty men afoot representing Australian and New Zealand horsemen, who had been engaged in the Sinai Desert and Palestine since the war broke out. Inside the walls were twenty French and twenty Italian soldiers, detachments from troops sent by Italy and France to take part in the Palestine operations.

Close by the Jaffa Gate, the iron doors of which were rarely opened, was seen the wide breach made in the walls in 1898 for the Kaiser's entry when he visited Jerusalem. Allenby passed that breach by and entered by the ancient gate. Inside the walls was a crowd more densely packed in narrow streets than the crowd outside. Preceded by aides-de-camp, Allenby had on his right the commander of the French, on his left the commander of the Italian detachment. At the base of the Tower of David, which was standing when Christ entered the city, the proclamation of military law was read. Every person was declared free to pursue his lawful business without interruption, and every sacred building, pious foundation, or customary place of prayer, whether Christian, Hebrew, or Moslem, was assured protection. The ceremony over, the procession returned to the Jaffa Gate, and Allenby left Jerusalem. Thus ended the simple and impressive ceremonial. In Jerusalem were found 750 wounded Turks without medical stores and practically without food.

The Roman Catholics at Westminster Cathedral in London were the first Europeans to celebrate the great event. The big bell, which had not been sounded since the beginning of the war, was rung. Its deep note caused a sensation in the neighborhood. A large congregation assembled before the altar of the Blessed Sacrament and, at the conclusion of the service, ''God Save the King'' was sung in English, a thing rarely done in Catholic churches. At St. Paul's Cathedral a solemn *Te Deum* was sung. Robed in magnificent capes of cloth of gold, Archdeacon Newbolt and Canon Alexander passed in procession to the altar, where tall candles were burning, while the choir sang the first verse of the hymn, ''Praise to the Holiest.'' Two canons representing the Eastern church had come from Serbia, in capes of a pattern strange to English eyes and glowing with the splendor of color. The whole cathedral rang with the strains of the national anthem. Manifestations of rejoicing were made by the Jewish community in Whitechapel, where broad pavements were studded with knots of people discussing the glad tidings which had become the one topic of discussion everywhere in London.

The erection of Palestine into an autonomous state under British protection seemed a natural sequel to the brilliant achievement of the troops under Allenby. Even to those among Jews who had little sympathy with the aspirations of their Zionist brethren for wresting the homeland of their people from the age-long domination of the Turks, the British victory brought a thrill of genuine emotion. But the future of Palestine had other and larger meaning. Christian, Jew, and Moslem, all sent pilgrims to Palestine, all had religious representatives in the country. Security of personal property, and freedom to enter and leave, were matters of the first importance to all of them. When at length Palestine should be provided with a government and people cooperating for its development, the world was surely to see the dawn of a new day. All competent authorities were unanimous in regard to the vast industrial and economic possibilities of Palestine. Sir Richard Burton had said long before that, when provided with railways and tramways, the Holy Land would offer ''the happiest blending of the ancient and modern worlds.'' It would become another Egypt, with the distinct advantage of a superior climate, and far nobler races of men. He had prophesied some fifty years ago that Syria and Palestine awaited the hour when, as the home of a free and energetic people, it would again "pour forth corn and oil, flow with milk and honey, and bear, with proper culture, almost all the good things that have been given to men."

Soon after Allenby entered Jerusalem he arranged to have it administered by a remarkable group of Britons— scholars who combined with academic learning an executive ability which became everywhere apparent in the management of the country. Almost every act of these men bore the mark of fine understanding of the native population and respect for their traditions. This attitude was seen in their official, as well as their unofficial, acts. They did not refer to Palestine as a conquered country, but made it known as "occupied enemy territory." Altho the British were in command, the British flag did not float over Palestine nor did any other. When a few Americans were about to hold their Fourth of July celebration, they were asked courteously not to run up the Stars and Stripes, and so they celebrated the Fourth without the flag. Allenby was not only a military man, but a student deeply interested in the historic background of the country. He spent one whole night with an American visitor pouring over the Bible and a standard historical work on the Holy Land, refreshing his mind as to spots of greatest interest.[16]

Dramatic possibilities lay in the British advance further north, which began early in 1918, in double column, along the coast toward Haifa and Beirut, and west of the Jordan toward Damascus. One resource was at the disposal of Allenby which his predecessors, all the way back to the time of Thothmes, had not possest, and that was naval power. With the establishment of a base at Jaffa, the difficult problem of transport had been greatly ameliorated, since British cruisers and gunboats could be employed to parallel the land advance. A successful naval demonstration against Haifa would threaten seriously the right flank of Turkish forces in the Plain of Esdraelon, just as a powerful cavalry movement east of the Jordan would menace their left flank. With British success, the way would be open to Beirut and

[16] Statement by Dr. John H. Finley on his return from his Red Cross Mission to Palestine in November, 1918.

Damascus, with serious implications for the entire campaign against Turkey in Asia Minor and the ultimate fate of Germany's Berlin-to-Bagdad enterprise. By January 22, because of the desertion of 160,000 Turkish troops between Constantinople and Palestine, Falkenhayn, who was believed then to be at Aleppo, abandoned his plan to reorganize the Turkish army. He had been credited with having an army of 300,000 men with which to take the offensive against the British, but Turkish officers refused to support his plan because they knew their troops were tired of the war, and so, in disgust, Falkenhayn, the eminent general who was formerly the Kaiser's Chief of Staff and who had lost the campaign for Verdun, returned to Constantinople.

By a brilliant operation Allenby, late in February, drove the Turks from mountain ridges east of Jerusalem, forced them out of Jericho, cleared the valley of that section of the Jordan, and compelled the Turks to burn their storehouses and pier at Rujm-del-Bahl, north of the Dead Sea, an important center of their grain-supply. Different phases of the operations lasted three days. No one who had not stood on the Mount of Olives and looked out on the rugged country that falls away to the Jordan and the Dead Sea could realize the great effort here required to turn an enemy out of trenches cut and blasted out of ridges and spurs of hills. The whole country is one succession of hills and valleys until it reaches marshy flats more than 1,000 feet below sea level. But the Turks, with all conditions in their favor, were completely defeated. At dawn the British attacked four important positions running almost due north and south on a line of about 2,000 yards, five miles east of Jerusalem. El Muntar, a bleak hill southeast of Jerusalem, lightly held by the Turks, was taken soon after 6 o'clock. Ras-et-Tawill, a brown knob dominating a wide district, was taken by a column which marched from Mukmas during the night, overcoming resistance at Splash Hill on the way. After a heavy bombardment the Turks were retreating from Tawill in a northerly direction, and the hill was won. At 9 o'clock the center column got Ras-umm-Desis and won Arak Sbrasim, north of the Jericho road, but on the high ground running eastward the Turks put up a stout resistance, one London battalion having to assault three times before bayoneting the enemy out of the trenches. The whole line was captured by 3 o'clock.

Nine miles east of Jerusalem lay Talteddumm, the key to Jericho. Winding up over its face was the Jerusalem-Jericho road. On the hill was the well-known Good Samaritan Inn, and standing out as a fine landmark of what the Arabs called the Hill of Blood, was a Crusaders' Castle, with little save the moat and vaults remaining of its past.

THE CITY OF BEIRUT IN SYRIA

London troops attacked this hill at daybreak. The preliminary bombardment was short but effective, after which the Turks were seen to rush in retreat across a broad green patch toward a defile. British infantry at this time were ascending the spurs of the hill, and before they reached the top the Turks had rallied and been brought back. When the British reached the top there was a brief fight, after which the Turks retreated, but they reformed and made one counter-attack, which was repulsed, and the position gained for the British by 8 o'clock. After that, they sniped at long range and shelled places where they thought the British were preparing to attack, but their fire was hopelessly out-classed, and soon after 10 o'clock their first-line trenches were carried. For a couple of hours there was fighting on Ektief, the Turks having a number of machine-guns hidden in rough ground, but they were routed, and, by afternoon, the whole range was in possession of the British. When darkness fell the British had won such commanding positions that the Turks moved off east and next morning the British entered Jericho where not one Turk was left. On March 6, fearing lest British troops would cross the Jordan, the Turks destroyed the bridge over the river at Chovaniyeh, east of Jericho. So far Allenby had confined his operations to the west of the Jordan, without attempting to cross the river and strike at the Hedjaz railway. His troops were advancing on a fifteen- to eighteen-mile front astride of the Jerusalem-Shechem road. On March 9 the dominating position of Tel Asur, 3,318 feet above sea level, was occupied. On March 20 the British army had reached a point about twenty miles north of Jerusalem and ten south of Shechem.

Momentous events were now taking place on the Western Front in the great German offensive of 1918, during which Allenby, in April, continued his slow but sure progress in a northeastward advance from Jerusalem, having two objects. One was to cut the Hedjaz railway on the eastern boundary and so isolate Turkish forces operating south at Medina. This he accomplished by taking Amman, while Medina, the last holy Mohammedan city in Ottoman hands, seemed about to surrender. His second object was, by advancing northward along the Jordan, to threaten the flank of the Turkish Syrian army facing him from Jerusalem to the sea. He had already arrived at Es-Salt, thirty-five miles northeast of Jerusalem. By proceeding further north, he could, by a flanking movement, force a retirement of the enemy beyond the boundaries of Palestine. By such strategy he could avoid the losses entailed by a frontal attack on strongly entrenched Turkish positions.

Not until autumn did any further notable event occur in Allenby's program. Then something happened which thrilled the whole Entente world. British forces, aided by

THE WAR AGAINST TURKEY

THE SHRINE OF THE HOLY SEPULCHRE
Christians and Moslems alike have made pilgrimages to this place for centuries. The jeweled lamps and other ornaments seen there were deposited by pilgrims

French, Anzacs, and Arabs, and themselves reinforced by troops from India, in the third week of September launched an attack on the Turkish line on a fifty-mile front from the Mediterranean to the Jordan. In smashing blows they broke through and swung forward nineteen miles in the coastal region and more than twelve miles inland. Three thousand prisoners and great quantities of stores were captured after 18,000 Turkish troops had been almost surrounded. The

Holy Land once more was aflame under the impetus of a great stroke. In less than a day Allenby's forces, with those under the flag of the King of the Hedjaz overran the Turkish defensive system. The railway and highway junction points were captured, strong forces of cavalry got well in advance of attacking troops, threatening to carry out a turning movement, while along the Mediterranean naval units cleared the coast-roads of Turks by gunfire. The predicament of the Turks was heightened by operations carried on by the Hedjaz tribesmen east of the Jordan which prevented them from taking refuge across the stream. The Turkish army was virtually annihilated. Allenby's forces, sweeping across Armageddon, soon advanced sixty miles, captured 25,000 prisoners and took 120 guns. Nazareth was occupied and the gateway opened to Damascus and even to Aleppo, the supply-base of the Turkish armies in Mesopotamia as well as those in Palestine. Allenby had completely crusht the main Turkish army; he had enveloped and destroyed it.

The event promised to free Syria as well as Palestine from the Turk. It gave control of the whole Turkish railway-system from southern Syria to a point not far south of Damascus. Strange memories and poignant associations were recalled by news that British cavalry, after galloping over the actual field of Armageddon, had occupied Nazareth. One more sacred place was in Allied hands. Armageddon overlooked the great plain of Esdraelon, southwest of Nazareth. It was one of the most famous battlefields of the world. It was there that Barak defeated the Canaanites, and Gideon the Midianites; there Saul was slain by the Philistines, and there Napoleon, in 1799, defeated the Turks.

British troops had advanced more than sixty miles. Two entire Turkish armies were wiped out. Twenty-five thousand prisoners and 260 guns were taken on the two sides of the Sea of Galilee. Forty thousand more had been trapt by the British and could not escape annihilation or capture. The British coup was probably the quickest and most successful of the war. The end of a hot summer had been the signal for a renewal of military operations in Palestine just as the beginning of spring had been on the plains of Picardy. The prospect seemed clear for a rapid march upon

Damascus and from there to Aleppo, carrying with it the collapse of Turkish resistance in Mesopotamia where the road already opened to Mosul carried a threat against the line which Turkish armies still held stretched out to the Caucasus. All Asia Minor had been shaken. Kut-el-Amara had been thrice avenged; first, when Maude's army took Bagdad and drove the Turks far up the Tigris toward Mosul; second, when the British entered Jerusalem; third, when virtual destruction came to the Turkish army that barred the Allied road to Damascus—the key to Syria— now practically undefended. When Damascus fell all British armies in Asiatic Turkey could be linked up with Aleppo, their common as well as ultimate objective. The Turks seemed now to have no forces in Syria or in Mesopotamia that were equal to stopping any British drive. The Allies had traveled a long way from Kut-el-Amara and Gallipoli. The military power of the Turk was fast waning. Bulgaria and Turkey alike were beginning to eat the bitter fruit of a covetous alliance with Teutonic powers.

Arab forces from Hedjaz successfully raided Derat, seventy miles north of the latitude of Jericho, and the

STREET SCENE IN DAMASCUS

junction of the Damascus-Hedjaz railway with a British line tapping the fertile Houran district and the country of Druses, from which the Turks had received grain. It was the first time the modern world had heard of Arab forces operating so far north. They were now in close touch with the Druses, who had never been well disposed to Turks at whose hands they had suffered much. Allenby's victory promised to make it possible to cut the Hedjaz railway permanently, which would enable the King of Hedjaz to clear the remaining Turks out of his territory and give him possession of Medina, the last of sacred cities remaining in Turkish hands. On September 25 more than 40,000 prisoners and 265 guns had been taken by the British. They were extending their occupation about the Sea of Galilee—had occupied Tiberias and Semakh and, east of the Jordan, the strategic town of Amman on the Hedjaz railway. Here the Fourth Turkish Army had been virtually surrounded. Its annihilation completed the clearing up of Turkish forces in Palestine and accounted in all for 70,000 men and 350 guns. Syria, with a large anti-Turk population, was now open to invasion.

For the first time since the World War began, we saw, not a huge territory occupied which might count for little, but an entire army in a given theater of operations destroyed, which was the object of war, and what all military commanders aim to achieve. The Turkish army in Palestine had ceased to exist. If Aleppo could be taken, the Turks for all practical purposes would be shut up behind the Taurus Mountains, with nothing of value left in Asia, everything in the hands of Great Britain and her Allies. Turkey's only hope was a peace with the Entente.

Damascus, the capital of Syria, was occupied by Allenby's forces on October 1, and more than 7,000 Turks were taken prisoners. This swift advance indicated a decided weakening of Turkish power in Syria. Damascus was a haven of desert caravans, a manufacturing center—the starting point of yearly pilgrimages to Mekka. Into Damascus, as into Bagdad and Jerusalem, the British came as deliverers from the Turks of its Christian, Jewish, and Arab population. Every advance in Syria had improved the British military situation. The port of Beirut was nearer Damascus than was Haifa, and beyond Rayak the railroad was standard gage. Approaching Aleppo from Homs, which apparently would soon fall, Allenby was coming at right angles to the advance of the British from Bagdad. There British armies would meet, at the key of Asia Minor, which was Aleppo, where with Falkenhayn and Sanders there would now be no fighting, for both had wisely fled. Reports that the Turks were on the point of surrender were made credible by their easy yielding of Damascus.

Aleppo, on the Constantinople-Bagdad railroad, was only 180 miles north. Damascus, 160 miles from Jerusalem and

THE FORTRESS OF ALEPPO

90 miles from the point where Allenby's offensive was launched on September 14, is the most beautiful and, after Bagdad, the most historically romantic city in Asiatic Turkey, situated in a fertile plain, at an altitude of 2,350 feet, its water-supply one of the marvels of Jewish engineering work, with many improvements made by Arabs, its population 150,000. More than any other city under Turkish rule, Damascus still possest its ancient buildings. The five-mile city wall, which, in 1148, Crusaders besieged in vain, was still there with its seven gates. Through the city still ran the "street called Straight," where St. Paul once took up his abode. Conquered by David, it had afterward achieved independence and attacked Israel. Conquered by Assyria,

it later became a colony of Greece and then of Rome. In the seventh century came the Arabs, who made it a great show city, a seat of learning and metal arts, the most famous of which was the making of steel sword-blades that still bear its name. From the sixteenth century it alternately surrendered to Egyptian and Turkish conquerors, and in 1841 was finally restored with Syria to Turkey.

As with Bulgaria's surrender, so with these British victories in Palestine and Syria, submarine activities in the Mediterranean were further curtailed. With Bulgaria now out of the war, not only were all Ægean ports west of the old Tchatalja line closed to U-boats, but a rapid advance of the Allies through Serbia was assured, which meant that the Albanian and Montenegrin coasts would also be sealed to them, and the whole Adriatic more easily bottled up by Italy. Allenby had gained possession of the Syrian sea-coast from which German submarines had issued to sink Entente vessels, among them a great British hospital ship with hundreds of wounded on board. This submarine menace to the eastern Mediterranean had, therefore, been removed. At the same time, near the other end of the great battle-front, the Belgian Channel-ports, still in German hands, were threatened by the Belgians. Thus the U-boats were going the way of the Zeppelins.

Zion, now cleared of the last of its Turkish oppressors, was the first of subject nations to reclaim its territory. The feat of Allenby, while less in a military way than that of D'Esperey on the Bulgarian front, yielded more prompt results. The land of the children of Moses had reverted to free use by its historic possessors a few days before the land of the sons of Kara George passed to its heroic remnant. The campaign in Palestine had been one of uninterrupted success since Allenby took over the British command. Australians, New Zealanders, Highlanders, Lowlanders, Indians, and, last but not least, British Territorials, or county-regiments, had vied with one another in advancing the Entente power. It had been open warfare, with cavalry playing a large part. Arab tribes, as allies of Great Britain, had had no mean share in the triumph. The British had fought hard for every mile of their advance, for if Turks were not always well equipped they were well led by their German generals. Turkish domination of the Arabian world had come to an end, and with the political went the religious authority. Syria, Mesopotamia, Palestine, and the Arab provinces were definitely separated from the Turkish Empire.

With the fall of Beirut, on October 7, the principal Turkish base in Syria collapsed. Its capture was an operation distinct from the land-movement which brought about the fall of Damascus. This stroke was ·made by the French, and would have effect on Constantinople, where it would throw confusion into the ruling element which was seeking to belittle the advance of Allenby's men. Syria had for many years been a sphere of French influence. The territory through which the Franco-British troops were advancing had been conceded to France by treaties concluded between the Entente nations. The landing of French troops was the first realization of the ·agreement. On the coast of Syria French protection already existed. After the massacre of Christians there in 1860, Napoleon III had occupied it for some months, in order to shelter Syrians from Turkish fury. Quite naturally the part of re-entering and succoring this stricken land fell to French warships.

The route from Beirut to Damascus, a journey of fifty miles through the Lebanon range, now lay in Allied hands, which had required a new advanced base-line for a push northward over the remaining 200 miles of coast to Alexandretta and the Allies had good prospects of going on unchecked. Lands south of Alexandretta would never again be in Turkish hands. The end of the Turkish might upon those shores was near. That Turkey, like Bulgaria, would have to bow to the inevitable was daily becoming more nearly certain. Syrians, whether Arabians, Jews, or Christians, had from the outbreak of the war been pro-Ally in sympathy and filled with a great hope that an Allied victory might free them from the hated yoke of the Turk. In fact, before Turkey formally entered the war, thousands of Lebanese had sailed from Beirut to enlist in the French army. Syria above all was pro-French. Syrians regarded France not only as their rightful protector but as their helpful foster-mother. Syria's railroads, her highways, and manufactures were French; her principal commerce was with France; her educational system was largely French; her people almost universally spoke fluently the French tongue. The province had often been called "the France of the Levant." During the war the Syrians had suffered cruelly; their men forced into the army; their horses, cattle and crops requisitioned. Deprived of food and of the means of producing food, they fell easy victims to famine and disease. The country seemed likely to be made into a semi-independent state under the protection of France.

On October 16, British cavalry occupied Tripoli, forty-five miles north of Beirut, and Homs, eighty-five miles north of Damascus. At Homs they were within 100 miles of Aleppo. On October 26 Aleppo was taken. Its capture was mainly the work of British cavalry and armored cars. Since September 19 the cavalry had made a march of about 400 miles. They found the enemy much stronger than reported—some 2,000 to 3,000 men with ten guns, who tried to counter-attack, but were heavily repulsed. An armistice was signed on October 31, when the British took 18 guns, nearly 1,000 prisoners, and a large quantity of rolling stock. Aleppo was six miles from the junction of the Damascus and Constantinople-Bagdad railroads. Its capture was the crowning event in Allenby's campaign. Men recalled the last words spoken by Othello in the play, as he kills himself:

> "In Aleppo once,
> Where a malignant and a turbanned Turk,
> Beat a Venetian and traduced the State,
> I took by the throat the circumcized dog,
> And smote him—thus."

The way was now open for an advance on Constantinople. Altho 650 miles from Aleppo in an air-line, the two cities were connected by the Berlin-Bagdad railway. It was believed that Allenby would seize, as a new base, Alexandretta, on the Mediterranean, sixty miles northwest of Aleppo. Alexandretta had a fine harbor and was connected with the railway from Aleppo to Constantinople by a branch line. On November 13 fifty British, French, and Italian battleships, cruisers, and destroyers anchored in the Bosporus. Newspapers and many people in Constantinople acclaimed the squadrons as deliverers. On the outskirts of the city headquarters were established with a British aerial force. About a thousand Germans and Austrians, including General Liman von Sanders, German commander in the Turkish army, who had fled before Allenby when he reached Damascus, were believed to be still living in Constantinople or the neighborhood, their exit across the Black Sea having been cut off by the Roumanians and by disorders in Odessa. The

BRITISH OFFICIAL PHOTO.

INDIAN CAVALRY PASSING THROUGH DAMASCUS

occupation was effected in a methodical way, with such lack of military display as to seem out of harmony with the famous city's history and traditions. Remembering Gibbon's account of the spectacular entry of the Turk 460 years before, there was something startling in the simple landing of the British commander from a motor-boat at the Galata bridge; in the anchoring of a small fleet of Allied ships in the Golden Horn, and in the gradual, almost imperceptible, sifting of soldiers throughout different quarters of the city.

The army of occupation made no exactions, it merely undertook the task of cleaning-up the city and restoring order.
Here on a landing pier D'Esperey met Allenby—an historic
occurrence, already represented in photoplay, but destined to
be preserved on canvas and in mural decorations in after
times.

In the tumult of the war the opening of a broad-gage
railway which the British had built from Cairo to Jerusalem
had passed almost unnoticed, but it was one of the great
improvements which Allenby's army left behind it, in its
way one of the greatest events which, next to the opening of
the Suez Canal, the Near East had known in modern times.
It was possible now to enter a sleeping-car at Cairo any
evening at dinner time and to reach a little hillside station
below the Bethlehem road, which was the terminus of the
Jerusalem line, at 4 o'clock the next afternoon. In former
times the overland route from Ismalia to Jerusalem, via El
Arish and Gaza, took three weeks and was not only expensive but dangerous. Starting from Kantara, on the
Suez Canal, where the line connects with the road from
Cairo, it skirts the sea to Gaza, the gateway to Palestine.
South of Gaza it branches off, one line going to Jerusalem
via Beersheba, the other hugging the coast.

One could not contemplate this road and the difficulties
which had beset its construction without acquiring a changed
vision of what army organization means. In the historic
wastes of the Sinai desert had been formed huge camps,
covering miles and laid out in perfect order, with fine roads,
thorough and complete sanitary arrangements, plentiful and
good food, and all other necessities for a huge army. All
this had been set up in a wilderness into which two years
before only the most intrepid traveler ever ventured. Now
an endless stream of motor-lorries, Red Cross vans, equip-
ment-vans, camels, soldiers, Arabs, Bedouins, Egyptians, and
motor-cycles had moved across the land. Water, which two
years before was nowhere to be had, was now to be had everywhere. Wet and dry canteens were so numerous that one
could buy almost anything anywhere in the desert. At night
a sky of stars, and a moon above fields of sand looked down
on the wonders which the British army had wrought in that

distant corner of the world. Under the Turk it had lain dormant for centuries and would have continued to lie dormant for centuries more.[17]

[17] Principal Sources: Cable dispatches from W. T. Massey in Palestine to The *Times*, The *Evening Sun*, New York; The *Times* (London); The *Evening Post*, the "Military Expert" of The *Times*, W. L. McPherson in The *Tribune*, The *Sun*, The *Journal of Commerce*, "Bulletins" of the National Geographic Society, New York.

THE TOMB OF ST. JOHN THE BAPTIST IN THE GREAT MOSQUE AT DAMASCUS

GENERAL ALLENBY MEETING THE JEWS OF JERUSALEM

A Scroll of the Law had been presented to him, and Allenby is making a speech in acknowledgment of the gift

IN THE EAST, NEAR EAST AND SOUTH

Part VI

THE BALKANS AND GREECE IN THE WAR

BULGARIAN TERRITORY

FROM THE LONDON "SPHERE." © IN THE U. S. BY THE N. Y. "HERALD" COMPANY.

SALONIKI AND THE HILLS BEYOND

In the distant part of the territory here shown, Bulgarian, Turkish, Austrian and German troops were entrenched in the winter 1915 and 1916

I

BALKAN PROBLEMS OF THE PAST, AND THE JOINT TEUTONIC-BULGARIAN CONQUEST OF SERBIA AND MONTENEGRO

September, 1915—January 25, 1916

THE Balkan country extends westward from the Black Sea about four hundred and fifty miles, and southward from the Carpathians to the Ægean about three hundred. It is not much larger than the State of Montana, but it has furnished the terrain for more than two thousand years of conflict between Europe and Asia. In one form or another the struggle has continued ever since Xerxes, five centuries before Christ, marched across the Hellespont to conquer Greece. Because its people have been on the world's natural highway from Europe to Asia, death and destruction have accompanied them from generation to generation. Long before modern Europe emerged from the wreck of the Roman Empire, some of the Balkan roads were already great world thoroughfares, the greatest of them the Via Egnatia, which ran from Durazzo on the Adriatic eastward by Monastir and Saloniki to Constantinople. Others ran from Belgrade, by Nish and Sofia, to the Bosporus; from Skutari to Nish and the Danube; from Monastir by Sofia to the Danube; from Saloniki by Uskub and Novi-Bazar to Serajevo.

If their inhabitants had ever been united, the Balkans might have played a great part in history. Including Roumania and Bosnia, their area of 190,000 square miles is not much less than the area of France, but the population is only about half that of France. Considering their defensive strength and favorable geographical situation between the Black, Ægean, and Adriatic Seas, the united Balkans might have made one powerful and prosperous state. The reason why they had not done so was the violent race rivalries that had existed there. While the

larger part of the population is Slav, there have been three
other vigorous race elements—Turks, Greeks, and Albanians.
Race divergencies within their own borders have often rent
these countries asunder.

The Roumanians have been infused with a belief that they
are a Roman race. Philologists have yet to decide whether
there are, or are not, any considerable remnants of the
Latin tongue in the present Roumanian tongue. As Roumania has been a highway for contending races for fourteen
hundred years, it does not seem reasonable to suppose that
the people are now much less Slav than are people to the
north, south, east, and west of them. At the same time there
is doubtless in Roumania a mixture of many races. As to
Bulgaria its people believe the original Bulgars were
Asiatics who adopted the language of those whom they
vanquished in Europe and so became politically, tho not
racially, a Slavonic nation. Serbia is a far more typical
Slav country, tho within her borders are many Wallachians,
Bulgarians, and Albanians. Bosnians are also mostly Slavs.
The modern Greeks are a tolerably definite race, linked
through the centuries with the great Greek race, but within
their borders are many Bulgarians. Within the small Balkan
area left to Turkey in 1913, including the city of Constantinople, are thousands of Greeks and some Bulgarians and
Armenians.

In addition to race differences there has been lack of religious unity in the Balkans. Roman Catholics live in
Albania and Bosnia, and many Moslems remained there after
Balkan lands were taken from the Turks in 1912. Otherwise the Balkan people are everywhere ministered to by the
Greek Church; but there are as many Greek churches as
there are Balkan countries. Bulgaria, Serbia, Greece, and
Roumania each has its own church organization, and none
of them is in organic relation to the greater Greek Church
of Russia. It is one of the curiosities of ecclesiasticism
that church services in Russia are held in the ancient Bulgarian tongue—which is no longer understood even in Bulgaria, the reason being that the earliest Christian missionaries among the Slavs first went into Bulgaria, and,
having converted the Bulgarian people, proceeded into

SERBIAN INFANTRY

Russia, using a ritual that had been compounded in the ancient Bulgarian tongue.

Language and religion, however, are not the only bases of an intense subdivision of racial and political sentiment in the Balkans. The whole region is more or less parceled out among race factions, some of which comprise not more than hamlets. Roumanians, Bulgarians, Serbians, and Greeks have a deep race consciousness, but each State has been threatened at times with a break-away by alien race-units within its borders. If Greece were peopled only by Greeks, Bulgaria only by Bulgarians, and Serbia only by Serbians, Balkan problems would have been easier. It has been the curse of the peninsula that so many alien groups in time past pushed their way forward wherever they found vacant land, or made vacant land by driving out holders and forming villages of their own. The result was the creation of certain "race-islands in race-seas." So long as the Turks were masters—and they were masters for about five centuries—these race rivalries lay somewhat dormant. Greeks and Bulgarians had their quarrels, and even their little wars, but their Turkish masters punished them impartially. The real depth of Balkan race feeling was most clearly revealed in 1913, when the question to be faced was how the territory they had taken from the Turks should be subdivided. While the successful Balkan war had seemed to mark the last chapter of Turkish rule and all western Europe rejoiced, it became the first chapter of violent internal struggles. Every one of the four Balkan Powers, now made independent, wanted more territory. Each was eager to become the leading Balkan State.

The investigator who gets behind "blue books," "red books," "white books," note-books, reports, and ultimatums, finds that the break in the strain between the Triple Alliance and the Triple Entente really came over the question whether Serbia should be allowed to grow up as the nucleus of a greater Balkan power and appropriate to herself the Slavs of Croatia, Slavonia, and Bosnia, then subjects of the Austro-Hungarian Empire, the murder of the Archduke being the match that touched off the bonfire. The ambition of Serbia to revive the empire of Czar Dunchan, who ruled in the Balkans before the Turks came, stood out clearly enough in that crime at Serajevo, altho there was neither proof nor likelihood that the Serbian Government had any hand in it. The accident served also to throw out into sharp relief the rivalry between Austro-Hungary and Russian influence. If Serbia were not to be punished for Gavrio Princip's crime, Austro-Hungarian prestige would be weakened, while, if Serbia were punished, Russia would cease to be the leading Power in the Balkans. The war, therefore, in its beginning, was a manifestation of an unquenchable rivalry between two empires external to the Balkans.

The reasons why Balkan peoples have not trusted each other are mainly blood-reasons, complicated by artificial national boundaries fixt arbitrarily by the Great Powers. In the Balkans is found a conglomerate blood-caldron, the product of a thousand or more years. Across that country went the Crusaders to and from the Holy Land. Then came the Turkish wave, which, subsiding, left a submerged people and further race confusion. But the racial ego, altho submerged, remained vital. It yearned all through the years for self-expression. The Balkan peoples in general have distrusted the Great Powers almost as much as they have distrusted each other, for which the Great Powers had themselves to thank. For nearly 500 years the Balkan States had been a buffer between Christian Europe and the Turk, but after the fall of Constantinople, in 1453, the whole peninsula terminating in Greece was submerged by the Turkish inundation. Mohammedanism threatened, in fact, to overwhelm all Christiandom, and was checked only after reaching high-water mark at Vienna. Christian Europe at Vienna saved itself, but it did not rescue from the Turk the Balkan peoples who were abandoned to the Turk's misrule. That was not the worst that followed. The Powers for centuries made use of the Balkan peninsula as an intermediate training ground. Unable or unwilling to put the Turk back into Asia, they made treaties with him in order to secure a thoroughfare to the Dardanelles. It was easier to bargain for the thoroughfare than to take it by force.

Early in the nineteenth century the Turkish population

in the Balkan peninsula began to decline and the Christians correspondingly increased. Except for the jealousies of the Great Powers, Turkish rule in Europe would have gone on decaying still faster. For a long time its security was actually fostered, in order that a state of equilibrium might be maintained in Europe. For all this the Balkan people paid the price, in religious, racial, and economic oppression. In the course of eighty-odd years, however, the Balkan States and Greece had slowly been shutting out the Turk. By 1829 the Greeks had won their independence from Turkey by fighting for it alone—in the war during which Byron lost his life—and a year later Serbia achieved partial independence. In 1877, after frightful massacres in Bulgaria, Russia, single-handed, moved against Turkey, and was successful; but her hand in its hour of triumph was stayed by the other Powers. The Treaty of San Stefano, forced by Russia on Turkey after the war, created the Principality of Bulgaria largely out of Turkey, but only to be torn up in the same year and superseded by the Treaty of Berlin, which greatly reduced the size of Bulgaria. The prospective strength of a new Bulgarian state had seriously alarmed the Great Powers, and especially Great Britain and Austria, and so Bulgaria was made to suffer under the treaty negotiated at Berlin, which gave full independence, not to Bulgaria but to Serbia, Roumania, and Montenegro, Bismarck, acting as "an honest brother."

In March, 1878, Russia was fast approaching the very walls of Constantinople, near which lay the small town of San Stefano, where the treaty was signed by the Turks, and Bulgaria was accorded boundaries which fulfilled her wildest dreams, including, as they did, every detached fragment of the Bulgarian race and something more. Her borders were made to run from the Black Sea to the Albanian hills, from the Danube to the Ægean, and included the port of Kavala on the Ægean, and most of Macedonia. By the Treaty of Berlin, signed on July 13, Bulgaria got only the territory between the Balkan range of mountains and the Danube, the country south of the Balkans being erected into an autonomous Turkish province called Eastern Roumelia. To Serbia was given Nish, and to Greece Thessaly. Bessarabia went to Russia, Roumania retained the Dobrudja, and Bosnia and Herzegovina were put under Austrian administration— an arrangement that led directly to the World War. Turkey was left with Macedonia, Albania, and Thrace, and remained the Suzerain of Bulgaria, Eastern Roumelia, Bosnia and Herzegovina. No authority was given to Austria to annex Bosnia and Herzegovina, as she audaciously did thirty years afterward, and thus prepared the way for the murder of the Archduke in June, 1914.

When, in 1912, Bulgaria, Serbia, Greece, and Montenegro, foregoing their separate quarrels in a new hatred of the Turk, formed the Balkan League, the Great Powers were aghast. It was now obvious that the Balkan States would fight together for what they wanted, and they did fight. They accomplished more toward putting the Turk back into Asia than the Great Powers had done in hundreds of years. But in their hour of triumph, the Balkan allies fell out over a division of the spoils and turned to fighting each other. This necessarily weakened them and the Great Powers interfered to limit their aspirations and especially those of Serbia, between which country and the Adriatic they created the new State of Albania in order to prevent Serbia from gaining her long coveted "window on the sea." Serbia thus remained, as she so long had been, land-locked. Austria was mainly responsible for that, but she was supported by her

THE SERBIAN CROWN PRINCE REGENT

allies, Germany and Italy. Each Balkan State was like Italy, in that it had an *irredenta* which could be reclaimed only through the dismemberment of Austria-Hungary, or that of Turkey, or that of one another. Each had long held to a policy of neutrality in the expectation of gaining territory eventually without the risks and losses of intervention.

But, as time passed, each drew nearer and nearer to the period when a choice had to be made between fighting for national ideals and taking chances of being ignored in a final settlement.

Bulgaria's action against Serbia in September, 1915, was influenced, if not actually determined, by the success of the great German drive against Russia. Nevertheless, if Bulgaria could have secured from Greece and Serbia pledges of the territorial concessions she had demanded in Macedonia, and from the Allied Powers a free hand in Thrace, her hopes of aggrandizement would have been substantially realized and she probably would not have allied herself with the Teutonic Powers. Many observers thought Serbia might well have yielded. Serbia had already invaded Albania, with Skutari and the northern Albanian ports as her objectives. She showed she was in cooperation with the Italian plans and that she expected to seek compensation in Albania, as well as in Bosnia and Herzegovina. Hence she apparently was in a position where she could well have yielded to Bulgaria such portions of her territory in Macedonia as were inhabited exclusively by Bulgars.[1]

Venizelos, the Premier of Greece, was known to be willing to cast his country's lot with the Allies. He believed that only in this course lay any chance of extending Greek territory and freeing Greek populations from Turkish sovereignty. The hindrance to Greek participation in the war lay, however, in the danger of Bulgarian aggression. Greece would fight for her future when the time arrived—the more so since all the forces of diplomacy which had detached Italy from the Triple Alliance and alined her as a belligerent with the Allies were now focussed on the problem of unifying the interests of the Balkan neutrals and seeking for them national ideals along the lines which Italy had elected to follow.

One reason why Bulgaria betrayed an unwillingness to pull chestnuts out of the fire, either for Russia or for Germany, was given in concrete form by M. Tsankoff, of the University of Sofia. According to his calculations the Balkan struggles of 1912 and 1913 had cost Bulgaria $256,-

[1] Albert Bushnell Hart in *The Outlook*.

000,000, apportioned among the following classes of expenditures: War credits, $70,000,000; requisitions, $30,000,-000; budget deficit, $10,000,000; materials of war of transportation, $30,000,000; various debts, as to the railways, $36,000,000; pension charges, $80,000,000. To this sum should be added the immense damage wrought to the economic structure of the nation by the loss of a large part of its laboring population—58,000 men between 20 and 45 years of age, of whom 6.7 per cent. were heads of families. In addition there were about 11,000 war-cripples now incapable of labor, who with their families had to be supported by the State. Professor Tsankoff, who made his estimate in 1915 before Bulgaria defied Russia, said he believed a loan of $100,000,000 was immediately needed, in order to put the nation on its feet. Such figures showed what was the immense burden which had already been shouldered by four and a half million people who, in spite of it, were now going to war again, and this time with Great Powers.

Every monarch in the Balkans was either a foreigner or, if he had been born in the country he ruled, was of Teutonic descent or under Teutonic influence through marriage, with the exception of the King of Serbia. It would be difficult to find a modern instance in which kings exercised greater personal influence than the sovereigns of Greece, Bulgaria, and Roumania in 1915. Everybody agreed that M. Venizelos was the ablest statesman modern Greece had produced, and yet a foreign prince on the Greek throne was able virtually to depose M. Venizelos, to counteract his policy, and to keep Greece neutral. The elections proved conclusively that the vast majority of the Greek people were on the side of Venizelos, but he and the Greek people were helpless because their King, whose wife was a sister of the German Emperor, refused to go to war with Germany. Here was a striking instance of the hold that monarchial institutions still had on a European people.

So also of Bulgaria, which had been called into political existence so late as 1877 and as the act of Russia. Bulgaria, in 1914, had seen Russia mobilizing to protect Serbia and yet she would not raise a hand to aid her. After eleven months of the war, with Russia still unable to carry out her policy of annexing Poland and disabling Germany, the Bulgars not only looked passively on but finally defied Russia, the Czar of Bulgaria being a Teutonic sovereign. On one side of French descent, on the other of German, his sympathies were all with the Central empires. For eleven months this king was able to paralyze both Greece and Roumania, and set them at defiance.

In Roumania the King was of the House of Hohenzollern and feared that if he drew the sword he might be attacked in the rear. A small Roumanian party argued that the true policy for Roumania was, not to wring Transylvania from Hungary, but to get back Bessarabia. The population of Transylvania, however, was three or four times as large as the Roumanian population of Bessarabia; and Bessarabia was being rapidly assimilated by Russia, while Roumanian Transylvania was still eager to rise against the Magyars. Balkan States, therefore, for eleven months in succession, had been paralyzed by the Czar of Bulgaria, a foreign prince, who not only refused to recognize the aspirations of his own people, but prevented his neighbor-Kings from recognizing the aspirations of theirs.

So it was that among the influences which shaped the course of Bulgaria, the personal character and ambitions of King Ferdinand ranked first. He was described as a man of considerable vanity and given to duplicity, but possest of political astuteness. He had been lured to disaster in the second Balkan war by a vision of being crowned Emperor of Byzantium, and so had chafed afterward under the consequences his own folly had brought upon his country. In craving for an opportunity for revenge on Serbia, Roumania, and Greece, King Ferdinand and his people thus had at least one dominant sentiment in common. The Treaty of Bucharest of 1913 was imposed on the defeated Bulgarians almost literally at the point of the bayonet, and as a matter of fact, that treaty was a bad treaty. It was not incorrectly described as providing for a series of grotesque frontiers, traced on vindictive lines, in violation of the principle of nationalities and in defiance of economic laws. It condemned probably more than a million beings to con-

248

ditions of life which caused some of them to regret their
loss of the rule of the Turks.

But the very States of whose vindictiveness the treaty
was the fruit, had now shown a readiness to revise its terms.
All three offered concessions so nearly approximating the
Bulgarian demands as to open a way for mediation. It was
here that the diplomacy of the King of Bulgaria and his
subservient ministers came in and spoiled the last chance of
a restored and reinvigorated Balkan confederation. Many
observers believed that, if a Russian, Serbian or Monte-

AN AUSTRIAN FLEET IN THE BAY OF CATTARO

negrin prince, instead of a Hohenzollern, had been reigning
at Sofia, Bulgaria would have resumed her place in the
Balkan alliance. In that case Turkey would never have
dared to declare war in 1914, for if she had done so, the
Dardanelles, with Balkan help, could have been forced, Constantinople captured, and tens of thousands of valuable lives
would have been spared.

What Bulgaria sought in 1915 was an incorporation in
her kingdom of something more than a million of her race
who had been separated from their fatherland by the Treaty
of Bucharest. It became with her purely a question which

of the two conflicting alliances of Great Powers could and would secure this incorporation. The action of Czar Ferdinand and his advisers in attacking Greece and Serbia in 1913 and so provoking the second Balkan war, had precipitated the ruin of Bulgarian hopes, and the consequences were afterward borne by something like a million Bulgars, innocent of complicity in the crime. A portion of Macedonia, which had always been recognized as Bulgar in race, language, and population, now became subject to Greek and Serbian masters. In the Serbo-Bulgar treaty which preceded the first Balkan war, Serbia had agreed to recognize Bulgaria's claim to all of Macedonia, east and south of a line drawn from Lake Ochrida to the point of contact of Serbia, Bulgaria, and the Turkish vilayet of Kossovo. This, had it been lived up to, would have given to Bulgaria Monastir, Ochrida, Kuprili, Istip, and Prilep. At the close of the war, Greece was prepared to surrender her claim to that portion of Macedonia which lies east of the Struma River, including Drama, Kavala, and Seres, but the Serbo-Bulgar agreement was based on the presupposition that Serbia would have Albania north of the Skumbi River. When Austria vetoed this Albanian arrangement, Serbia claimed as "compensation" that portion of Macedonia which her armies had conquered and which embraced Monastir, Kuprili, Ochrida and Prilep. Bulgaria declined to accede to this demand. She held that Serbia was bound by her agreement with Bulgaria and naturally refused to give up territory that was inhabited by a population which desired to join Bulgaria.

The question was in debate when Bulgaria in 1913 struck at Serbia and Greece. In this second Balkan war the Bulgarian troops were driven out of Macedonia by combined Serb and Greek armies. At the same time Turkey retook Adrianople, while Roumania invaded Bulgaria from the north and seized a wide district about Silistria and between the Danube and the Black Sea. At Bucharest the victors divided the spoils. Serbia kept all of Macedonia west of the mountains, including Istip, Monastir, and Prilep; Greece took Kavala and Drama and pushed her frontier east to the Kara-Su; Turkey retook all of Thrace, save a small district between the

Ægean and the Rhodopians, west of the Maritza; Roumania, as her share, annexed the region between the Danube and the Black Sea. By these processes there were taken from Bulgaria 1,250,000 people, who inhabited regions that Bulgarian troops had conquered, or districts which were Bulgarian before the war. Moreover, Bulgaria had laid claim to some 500,000 people in Macedonia in and about Monastir, lands which she had forfeited to Serbia. So that, out of two wars, Bulgaria emerged with a gain of less than 500,000 in population, while at least 1,000,000 Bulgars were placed under Greek, Roumanian, or Serbian rule.

What Bulgaria asked of Serbia in 1915 was to return to her upward of 500,000 Bulgarian people and their lands in Macedonia, a large majority of whom desired to become Bulgarians. Serbia could well have done this, because the enemies of Germany, if successful, would have been able not only to restore the old situation, but with Austria out of the reckoning, to permit Serbia to annex Albanian regions. Italian consent, however, would have been necessary in restoring the conditions on which the Serbo-Bulgarian treaty of 1912 was based. In addition the enemies of Germany were prepared to promise to Serbia, Bosnia, Herzegovina, and Dalmatia as far south as the mouth of the Barenta, regions which, except for an Albanian district, were inhabited largely by Serbs. Serbia would thus have gained 2,500,000 people and have lost to Bulgaria some 750,000. Moreover, she would have been surrendering Bulgars for Serbs.

Bulgaria opened to the Teutonic Powers the path which some of the Crusaders had taken from Europe to the Holy Land, that is, the road that runs across a little neck of Serbia that was all that separated Bulgaria from Hungary. With this and a thoroughfare across Bulgaria, the Teutonic Powers could have marched to the assistance of the Turks. Thus the Allies in 1915, when Bulgaria deserted them, suffered a serious diplomatic defeat and were facing a difficult military problem. With Serbia crusht between the Teutonic hammer and the Bulgarian anvil, with Allied forces driven from Gallipoli, came the failure of a brilliant hope, tho hardly more, since the Allies would remain about where they were before they made their attempt against the Dardanelles. That move had for its aim the winning of the war by a dramatic coup. Beyond question the winning of Constantinople would have meant the winning of the Balkans as a unit for the Allies. If Constantinople had fallen in the late spring or summer of 1915, when the Russian armies were hammering at the Carpathian gateway, if at the same time Roumania had thrown her armies into Transylvania, a much-talked-of separate peace by Austria might have become a reality. But the Dardanelles venture failed and then came loss in prestige and the discouraging after effects in Allied homes.

The Allied move against the Dardanelles had been more than a thrust against a vital spot in the Teutonic armor, for it was intended at the same time to avert any possible attack on Britain's vital interests outside of Europe. By keeping the Turks busy at home the safety of Egypt could be assured, and Egypt meant India. The campaign of Gallipoli meant, not only the safeguarding of the Suez Canal, but the prevention of any formidable display of Turkish strength in Mesopotamia. It kept the war from drawing too perilously close to India, with possible disaffection among Indian tribes. If the Allies had permanently failed in the Balkans, it would have meant a renewal of Britain's concern for her African and Asiatic possessions.

That was the purpose of the Teutonic invasion of Serbia under Mackensen in 1915. Perhaps half a million men were thrown into the scales against the Allies in the Balkans, a number far larger than the Turkish army which the Allies had had to deal with, and it meant the release also of a Turkish army for a renewed offensive against the Suez Canal and in the valleys of the Euphrates. Had the Balkan struggle ended in complete Allied defeat the problem would have become formidable, because what German leadership had done for the Austrian armies and for the Turks in Europe, it would then have attempted with the Balkan States.

To create a Greater Roumania, by annexing the Bukowina and the Roumanian portion of Transylvania, was the natural ambition of the Latins of the Danube delta. Their brethren in the Bukowina and Transylvania had suffered under the

Hungarian yoke as much as the Italians of Trieste and the Trentino had suffered under the Austrian yoke. In a military sense, however, the Austro-German victories in Galicia, in the spring of 1915, had made an invasion of Transylvania far more difficult to Roumania than it would have been when the victorious Russians were threatening northern and eastern Hungary. But Italy's strength, when thrown into the opposite scale, had counterbalanced, so far at least as Austria-Hungary was concerned, the collapse of the Russian offensive in the summer of 1915. Roumania's problem remained, therefore, almost what it had been—to choose the right moment for the occupation of Transylvania, after securing herself from an attack in the rear by Bulgaria.

Roumania is composed of two principalities, Moldavia and Wallachia, the first of which found freedom from the Turk in the Treaty of Paris, signed in 1856. The two were united in government almost from the start; and under the rule of their second Prince, Charles of Hohenzollern, a vigorous spirit of nationalism was instilled into all classes. After the defeat of the Turks by their soldiers at Plevna, in 1877, the little principality was recognized as a kingdom. The Roumanian King of 1914, a nephew of Prince Charles, ruled over a land of 53,489 square miles, or a little less in area than Massachusetts and New York combined. Within this territory were 7,800,000 inhabitants, showing a density of population slightly greater than that of Maryland.

A generation had passed since the Great Powers sat about a table at the Berlin Congress and willed that certain things should be done. Their main purpose at that time was to protect their own States from war, and to prevent their rivals from gaining, through the Treaty of San Stefano, disproportionate profits from the Russo-Turkish war. But in the process the statesmen in Berlin turned back to the gentle mercies of the Turk in Thrace and Macedonia two million Bulgarians. Similarly the Serbs of Bosnia were transferred to the actual, tho not the titular, sovereignty of Austria, while the Greeks in Epirus, Macedonia, and the Ægean Islands were left to dwell beneath the Turkish yoke. To placate Russia, leave was given her to rob her Roumanian ally of Bessarabia, which was inhabited by Roumanians, while Roumania was quieted by a permit to seize the Bulgar land, Dobrudja. For a generation afterward, each succeeding spring saw men in revolt in Macedonia, women dishonored, children murdered. From the Danube to the Ægean islands some millions continued to live in pain and die in misery in order that there might be peace and prosperity in London and Berlin.

To all suggestions from the Powers in 1915 Bulgaria answered simply that she desired to have back her lost provinces and her stolen children. Let Roumania as a prelude to the liberation of Roumania, first free her Bulgarians. Such was the Bulgar demand—that some 3,500 square miles and some 500,000 souls be restored by Roumania. Of all her losses, the one felt most keenly by Bulgaria was the Macedonian loss. Here people spoke her dialect. In the Treaty of San Stefano this region had been assigned to her. In Bulgarian hearts the frontiers made by that rescinded treaty were still a living fact. From Serbia, Bulgaria merely asked that the old bargain be fulfilled; until Monastir and Istip were returned to her, she would yield to none of Serbia's appeals for sympathy and aid.

The picture of Germany late in 1915 driven from the sea by the British fleet, checked in the east after an astonishing drive which had lost to Russia thousands of square miles of territory and facing in the west a new offensive in the Champagne and Artois which threatened to break through Germany's hitherto impregnable line of defense, now suddenly striking south, with an army estimated at half a million, in an endeavor to win a way through hostile territory to the relief of a small and almost exhausted ally, startled anew the imaginations of men and compelled admiration once more for her powers in colossal military activity. Germany, in the alliance now concluded with Bulgaria, was believed to aim at India and Egypt. To burst through her "iron ring" and to seize an Oriental empire, all by one great stroke, was a colossal scheme which seemed too wonderful ever to come true. A people who had lost access to the sea, who had not one warship, nor one merchant vessel free to sail, was going forth to compass an ocean-spaced empire by setting out on a military expedition of hundreds of miles across mountains and through deserts. Taken not seriously, but as a piece of imaginative audacity, the German scheme probably had its value. As a distraction even, it might prove important, especially if it should succeed in worrying the Anglo-French forces into a contest, in a theater of the Germans' own choosing, and at a time when the main Allied strength was devoted to a drive on the Western Front.

The Austro-German attack on Serbia in October, 1915, was more than a menace to the little Serbian nation, more than an attempt to give relief to Turkey. It was an indication that Germany had not abandoned her expectation of controlling the direct line of communication between Central Europe and the Near East, and indirectly was a threat against British sovereignty in the Mohammedan world. If completely successful, it would have done much to destroy such British prestige as was won at the outset of the war by the suppression of Teutonic intrigue in Egypt and India, and by the bold attack made at Gallipoli in 1915 on the seat of the Califate itself at Constantinople. Little Serbia was caught between the upper and lower millstones of an Austro-German advance on the north and a Bulgarian advance on the southeast. For the moment, her safety and independence rested on the activity of perhaps a quarter of a million of her own troops and the expeditionary force of French and British coming by way of the Ægean Sea and in camp at or near Saloniki, a Greek port. The Bulgarian and Austro-German armies had for their immediate problem to overcome the entire Serbian forces before they could unite.

The German drive thus revealed itself, not as a punitive expedition against Serbia, nor as a relief expedition for the Turkish forces fighting to hold Gallipoli, but as an effort to gain, by force of arms, an advantage that years of diplomacy and peace had failed to secure. It was, according to semi-official pronouncement, a stroke to secure a swift passage of the Balkan mountain-lands and eventually to complete an unbroken German line from the North Sea to the Bosporus, thence across Asia Minor to the Persian Gulf and India, and finally to envelop the Suez Canal, Egypt, Tripoli, and Algeria, all of which were the hard won North-African possessions of Great Britain, France and Italy. If this was the ultimate purpose, the enterprise was startlingly bold and daring, for Germany could not count on any movements by sea to aid it. It had to be a land operation entirely, and must be accomplished in part literally on foot.

For the German press it was natural to speak of it as the beginning of a German thrust at the British in Egypt and India. In its distant implications it might hold such a threat. But it was altogether too early to speak of a campaign against Egypt as an actuality of the near future. Before that could come about, a decision had to be reached in the Balkans, and if precedent counted for anything, operations in the Balkans would not be completed as a matter of rush or dash, but would be a slow and grinding process, with a possible deadlock, like that in Gallipoli, for months afterward. Even should the tide turn definitely against the Allies, the menace to Egypt would have to take the form of a Turkish move against the Suez Canal under German leadership. It was hardly to be supposed that German troops would actually be thrown into Asia Minor in order to perform a difficult march through the desert. But that was the only way in which an attack could come, if it came at all. The sea would continue to be held by the Allies.[1a]

A battle-front of 1,200 miles had been lengthened out by something like another 600 miles. For the defense of this new frontier, as of the old, the Germans became responsible. While they had gained a new ally in Bulgaria, this did not alter the fact that they had added to their own vulnerability. For the Allies the campaign became, by force of circumstances, strategical rather than political, and a naval and military operation of the first significance. If they were to allow the Germans to subjugate Serbia, seize Constantinople, and obtain the hegemony of the Balkan Peninsula, the Germans would succeed in doing in the South of Europe what they had failed to do in the West and East. Occupation of Constantinople by a German force would have dealt a tremendous blow to British prestige in India, and have been a standing menace to Egypt.

[1a] The *Tribune* (New York).

256

AN HISTORIC MEETING AT NISH

Here are seen the Kaiser (on the left), with one of his General Staff, and King Ferdinand of Bulgaria (on the right) talking with Field-Marshal von Mackensen

VIII.

THE BALKANS AND GREECE IN THE WAR

The invasion of Serbia was undertaken on a carefully-considered plan arranged between the German and Bulgarian General Staffs. An Austro-German army, composed, as was believed, of 300,000 men, with a reserve of 100,000, crossed the Danube in two main groups, one under the Austrian General Koevess, the other under the German General Gallwitz, Field-marshal von Mackensen being in supreme command of both groups. The lower Morava Valley was the

CONCENTRATION OF TEUTONIC TROOPS FOR THE
INVASION OF SERBIA

dividing line between the two armies, which were to advance in a southerly direction, and secure the line of the Western Morava. On the west an Austrian army, which was not thought to exceed two divisions, was to assemble at Vishegrad, across the Drina, and after detaching a force to Koevess's right wing, was to move into the old sandjak of Novi-Bazar and drive a wedge between Montenegro and the Serbian army retreating south. On the east two Bulgarian armies were to take part in the enveloping movement, the first army (200,000 strong), under General Bojadjeff, being concentrated on the northern part of the Serbian frontier, while the second (100,000 strong), under General Toucheff, was assembled at Kustendil and Strumnitza. The third Bulgarian army, commanded by General Teodoroff, was to watch the Roumanian frontier. Bojadjeff's share in the plain was to march into the Timak Valley, seize Nish, and drive the Serbians westward; while Toucheff was to take Uskub, hem the Serbians in on the south, and prevent their retreat down the valley of the Vardar.

After a month the Teutonic forces advanced about thirty miles, and then waited for reinforcements, for once they had cleared a way to the railroad, they would be obliged to patrol every mile of it and Constantinople was still 400 miles away. The Allies naturally would attempt to "break" this line. Anglo-French forces landing at Saloniki could strike at Nish, or even at Sofia. They might capture the pass at Strumnitza, whence a thrust to the northeast would strike Bulgaria. Forces landed at Enos and Dedeagatch on the Ægean might fight their way up the Maritza Valley and deliver a body blow between Adrianople and Constantinople. Russia, in addition, was to be reckoned with. The first purpose of the Anglo-French troops was to protect the Serbian communications with Saloniki, and the second to hasten troops inland toward Nish to protect the Serbian rear from attack from Bulgaria. Serbia, after a Bulgarian declaration of war, occupied a position between the German hammer and the Bulgarian anvil. She might for a time hold back the Germans, but she could not ward off blows from both Bulgaria and Germany.

About the middle of July it had been learned that Roumania refused to allow weapons and ammunition to pass through her territory from Germany to Turkey; to Berlin's demand she had sent an emphatic rejection. Here was a premonitory symptom. Tne pinch of scant ammunition-supplies obviously was being severely felt by the Turks at Gallipoli, and found expression in such Franco-British gains as were made after their severe early checks. Since the direct line to Constantinople through Serbia was closed by the war, German co-operation with Turkey had been established through Roumania. Along the route which passed from Vienna through Budapest, Bucharest, Sofia, and Adrianople, German officers had traveled to Constantinople to train the Turks in scientific warfare and to lead their armies in the field. Along that route also arms and ammunition had been carried to the Turks until now when Roumania, evidently under pressure of the Allies, closed her railroad to shell- and powder-trains. With the only land route to her Turkish ally thus cut off, Germany, since the middle of June, had not been able to send Turkey any more weapons. The Turks, thus suffering from a scarcity of ammunition, were also faced with possible famine. Meanwhile, the Teutonic Allies were exerting every effort to keep Roumania neutral. On July 7 they offered her, as the price of her neutrality, the Bukowina, as far as Czernowitz and better treatment of Roumanian peoples there and elsewhere in the Dual Monarchy. The only restraining influence on Roumania was the Bulgarian menace. Bulgaria was itching to avenge the coup of the Second Balkan War, when the Bucharest Government, joined with Serbia and Greece, brought about Bulgarian defeat, and took from her territorial spoils of victory.

By the end of September, when the situation had grown tense, slight relief was given by an announcement that Bulgaria would merely mobilize her army and then assume a stand of "armed neutrality." The Bulgarian Premier, M. Radoslavoff, confirmed a statement made in a semi-official note issued at Sofia on September 23, that Bulgaria had been forced to adopt armed neutrality because of the development of political and military events in the war, but that her mobilization was not directed against either Roumania or Greece. "Our mobilization at present," said he, "is purely a defensive measure." Bulgaria had "no aggressive designs against Roumania and Greece, a fact which she wished emphatically to point out." Had Bulgaria attacked Serbia at that time, it was clear that she would have found herself arrayed against the army of Greece and, in all likelihood, that of Roumania, aided by a force of British and French troops. Only two days later, two members of the Bulgarian Cabinet resigned because Czar Ferdinand refused to approve an immediate attack on Serbia. Russia then, early in October, issued her ultimatum to Bulgaria demanding a reply within 24 hours. Receiving none, she sent warships to Varna, the Black Sea port of Bulgaria, and British and French troops were ordered to Saloniki. Meanwhile, Bulgarian troops were massed along the Serbian borders. Reports then came from the Central Powers that men and metal had been collected preparatory to a blow against Serbia as the first step in what the popular imagination accepted as a fact—German determination to smash through Serbia and line up with Bulgaria, thus creating a new battle-front from the Austrian border to Constantinople.

The most obvious fact in the Balkan negotiations was that the Allies had suffered a crushing diplomatic defeat. Germany had the advantage of being able to offer Bulgaria territorial compensation which could be taken from enemies, while the Allies had to rely on concessions obtained from friends. Germany successfully induced her ally, Turkey, to surrender territory to Bulgaria, while the Allies failed in a like enterprise. German diplomacy had found a fertile field in the Balkans and cultivated it with skill. The Russian reverses and the failure of the Allies in the Dardanelles, both happening at Bulgaria's very door, had influence with King Ferdinand and his advisers. They produced upon their minds that certainty of German victory which made the Bulgarian Government declare in its official statement of reasons for joining Germany and Austria that "Bulgaria must fight on the victors' side," and that "Bulgaria would commit suicide if she did not fight on the side of the Central Powers."

In England Bulgaria's act was attributed solely to her King. In Paris it was asserted that King Ferdinand was so anxious to retrieve the territory he lost in 1913 that he was "blind to larger issues." On the side of the Allies, Bulgarian intervention and the reopening of the Balkan campaign was viewed with not a little misgiving, altho a ray of hope was seen by most London papers in an eventual participation of both Greece and Roumania on the side of the Entente.

That Austria would accept as final her humiliation and defeat by Serbia in December, 1914, was not expected. In the same winter preparations had virtually been set on foot for a second invasion. Perhaps 200,000 men were massed

GERMAN SUPPLIES EN ROUTE INTO SERBIA

at Serajevo, and there was talk of a combined Austro-German force, but the plans were afterward abandoned for the much greater offensive against the Russians in Galicia. The Serbian army numbered at this time about 240,000 men of all arms, with some 700 miles of frontier exposed to attack from east and west. Exposed as she was on the Austrian side, Serbia herself held that her danger from Bulgaria was even greater and throughout the summer stood on guard. By French airmen she was kept well informed of all movements within striking distance of the frontier. The summer had passed without any serious threats of immediate danger.

The first actual invasion of Serbia by Bulgarian troops seems to have taken place on October 11 at a point near Kniashevatz, to the northeast of Nish. Later Bulgarian troops crossed the frontier near Leskovatz, about an equal distance to the southeast of the temporary Serbian capital. The situation in which Serbia found herself was the worst that her fears could have pictured. She faced enemies on all sides except the south and the extreme southwest. On the north and west the Austro-German forces may not at this period have exceeded 150,000 men, but they had an overwhelming weight of guns. On the east Bulgaria's army probably exceeded 300,000. In all, Serbia's foes in the field may have amounted to 600,000; against which she had only 240,000 men, inferior in all details of equipment and hopelessly outclassed in artillery. Greece, as her ally, had failed, while the others—Great Britain, France, Russia and Italy—moving slowly, were too far away to render any effective help. The tale of the next two months is one of pure national tragedy.

For some weeks an Austro-German army of invasion had been assembling north of the Danube. Mackensen's objective was both strategically and tactically simple, the motive being to win a way to Constantinople. Two routes were possible—the Danube and the Ottoman railway. But before the Ottoman railway could be used there had to be a considerable amount of campaigning done; the great bridge over the Save which had been blown up by the Serbians a year before, had to be repaired and bridges and embankments restored between Belgrade and the Bulgarian frontier. To cross the river, however, was an easy task. The other route would be much slower to win, as it involved the capture of Belgrade and ridges to the south of it, and an advance to the southwest which would clear the Morava Valley up to Nish and the tributary Nishava Valley as far as the Bulgarian frontier. To secure both routes, the German plan of campaign was one of converging attacks. On the 7th both the Save and the Danube were crossed, the latter at Belgrade. An immense weight of artillery-fire made the city untenable, and on the 8th the Serbians began to evacuate it. During the day fierce fighting continued at

SERBIAN PEASANTS FLEEING BEFORE THE TEUTONIC INVADERS

quays and in the lower part of the town, but by evening the Citadel and the royal palace were taken. There was a desperate guerrilla struggle in some of the streets. It was not till the morning of the 9th that Koevess had the whole place in his hands. Next day Bulgaria entered the war, having waited till assured of Mackensen's ability to force the line of the rivers.

In the bombardment of Belgrade the guns included 9-inch and 12-inch howitzers. In the course of 24 hours probably more than 40,000 shells of all sorts were thrown into the area of the Belgrade defenses. Meanwhile aeroplanes were kept flying low over the city and dropping bombs. To this terrific assault the city was unable to reply effectively. The only Allied guns which were in position to offer active resistance were Russian guns in the fortress. The destruction was almost complete. The city was on fire at many points, and the whole river front was pulverized. During the night of the 6th the Teutonic force began landing operations, using flotillas of flat-bottomed boats which had been prepared at Jakevo, on the Save, and behind Semlin. The landing was made in two places—on the west of Tziganlia Island, which was connected with the Serbian shore by a bridge; and at the Danube quays on the front of the city itself. By daybreak between 4,000 and 5,000 men had made good their footing at these two points. The eastern portion of Tziganlia Island was still held by a small force of Serbian infantry; but in the course of that day, the survivors were compelled to evacuate.

The crossing of the Drina offered as much trouble to troops as the Vistula and Dneister had given in the early summer because of the mountains along the banks, which gave fine positions for hidden artillery and machine-guns. The stream itself is in some places rapid, yet silent. Every sound was re-echoed at night from these mountains. When the Teutonic engineers got to work on pontoon bridges, the launching of timber and boats drew fire. Crossings were effected only after the Serbian guns had been overpowered by superior artillery.

During the first operations, about a thousand Teutons succeeded in reaching the opposite bank across the pontoon-bridges, amid a shower of shrapnel and machine-gun fire. While the bridges were being constructed and finished, a sanguinary hand-to-hand battle was fought. Bridges were destroyed half a dozen times before the first man could reach the other bank. At night under searchlights the grimness of the scene made men shudder. An Austrian officer estimated the losses of the Austro-Hungarians on the Drina sector on the night of the actual crossing as over four thousand in killed and wounded. When he himself was passing over a bridge it was blown up and three hundred men were thrown into the river, mostly wounded. The officer was rescued only after he had hung on to débris

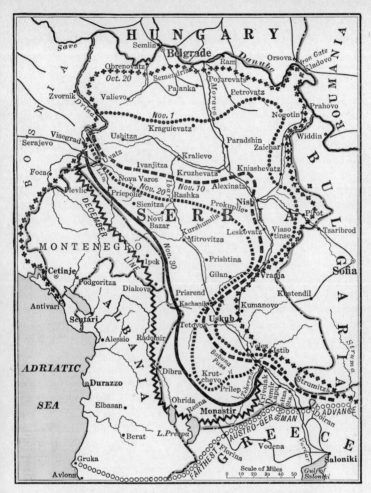

THE TRAGIC, BUT EASY, CONQUEST OF SERBIA

After Austro-German forces under Mackensen had effected a crossing of
the Danube at Belgrade and elsewhere, their progress across the country
was rapid, assisted as it was by Bulgarian attacks on Serbia's right flank.
Less than two months were required by the three stronger powers to conquer the one weak little state. The fall of Montenegro was effected no less
rapidly, and then the greater part of Albania was overrun. The reader will
note in Albania the two towns Berat and Elbasan, both of which were recovered early in 1918 by a Franco-Italian force, and thus became the first
steps in the decisive campaign won in Serbia later in the season by the
Entente forces under General Francinet D'Esperez.

for several hours. During the time he was in the water, the same bridge was repaired and blown up four times, hundreds of men being thrown into the water each time. When the invading troops finally got across the river, the Serbians attacked them with great vigor, at first pinning them to the river banks and preventing them from debouching from bridge-heads. In the bombardment huge shells threw up débris to the height of five-story houses. Every square yard of the city was systematically searched by machine-gun fire. When crowds of refugees streamed out, German airmen dropt bombs on them. Attack after attack was driven back before the Germans gained a footing. Then their most formidable task began, for they had to win the capital, street by street. As George Renwick [1b] said, they "had to pay a price for every paving-stone." Prisoners told him it was appalling work. Every street-corner seemed a citadel. Before the Germans were masters of Belgrade the city had become "a mass of smouldering ruins, strewn in the grimmest horror with a covering of the dead."

Once in possession, the Germans opened fire on the Serbian positions behind it. Lines of trenches were searched one by one. Facing Belgrade and Semendria, the river bank was often a long-continuing line of flame. The capture of a hill was frightfully expensive. Every hill had to be covered with dead before it could be won. After 12 days' onslaught, General Mackensen succeeded in obtaining little more than a foothill on the southern side of the river. On the Drina front he found his task equally heavy. Time after time the attacking forces were driven back. After ten days of severe fighting, he concentrated his forces on positions beyond Belgrade and Semendria, the object evidently being to drive south from the former place to Kraguyevats, while the Semendria army was to ascend the Morava Valley—the historic highway to Central Europe, by which the Turks in the seventeenth century invaded Hungary in their progress to the gates of Vienna. A second crossing of the Danube was made at Semendria, where the attack began a day later than the one on Belgrade, the bombardment being equally fierce and overwhelming. It was estimated that the Germans and

---

[1b] Correspondent of The *Daily Chronicle* (London).

Austrians had in action against Semendria no fewer than 200 guns of all calibers. There was practically nothing with which to reply to this tremendous fire. After two days the Teutons crossed the river in force and occupied the town, altho not until after desperate fighting had occurred with Serbian infantry.

On October 18, after showering 10,000 shells on the Serbian position, the Teutons took Malakresna, but a strong force of Serbian infantry, concealed in the forest, attacked and drove them out. On the 19th the Teutons took Rawla, south of Belgrade. The heights of Avala were also captured after heavy fighting from October 18 to October 19. Meanwhile, in the Morava Valley, progress was equally difficult. On October 19 the Teutonic advance lines were no farther south than a line extending from north of the Lubejevo bridge eastward to slightly north of Passarowitz.

Mr. Renwick motored north from Palanka to the neighborhood of Azanya, when a most imposing spectacle was presented in that angle of the Danube and Morava. Far in front were "the purple-blue" mountains of Hungary, their dark sides lit up with the constant lurid flare of Germany's heavy artillery. Six miles away could be seen the Danube. General Mackensen's machinery had then been battering away for two weeks. From a little hill called Ossoie Mr. Renwick could plainly see the positions of the Teutonic cavalry. During the morning two heights nearer at hand, on both of which the Serbians were in position, had been subjected to "perhaps one of the most appalling deluges of shells of all sizes that the war has yet seen." The hill and its neighbor were "simply blown out of existence." From fair green hills they were altered to "shapeless masses of iron-shard, on which nothing could live."

The Serbians were described as being "as gay as a holiday." They had so hampered the Teutonic advance that it seemed as if General Mackensen would need months to carry out his scheme. And in these months succor from the Allies, coming from the south, might wreck him. Mackensen's army probably did not consist of more than 150,000 men, but was provided with artillery which would be considered ample were his army composed of a million. Into

Belgrade alone 50,000 shells were poured. Mr. Renwick thought the German army a "scratch force gathered together from all quarters." He spoke with prisoners who had come from the Flanders, French, Italian, and Russian fronts, from garrisons in Germany and from throughout the conquered territory. Many were young men of 18, who had left their homes only a few months before. It was an army fighting without reserves.

The Bulgarian attacks were delivered at eight different points. On October 21 the army of General von Koevess, from Belgrade, had forced its way as far as Leskovatz and

GERMAN BRIDGE ACROSS THE MORAVA IN SERBIA

Stepoyavevatz, about thirty miles south and southwest of Belgrade, and was threatening Sopot, slightly to the east of those places. Keeping pace with Koevess on his left, was General von Gallwitz, from Semendria, who had occupied Selevatz and was pushing up the valley near Ranovatz. On the east fighting was in progress along the whole length of the Bulgarian frontier. Commencing from the north, the Bulgarians had occupied Negotin and Zaitchar, and desperate combats were going on near both Pirot and Kniashevatz. The Bulgarians were close to Kumanovo. Pushing up the valley of the Bregalnitsa, a Bulgarian column reached the railway at Veles, and occupied half of the town on the eastern bank of the river.

Forlorn was Serbia's plight, with an enemy outnumbering her armies by three to one, and with ten times the weight of guns. Not only was the fate of the country sealed, but the whole Serbian army, as well as the Government, with the King, the Crown Prince and all the foreign missions, were in imminent danger of being surrounded and compelled to let themselves fall into the enemy's hands. The sole ray of light was the fact that the Allies were landing troops at Saloniki, and that small French and British columns had come up along the railway across the frontier. In any encounters the Serbs alone would be outnumbered by as many as five to one. This was the case in a valiant eleven days' battle which raged before Uskup. For the greater part of that struggle the contending Serbian and Bulgarian armies were at a distance of only two hundred yards from one another. Hand-to-hand encounters were frequent with heavy losses on both sides.

The Morava Valley, along which the allied German and Austro-Hungarian troops pushed forward from a junction with the Bulgarians, forms the core of old Serbia. The greatest part of Serbia's trade flows through this valley. Here, also, is much of the small kingdom's richest agricultural land. Through this narrow strip, the mountainous Balkan country has maintained contact with the West. The valley forms one of those famed thoroughfares along which armies have poured through all history. Many powerful conquerors in past ages have traversed the very course now to be taken by Teutonic soldiers. When Roman Constantinople was in its zenith, its generals, with armies in the Morava Valley, held back Slav incursions. Crusaders marched this way to cross into Asia Minor. On their way exuberant Franks and Teutons often kept people guessing as to whether the Crusade was planned against the Eastern Church or against the Mohammedans. In a later age conquering Turks, pressing westward, reversed the lines of march, and swarmed along the Morava Valley to the gates of Vienna. Since the break in the Ottoman power, German peoples have long looked to this valley as leading to commercial expansion in the rich tho stagnant areas of Asia Minor and Mesopotamia. The Morava is not only Serbia's largest river, but one of the most important streams in the Balkans. The line of the Orient Express, coming from Paris, Munich, and Vienna, parallels this river.

After the Bulgarians took Uskup, 5,000 of the 20,000 men in garrison made a last stand in the hills midway between Uskup and Kaschanith. The Bulgarians, having outflanked them from the Tetovo plain, forced them to take up a position at the entrance to the Kaschanik defile. Louis Edgar Brown [2], who saw this battle, described how the Serbian artillery began the fray. Thousands upon thousand of shrapnel and high-explosive shells were thrown to the enemy. Bulgarian prisoners said shells fell on first and second line trenches and barricades continuously, with a roar of "a siren on an ocean liner." Everything was drowned by the continuous exploding of Serbian shells.

The Serbians calmly dug themselves out of the mud, and, with fixt bayonets, prepared to sell their lives dearly. The first attack struck the Bulgarians in the dusk of evening. The Serbians drove on like huge waves, accepting only hand encounters, and not pausing to aim the fire of their rifles. They seemed to be obsessed with a determination to get their bayonets into the Bulgarians, "laughing at their foes as they lay mortally wounded on the ground." Detached groups, at hundred paces along the battle-front, "stabbed, clubbed, bit and choked savagely." The battle became a mêlée such as only Bulgarians and Serbians as traditional enemies were capable of fighting. Their ruling passions were hatred and revenge. When the battle ended the Serbians had lost the road to Uskup. Realizing that their retreat was cut off, they "fought like cornered wolves." While the Serbian nation knew its cause was lost, the army was determined to die resisting to the last shell and last man. The Bulgars entered Uskup on the evening of October 23. Next morning the battle was resumed on the western side of the town. There, too, in face of superior forces, the Serbs put up a splendid fight.

[2] Correspondent of The *Daily News* (Chicago), whose account in part is summarized here.

IN THE EAST, NEAR EAST, AND SOUTH

The loss of Uskup was a misfortune of the first magnitude. It cut off all communications between the Vardar and Morava valleys; it blocked the routes to Prilep and Monastir in the south and access to Kossovo and Novi-Bazar in the north. The outlook for Serbia was black indeed, struggling as she was against three powerful enemies—Germany, Austria, and Bulgaria—and she made a last despairing appeal to the Allies for aid. Throughout the land a mass of fugitives of every age and condition fled distractedly by the few routes left open to the southwest. Nish became a beleaguered city. Food was scarce, and vehicles could hardly be obtained for love or money. By the 26th, disaster had followed disaster.

On October 14, after fighting for a week, Gallwitz had stormed the fortifications of Passarowitz, and, deploying his army on a forty-mile front, began to advance slowly up the right bank of the Morava, having reached the Vodonj-Misljenova line on the 18th, these two points being respectively six and nine miles from the Danube. Koevess, who was moving up the left bank of the Morava, having captured Belgrade on the 14th, stormed the strong Serbian positions on Mount Avala about eight miles south of the town, and then pushed forward in a southerly direction, his right detained for some days till he captured the fortified town of Obrenovatz.[3] Nish was Mackensen's objective. When he reached it, the Orient railway through Bulgaria would be at his disposal. How to block his way was the problem the Allies had to solve.

The Rhodope Mountains, stretching the whole length of the Ægean Coast from the Struma to the Maritza, offered an impenetrable barrier to an army attempting to reach the railway from the south until it reached Dedeagatch, where the railway from Saloniki turns up the Maritza valley and joins the Orient line at Kuleli Burgas. Dedeagatch was therefore a point of strategical importance. It could be reached both by sea and land from Saloniki. From Nish to Constantinople, allowing for the winding route of the Orient railway, the distance is more than 400 miles, so that, unless Germany was assured of the neutrality of

[3] The Cologne *Gazette*.

Greece and Roumania, Mackensen's advancing army might be in a precarious position. German prisoners taken by Serbians admitted that on various battlefields they had experienced nothing so extraordinary as the stubborn way in which men on the Morava slowed down the German advance. Nothing, in the opinion of the Serbians, could drive them out of their positions, save, perhaps, the heaviest howitzers. In one encounter with the Bulgarians 5,000 Serbs held a pass against 20,000. For some time the Teutonic invaders, it was expected, would fight only rearguards, the Serbians, doing as they had done on previous occasions, falling back until they reached positions where they could hold their ground. The attack for a time met with real resistance. The Serbians gave ground foot by foot, and after the fall of Nish Mackensen's drive slackened. But he had what he set out to get—the Danube route and the Ottoman railway, and the campaign was left in Bulgarian hands, where it became a campaign of long-cherished and bitter revenge.

A blockade of the Bulgarian coast in the Ægean Sea by Entente Allied warships was put into effect on October 16. This strip of Bulgarian coast runs from Saritchahan, in Greece, to Enos, in European Turkey, a distance of about eighty miles, and consists of territory obtained from Turkey as a result of the Balkan wars. The chief seaports are Dedeagatch, Porto Lagos, Maronia and Mecri. Running parallel with the short line, at a distance back of from five to ten miles, is the Saloniki-Constantinople railroad. Late in October occurred a bombardment of this coast by British, French and Russian ships, mostly monitors, destroyers and cruisers, under direction of Vice-Admiral de Robeck. The first shots were fired at the barracks in Dedeagatch, which were full of soldiers, who ran in hundreds out of the building to and fro, seeking shelter. Heavy guns shelled the barracks, while destroyers trained their guns on fleeing soldiers and inflicted heavy punishment. Every building of military importance came under fire and was razed to the ground. While the bombardment was proceeding, a train sped along at top speed, and the destroyers subjected it to heavy shelling. The railway line was torn up, the station completely wrecked and loaded railway-trucks along the line caught fire.

The Allied forces from Saloniki now began operations against the Bulgarians. An advance guard of French troops crossed the Greek frontier into Macedonia on October 21. The first encounter took place on the 23d at Robrovo, an important tactical point on the road from the town of Strumitza to the Strumitza station, which it was necessary to occupy in order to safeguard the railway. The French then pushed on to Krivolak, where the Bulgarians, who held an entrenched position at Istip, unsuccessfully attacked them on the 30th. On November 2 a further advance up the railway was made to Gradsko, at the confluence of the Cerna and Vardar rivers. The whole of the Vardar Valley from Gradsko to the Greek frontier was in French possession, the French being able to advance north of the Cerna. The Serbians were helped by the weather, which was cold and wintery. Then rains set in and impeded the movements of enemy troops and guns, which, at the best, had to move slowly over what answered for roads. For two weeks the Serbians offered stubborn resistance to Austro-Germans in the north, and for more than a week fought the Bulgarians along their eastern frontier, where lines were broken at places and towns captured. In the meantime, additional French and British forces were landed at Saloniki.

Throughout November the situation in Macedonia was dependent on results of the campaign in Serbia. Altho the Bulgarian General Teodoroff was firmly established at Uskup until the First Bulgarian army was free to reinforce him, he was not strong enough to do more than hold up the French in the Cerna-Vardar salient, and at the same time prevent the Serbian army of the north from breaking through into Macedonia. What he did, was to occupy Tetovo and Katchanik, and by so doing sever communication between Serbia and Macedonia except by a circuitous route through Albania. But he did more than this. He kept a sufficient force at Istip and Strumitza to prevent a further advance of the Allies northward, and placed nearly a whole division in and about Mount Archangel, a formidable ridge some four or five miles west of the Cerna, in order to check any attempt of the French to advance westward with the purpose of linking up w.th the Serbian troops that were holding the Babuna Pass.

These dispositions were successful. The French crossed the Cerna on November 5, driving in Bulgarian outposts before their advance, but before they got far on their way were pulled up in front of the enemy's main position on Mount Archangel, and were unable to get nearer than within ten miles of the Babuna Pass. No reserves were immediately available, and Colonel Vassitch's small Serbian army, being unable to wait, because in danger of being enveloped, fell back toward Monastir, abandoning the Babuna Pass. Then the Bulgarians turned on the French, and counter-attacked with great violence, but with no real gain to show for the loss of 4,000 men. The French retained and reinforced all their positions up to November 27, when Sarrail, perceiving that the Bulgarians were being reinforced from the north, and that there was no further hope of saving the Serbian army, began to retire from a position which had been rendered precarious by the Serbian retreat.

The Austro-German offensive had become more pronounced as the Serbian resistance weakened. General Koevess continued his advance south of the Western Morava toward the Sanjak, and occupied Novi-Bazar, while two days later his right wing entered Prijpolye. The Serbian Government, which after the fall of Nish had gone to Mitrovitza, left that town for Prisrend, and General Koevess occupied it, while the right wing of General Gallwitz's army, forestalling the Bulgarians, who had a temporary setback west of Leskovatz, occupied Prishtina. The enemy's rapid advances decided the Serbian Government to leave Pr.srend and establish itself at Skutari, the ancient capital of Stephen Dunshan, where Prince Alexander arrived with M. Passitch and the foreign ministers, after a rough cross-country journey through Albania. With the fall of Mitrovitza and Prishtina the historic plain of Kossovo, where Sultan Amurath overwhelmed the Serbian army under the Tsar Lazar in 1389, was again delivered into an enemy's hand, and the Serbians forced to seek shelter in the mountains of Albania and Montenegro.

Mackensen now left Generals Koevess and Bojadjeff to

continue the pursuit of the Serbians into Albania, while he drew off General Gallwitz's army for operations elsewhere. On November 29 the Bulgarians captured Prisrend, where they claimed to have taken between 16,000 and 17,000 prisoners, 50 field-guns, and a quantity of war-material. Koevess with his Austro-Hungarian troops meanwhile continued his advance across the Lim River, but not without encountering a tough resistance from the Montenegrin army, which was bravely keeping the field under command of the old King Nicholas. The Montenegrin frontier was crossed on December 1, and Plevlie, the former headquarters of the Austrian army when in occupation of the Sanjak, was occupied on the 2d. Farther south the Bulgarians, following up the retreating Serbians, occupied Dibra on December 4, and Djakova on the 7th. The German troops of Koevess's army reached Ipek on the same day. Pursuit came to an end as the Serbian troops, dispersed and broken up into small detachments, found their way as best they could along mountain-tracks converging on Skutari.

By December 2 the long struggle for Monastir had ended. The Serbians evacuated the town and their positions in front of it, and the enemy took possession. The force which occupied it included Austrians and Germans. Automobiles containing Austro-German and Bulgarian officers, entered first, followed by detachments of German, Bulgarian and Austrian cavalry officers. The officers proceeded to the Government buildings, where they hoisted the national flags of the Central Powers and their allies. The Bulgarian inhabitants displayed their joy by firing guns and pistols. Public and private buildings displayed flags of the conquerors. The hated Star and Crescent flag of Turkey was now seen once more in Monastir side by side with that of Germany.

Monastir was one of the most prized acquisitions made by the Serbians in the war of 1912. By means of schools, propaganda, Serbian committees, and Serbian priests, the people had long been prepared for an ultimate union with the Serbian kingdom. The Serbians pursued the same tactics here that the Bulgarians and Greeks had pursued for years in endeavors to win the upper hand in the Turkish

province of Macedonia. Monastir was to Serbian ambitions
what the port of Saloniki was to Greeks and Bulgarians.
It was the second city of Turkish Macedonia, and did a
thriving business even under Turkish rule, when it was a
base of military defense and offense of the same rank as
Adrianople. Here were the headquarters of a Turkish army
corps. Roads from the port of Saloniki, on the Ægean,
from the port of Durazzo, on the Adriatic Sea, from Nish,
the ancient capital of Serbia, and from the important
fortresses of Adrianople, meet and cross here. The Serbians
strengthened its defensive works after their occupation.

SERBIAN BATTERY IN THE FIELD

General Sarrail, who had come from the Western Front,
and now commanded a considerable body of Allied troops
based on Saloniki, had for his problem in the Balkans
to bring back the French left and center till a continuous
frontal line could be formed with British troops who occupied the right flank. Quick to appreciate the position, the
Bulgarian commander determined to prevent Sarrail from
effecting his object. Concentrating the bulk of his troops
on the right and left of the Strumitza-Dorian road, he
sought to drive a wedge between British and French troops,

throw the former back on the Greek frontier, and intercept the French line of retreat down the Vardar Valley. The plan was well conceived, but failed owing to the stand made by the Tenth British Division. On December 5 the French, who had withdrawn from Krivolak two days earlier, reached the Demir-Kapu defile, and were continuing their retreat on the 6th when, after a heavy bombardment, a Bulgarian attack was launched on the British position, and pushed home with great determination. Under cover of a mist, small parties of the Bulgarians got into British trenches, but were immediately driven out. Undaunted by failure, the Bulgarians next day renewed the attack, and by weight of superior numbers pushed the British out of their first position, and compelled them under cover of darkness to withdraw to a second line of trenches. On the 8th the attack was again renewed, but this time the British troops held their ground till it was necessary to retire to a third position in order to conform with the French movements. The British casualties were 1,500. The Bulgarian losses must have been correspondingly heavy.

The joint Teutonic-Bulgarian conquest of Serbia was thus accomplished after a two months' campaign, in which the Serbian Army of not more than 250,000 men had to fight against odds of probably three to one. The result was a foregone conclusion as soon as it was clear that little aid could be expected from the Allied Powers. The Serbians fought with heroic courage, to which the Germans paid testimony, but there is a limit to what heroism can accomplish against superior force. The Serbian Army was completely broken up and lost the bulk of its guns and equipment, but its fighting spirit remained. There was reason to believe that, after recuperation and refitting, it would be able to resume the offensive in the spring in conjunction with the army of the Allies, which was concentrating at Saloniki.

Heavy fighting continued well into December, when in the neighborhood of Lake Doiran, the British and French were simultaneously attacked; but because of reinforcements they were able to repel the onsets. More than 8,000 dead and wounded were said to have been left on the field by the Bulgarians during two assaults on the British lines. At the

THE BALKANS AND GREECE IN THE WAR

second assault, the fire of artillery, rifles and mitrailleuses
was opened on advancing masses. The Bulgarians faced
the murderous hail at a run for 300 yards. Those who
survived could not approach nearer and so broke into flight,
which became a helter-skelter rout. The Bulgars started
frenzied and simultaneous attacks on both banks of the
Vardar, and strove to drive a wedge between Dublyani and
Predevo. The French had no fewer than 200 cannon vomit-
ing fire on a restricted three-mile front, and the battlefield
was strewn with corpses. But on December 12 the last
yard of Serbian territory passed into the occupation of the

THE SERBIAN CROWN PRINCE INSPECTING
JUGO-SLAV TROOPS

Teutonic allies and the Bulgarians. Within a few miles of
Greek territory, the Bulgars, led by German officers, made
attempts to annihilate the Anglo-French rear-guard, which
escaped, retiring down the Vardar in order to occupy the
first series of defensive positions already prepared.

No mere outline can give any idea of the dreadful nature
of the Serbian retreat. It must be remembered that it was
not the mere retirement of an army. It was probably
unique in that not one active army, but all the armed forces
of the nation were withdrawing from the country. And

with those armies went the King and members of the royal family, the Government and all its civil personnel; the foreign legations and the doctors, nurses, and staffs of the hospitals of the Allied peoples. Most pathetic of all was the great mass of peasant refugees, villagers, peasants and people of the towns who fled in sheer terror. Rather than face the Austro-German occupation, the entire Serbian population, save a few who were held back by some unbreakable tie, gathered together what little household goods they could and took flight. A great proportion were physically unfit to face the difficulties of the road. Almost none had food to last through the journey. It was not only armies which retired, it was almost a nation which fled. Swelling the number of those who had to be fed upon the road were some 20,000 Austrian prisoners who had been captured the year before. The road which the multitude had to travel, for a great part of the way, lay through and over rugged mountains, often by paths dangerous at any time; and these mountains were peopled by a population of hereditary enemies, largely brigands, who fell on small parties and robbed and murdered whenever they dared. The crowning burden was the fact that the weather was most bitter, heavy snow falling for many days with the temperature in the mountains for the most part intensely cold. It seems as if no detail that could add to the horror of the march was omitted. Terrible scenes were witnessed on the road to Prisrend. Deep snow lay everywhere. There was practically no supply-column or commissariat. The men sustained life largely on the carcases of cattle and horses that fell on the road.

At Prisrend 150,000 refugees, among whom the destitution and suffering were terrible, were massed. From here the only path of escape lay over the forbidden mountains of Albania, to Skutari, over 100 miles away. All motor-cars, carriages, guns and stores had to be destroyed or thrown into the waters of the Ibar, for to get them over the mountains was impossible. Here Marshal Putinik, very ill, as he had been since midsummer, arrived in a motor-car and had to be carried in a chair. Here King Peter left his ox-wagon, and with two officers as companions, went on foot, with an

KING PETER OF SERBIA WATCHING A BATTLE

279

escort of twelve men. The Crown Prince also went on foot, with an escort of twelve of the Royal Guard. All arrived finally at their destination, but suffering and broken, the Crown Prince lying for some time seriously ill at Alessio.

Part of the Serbian troops, instead of taking the road by Prisrend, struck west from Prishtina to Ipek in Montenegro, and so reached Skutari. These succeeded in taking with them some batteries of field- and mountain-guns. Over the Albanian Mountains it was not possible to take larger guns. The road was in parts of a precipitous and dangerous character. In the snow, there was ever a likelihood of detached parties missing the route, which was often marked by the corpses of those who had fallen. Immense numbers of people, both soldiers and civilians, died from sheer exhaustion, from weakness and hunger, lying down at the roadside to die. Where a road was steep, or where a small stream had to be forced, the road might be marked by accumulations of the dead. Not a few people and great numbers of transport-animals lost their lives by falling out of narrow paths down mountain-sides. Many died from frostbite and dysentery, and not a few, both Serbian soldiers and civilians, fell victims to Albanian inhabitants of the mountains.

This flight of the Serbians from their country was one of the tragic episodes of history. For many who took part in the exodus, the retreat lasted over two months. For those who started from the center of the country, as from Kragujevatz or Krushevatz, the time taken was from six to eight weeks. The journey was made in all cases under conditions of great hardship, from lack of food, from the physical difficulties of the latter part of the road, and from the bitter weather. The Serbian Army, by the time it reached the Adriatic, had lost about 120,000 men, or one-half its original strength. The mortality among the civilian population will never be known, but it was very great. Hardly any country in any age has seen so terrible a calamity.

Skutari was the sixth capital Serbia had had during two months. After Nish came Kraljevo, Raska, Mitrovitza, Prisrend, and then Skutari. In their flight to Skutari, men composing the Serbian Government rode little mountain-ponies, but often had to abandon their mounts and go on foot. So dangerous were mountain-roads that horses often slipt and fell into abysses. Sometimes a man had to go on all fours; others, to avoid vertigo, had to be guided. Roads in places were worn through the snow a yard deep. Through such a country the army could not bring guns and convoys. Officers and soldiers wept as they demolished guns, pieces of steel which they called their "French friends," and which had been made at Creusot. After suffering from cold, hunger, and fatigue, many soldiers now barefoot, reached Skutari. Altogether there arrived by various routes 6,000 women and children. The tragedy of the situation was that the army had had almost nothing to eat for four days. Small quantities of flour were kept and baked for women and children. Skutari, altho a temporary haven of refuge at which the Serbians gained rest after their exhaustion, was by no means a place of permanent safety. It was necessary to get everybody, soldier and civilian alike, first to the coast, and then to some place across the water beyond the reach of danger.

On January 11 the Austrians had captured Mount Lovtchen in Montenegro, and then they occupied Antivari, which gave them command of Skutari Lake, and on the 19th Dulcigno. On January 18 the Queen and royal family of Montenegro embarked at Medua for Brindisi, and on January 20 the King followed. Later he went to France. By this time all members of foreign missions and the hospital staffs had got away. Serbia's armies had to march by land yet one more stage southward to Durazzo. At Durazzo the work of transferring them to a place of safety, chiefly to Corfu, and of there nursing them back to health and fighting strength, was taken over by the French, under General Mondesir, who had been sent out for the purpose.

The war in January invaded the peaceful seclusion of Mount Athos, where Bulgarian monks, from the monastery of Zographu, endeavored to oust their Serbian brethren from the neighboring monastery of Chilandari. The attack failed, owing to the strength of the Serbian defenses. The Bulgarians then set fire to a portion of the Serbian structure. All the monasteries on this Holy Mountain were fortified in the early Middle Ages, in order to resist the attacks of pirates. Athos, or the Holy Mountain, is well known as the third and most easterly spur of the Chalcidice peninsula, which is bounded by the gulfs of Saloniki and Orfano, and thus came within the Allied sphere in the Ægean. On lofty heights overlooking land and sea are situated three monasteries. They constitute a curious monastic survival and date in actual origin from the eleventh century. The most recent phase in their evolution, the advent of Russian monks during the last century, exerted a more profound influence on them than any other single event. Of the two rival monasteries, the Serbian is the more ancient, dating from 1197. Its treasure-chest contains valuable specimens of Serbian ecclesiastical art. The Bulgarian monastery of Zographu (named in honor of St. George "the Painter") has a church that was built early in the sixteenth century.

In co-operation with the Serbians during the winter, British troops seized the island of Corfu of the Ionian group, about 60 miles south of Valona. Here the German Kaiser had a beautiful villa. Every power and alliance of powers, which has sought mastery of Adriatic waters, from the Delian League of the fifth century B.C., to the Entente Allies in the twentieth century A.D., has warred for possession of Corfu. Corfu lies like a watch-tower before the narrowing entrance of the Straits of Otranto. To the north is a rugged finger of Albanian mountain-land that reaches out into a strait, and, bending back, forms the splendid naval harbor of Valona. To the northwest the long Italian heel cuts out into the sea. There is great fertility and much picturesque beauty at Corfu. It was originally settled in 734 B.C. by colonists from Corinth. The colony grew rapidly in wealth, maritime power, and independence. In a dispute with its mother-city, it allied itself with Athens, and thus became one of the causes of the Peloponnesian War, that world-war of classic times which had for historian one of its soldiers—Thucydides.

The occupation of the Greek island of Cephalonia by French and British forces later in the winter was made for

READING THE BRITISH PROCLAMATION IN JERUSALEM

A priest is reading it from a platform in front of the Tower of David (in the center of the picture), a building that was standing in the time of Christ

VIII.

strategic purposes. The event marked another cycle in the strange history of a little island in the Ionian Sea about 100 miles south of Corfu. With an area about three times as great as that of Martha's Vineyard, Cephalonia is the largest of the seven Ionian islands. From the year of its surrender to the Romans, 189 B.C., its history has been marked by a succession of changes in ownership. After the Roman Emperor Hadrian made a gift of it to Athens, Cephalonia and the six other islands of the group became "free and autonomous," but during the ascendency of the Byzantine Empire were subject to its power. Cyclopean and Hellenic walls still stand on the sites of ancient cities.

THE HARBOR OF CORFU

Early in the New Year, Montenegro had met with an attack similar to that which had crumpled up so completely her friend and neighbor, Serbia. The Austrian onslaught, which had been a long time in preparation, was prosecuted with violence, and menaced several important positions close to and on the Adriatic coast. The great Montenegrin stronghold, Mount Lovtchen, behind but overlooking Cattaro, had been easily taken. The Austrians here delivered furious attacks, supported by a hurricane of uninterrupted fire from warships and forts off or near Cattaro. The capture of the mountain was not only a severe blow to Montenegro, but to Italian prestige in the Adriatic. Mount Lovtchen dominates the Austrian naval port of Cattaro, and Cattaro con-

trols the Dalmatian coast. To reduce Cattaro and its guardian forts at Vermatz, and to force the Austrian fleet
hiding in the Bocche di Cattaro out into the open sea, had
been an objective of the Allies since the war began. From
behind the mountain islands which obstruct the waters of
Cattaro had issued the submarines, which successively sank
the French battleship *Leon Gambetta* and the Italian armored cruisers *Amalfi* and *Giuseppe Garibaldi*.

The Bocche di Cattaro is famous for wild scenery, but
no other part compares with Cattaro itself, surrounded as
it is by mountains which soar aloft as superbly as those
of any Norwegian fjord. The mountains which comprise
Montenegro, dull and cold, gaunt and bare, rise majestically
from the smiling blue waters of the bay to a smiling blue
sky above. To the right of the town is Lovtchen, or Monte
Cella, as it is also called, hanging threateningly over the
city "like a frowning demon awaiting an opportune moment to pounce upon and devour the frightened little town
crouching at its feet." A new road, constructed by the
Austrians, and a splendid feat of modern engineering, has
replaced a perilously steep and rough foot-path that was
in use for centuries by peasants in their long journeys
over the mountains. This "Ladder of Cattaro," as it is
called, mounts the steep side of the Lovtchen, seeming to
lurch from side to side like a drunken man, onward and
onward, passing the castle and zigzagging its weary way
over a wilderness of rock.

Small as was Montenegro, with fewer people than Rhode
Island, on slightly more than the area of Connecticut, it
had been twice greatly enlarged under King Nicholas, who
won Nikshidsh and a window on the sea in 1877 and in
subsequent fighting, and had again profited from the Balkan
Wars. Its heroic little people, who, alone among all Balkan
people, have never yielded to the Turk, now retired before
a mightier foe. In losing Lovtchen, Montenegro lost its western bastion, and Austria gained a height which had threatened its best naval base in Dalmatia. There was world-wide
sympathy for the Montenegrins. Their political course had
been singularly free from causes of war, at least during
the long reign of Nicholas. Under him their development,

THE BALKANS AND GREECE IN THE WAR

tho still primitive, had been rapid. Wonder grew why Italy, whose Queen was a Montenegrin Princess, and which must have had a million armed men in reserve, did not take some effectual step to aid the gallant little land—not to mention to defend its own power and prestige in the Adriatic.

By the middle of the month, the capture of Cettinje, the

THE GERMAN EMPEROR AND BULGARIAN KING REVIEWING
TROOPS AT NISH

capital, was announced. Its fall, after the fall of Mount Lovtchen, had been regarded as a matter of only a short time. Cettinje is only six miles from that stronghold. With Cettinje in the hands of the Austrians, the Montenegrins were hemmed in on almost every side, and, unlike the Serbians, had little opportunity to retreat beyond the borders of their own country. It was doubtful whether they would be able to escape into northern Albania, but, had they done so, they would have been opposed by hostile tribes in that region. Cettinje is a small town. Its population twenty years ago was less than 3,000. It is situated in a narrow valley, at an elevation of 2,000 feet.

Fighting between Austria and Montenegro was resumed late in January, King Nicholas having rejected the terms Austria offered. The Montenegrin Government was then installed at Skutari, but Skutari, which is in northern Albania, was taken by Austro-Hungarian troops late in January, after a desperate battle of two days, in which the Montenegrins made their last resistance on the Tarabosch Mountains. Finding they could look for no aid from Italy, they gave up the fight. This opened the road for the Austrians to descend along the shore of the Adriatic, to penetrate into Albania, march upon Durazzo and organize a campaign against Valona. The Serbs, so far as they were able, fled to the coast and were transported thence to Corfu, Tunis and Saloniki, while King Peter took refuge in France. There was left only a small Italian force at Valona and a few Serbs to meet the oncoming Austrian storm, which was now directed against Valona. In five hundred odd years of existence Montenegro had never before acknowledged herself beaten, altho her mountains had on several occasions been overrun by invading forces, her towns burned, and her fields laid waste. The entrance of this miniature mountain State, with its area of only 5,606 square miles, its population of a little over half a million, its army of 50,000, and its aged monarch into the war was purely sympathetic and ideal—to defend their brethren, the Serbians.

The Germans and Austrians thought they saw in their victory proof of their final success, but the Allies saw no warrant for subjective conclusions. On Franco-Belgian fields the war would still have to be decided. Only a few thousand Allied troops had been engaged in the Balkans, and even if the Allies had to quit the Balkans, and defend Egypt or Suez, the actual military effect would not have been overwhelming. Maps and reports showed great German successes, but neither maps nor reports showed the work of the British fleet, or indicated the extent to which Germany was isolated and beleaguered. A sortie like the Serbian expedition had expanded the area of occupied territories, but had not broken the lines that enveloped Germany.

CATTARO, ON THE GULF OF THE SAME NAME

Cattaro lies near the base of Mount Lovtchen and is encircled by a medieval wall. Above it, where crosses are seen, are forts dating from the time of the Venetian occupation

MOUNT LOVTCHEN, IN MONTENEGRO, TAKEN BY THE AUSTRIANS

Along the slopes of this mountain is seen a road, built by the Austrians, with hairpin curves. The mountain dominates the southern end of the Gulf of Cattaro. At its top lies Cetinje, the capital of Montenegro. About half-way up the mountain, at the extreme right, is a rest-house. Before reaching it one makes nearly twenty hairpin turns

IN THE EAST, NEAR EAST, AND SOUTH

Economically, Germany had been practically eliminated from the outside world, her world commerce gone, and she had to finance not merely her own armies, but those of Austria, Turkey and Bulgaria. Germany had won a campaign and probably accomplished all she set out to accomplish, save only to obtain peace. Peace, however, was not to be obtained as a consequence of a minor campaign in a remote field. The essential object of the war had thus far eluded her pursuit. East and west the decision she sought to reach swiftly had not been reached. Her fleet still lay in hiding in the North Sea; the ocean was stript of her commerce; her colonies were lost. Her real enemies, Great Britain, France and Italy, were still unbeaten, despite all she had been able to do. In Serbia, the boasted might of militant Germany, aided by Austria and Bulgaria, had merely beaten an exhausted small State. More than conquests in Belgium and Serbia were needed to save the reputation of militant Germany.[4]

[4] Principal Sources: The Cologne *Gazette;* The *Times,* The *Daily Chronicle,* The *Standard,* The *Morning Post,* London; The *Daily News* (Chicago), The *Temps* (Paris), The London *Times'* "History of the War"; The *Times,* Albert Bushnell Hart in *The Outlook,* The *Sun,* The *Evening Post, The Literary Digest,* New York; The *Daily News* (London), *The Wall Street Journal* (New York), The *Economist* (London), "Bulletins" of the National Geographic Society (New York), Associated Press correspondence, *The Fortnightly Review* (London), The *World* (New York), Alice Lee Mogue's "Delightful Dalmatia" (Funk & Wagnalls Company), The *Tribune* (New York).

KING PETER MOUNTING A HORSE DURING HIS RETREAT

II

WITH THE ALLIES AT SALONIKI—BULGARIA INVADES GREECE, BUT MONASTIR IS RECOVERED AND CONSTANTINE ABDICATES

May 29, 1916—June 19, 1917

WHEN the Anglo-French Army withdrew from Macedonia, and retreated to the neutral territory of Greece, an unprecedented situation arose. It was understood that, as a result of meetings in Paris of the War Councils and General Staffs of the Allied Powers, it had been decided that Saloniki should be retained as a base of operations in the Balkans. No other decision, in fact, had been possible, in view of the declaration of the Allies that they would stand by the Serbians and help them recover their lost territory. As Serbia had to be reconquered Saloniki was the natural base for operations. With its environs the city lent itself to all the purposes of a great entrenched camp. On the south it could only be approached through a practically land-locked harbor, defended by shore-batteries and mines, and by various contrivances designed by the admiralty as a protection against submarine attacks. There was deep water close to the harbor-shore. On the west at a distance of twelve miles from the town was the river Vardar, unfordable at all times of the year, with marshy banks extending for some distance on either side of the stream, and contributing to the difficulties which the river placed in the way of an attack coming from the west.

Saloniki resembles other ports of the eastern Mediterranean in being a picture of beauty from a distance and a sty of squalor near at hand. Sailors on board warships in the gulf, who looked at it through morning mists, envied soldiers who were quartered in Saloniki, while the soldiers who stumbled through its muddy-paved, ill-smelling streets, wondered why a sailor aboard ship, with a comfortable ward-room to live in, should ever want to go ashore. It is a slatternly, Levantine town, in a beautiful medieval setting, comely in the mass, but unpleasant in detail. This ancient city has witnessed notable events and suffered many vicissitudes in the two and twenty centuries that have passed since a brother-in-law of Alexander the Great restored it and named it after his wife, Thessaloniki. Under its earlier

GENERAL SARRAIL

name of Therma, which was derived from its hot springs, it witnessed the march of Xerxes into Greece, and was occupied by Athenians in the Peloponnesian War. Near its walls is Philippi, where the fate of the known world was decided after the assassination of Julius Cæsar. In commemoration of that event, a Roman arch still stands near the Vardar gate, but it had been greatly injured by the Turks in 1867 in repairing their defenses. This arch was probably reared in honor of the victory of Octavius and Anthony over Cassius and Brutus. Saloniki had flourished afterward under successive Roman emperors.

With the coming of war to her door, Saloniki became a picturesque Babel. Her harbor gulf was filled with many ships of many flags and her streets became gay with uniforms. The long reach of the gulf revealed a continuous procession of ships going and coming, and from their standards trailed the most unexpected flags, Roumanian, Belgian, Dutch, Russian, Egyptian, all engaged in some way in indicating the foreign troops concentrated here on the doorstep of the Balkans. Huge trans-Atlantic liners, French and British, laden with soldiers, glided into the harbor, whose entrance was guarded by a common tug metamorphosed into a warship by use of armor and a mounted gun or two. This warship flew the French, not the Greek, flag. Each entering vessel was hailed and, while not visited, was requested to give an account of itself before it was permitted to pass through the gateway guarded by a steel net stretched across the narrows and marked by a line of floats. Within the harbor, whose safety was secured against submarines by this net, the scene was even more animated. Out in the roadstead lay French and British warships, and one Italian man-o'-war. To defend the interests of Greece a tiny Greek destroyer hugged the shore, a pigmy among giants.

If the harbor was a conglomeration of strange flags and of every class of ship, it was as nothing in comparison with the quays. No Port Said or Marseilles ever knew so polygot a babel, or saw such a kaleidoscope of costumes. There were French "poilus" in their sky-bue uniforms; French Alpine chasseurs with tam-o'-shanters on the side of the head, French Colonial troops—Turcos and Senegalais—in baggy khaki bloomers and short gaiters; French marines, with red pompons on their round caps; French dragoons, with horse-tails in their helmets; French officers of every description; French sailors and, commonest of all, calm, red-trousered French Territorials. Now and then carts drew to one side to make room for a column of Greek mountain-artillery or straggling lines of Greek infantry would take the right of way. Afoot, bands of British "Tommies" pushed their way down crowded streets. British officers, canes in hand, swept the sidewalks from side to side driving countless itinerant vendors into the street. French saluted Greeks; Greeks saluted French. But the British saluted only the British. Cosmopolitan as are the inhabitants of Saloniki at any time, they were more so now than ever, increased as the population was by refugees from Serbia, Macedonia and Thrace. Among the permanent inhabitants, Turks seemed to predominate.

The city always had too many people—120,000—for her narrow quarters, but suddenly there had come 100,000 Greek soldiers with officers, and many with their families; 60,000 British soldiers and sailors; 110,000 French soldiers and sailors; and no one knew how many thousand Serbian soldiers and refugees. It was found impossible for four men to sleep on the floor space needed for one, or for four men to sit in one chair in a restaurant, or for four men to stand in a spot on the street where there was hardly room for one. Even more impossible was it for motor-trucks to occupy the space designed for a donkey. The clamor of the streets became indescribable. Richard Harding Davis [5], who visited Saloniki in 1915, stayed where half a dozen other American correspondents had taken quarters, formerly an Austrian club, sleeping on a sofa two feet too short for him. In this hotel, and especially its corridors, English, French, Serbians, Greeks, men, women, and children—wounded and well—all slept together. Meals became a continuous performance. The dining-room was so crowded that one set of customers ordered as another paid their bills. In order to clear the table, a waiter with a napkin swept everything on the floor. Sixpenny worth of tobacco cost $2, and Scotch whiskey rose from four francs to fifteen.

The Allies, in their entrenched camps at Saloniki, were now to become a menace on the flank of the German line of communication with Constantinople. They were in possession of ground suitable for an offensive in the spring of 1916. All through the autumn and winter there had been seen in Saloniki that indescribable, seething crowd, at once exotic and yet familiar, dominated by the pink and white British "Tommy," doubly fair in that southern land with his cleanly shaven cheeks and mud-bespattered uniform. A variety of uniforms told of the presence of French, Greeks, and Serbs, the last-named arriving in not inconsiderable numbers, from remnants of Serbia's little army after its flight. It was essentially a military crowd, and yet the civilian was not wanting—Christian, Jew, and Turk, drest in every fashion, from the smart morning-coat to the long fur-lined dressing-gown and turban—every class and every nationality. Never had such wealth poured into Saloniki. Hotel proprietors, shopkeepers, owners of cafés, bars and "movie" shows revelled in a golden harvest.

Among foot-passengers rolled wheeled traffic, presenting strange anomalies and infinite variety. With a regularity

[5] Correspondent of The *Tribune* (New York).

that was almost wearisome, electric street-cars passed at intervals of perhaps half a minute, to the clanging of warning bells. Between street-cars, round them, before and behind them, were motor-lorries, strange dog-carts, broken down victorias, bullock-wagons, Red Cross ambulances, and great drays drawn by Clydesdale horses, freshly arrived from England and laden with goods. There were carts full of boxes, carts full of meat, and carts full of men, long trains of pack mules, little pack ponies carrying goods and chattels, and often the families of peasant refugees, and smart motor-cars full of officers of general staffs. In a sort of orderly disorder, this varied traffic passed and repassed, bumping and squeezing, now backing into a side street to let some great mechanical monster pass by, now arrested in what looked like an eternal block, and yet ever going on again without apparent difficulty or danger, self-directed, with restraint and good humor, and bearing in all its details the stamp of efficiency and control.

In the first days of 1916, Russia had begun to push her campaign southward toward the Balkan country. From the Pripet to the Roumanian frontier, over a front of at least three hundred miles, Brusiloff, with great strength and confidence, began delivering blows at opposing Austro-German armies. Heights on the Pruth near Czernowitz, the Bukowina capital, were soon taken and prisoners captured. This drive made from Bessarabia was in some quarters regarded as one of the most ambitious plans in war strategy that had been devised since beginning of hostilities. It promised much as an attempt to break the backbone of the whole Teutonic line across the Balkans. The apparent plan was that Russia and the other Allies, moving from different sides should meet in the Balkans and gain complete mastery of the peninsula. If they succeeded Turkey would be subdued. The work of the Russian Army was thus directed to making a gap between the German Army in the center and the Austrian forces in the south. Desperate Austrian counter-attacks in the region of Kolki were designed to prevent this. An outstanding success by the Russians at this time promised to have far-reaching effects on Roumania. This offensive in its early phases had the effect of diverting large contingents of German troops from the Macedonian theater of war, and by this means gained time for the Allies to complete the construction of their entrenched camp at Saloniki and to land reinforcements of men and material.

By the end of June it was known that a successful movement of the Serbian Army from Corfu to Saloniki had been effected. Over 100,000 men had been taken through seas infested with submarines without a mishap or the loss of one man. There had been a steady flow of troops into Saloniki regularly, methodically, and unceasingly for four weeks. The transports were French. The achievement, however, would not have been possible without British warships. Unceasing patrolling by the British had made the seaways clear and safe. Over a hundred thousand Serbians were now encamped on the plains and in the valleys near Saloniki, tall, thickset fellows showing no traces of the hardships and sufferings of their retreat and exposure through Albania. Four months' recuperation in Corfu had sloughed away all marks of sickness, toil and privation. Few had heard anything from their families for over six months. At the Serbian camp, all the talent of the regiment was employed to entertain guests. Some of the songs were stirring, even tho the words could not be understood. What everybody most enjoyed was the dance, the famous *hora* of the Balkans, very simple as far as the steps went. Goodfellowship prevailed between officers and men as they joined hands in a huge semicircle which to rhythm and measure slowly revolved on the green. Seeing these men it was difficult to realize that each of them had been more than once wounded and that the commanding officer had been wounded nine times; that they had been fighting almost continuously for four years; that they had been through scenes and experiences that might excusably have shattered the nerves and broken the bodies of the strongest.

Saloniki had seen many strange sights since Alexander's time, but never such as now. The armies of twelve nations had been brought to that region, to fight over neutral territory which belonged to none of them, and to which none of them laid any claim. Here Bulgars and Serbs were contesting for ground which four years before they had jointly conquered from the Turks and given to the Greeks. Russians and British were on one side and Bulgars and Turks on the other. The line-up of this international contest was as follows: *Allied Powers*—French, British, Serbs, Italians, Russians, Montenegrins, Albanians, Greeks. *Central Powers* —Bulgars, Austrians, Hungarians, Germans, Turks. Greeks were among the belligerents because, altho officially neutral, they had been doing as hard fighting as anybody. Greek garrisons on the Struma had disobeyed the orders of their government to surrender their forts to the Bulgars, and instead had put up a resistance that reminded Greek journalists of the heroism of their ancestors at Thermopylæ.

Early in November, 1915, a Zeppelin had bombarded Saloniki while the French and English were assembling troops. It was of large dimensions. After making a wide détour, it began real operations by dropping five bombs, which fell into the sea. Warships opened fire on it, but after fourteen shots the ships were obliged to cease for fear of wounding the population, now filling the streets. The air raiders missed the next target, but blew a woman to pieces and wounded a small boy. A bomb set fire to warehouses filled with fats, oils, benzine and sugar. The building flared up like a torch, and the population became wildly excited. The Zeppelin continued to rain down its missiles, one of which demolished the mosque of Yussof Pasha, killing three and injuring eleven Greek refugees from Asia Minor who were sheltered in it. Another crashed through the roof of a house and instantly killed five persons. The flames from the blazing warehouse lit up the whole harbor with a red glow, against which stood out the white sails of coasting-ships, fleeing under canvas. Fast aeroplanes rose in pursuit of the Zeppelin, while British, French, Italian and Russian sailors operated a fireboat at a wharf and poured torrents of water on the fire. The bombs thrown from the Zeppelin weighed about 100 pounds, and were dropt from a height estimated at 2,000 feet. The total number of victims in the raid was eighteen killed and thirty-seven wounded. The material damage was estimated at nearly 5,000,000 francs.

Early in February Saloniki again experienced the "thrills" of a Zeppelin raid. Persons lying awake at 2.45 heard a buzz that differed from the familiar whirr of the aeroplane. Between then and 3 o'clock 25 large bombs fell with terrific crashes in the harbor and on the town. People with windows facing south distinctly saw the airship. From the roofs of some house might be seen the crowded dwellings of the town which rise amphitheater-like on a hill, flickering one after another into light, as the streets filled quickly. Greek firemen worked hard with hand-pumps. Blue-jackets, hurriedly landed from the ships, came along at the double, carrying hose. Several wounded Greeks were in the streets. Seven others were killed near the docks and ten in the town. A man and his wife were killed in bed. In all, two Greek soldiers were killed and 28 persons wounded.

Between two and three o'clock on the morning of May 5, the people of Saloniki witnessed a fight against, and the destruction of, a third raiding Zeppelin. The giant airship afterward lay in shallow water near the mouth of the river Vardar. Shortly after 1 o'clock that night the city had been plunged into darkness, a warning having been received that a Zeppelin had crossed the lines and was flying toward the city. About 2.15 the hum of engines was clearly heard by those whom the turning out of the lights had put on the alert. With the night cloudless and flying at a great altitude, the Zeppelin steered a course straight across the city. When over the gulf, searchlights caught in their glare the silvery form of the raider remaining clearly visible for fully a quarter of an hour. Anti-aircraft guns opened fire, a hurricane of shells bursting round the airship, some very close to it, while it remained practically stationary for some time. At 2.30 a shell appeared to onlookers to have struck and passed clean through it, while another seemed to have burst in its center. Then two blazing shells fell from near the tail of the airship. These were incendiary shells dropt by an aeroplane which had gone up when the first alarm was given, and was waiting for the raider. The Zeppelin seemed at once to be out of control; it turned to the left, as if to return, and then veered to the right, with a dip in front. Another shower of shells burst round it, and a minute afterward searchlights lost its position. For nearly half an hour people waited for the Zeppelin's reappearance, and then at 3 o'clock a gigantic burst of flame, accompanied by a dull roar, lit up the horizon out to sea. This signalled the end of the raider. Apparently, when the searchlights lost it, the aircraft, badly hit, fell rapidly to the sea, and then blew up. A few minutes later a warship sent out a flashlight message announcing to the rest of the fleet the destruction of the Zeppelin. Following that came

© INTERNATIONAL FILM SERVICE, N. Y.

THE WATERFRONT AT SALONIKI

In the foreground is a German aeroplane that was brought down by French scouts during a raid

cheering from all the warships in the harbor. The Zeppelin lay in the shallow waters of a marsh, near where the Vardar empties itself into the sea. The crew consisted of about 36 men. After lying in this shallow water for 20 minutes, the Zeppelin exploded or was set on fire by its crew. Five unexploded bombs were found in the wreckage.[6]

Twelve men of the Zeppelin crew were captured by the French as they came out of the thick reeds of the marsh.

[6] Dispatch from George Renwick in The *Daily Chronicle* (London).

They said the Zeppelin had come from Temesvar in Hungary, a very long journey, over mountain ranges. Directly they got over Saloniki, they found the searchlights that picked them up were of such unusual power that they were dazzled and unable to pick up their bearings. At the same time shells began to burst all around them. They were hit several times, one balloonet being burst, and one of the four motors hit and stopt. It was probably a shell from an anti-aircraft 12-pounder on the fore-bridge of a British battleship lying in the gulf that actually brought the Zeppelin down. A shell was clearly seen to strike her. From that moment she drifted gradually down to the marshes, the fall taking over a quarter of an hour. The prisoners were lodged in a building that was formerly the German school at Saloniki. The gaunt skeleton as it lay there reared itself up 50 feet above the marsh, and became a conspicuous landmark for vessels entering the Gulf. All around the framework were semicircular brackets in which the bombs were carried. Men found one that weighed 150 pounds still in position. This Zeppelin seems to have been nearly 600 feet long. The propellers were polished walnut-wood, built in layers, and edged with copper. From a letter found on one of the Zeppelin's crew, the fact was established that this was the same Zeppelin that had bombarded Saloniki in February. Confronted with this evidence, the prisoners admitted the fact.

In the spring of 1916 it had been repeatedly rumored that Allied troops at Saloniki were preparing to invade the Balkans as soon as the season should permit. French and British troops stationed there during the winter, and supposed to number from two to three hundred thousand men, had been reinforced in April by Serbians. The opposing lines were held by some three hundred thousand Bulgars, and such Austrian and German troops as still remained on the Balkan Front, but it was reported that some of the Bulgarian soldiers were with the Austrians in Italy and the Germans in France. Meanwhile the Bulgarian army, under German management, was following the German plan of an anticipatory offensive. Just as the world was expecting in the spring an Anglo-French drive on the Western Front, and the Germans forestalled it by attacking Verdun in February, so again while the British and French at Saloniki were preparing for the invasion of Bulgaria, the Bulgars got ahead of them by invading Greece.

Allied dispatches at first represented this movement as merely the raids of Bulgarian irregulars, but it was soon evident that it was a well-considered and skilful stroke of strategy, that quite disconcerted the plans of the Allies. By advancing toward the sea east and west of Saloniki,

© INTERNATIONAL FILM SERVICE. N. Y.

FRENCH TROOPS DISEMBARKING AT SALONIKI

the Bulgars secured positions on both flanks. Three railroads ran out from Saloniki. The middle one that went up the Vardar River was to be used for the Allied advance into Serbia. The two others ran respectively to the west and east, and both were now in Bulgarian possession. The western road had been undertaken for the purpose of connecting Saloniki with the Adriatic at Durazzo, but owing to the disturbed state of Albania was never extended beyond Monastir, which was just over the boundary in Serbia.

IN THE EAST, NEAR EAST, AND SOUTH

The Bulgars, who had taken Monastir late in 1915, now advanced down the railroad nearly half way to Saloniki. Serbian troops, which had been stationed along the border opposite Monastir, were compelled to evacuate Florina and fall back. Since then the Serbs had made furious attempts to regain their lost positions, but without success. If the Bulgars could now hold this ground it would cut off the Italians who were at the Albanian port of Valona from co-operation with the Italians at Saloniki.

On the east the position occupied by the Bulgars was stronger. They entered Greece on May 29 through the Rupel defile by which the Struma makes its way through the Belashitza range to the sea. This gave them possession of Demirhissar and other Greek forts along the Struma, down which they advanced to the sea. The Greek garrisons were under instructions from their government to surrender their forts on the approach of the Bulgars; but in some cases they refused to yield. The demobilization of the Greek army which the Allies had forced by means of the blockade, had made it impossible for the Greeks to offer any substantial resistance, however much they hated to see the Bulgars regaining territory which they had taken from them in the Second Balkan War. This move secured for the Bulgars command of the railroad running east from Saloniki to Constantinople, and offered them an opportunity to attack the Allies on their right flank if they should advance north into Serbia. By May 29 the Bulgarian forces were making their way southwestward toward the Ægean seaport of Kavalla, which lies northeast of Saloniki. Along the Struma River the Greeks had evacuated forts Rupel, Bragotin, Spatovo and Kaneov.

With Bulgarian soldiers on her soil, the neutrality of the Greeks ceased to be farce-comedy and became a tragedy. Neutrality, as Greece had practised it for many months, had become an elastic condition. In turn French and British troops had occupied the Saloniki district, and Serbian armies, reorganized on Corfu and other Greek islands, now occupied it. This Allied occupation, however, was an entirely friendly one, justified in a measure by an informal invitation received from the former (Venizelos) Greek Government. King Constantine had writhed at the presence of Allied forces on Greek soil, but, lacking support from his people, he had not ventured to do anything more than issue ineffectual diplomatic protests. Beyond question he would have confined himself to similar empty protests in case German and Austro-Hungarian soldiers had invaded Greece. Constantine was, however, pro-German, and the Greek people were neither violently anti-German nor anti-Austrian, but, when it came to a violation of Greek sovereignty by Bulgars, the inveterate enemies and most dangerous rivals of the Greeks in the Ægean littoral, no strained interpretation of the Greek Government's doctrine of passive neutrality could mollify the national passion or salve the national pride.

Greece had acquired Saloniki and the region beyond it as far as Kavalla and Drama at the expense of Bulgaria. The Bulgars had afterwards allied themselves with the Teutonic powers in order to recoup themselves for losses. Every Greek knew this. Universal fear and hatred of Bulgarians made it impossible for King Constantine and his Government to maintain any pretense of dignified acquiescence in Bulgaria's seizure of positions in Greek soil that were held by Greek troops. King Constantine's neutrality policy, therefore, became bankrupt. Moreover, he had thrown away the great chance which Venizelos had been willing to take in the early spring of 1915. The fortunes of Greece were tied up with the war almost as much as if she were actually a participator in it, and yet she had lost for good and all an opportunity of figuring in the adjustments that would follow the war, except as a suppliant. She had a statesman who had seen the golden opportunity, but she had a king who could not see it, and she followed Constantine, the over-canny, instead of Venizelos, the imaginative and heroic.

By June 21, under heavy pressure from the Entente Powers, Greece accepted without reserve certain demands presented in a joint note from Great Britain, France, and Russia. Greece was now without a government. Premier Skouloudis had announced to the Chamber of Deputies the resignation of himself and his associates and their failure

for the present to obtain successors. The action of the
Entente Powers came on one of the hottest days Greece
had known in many years. The palace at Athens was
darkened, the King at Château Latoy, shops closed, and the
Ministries deserted. People were unaware of what had occurred that day until well on toward evening, when newspapers and hand-bills distributed broadcast made known the
text of the Entente demands. King Constantine then returned hastily to Athens and all the troops in the city were
ordered under arms and the Deputies summoned to the
Chamber, where Premier Skouloudis announced that he had
resigned. Talk of non-compliance with the demands of the
Allies awakened no serious resistance. These demands as
accepted unconditionally were as follows: (1) Complete
general demobilization. (2) Removal of the Chief of Police
at Athens. (3) Popular pro-Entente sentiment not to be
supprest. (4) Deportation of agents spreading German propaganda.

An Allied fleet was ordered to cruise before the Piræus, the
port of Athens, the fleet eventually to be supported by a
landing party. Piræus, the second largest city of Greece,
is five miles southwest of Athens and 200 miles below
Saloniki, the base of the Allied forces in Greece. This
Allied action linked itself up closely with military events
on the Russian front. The unfriendly attitude of the
Skouloudis Ministry had been at all times a source of vexa-

FRENCH OFFICIAL PHOTOS.

FRENCH SOLDIERS IN SALONIKI

tion, and might have become a menace, if the military situation had reached a point where an Allied advance from Saloniki was feasible. Should the demobilization of the Greek army not be carried out according to promise, the possibility would exist of an attack from the rear, in case a northward move was made by the Allied forces under General Sarrail. Benevolent neutrality was what the Allies insisted upon as their right. The contention that there was no desire to force Greece into war was sound.

Greece could no longer bear the burden of the expenditure that her army imposed upon her. She had to demobilize. The nations that had given Greece her liberty early in the nineteenth century, and had continued to supply her with guns—France, Russia, and Great Britain—had a good case in insisting that the will of the majority of Greek citizens should not be thwarted by a Germanophile ruler who had bound Greece to Teutonic leading-strings. Since the Allies controlled the sea, Greece could not resist and the Austrian defeats in Galicia gave new strength to Venizelos. In this treatment of Greece by Allied Powers there was nothing really parallel to the treatment of Belgium by Germany, but the Germans insisted that there was. Altho the ends sought to be attained were in both cases the same, and the neutrality of Greece as a matter of fact had been coerced, the parallel otherwise failed. The neutrality of Belgium had not merely been violated, it had literally been

ITALIAN TROOPS, ARRIVING IN SALONIKI, REVIEWED BY
GENERAL SARRAIL

murdered. What the Allied Powers did to Greece was to restore her neutrality; as, indeed, it was their treaty right to do. That to do this happened to favor their interests—to insist on the fulfilment of a moral obligation did not lessen the force of that obligation.

By the Treaty of London of 1831 the neutrality of Belgium as an independent kingdom had been guaranteed by Austria, Prussia, Great Britain and Russia, but in 1914 Germany had declined to be bound by a "scrap of paper" and so invaded Belgium, in order more quickly to reach an enemy on the other side—only for that, and not because she had any quarrel with the Belgians. She was sorry for them at first and spoke of making amends. Belgium, said German apologists afterward, had really grown unneutral at heart, and therefore she invited her fate. By the protocol of London, in 1830, and again by the Treaty of London in 1863, the independence and neutrality of Greece had been guaranteed by Great Britain, France, and Russia. They had since been for nearly a century the guarantors of her national liberty and her protectors. To them as a matter of fact she had owed her existence. Nations are notoriously ingrates, but this fact of history did emphasize the nature of a relationship giving the Allied Powers a right, and imposing upon them a duty, to preserve the neutrality of their ward. As measures to this end they made their demands. The coercion of Greek neutrality by the Allied Powers consisted, therefore, in delivering the Government of Greece into the hands of the Greek people. While Belgium neutrality had been violated and prostrated by German arms, Greece was rescued from a government that was willing to deliver its people into German hands.

While the Allied drive was not officially launched until August 20, fighting along the 150-mile Saloniki front had been reported as early as the first of the month. General Sarrail, who had defended Verdun in the opening of the western campaign, but who was removed by Joffre because of differences of opinion, had been sent to the Near East in command of the Allies. Why did the Allies, under Sarrail, so long postpone their thrust? The answer was found in political as well as military considerations. The longer the

Allies waited at Saloniki while the pressure against the Central Powers on all the other fronts was growing, the fewer Germans and Austrians would remain to bar their way to the Danube, and the more certain they would be of a decisive success, and the less would be the Bulgarians' liking for remaining with their Teutonic partners.

By the end of August it was believed that Greece was on the verge of joining the Allies, that she would at last abandon her neutrality. Greece, however, was soon shaken by revolt. Stirred to action by the Bulgar advance in Macedonia and the failure of their Government to withstand it, adherents of the Allied cause in Greece took things into their own hands, and seized the barracks of Greek troops at Saloniki, Vodena, and Fort Little. Behind the banner of these rebels many more Greeks fell into line, until the revolt spread to other sections of Macedonia. The rebels were determined that the Government should abandon its neutrality and join the Allies. The ousting of Zaimis and the restoration to power of Venizelos and the pro-Ally party seemed likely. King Constantine all but lost control of the situation. At the same time an Entente fleet of twenty-three warships and seven transports arrived off the Piræus.

On September 4 Great Britain and France demanded control of the Greek posts and telegraphs, including the wireless system, that German agents employed in espionage

BRITISH TROOPS NEAR SALONIKI

should immediately leave Greece not to return until the conclusion of hostilities, and that necessary measures be taken against "such Greek subjects as rendered themselves guilty of complicity in corruption and espionage." The Zaimis government agreed to all these demands, and Greek intervention seemed to rest almost entirely with the Allies. In case Greek forces should be considered of value in the Balkan battles, the Hellenic nation, apparently, would take up arms with the Allies. But there were many among the Allied commands who held that benevolent neutrality, and free scope for Allied forces operating in the Balkans, were all that the Allies needed from Grece. Premier Zaimis now assumed unobtrusively what amounted virtually to dictatorial powers. He was to all appearances in a position to swing the whole country as he wished, unembarrassed by any dissenting popular opinion.

To Greece, one year before, when the German thrust through Serbia was about to begin, the Allies had offered Smyrna, the coast of Magna Græcia, which once had been Greek, the Greek islands in the Ægean held by Italy, and the British island of Cyprus. More than two million Greeks, a commanding position in the Ægean, a future in Asia Minor, were the prizes thus offered. But the Hellenic monarch, convinced that German victory was inevitable, took the reins of government from Venizelos, who had half

RUSSIAN TROOPS IN SALONIKI
General Sarrail, the Allied commander, is reviewing the troops from a stand

achieved the work of the reunion of the Hellenic race, dismissed cabinets, defied majorities, tore up the treaty which bound Greece to support her Serbian ally, and made inevitable, by this act, the success of the German attack on Serbia. No man ever gambled more than did Constantine; but when all his calculations went wrong; when the Bulgars entered Kavala and Drama; when the Italians landed troops in Saloniki, and when Roumania cast her lot with the enemies of the Central Powers, the days of Constantine, "the Bulgar-Killer," had apparently ended—at least his abdication seemed bound eventually to come as a demand from his own people.

On September 25 Venizelos fled from Athens at 5 o'clock in an open boat and was picked up at sea by a Greek merchant-steamship on its way to Crete, whence Venizelos was to go to Saloniki to head a revolution. Venizelos was accompanied by Rear-Admiral Condouriotis, commander-in-chief of the Greek navy, several of the higher officers and many other supporters. In Crete he found the revolutionists in complete control. Venizelos himself was a Cretan and the personal loyalty of the islanders to him had been generally admitted. Practically every garrison in old Greece joined the revolutionary movement. A large number of naval officers left the Piræus, and the Greek cruiser *Lonchi*, under control of the revolutionists, slipt out of the harbor for Crete or Saloniki.

The revolt in Crete occurred near the fourth anniversary of the announcement of the island's annexation to Greece as made by the Greek Premier on October 14, 1912. Up to that time the Cretans had been in an almost constant state of revolt against the Turkish and Egyptian domination for the great part of the nineteenth and the first decade of the twentieth centuries. Crete and Corsica were practically equal claimants for the distinction of being the fourth island in size in the Mediterranean, each having an area somewhat in excess of 3,300 square miles and being surpassed in size only by Sicily, Sardinia, and Cyprus. While Corsica has sustained a comparatively inconspicuous rôle in world history, if one excepts the fact that it was the birthplace of and sometime refuge of Napoleon, Crete had played a stellar part for more than 4,000 years. Crete was a civilized land long before Greece and Rome were founded.

This uprising in Greece was a most unusual revolutionary movement. It was not a movement to dethrone a royal house, or even a king, or to substitute one form of government for another, but a rebellion the object of which was to compel the King to obey the will of the people, and to leave him on the throne to carry out that will after he had been coerced into doing it. It followed the course of other revolutions in purposing to form a provisional government, but this provisional government was to have the single object of defending Greece from invasion and protecting her interests by bringing her into the war. It was a revolution "to induce the King to come forth as King and follow the path of duty in the protection of his subjects." So declared Venizelos, who added: "As soon as he takes this course, we all of us shall be only too glad and ready at once to follow his flag as loyal citizens led by him against our country's foe." Thus they made war on their King in order that he might obey the will of his people and that they might be able to obey him.

On September 27 the air seemed cleared by the announcement that the Greek Ministry had decided to join the Allies. An actual agreement for military cooperation with the Entente, it was said, had been reached by King Constantine. With Greece in the war, there were now to be sixteen belligerents, including the little Republic of San Marino—four on the side of the Central Powers, and twelve on the side of the Quadruple Entente. From appearances it seemed that King Constantine's hand had been forced and that he had as his alternative abdication or war. But it was to be remembered that no revolutionary party, not even that in Crete, which Venizelos had taken in hand, had demanded abdication, while the King had repeatedly stated that the continued neutrality of his country depended on events.

Greek military resources were quite sufficient to turn the scale in the Balkans hopelessly against the Teuton-Turkish-Bulgarian alliance, and so the military situation in Bulgaria became at once precarious. A successful defensive might be maintained through the winter, but the outlook for the spring of 1917, when Greece's full strength would be developed, was uncertain. The entry into the war on the side of the Allies, first of Roumania and then of Greece, would definitely have reversed the balance that had been established in the Balkans in 1915, when Ferdinand of Bulgaria joined the Kaiser's cause and victorious Teutonic columns overran Serbia, Montenegro, and Albania, without once encountering any serious resistance.

With a population of a little less than five millions, or about the same as that of Bulgaria, it was estimated that Greece could bring to the side of the Allies a minimum strength of 200,000 men. The number would have been larger if eastern Macedonia had not been occupied by the Bulgarians and but for the loss of the garrison in that region, including about 400 officers. Nevertheless, the entry of Greece actually meant ten more divisions thrown at once against the Bulgarian flanks. The account in the Balkans now stood about 700,000 men for the Central Powers— 350,000 Bulgars, 200,000 Turks, and 150,000 Austro-Germans —as a maximum; while on the Allied side there were the 200,000 Russo-Roumanians in the Dobrudja, the 200,000 Greeks, and the Saloniki army, which had been rated as high as 600,000, and might be half a million, all of which would make the Allies as 9 to 7 in the Balkans, with Greece capable of greater efforts and indefinite reinforcements from Russia.

A clearer way of estimating the effect of Greek aid was to judge what the result would be of throwing as many as 100,000 fresh troops against the Bulgar flank south of Monastir, which was hard prest. If the Greek army acted as a unit it meant the addition of 200,000 men for the re-conquest of Serbia and the cutting open of the famous German corridor leading by rail to Asia. The Greek army represented not the only increase of strength which the Allies expected to receive. With that country openly on their side would come a new sense of security for the army of Saloniki, lack of which had hampered the full development of its operations. Espionage at Athens and Saloniki would be greatly reduced and facilities for Austro-German submarine warfare in the eastern Mediterranean would disappear, so far as the resources of Greek harbors and islands were concerned.

With the occupation of Athens and the Piræus by French marines on October 17, a tense situation arose in Athens. Great crowds of Royalists paraded the streets and cordons of Greek troops and marines were thrown about the railway-stations, city hall and other points occupied by Entente forces in order to prevent clashes between them and the Royalists. An unofficial dispatch said Admiral du Fournet was hissed by throngs of men in the streets of Athens and that a detachment of French sailors was driven back by a hostile crowd. About a thousand marines landed and occupied the railway-station at the Piræus and several buildings in Athens. Immediately this became known the streets swarmed with Greeks frantically cheering King Constantine and chanting the Greek national anthem. Great crowds marched, thousands gathering in the neighborhood of the post-office square. The War Minister, General Dracos, ordered troops and marines to guard every approach to the square, in order to prevent any clash between Greek civilians and the French, who occupied that section, establishing a complete cordon about the French and taking all precautions to avoid any incident or accident capable of starting strife.

Modern Greece had come into being through the action of Great Britain, France, and Russia, whose fleets, in the battle of Navarino ninety years before the World War, broke the Turkish power, and these three had now recognized the independent government which Venizelos had set up in Crete. By all diplomatic and international precedent, the situation was impossible. Probably if the removal of Constantine from power could at that time have been effected with little trouble, the Allies would not have hesitated to effect it, for they would have had the sanction of half the nation behind them, and, more than that, the plea of self-defense. King Constantine's firmness in holding out against the Allies was attributed to the exact knowledge he had of the preparations made for the great Teuton stroke in Transylvania. That he knew what was going on at Saloniki went without saying. It was to prevent such

AN ALLIED CAMP AT SALONIKI

A BRITISH FIELD-BAKERY AT SALONIKI

311

information from getting to the Germans that the Allies
interfered in the internal administration of the country.
The entry of the French into Athens occurred in the third
week of October. It was part of a course which the Allies
took in an effort to deTeutonize Greece without antagonizing
the population of the country. The difficult thing with the
Allies was not to act more vigorously than their best advantage required. It was now somewhat more than a year
since official Greece, in the person of King Constantine, had
repudiated the "scrap of paper" that bound her to take the
field in Serbia's defense in case of an attack by Bulgaria.

The mission of the Sarrail force at Saloniki had a twofold purpose: to oppose the Bulgars on the north and to
repress any final espousal of the Teuton cause by Constantine on the south. The Entente strongly suspected
Athens. It was only on the disbandment of a large part of
the Greek army that Sarrail could venture to start any
operations at all toward Monastir. The wonder was that
the Entente had refrained for a year from marching hot-
foot to Athens, seizing the hostile and unrepresentative
ruler and setting up Venizelos as President.

Of progressive steps the entry of the French into Athens
was the most significant. It snuffed out the discredited
King's authority in his own capital, as it had been snuffed
out already in a large part of his dominions. He was
gradually being edged off the map and out of the honorable
regard of Greece, with violence to no one. The process was
slow; but it was more merciful than was Germany's assault
on Belgium and it was more definitive. The trouble in
Greece was chiefly at Athens and the Piræus and seemed
entirely due to King Constantine as a brother-in-law to the
Kaiser. It was natural that the excitable populace of
Athens, wrought upon by friends of Germany, should re-
sent the seizing of naval vessels of their country and the
landing of troops on their soil, without the consent of the
only government they had. But the Allies not only had
the right under the protocol of 1830 and the Treaty of London of 1863, but they had of necessity to proceed against
Bulgaria.

It was not merely the British who were engaged in quieting the Greeks, but the French, some of whose troops were in Athens. The Allies had gone to Saloniki on the invitation of the Greek Premier Ven zelos, and his consent was not then opposed by King Constantine. Venizelos desired to join the Allies, but Constantine declined, and so abrogated Constitutional Government in Greece. A new general election, despite the influence of the throne, resulted in a victory for Venizelos. Thereupon the K'ng again upset the Constitution, drove Venizelos out of power, and, in fact, ruled Greece without regard to the will of the people, and when more than half of Greece was in revolt against him. A separate government having been set up by Venizelos and large sections of Greece having joined in supporting it, Constantine's policy had wrecked his country's future and produced civil war. If the Allies had had more courage it would have cost him his throne long before. Sarrail, already handicapped by lack of resources, was unable at once to take advantage of the Roumanian declaration of war because he had to protect his rear against Constantine, the hero of Larissa of April 24, 1897, who had no other purpose than to serve German ends and to earn in the field that decoration of field-marshal in the German army bestowed upon him by his brother-in-law in recognition of his military achievements in the second Balkan War against the Bulgars, whom he had now permitted to occupy Hellenic territory.

The surprize and sensation of the war news in the third week of August was the landing of Russian and Italian troops at Saloniki to join in the "great push." In the army now moving north from Saloniki along the two railways which led to Monastir and Nish, and up the Vardar River toward the line between Nish and Sofia, there were five nations represented—Great Britain, France, Serbia, Italy and Russia, and it was rumored that a sixth, Greece, had clashed with Bulgars at the eastern end of the battle-line, where they were advancing near Seres and threatening Kavala on the Ægean. No one knew how many Italians or Russians had been landed at Saloniki; one report said the Russians would eventually number 80,000. They were put into service side by side with the Serbians, who rejoiced at the political as well as the military significance of this comradeship. As to the Italians, one result seemed almost certain. If they fought Austrians on Balkan soil, they would be fighting Germans also, so that at last Italy would be at war with Germany. Italy's force at Valona, on the Adriatic, while at some distance from the main Allied line, might eventually move on Montenegro. Whether the Balkan advance was really aimed at Nish, which is on the direct rail-line running north into Serbia, or at cutting the line between Nish and Sofia, and thus severing Teutonic communication between Turkey and Bulgaria, was uncertain; but if the latter was the immediate purpose and it succeeded, express trains from Antwerp to Constantinople would cease.

The army under Sarrail was in composition the most extraordinary ever united under a single general. The only precedent was the international expedition to China under Marshal von Waldersee; but the difference between that force and the one under Sarrail was that the former had no homogeneity. Every section regarded the others with distrust to such an extent that von Waldersee never gave an order without first assuring himself privately that it met with the approval of the commanders of the various units, whereas the army of Saloniki had blind confidence in its commander. In the complicated problems that faced Sarrail the first of the difficulties was the international character of his force—British, French, Italian, Russians, Serbians, and Albanians. Such a force had to be distributed in sections, each holding a certain part of the line. They could not be mixed without reviving Babel and the confusion of tongues. The debarking of an army of hundreds of thousands of men, hundreds of miles from their base, had been a long and difficult matter. It meant the accumulation of hundreds of thousands of tons of food, munitions, and war-stores of every kind. No advance was possible until its base had been prepared for all emergencies.

By August 19 the Allied forces were attacking along a front of 115 miles, and had regained five villages. From Florina, where a Bulgarian counter-thrust had been halted, to the sector north of the Gulf of Orfani, well east of Saloniki, a battle was in progress. From August 1 the

Allies had been feeling the line. Their artillery had been active night and day, airmen gaging the strength of the enemy. To military observers this seemed a moment when an Allied drive to win back Serbia stood the greatest chance of success. The Teutonic Allies had begun two attacks. Bulgars had taken Florina, south of Monastir, and Germans had begun an advance east of the Struma River at a point east of the Saloniki railway. Both attacks were finally stemmed. The Serbs then began a counter-thrust, while Sarrail's forces widened their assault in both directions from the Saloniki road. The general engagement represented an irregular line upward of 150 miles long. Sarrail was direct-

FRENCH SOLDIERS IN A VARDAR RIVER MARSH

ing the united operations of the Allies, with General Cordonnier commanding the French.

Sarrail in taking Doiran late in August recovered a strong strategic point. Its loss in the previous year had forced the retirement to Saloniki. It lies on high land between the Vardar and the Struma, on a direct line north from Saloniki to Sofia, the Bulgarian capital. Its possession opened the way for a plan of campaign against western Bulgaria. Success for this movement promised not only to restore the Serbians to their lands, but to bring to a decision Roumania and Greece, which before entering the war had been waiting for a decisive victory in southern Europe.

Allied success might also isolate Bulgaria and bring from her a separate peace. By August 15 the Italians, in co-operation with the French and British, had started opera-tions in Albania, a little north of Valona, where they had an army of about 100,000 men, forming the extreme left of the Allied line across northern Greece and southern Albania. There was nothing to indicate thus far that a general offensive had begun, but it was apparent that the entire Allied force in the Balkans was trying-out the Teutonic positions.

Such was the inconsequential fighting of the summer on this front. It had been political mainly. There was no real offensive and no sign of one. Sarrail's army remained much of the time passive. While the Russians held Ger-mans in the north and drove Austrians before them in the south, Sarrail was motionless. When Joffre and Haig began the Franco-British offensive on the Somme there was no sign from Sarrail. When Cadorna captured Goritza and so added his share to the hammering of Austria, Sarrail still did not move. When news came that Russian and Italian forces had been added to French and British at Saloniki, an advance was expected, but none came. When some fight-ing was reported, this was announced as not being the real Saloniki drive; on the contrary the Bulgarians were making an incursion into Greece. Roumania entered the war and invaded Transylvania, whereupon the Bulgarians and their Teutonic Allies sought to disconcert them by an advance into southeastern Roumania. It was to prevent the disloca-tion of this Roumanian plan that French and British went to the rescue, with an assault on Bulgaria from the south, its object being the protection of Roumania while she was proceeding with her attack on Transylvania.

This torpor of Sarrail, a torpor imposed upon him by Joffre, was a mystery of the war. It was a political torpor only, just as the Bulgarian attack on Greece, misinterpreted at first as the beginning of a drive, was a political attack. The Franco-British army at Saloniki was held inactive while political negotiations were going on. The Bulgarian attack on Greece, apparently a foolhardy thing, was made because the Bulgarians knew the Saloniki army would not, or could not, stop them. They knew the political situation, and counting on its continuance, attacked Roumania. The Allies then stirred, but only enough to help Roumania, not enough to bring on a great battle in the Balkans. Finally, on September 11, the British, forcing their way over the Struma River, engaged the Bulgarians in battle. Four villages in Macedonia were taken. The French at the same time assailed the Teuton line along the Vardar. North of Majadag, in the Lake Doiran region, Allied forces fought the Bulgars for thirty-six hours. Trenches on a front of two miles, and extending to a depth of 800 yards, were taken. The British, pushing further east into Macedonia, won a stronger hold on the east bank of the Struma and captured two more villages. In this attack French troops cooperated until the Struma line was firmly held by Allied forces. One of the first results of the push eastward was a menace to the Bulgars before Kavala. King Peter's Serbian troops, after capturing Bulgarian trenches between Koveal and Veterenik at the point of the bayonet, carried the first line and northeast of Lake Ostrovo seized an important strategic height. Meanwhile Bulgars and Germans, their flanks protected by the withdrawal of British forces behind the Struma, advanced to the Ægean and obtained possession of Kavala.

On September 15 the Serbians, after several days of fighting, overwhelmed Bulgar positions in front of them, capturing twenty-five guns and a large number of prisoners. The French captured positions half a mile deep to the east of the Vardar, while the British west of that river, near the center of the Allied front, had taken by assault the town of Makukovo from a mixed Bulgar and German force. Serbians, French, and Russians continued to follow up their successes until the Bulgar retreat was developing apparently into a route. They tried to make a stand on the right bank of the Cerna, but failed. Florina was captured as a result of an encircling movement by French and Russian troops, which crusht the Bulgar's flank and drove them back in confusion toward Monastir. Florina is fifteen miles south of Monastir and the main railroad station on the road running from Saloniki around Ostrovo Lake to Monastir. It marks practically the beginning of a wide plain stretching out toward the north, paralleling the valley of the Cerna River. The railroad to Monastir divided this plain almost exactly in half. The western border of the plain is a wall of mountains, rising rapidly and penetrated at several points by streams which flow through narrow valleys into a lake. Florina itself lies at the foothills of these mountains, while the Florina station is in the middle plain.

For many days the fighting centered around the height of Kaimakchalan, the highest peak of the Starkov Grob range of hills. This peak had great strategical significance. It is the highest point in the whole region south of Monastir, and completely dominated the great Florina plain in which the Serbs and Bulgarians were facing each other. When this height fell into the hands of the Serbians the entire Bulgarian line was outflanked from a dominating height and was therefore forced to retire. This retirement was continued for over five miles on a front of nearly twenty and carried the Serbian trenches forward as far as Kenali, just ten miles south of Monastir, on the Saloniki-Monastir railroad. The bend or loop of the Cerna River had been crossed and was now well to the rear of the Serbs; their right had moved forward as far as Petalino, while the left was but seven or eight miles south of Monastir. This campaign in the south was just beginning to take form in October. There was reason to think that, from a military standpoint, it would prove most interesting. It was a long way off, the country but little known, the names strange. But there was a wide field for strategical plans such as would not be possible in the west; a wider possibility, therefore, for the display of military genius.

The Serbians on October 5 were only eight miles from Monastir, the British had established themselves firmly on the east bank of the Struma, and the French were preparing for a blow along the Vardar. North of Florina Allied troops were nearing the border directly south of Monastir, while further east they had begun to cross the Cerna. A desperate battle was expected, for the Bulgars had a strong line four miles to the south. A battle around Yenikeui on the Struma front resulted in a British victory, the whole village passing into their hands. French troops operating against Monastir crossed the Tcherna and occupied Buf, which lay about six miles north of Florina, and twelve from Monastir. British troops next day were driving back Bulgars. The town of Nevolen was occupied without loss, after a brief artillery-attack. French and Serbs were striking toward Monastir, fighting being in progress along the whole Medzili-Kenali-Gradesnika line. Finally, on November 19, the city fell into Allied hands. Ward Prince,[7] the first

BRITISH OFFICIAL PHOTO.

BRITISH HIGHLANDERS MARCHING TO THE FRONT FROM SALONIKI

Englishman to arrive after its recapture, wrote of what he saw:

"Down the streets, with their black vistas of closed iron shutters came French cavalry, the first to enter. Their horses' necks were hung with wreaths of flowers, for the inhabitants, after peeping timidly from behind barred windows, had ventured out and were offering posies and garlands to the French and Russian soldiers as they constantly came marching in. At 8.15 the last battalion of

[7] Correspondent of The *Times* (London).

IN THE EAST, NEAR EAST, AND SOUTH

Germans marched out at the northern end of Monastir, and were
seen by French scouts pouring along the Prilep road. Thus Monastir became Serbian again, for altho the French and Russian troops
had the privilege of arriving first, they were anxious to admit that
it was chiefly the tireless advance of the Serbians among the mountains that forced the Bulgars and Germans to evacuate Monastir."

The capture of Monastir was the most dramatic achievement to the credit of the Allies since Brusiloff's advance in
June and his capture of Lutsk. But Monastir had greater
significance in that its fall was brought about, not by an
unexpected blow and the smashing of an entrenched front,
but by a mixture of straight fighting and the kind of flanking work of which the German leaders had so far been the
most successful practitioners. It was a source of encourage-
ment for the Allies that the rushing forward of German
reinforcements, which had almost invariably been the signal
for a bracing up of wavering lines, was not effective at
Monastir. To lose Monastir, and with it Ochrida and the
region west of the Vardar, was to lose the chief prize of
the war for which Bulgaria had been fighting. With the loss
went a heavy casualty list, for the main burden of resisting
the Entente forces in Macedonia was carried by the Bulgars.
The Bulgars had to retreat north over the Babuna Pass,
making their first stand at Prilep, on the heights between
the Monastir plain and the Vardar valley.

The progress made by the Allies in Macedonia after a
month had been at least respectable. On the left wing the
Serbs, Russians, and French had made headway in the
direction of Monastir. On the right the British had
definitely broken the line of the Struma. Yet, compared
with the swift progress of the Roumanian invasion of
Transylvania, and the still quicker recoil, Sarrail's pace
had not been altogether impressive. The numbers engaged
on either side were not large. Allied reports spoke of Bulgars "reinforced by a battalion," or "reinforced by a regiment," making strong counter-attacks against victorious
Serbs. Here, the addition of a thousand men, or of even
three thousand, played the same rôle that entire divisions
and army corps played in the west. On both sides the

FORMER KING CONSTANTINE OF GREECE AND HIS FAMILY

flanks, or at least one flank, were thinly held, while heavy forces were massed along the center.

The long expected fall of King Constantine took place on June 10, 1917. His abdication, made in response to the demands of Great Britain, France, and Russia, was accompanied by the waiving of the claims of the Crown Prince in favor of Constantine's second son, Prince Alexander, who was regarded as likely to deal with the political situation more independently. Venizelos represented the true sentiment of Greece; now the Provisional Government and the armed forces Venizelos headed would have an opportunity to take their proper places in Greek affairs. The abdication was finally brought about through M. Jonnart, a French senator, who had held posts in several French Cabinets and had gone to Athens as the representative of France, Great Britain, and Russia, and had previously visited Saloniki. It had been substantially proved that the King was in close touch with Berlin by wireless, and that the German submarines were using Greek islands as bases of submarine operations against Entente shipping, with the approval, if not the secret connivance of the King. After the abdication, the former King and Queen, with Prince George, embarked on a British warship for Switzerland by way of Italy. Prince Alexander, the new King, was only twenty-four years of age.

Constantine had held on too long. He might have made favorable terms with the Allies by quitting a year or a year and a half before. He might have insured Greece substantial recognition in the settlements which were to follow the war, but he had no thought for Greece's future. He chose to serve Germany, not Greece, and was willing to sacrifice all that Greece was, or could hope to be, to an indulgence of his pro-Teuton sympathies. No king ever rode more recklessly for a fall. Greece had had a rebirth of energy and prosperity under Venizelos whom Constantine plotted against. His fate awakened no sympathy except among those whose tool he had chosen to be. But Greece's plight—due to her ineffective protest against his ruinous policies—excited pity. She was already partially dismembered and no one could tell how far the process of dismemberment might go. Venizelos deserved recognition from the Allies, but apparently the golden hour had passed for the establishment of a Greek republic under his leadership.

Constantine arrived at Lugano, in northern Italy, on June 20. Officers and delegates of the Swiss Government met him at the frontier and welcomed him in the name of Switzerland. He had landed in Italy at Villa San Giovanni, a village facing Messina on the Italian mainland and the starting-point of the railway to Naples. A large number of German personages waited for him at the station in Lugano, including Prince and Princess von Bülow and Dr. Mühlberg, German Minister to the Vatican. The Greek Minister to Berne was also present. Constantine and his suite drove directly to a hotel where rooms had been reserved for him, but was coldly received by the crowds. After dinner he attended an open-air concert, where on being recognized he was hissed and jostled. He left by a rear door to avoid further hostile acts, but met a rough reception in front of a restaurant where he was quietly sipping a glass of beer. A mob gathered and followed him through the streets to a hotel where all the doors and windows had to be shut down to protect him against a riotous crowd that quickly swelled to thousands. He was ultimately rescued from this hotel and taken to another by the military.

Nine months after Venizelos had left Athens to put himself at the head of a revolutionary movement, he had now returned to head the government of Greece. His object in both cases was the same, to obtain and secure for Greece a constitutional government. His return put an end to the separation of Greece into two countries, which had been her state during most of his absence from Athens. He had a difficult task before him—the most difficult in his distinguished and patriotic career—to save his country from its three years of ruinous, treacherous misrule, and to redirect it to the destiny that his broad vision had foreseen. By June 29 the Greek Government considered that a state of war existed and broke off diplomatic relations with Germany, Austria-Hungary, Bulgaria, and Turkey.

The return of Venizelos to the Piræus called forth the

most enthusiastic welcome, showing how he still maintained his hold on the great mass of the Greek people. Only in Athens and its immediate vicinity was there any reason to question his strength. Here Constantine and his pro-German followers had sought by every possible intrigue to discredit him and to weaken his power. In a speech to the Crown after taking the oath of office at the palace on June 29, he said that Greece's place was beside democracy. The nation was struggling for freedom against two Central Powers with whom Greece's hereditary enemies were allied.[8]

[8] Principal Sources: *The Fortnightly Review* (London); The *Evening Post, The Independent,* New York; S. Ward Price in The *Times* (London), Associated Press dispatches, "Nelson's History of the War" by John Buchan, "Bulletins" of the National Geographic Society (New York), The *Daily Chronicle* (London); The *Tribune,* The *Evening Sun,* the "Military Expert" of The *Times,* New York.

A CORNER OF THE PARTHENON BY MOONLIGHT
The Balkans Relief Commission of the Red Cross for a time had its headquarters in Athens. This picture was made by one of its attachés

III

MACKENSEN AND FALKENHAYN, WITH BULGARIAN AND TURKISH HELP, OVERWHELM THE ROUMANIANS

August 30, 1916—January 31, 1918

OWING to the conformation of her territory and to the fact that Austria-Hungary and Bulgaria were both now her enemies, Roumania had perhaps the longest frontier to defend, in proportion to her size and military resources, of all the belligerent powers. She had to carry on war on two extensive fronts, the Transylvania frontier on the northwest and the Bulgarian on the south. Neither front, however, was vulnerable along its entire extent. Transylvania is separated from Roumania by the Transylvania Alps, a barrier which could be crossed only by a few mountain passes. Through these Roumania at once sent the greater part of her army in a vigorous drive, aiming to force the Hungarians and their allies to evacuate the country. Her southern frontier, at the same time, was in large part protected by the course of the Danube, tho not at its easterly extremity, where a part of the territory called the Dobrudja lies on the other side of the Danube and adjacent to the Black Sea, and thus is open to invasion on the south. Being vulnerable it was selected by the Bulgarians as the best place to attack, not only because it lay open, but because a victory in this region might cut off the rest of Roumania from access to the Black Sea.

The importance of Roumania's decision to enter the war was both military and political. It was a diplomatic victory for the Allies and atoned for former failures in their Balkan diplomacy. Austria-Hungary and particularly Hungary, were now in what seemed to be an almost precarious state. Austria had to fight enemies on several fronts. Italy's recent capture of Gorizia and her repulse of the Austrian offensive from the Trentino had shown that heavy forces would have to be used to hold that part of the Austrian line. Austro-German armies which had swept through Serbia were now facing an impending advance from the Allies in Greece. On the Roumanian border the appearance of a third battle-line in these circumstances was of no little importance, while farther north the Russian attack in Galicia and the Russian attack near Lemberg still met no force which could check them. The situation of Turkey was hardly less desperate. A recent serious blow to Turkey had been the reoccupation of Bitlis, in Asia, by Russian troops, and the recapture of Mush. The fact that a new body of troops of perhaps half a million men had entered the field on the side of the Allies seemed bound to have some effect on the situation for the time being. That Greece, after long hesitation and uncertainty was actually to declare war, was probable, the more so because of Bulgaria's recent invasion of her territory. Berlin took the new situation seriously but without outward confidence. It was reported that Germany had already made plans to afford substantial military assistance to Austria and Bulgaria. Meanwhile had come the removal by the Kaiser of the former chief of staff of the German army, Falkenhayn, and the appointment in his place of Hindenburg.

Within three days of Roumania's declaration, her troops had crossed the Transylvania Alps in a wide encircling movement and captured Brasso, or Kronstadt, Transylvania's leading commercial and industrial center. At the same time a large Russian force, concentrated at the junction of the Pruth and Danube, had moved through Roumania in a drive against Bulgaria. Contrary to all previous Teutonic strategy, the Austrian forces, instead of seizing the offensive, fell back before the Roumanians in Transylvania to a second line of defense. Roumania's advance was rapid and successful. Apparently she had all but got through some of the Carpathian passes before war was actually declared, had quickly seized Kronstadt, almost as quickly taken Hermannstadt, and later occupied the important town of Orsova, not far from the "Iron Gates." She seemed at once to be firmly established in Transylvania. What this meant was evident from a glance at the map. Transylvania was a nut

KING FERDINAND OF ROUMANIA

between two halves of a nutcracker made by the northern boundary of western Roumania, on Transylvania's south, and the western boundary of northern Roumania, on Transylvania's east. One-half of the Roumanian nutcracker almost joined the Russian advance in Galicia, so that Russia and Roumania had every opportunity to act in concert. Russia was free to send troops south through eastern Roumania and Bulgaria in an advance on Constantinople—free, that is, except for the resistance which might be offered by Bulgaria and her allies.

About August 21 the Teuton leaders first knew that Roumania would declare for the Entente. Operations under Hindenburg on the northerly Russian front were at once given up, and a body of 50,000 troops sent by train to Shumla, in eastern Bulgaria. Six days later—on August 27—Roumania declared war on Austria-Hungary and immediately struck north into Transylvania. A council of the three Kaisers, German, Austrian, and Bulgarian, followed in Berlin, in which Ferdinand of Bulgaria apparently exacted German support at the cost of Austria, as the price of his continued allegiance. Following that conference, Hindenburg was put in supreme charge of the forces of the Central Empires. By September 9 the Roumanians had taken Olah Toplitza and five other towns in northern Transylvania. This represented an advance of nearly thirty miles into the country. Hundreds of thousands of Germans and Magyars fled westward before the invasion. While more than half the people were Roumanian by race, there were a million Magyars and Germans in the regions into which the Roumanian armies were overflowing. When the first refugees reached Budapest, they brought with them every evidence of such misery and suffering as the world had seen in Belgium two years before, save for such deeds as made Louvain memorable. Belgians now read of long processions of Hungarian peasants, with their families loaded on ox-carts, fleeing through mountains, into which winter was coming, leaving behind them homes and all but the smallest fraction of other possessions, and going into an exile that might be permanent. Roumania occupied something like the same area in Hungary that Germany occupied

The map legend reads:

Line of Roumanian
Farthest Advance, 1916 ++++++
Line of German
Farthest Advance, 1917 ■■■■■■
Railroads———— Oil Fields ·:·:·:·
Scale of Miles
0 10 20 40 60 80 100

THE MATTHEWS-NORTHRUP WORKS, BUFFALO, N.Y.

THE CONQUEST OF ROUMANIA

That the hopes entertained in Entente circles of Roumania's activities in the war should have come to naught, may be understood from a study of this map, provided one remembers what were the effects on Roumania of Russia gradually ceasing to remain a military power and an ally that could be reckoned on. Roumanian armies at the beginning had prest across the Carpathians, through the Vulcan, Red Tower and Predeal passes, and had easily taken Transylvanian territory, including the important towns of Hermanstadt and Kronstadt, besides the Danubian base at Orsova, near the Iron Gates. Alone on her western front, Roumania had to combat fresh German military forces led by Falkenhayn, while in the Dobrudja with such help as Russia could give her, she had to meet Mackensen with Germans, Bulgarians and Turks. With Mackensen crossing the lower Danube and moving north, and with Falkenhayn's forces advancing eastward from the Carpathian foothills, the end of Roumanian resistance had been fore-shadowed long before the capital was abandoned and the whole country by the end of 1916 overrun. While she was able, in 1917, under tutelage from the French General Berthelot, to make a new and promising stand on the Pruth, to which she had been forced in 1917, and to drive the Central Powers back into the Vrancea Mountains beyond the Sereth, Russia under the revolution collapsed as an ally, and Roumania had to sign the crushing peace imposed upon her by her conquerors.

in France, and Russia in Bukowina and Galicia held almost as much territory as Germany held in Belgium, and both the Roumanian and Russian armies were still advancing.

Transylvania is high land, broken into innumerable hills with plains scattered about. From the west the country rises toward a mountain-barrier that separates it from Roumania in a comparatively gentle slope to the heights of the southeastern and southern Carpathians. On the east the mountains break into huge and precipitous walls forming a tremendous natural fortress. The northern part of the frontier is formed by the eastern Carpathians, which are cut by the Strol or Kirlibaba Pass almost at the point where the frontier of Bukowina joins that of Roumania. Thence the eastern Carpathians go south in a great semi-circle to the point where the Predeal or Tomos Pass provides a gateway for the railway from Kronstadt to Bucharest. Rising on the southwestern side of the Predeal Pass the Transylvanian Alps form almost the whole of the northwestern frontier of Roumania. They merge into the Stretenye Mountains, which go to the bank of the Danube, and there, with the heights on the Serbian side of the river, form the famous gorge of the Iron Gates, near Orsova. The highland of Transylvania has a mean altitude of from 1,000 to 1,600 feet above sea-level. A fertile plain about sixty miles in length and fifty in breadth lies almost in the center of the country.

The mountains on the frontier of the country attain at points to great heights. Thus Negoi, just west of the Roten Turm Pass, reaches 8,345 feet; Busecz, just west of the Predeal Pass, 8,239 feet; Pietrosu and Konigstein, farther north, 7,544 and 7,352 feet. Transylvania has three "privileged nations"—the Hungarians, Szeklers, and "Saxons." The Hungarians are descendants of the Magyar conquerors. The Szeklers are closely akin to them. The "Saxons" are descendants of German emigrants who came from Flanders and the Lower Rhine in the twelfth century to re-people the Hungarian plains, desolated by constant invasions of migrating peoples. These races, however, are altogether outnumbered by the Roumanians, who are spread all over the country but had long been excluded from power and political equality. In 1868 Transylvania was deprived of the last remnant of her autonomy and formally embodied in the Kingdom of Hungary. Political control by the Magyars had since been steadily strengthened, in spite of all protests sent to Budapest from Transylvania, Hungarian became the chief language and the official one. In 1872 a Hungarian university was set up at Kolozsvar.

The Bulgarians were between two millstones. French, British, Italian, Russian and Serb troops were operating from Saloniki, Russian and Roumanian troops in the Dobrudja and along the Danube. Hitherto the whole Bulgarian army had been able to cover Saloniki; but now it would have to be divided, unless Germany, Austria, and Turkey could furnish troops to defend northern Bulgaria. The new situation had demanded a new Austro-German army at the moment when the invasion of Transylvania suddenly produced another demand. Fresh troops were wanted also to defend Lemberg against the advancing Brusiloff, not to mention the heavy claims made on German reserves to replace losses in the Anglo-French offensive on the Somme. At the same time the Italian operations about Gorizia were calling for greater Austrian forces.

There was no question as to what the Germans had to do. Bulgaria was vital to them. If Bulgaria had been conquered by the Allies, the road to the Near East would have been cut. If Bulgaria were threatened with conquest, there was little question as to what she would do, for there was a strong Russophile party in Bulgaria. Thus Berlin had demands for reinforcements from Vienna to save Lemberg, from Budapest to save Transylvania, from Sofia to save Bulgaria, and from Turkey to save Constantinople. Should Bulgaria desert the Teutons or be conquered, the collapse of Austro-German influence in the Balkans and Near East would be instant and the fall of Constantinople could not be long delayed. Incidentally the liberation of Serbia would be prompt and the gap in the circle of fire and steel about the Central Powers, opened by Mackensen a year before, would be closed. The war had seen few more dramatic moments and few more interesting campaigns than that which was opening in the Balkans.

But when Roumania entered the war, she did not have sufficient troops to defend her entire frontier. If she attacked in the south, the Transylvania passes could be forced by the Teutons, while, if she directed her attention to the passes, and temporarily, or even permanently, avoided her opportunity of striking south, her southern frontier would be in danger. Russia, with enormous reserves in man-power, was, however, on her northern and eastern border with great numbers of troops concentrated and waiting for Roumania to say the word when they should pour across and lend her aid. The point of concentration was at Reni, where the Pruth falls into the Danube. There was a political condition here which undoubtedly exercised a certain control over the situation. Roumania wanted Transylvania and naturally she did not want the forces of any other nation to be in possession of that province when the time came to discuss peace. Russia wanted Constantinople and, for the same reason, did not want any one else to participate in a movement which might result in the fall of the Turkish capital. Accordingly, Roumania reserved to herself the task of invading and occupying Transylvania with all its mineral wealth, while to Russia was awarded the problem, first, of assisting the Roumanians in guarding the unprotected stretch of her frontier and then, with the time ripe and a sufficient concentration secure, to invade Bulgaria and cut a way through to Constantinople. Acting on these plans, the Roumanians had immediately struck westward against Kronstadt and Hermannstadt. The Austrians fought a delaying action, retreating slowly as pressure was applied. Kronstadt and Hermannstadt fell and on the Roumanian left the town of Orsovo fell, which secured the flank. Further to the north, near Bukowina, the Roumanian right effected its junction with the Russians south of Kimpolung. The Roumanian line of attack seemed well established.

By the second week of September the Roumanian situation took on a portentous aspect in another field. Bulgaria, following the action of Italy against Germany, and of Roumania against Austria, had declared war on Roumania, and a Teuton-Bulgar force, supported by Turks, had crossed the northeast frontier of Bulgaria and hastened into the Roumanian province of the Dobrudja. Two days later this force, commanded by Mackensen, engaged a Russian army, then landing at the Roumanian Black Sea port of Constanza, and, driving the Russians before them, entered the city of Bobric, winners in the race for position. While the right wing of the invasion was thus employed, the left, moving down the south bank of the Danube, fell upon Tutrakan, a city which constituted a bridgehead, or sally-port, at the uppermost point of Roumanian territory south of the Danube, and the natural point of departure for any future Roumanian offensive against eastern Bulgaria. Tho strongly fortified, Tutrakan was taken in less time than was the famous Belgian fortress of Liége, in August, 1914. Seven of its forts fell before September 6, and then the town itself fell. Three days later the Teuton onrush took the greater, but less well defended, city of Silistria.

The immediate purpose of the Teutonic blow was to protect Bulgaria from an expected offensive by the Roumanians and Russians. Holding Tutrakan, the Roumanians would have been in sufficient force within a fortnight to move in boats up the Danube toward central Bulgaria. From Tutrakan east to the Black Sea coast, by water, is nearly 100 miles; from Silistria the distance by land is only seventy. If the Teutons had prest on, they would have reached a point where the neck of the Dobrudja between the Danube and the Black Sea narrows to barely thirty-five miles. Even by stopping short of this point, they could have reached a place where the neck is only fifty or sixty miles wide, and where 150,000 soldiers well entrenched might hold off the chief danger from Roumanians to Bulgaria. The capture of Dobric by a Russian force, supervening upon the headlong Teuton rush toward Silistria, offered a serious menace to the Teutonic right flank and at the same time to the Bulgarian port of Varna, immediately south.

Mackensen's thrust into the Dobrudja was well conceived. It was the best reply Germany could have made to the Roumanian declaration of war. While the bulk of the Roumanian army was marching into Transylvania, the Dobrudja was weakly held in expectation of the arrival of a Russian army to invade Bulgaria. The Danube was unbridged from Belgrade to Cernavoda, where a famous railway bridge, protected by batteries on both banks of the river, facilitated communication between the Russians and Roumanian armies. Mackensen determined to seize this bridge if he could, and, by so doing, isolate the Dobrudja and prevent Russians and Roumanians from cooperating. Surprized by the German commander's sudden and rapid movement, the Roumanians did the best they could to check his advance, but only one division of the Russian army arrived, and there was no railway by which troops could quickly be transferred from the Danube delta to the southern frontier of the Dobrudja. A large percentage of the Czar's fighting men who passed into the Dobrudja embarked from Odessa, 170 miles northeast of Constanza, going thence by the Black Sea lane traversed in peace times by passenger-ships of the Roumanian state-owned steamship-lines. Some 190 miles south of Constanza lies Constantinople, through which the Allies hoped eventually to send vast stores of grain from southern Russia and Roumania.

Until hostilities began in 1914, Constanza was the transfer point for an extensive passenger-service from London, Paris, Brussels, Berlin, Vienna, and Budapest to Constantinople and the Near East. Here express steamers, connected with *de-luxe* trains from the west, made the run to Constantinople over-night. Millions of dollars had been spent on the harbor and docks of Constanza since the town was made a Roumanian possession by the Treaty of Berlin in 1878. The principal improvements were begun in 1896. With wide, clean streets, numerous mosques, synagogs and churches, Constanza occupies the site of the ancient Tomi, Tomsi, or Tomes, the metropolis of the Euxine country. Many broken columns and fragments of statuary testify to the importance and wealth of the city in Roman days. In the fourth century Constantine the Great changed its name to Constanza, in honor of his sister. Probably the most noteworthy event in its history was its designation by the Emperor Augustus as the place of exile of the great Latin poet, Publius Ovidius Naso, familiarly known as Ovid. The poet's offense was the publication of *"Ars Amatoria,"* which enjoys the questionable distinction of being perhaps the most immoral work ever written by a man of genius. Ovid was ordered to leave Rome and took up his residence at Tomi, where he remained for the last eight years of his life, bitterly complaining of his fate in a series of letters, afterward compiled as the five books of *Tristia*.

The Dobrudja is now largely a fertile plain, but it was a low-lying, treeless, largely fen-and-swamp province, when ceded to Roumania in 1878 in exchange for her thickly populated province of Bessarabia, which had been a part of her domain since it was taken from Russia after the Crimean War. In thirty-eight years the Dobrudja had taken rapid strides, thanks to improvements in drainage and agriculture and to the prosperity of several Black Sea ports in the province. At the conclusion of the second Balkan War, in 1913, Roumania demanded and obtained as her share of the spoils from Bulgaria an enlargement of this formerly despised area. Including territory thus newly acquired, the Dobrudja now embraced nearly 9,500 square miles, with a population of 500,000, made up of many elements—Bulgars, Roumanians, Gypsies, and Jews. It produces important cereals, tobacco, sugar-beets, vines, and mulberries. Bounded on the north and west by the Danube, on the east by the Black Sea, and on the south by Bulgaria, it is of great strategic importance, a fact recognized by the Romans, who defended it on the south by Trajan's wall, a double rampart extending from the Black Sea, at a point near Constanza, to the banks of the Danube. The Roumanian-Bulgarian frontier was some sixty miles southwest of this ancient fortification.

The earliest history of the Dobrudja region begins when it was the home of the Dacians, of whom Herodotus speaks as "the bravest and most honorable of all the Thracian tribe." Along the coast from Constanza, northward, runs a belt of lagoons, the remainder of the coast steep and high. Its most striking feature is the delta of the Danube, which occupies an immense triangular plain completely covered with reeds, and dotted with lakes, connected by small canals, acting as reservoirs for the three main arms of the Danube, the Kilia, Sulina, and St. George arms. Owing to strong currents and deposits of silt, the Kilia arm, altho the largest, is almost useless for navigation, and the same is true of the St. George arm. Through the activities of the Danube Commission the Sulina arm has been made to offer easy and secure navigation. For ages the delta of the Danube remained practically unexplored. Accounts of its extraordinary life, where plants as well as animals have had to develop a new type adjusted to the regular interchange of floods and dry season, read like bits of a new "Jungle Book." It a paradise for animals. Man alone can find no permanent footing here.

On the railway line that runs from Bucharest to Constanza, the Danube is crossed by a bridge eleven miles long between Fateshti and Cernavoda. This bridge consists of an iron structure 1,000 yards in length over the Bartha arm, with viaducts eight miles long and eighteen feet high, running over marshy lands, and a second bridge, about one mile long, over the main Danube arm at Cernavoda. The most important port is Constanza, which has great military value because it forms, with Mangolia, the only point where a safe landing can be made, and because possession of it determines the control of a powerful defensive line, the "wall of Trajan." Constanza lies at the end of the shortest route from the Danube to the Black Sea and is free from ice in winter.

Once more the war in this region thrust tongues of flame into scenes associated with the beginning of human history. In Asia the war had invaded the traditional site of the Garden of Eden, and made it a battlefield with camps on the shores of rivers that are supposed to have watered man's early paradise, and it had reached Mount Ararat, Mount Sinai, and Mount Lebanon. Remains of Assyrian, Babylonian, Egyptian, Parthian, and Roman empires had been visited by it, including places closely connected with the rise of Judaism, Zoroastrianism, Christianity and Mohammedanism. Men were reminded by fighting at Ctesiphon on the Tigris that in that same place the Parthians had defeated Trajan. In the Dobrudja came mention of Trajan's wall as a battle-line between Russians and Roumanians on the north, and Germans and Bulgarians on the south.

Eighteen hundred years before, in the year 101 A.D., Trajan had led his legions hither to conquer the Dacians, whose country comprised all those provinces of Moldavia, Wallachia, and Transylvania, which the Roumanians had long desired to reunite under one sovereign. Dacia's warrior-king, Decebalus, defended his land so well that Trajan had to start a second campaign four years after the first. Not until then was Dacia forced to acknowledge Roman rule.

On September 16 a telegram in Berlin received by the Empress from the Kaiser announced that the Bulgar-Turkish-German troops in the Dobrudja, under Mackensen, had "gained a decisive victory over the Russo-Roumanian forces." The Russian and Roumanian forces had retreated to a line running from the Danube at Rosova through Copadinu to the Black Sea at Tuzla, and there intended to make a stand to protect Constanza and the railway running west to Bucharest. Russian troops from the north had reinforced the line. Some military observers vainly believed that Mackensen's drive would be permanently halted, for on an effective resistance hung the fate of Roumania's most accessible route for operations against Bulgaria. Along the Danube the Roumanians developed a vigorous artillery offensive, German positions being swept by shell-fire. Signs were not long wanting that the Bulgarian offensive was weakening.

Its regiments that had been hurriedly dispatched to the Danube front at the opening of hostilities were below full war-strength and had further been depleted by heavy fighting. By September 21 it was announced from London that the battle of the Dobrudja had been won by the Roumanians. After five days of furious fighting Mackensen's troops were in retreat before King Ferdinand's forces, as reinforced by the Russians. The Teuton-Bulgarian army had made a desperate effort to break through the Roumanian line guarding the Danube crossing, but this was hurled back by troops turning to the offensive. Mackensen's stroke had been a heavy blow, and for a time it had seemed as if Cernavoda would be threatened, but reinforcements from Bessarabia strengthened the Roumanian line, which was now able to

A ROUMANIAN WHITE BULL ADOPTED BY THE ARMY AS A MASCOT

mass its forces for a counter-blow. A violent battle followed, until fortune turned to the Allies, who, pressing their advantage, put the Teutons to flight. With reference to these operations, Berlin admitted that the "fighting in Dobrudja had come to a standstill." But next day Mackensen struck back. Directing a counter-drive against the flank, he turned it back, encircled it, and then dashed in on the rear, until the opposing forces fell back in disorder. Confidence prevailed among the Roumanians, however, that their main line would hold. The successful operation by Mackensen was only a temporary success, due to some rash move on the part of an over-confident Roumanian commander. Mackensen's army was known to be in serious plight by inability to obtain supplies, while rain had ruined roads and cut communications, and his army found itself without food and munitions. Convoys of food coming down the Danube from Rustchuk had been sunk by Roumanian artillery.

As with the Russian campaigns in Asia, so with this, the ultimate object of Russian operations with the Roumanians was Constantinople, which is only 175 miles south of the southern border of the Dobrudja. Should Constantinople fall into Russian hands, or should the Russians advance to a point where that city was in any way threatened, this would have meant the collapse of the entire Teutonic defense of the Saloniki position. Turkey, meanwhile, would have been completely cut off from her allies and forced to capitulate. Bulgaria would have been so seriously threatened that she would in all probability have had to sue for a separate peace and the Central Powers would have been forced to retire within the borders which enclosed them before Turkey entered the war. Constantinople thus was the prize for which the Russians fought. In order to achieve her ambition, Russia had undertaken one of the greatest military tasks in modern history—her campaign in Asiatic Turkey against the back door of the Turkish capital. Altho generally successful in Asia, she still had before her hundreds of miles of the most difficult military country imaginable, a country full of mountains, with few roads, and almost entirely without railroad communications. Distances in Europe were so much less, that in every way the campaign against Constantinople by way of Bulgaria, was attractive as compared with a continuation of the campaign from the Caucasus. Constanza was necessary to the plan.

Russia controlled the Black Sea as surely as her Allies controlled the Atlantic Ocean, and possessing Constantinople, the work of transportation of her troops would have been almost without restraints. She could deliver troops at Constanza, a port near the center of her operations, with a minimum of land travel. These considerations made Constanza and retention of control of the railroad of the greatest importance. In early times, as the old Byzantine Empire weakened, the Russians went down to Constantinople by this very route. In modern times efforts to regain the route had been continued from time to time for a thousand years. Four invasions of the Dobrudja were made by Russia in the 19th century—in 1810, 1829, 1854, and 1878—and now again Russia was fighting in that region for Constantinople. This time Great Britain, which formerly had stood in her way, was helping her in efforts to get it.

Mackensen's forces continued late in September trying to gain the offensive and renew their thrust against the Constanza-Cernavoda railroad-line. Three strong assaults were launched against the right flank of the Allied army northeast of Silistria. Bucharest announced that all three attacks were repulsed, while the Roumanian lines in the Dobrudja seemed in little danger of being turned, as both

THE PREDEAL PASS FROM ROUMANIA TO KRONSTADT

flanks were protected and the Allied armies were in strong force, with unexcelled means of communication and supply. Apparently the Mackensen menace—for the time at least—had been checked. The most interesting sector in the whole European battle-line was now the Dobrudja. Dramatic action and suspense it did not lack, for this one repulse of the Teuto-Bulgars was followed within twelve hours by a defeat of the Russo-Roumanians and their retreat in disorder.

What stood out from various reports was the apparent fact that Mackensen's great march around the Roumanian flank had been brought to a temporary standstill only, but that the situation was settling down to the familior deadlock of trenches. Mackensen's enterprise had been held up, but he had not set out to win a victory in a particular sector. His was rather the great counter-stroke for which observers had been waiting ever since the beginning of the Allied forward march under Brusiloff, Cadorna, Foch, and Haig. The Mackensen phalanx was expected to repeat its work of May, 1915, its aim being to smash a hole in the Allied line, as wide as the gap which the German guns had laid open before Krakow and the Carpathians. Through another gap it expected to throw an army, in the rear of the Roumanians on the one hand and of the Russians in Bukowina on the other, precisely as the Mackensen phalanx did in the rear of the Russians in Poland and the Carpathians. Just as the Russians in northern Poland fell back before Hindenburg, because of what Mackensen did to them in Galicia, so Brusiloff was now to be forced away from Kovel and Lemberg by a shattering blow near the Danube.

At the beginning, the Mackensen steam-roller seemed in as good condition as ever. The sudden capture of the Turtukai fortress, with nearly 25,000 prisoners, was a characteristic opening smash. It was as large a haul of captives as was announced in the first day's report of the battle in Galicia in May, 1915, and that first day's record was the initial instalment in an account that mounted up in four months to a million prisoners. Would the event be repeated in the Dobrudja? For a week the thing seemed possible. Turtukai fell on September 7, and on September 15 Berlin announced a "decisive victory" over the Russo-Roumanians, while Sofia spoke of the "destruction" of the Roumanian forces. The tide of battle might still surge back and forth in the Dobrudja, but the important thing was that the conflict apparently had been localized. Mackensen's operations seemed now only a detail in the European conflict.

On October 2, the Roumanians invaded Bulgaria on the upper reaches of the Danube, between the fortified towns of Rustchuk and Turtukai, where the river begins its bend northeastward, leaves Bulgarian territory and separates Roumanian proper from the Dobrudja. Here troops of Roumania made their way to the southern bank of the stream. Just how many men were thrown across the river was not disclosed, but the strategic value of the maneuver seemingly was twofold. Ninety miles eastward from Turtukai was Varna, Bulgaria's chief seaport on the Black Sea. If sufficient men could have been sent across the river and driven along the Dobrudja-Bulgarian frontier toward Varna, not alone would that seaport be in danger, but the move would constitute a serious menace toward the isolation of the Teutonic, Bulgarian and Turkish forces operating against the Roumanians to the north. Simultaneously with the announcement of the crossing of the Danube, came a report from Bucharest that a fresh attack along the entire front in the Dobrudja had resulted in the defeat of the center and right flank of the Central Powers. Thus a new phase of the great battle in the Balkans seemed to have opened. In this movement the Roumanian and Russian troops cooperated by thrusting forward against Mackensen's whole front and pressing its lines back in the center and on the right flank along the Danube.

On October 3 Bulgarian forces attacked the Roumanian army that had crossed the Danube. A violent battle took place east of Rustchuk. On October 4, the repulse of about 15,000 Roumanians was announced. They had been driven off by troops from the garrisons at Rustchuk and Turtukai. By October 5, the Roumanian invasion had proved abortive, according to Berlin, as the result of an encircling movement put in operation by Mackensen. The force which flanked him by crossing the Danube had retreated back into

Roumania. The Russo-Roumanian attack on Mackensen's line across the Dobrudja, however, continued to make progress in the center and on the left, where 1,000 men and seven guns were captured, the Roumanians pushing a successful offensive and taking 2,000 prisoners. In the face of violent attacks by the Teutonic Allies, the Roumanians and their Russian allies fell back on October 22. The towns of Toprai Sari, fourteen miles southwest of Constanza and Cobadin, seventeen miles southeast of Rachova, were taken. On October 23, the Roumanian port of Constanza was captured. Troops of the Central Powers crossed the railway-line between Constanza and the Danube, at a point to the east of Murfatlar, Constanza being one of the principal objectives of Mackensen. As it had been notably useful in offering a seaport and railway entrance for Russian troops and ammunition sent to the aid of Roumania, its capture cut off the most convenient water-route for Roumanian replenishments, especially munitions, of which the Roumanians had been reported badly in need.

The right wing of the combined Bulgarian, Teutonic, and Turkish force marched ahead after taking Constanza, and in a powerful push advanced about twelve miles beyond that place. The capture of Medjide became only a question of a few hours. The Teutonic allies now stood before the strong Danube bridge-head of Cernavoda, which served as a cover for the hasty retreat of the defeated Russians and Roumanians. The railroad-line from Constanza to Cernavoda, now in the hands of the Teutonic allies, constituted, with valuable material in locomotives and railroad-cars taken with it, a base for strategic operations. This material had been abandoned by the Russians and Roumanians. The defeated army was separated into two parts. Those who did not remain in the battlefield, or were not taken prisoners, saved themselves by flight across the Cernavoda bridge, or to the northward in the Dobrudja. The Roumanians blew up the bridge which, after the capture of Cernavoda, was dominated by Mackensen's guns. This bridge is the largest in Europe. Completed in 1896 and the longest railroad-bridge in the world, it cost some $35,000,000.

Strong German forces, under command of Falkenhayn,

had now won a three-day battle at Hermannstadt, in Transylvania, driving sectors of the First Roumanian Army south in the mountains by the end of September. The official report of the battle from Bucharest admitted this setback, saying the Roumanians were attacked on all sides at Hermannstadt and had retreated with difficulty. By what Berlin called "a bold mountain march," German troops had succeeded in getting in the rear of the Roumanians, seized the Rothen Thurm or Red Tower pass, directly south of Hermannstadt, and thus had cut the Roumanian line of retreat. The fighting in the mountains was fierce, but the Roumanians cut their way through and reestablished their communications. More than 3,000 prisoners were taken by the Germans. Thirteen guns and a large quantity of war-supplies were captured. The Roumanians had evidently suffered a severe defeat.

In his report to the Kaiser detailing these operations, on September 26, Falkenhayn claimed to have "utterly crusht" the Roumanian army. But Falkenhayn took an exaggerated view of his victory. That he out-generaled his adversary, compelling the Roumanians to fight on four fronts at the same time, was indisputable, but all reports except that of Falkenhayn agreed that, when the Roumanians found themselves caught in a trap, they fought their way out with courage and without sign of panic. Their army was not annihilated, but bursting through the cordon north and south of the Red Tower pass, fell back into Roumania by numerous mountain roads adjacent to the pass, breaking up into detachments for this purpose and recovering homogeneity behind the frontier. Only 3,000 prisoners fell into Falkenhayn's hands, which was not a large number for an army of 150,000 men to lose after suffering defeat in the circumstances mentioned. The principal loss was in material, 13 guns, 300 ammunition-wagons, 200 transports and 10 locomotives being abandoned to the enemy. After making their way across the mountains the dispersed units rallied at Tzaineni, five miles south of the Red Tower pass.

Against Roumania, the Teutons were employing their ancient rule of concentrating blows against the weakest point. Altho not the rule by which an adversary can necessarily be overwhelmed, it was that to which the warring forces of the Central Empires were now reduced. This was not the principle upon which the Kaiser had acted when he began the war, and all but ended it, with the great blow through Belgium against Paris. He then sought to overwhelm all by crushing the strongest part. The policy now adopted against Roumania was a repetition of that used against Serbia in 1915. Roumania was the weakest member of the Entente Alliance—weaker than Serbia—because she had the fewest forces in proportion to her front, and was the least provided with facilities for replenishing her munitions. But Roumania excelled Serbia in numbers, in ability to import supplies and, above all, in proximity to Russia. Serbia had been totally cut off from reinforcement until the Bulgar attack gave the French an excuse for landing a hastily improvised force at Saloniki, while Roumania was accessible to Russian supporting troops, which could be poured in by land, by the Black Sea, or by the Danube waterway. About Hermannstadt the Teutons, having concentrated a superior force, carried out a skilful enveloping movement, and were able to expel the Roumanians with serious loss from an important part of their earlier conquests. In placing these Transylvanian forces under command of Falkenhayn, the Teutons showed that no petty operation was intended. The difficulties of advancing in a well-defended country with a mountain range in the rear cast some doubts, however, on Falkenhayn's ability to accomplish much before Roumanian and Russian co-operation had made secure this front.

Neither Mackensen nor Falkenhayn, the two projectors of the great Galician offensive of May, 1915, of which the Dunajec battle was the beginning, appeared to be strong enough to deliver a smashing blow. The gains they scored seemed more local than strategic, the power of the German stroke not in evidence, and the strain on German resources enormous. Austria was plainly failing. Everywhere in the bulletins it was the same story; where the Germans were, the Teutons won or held their own; where the Austrians alone were, they lost. In such conditions, Germany apparently might well have been content to keep what she had.

The meager results of her offensive compared strikingly with the price she was making her enemies pay in the west, where she stood on the defensive. Since the beginning of July, the British had lost 300,000 men. A fraction of this number might be assigned to other fronts, the Balkans and Mesopotamia, but it would still be true that on the Somme alone the British casualties were close to

A BOULEVARD IN BUCHAREST

300,000. By adding the losses of the French, we would get the half million casualties which Berlin ascribed to the Allies on the Somme, which was about the same price that the Germans paid for their venture against Verdun. The Allies, however, had got more for their money than the Crown Prince did, and they could have afforded to pay a price in men that Germany could not pay, but it did not follow that the Anglo-French armies would have to keep on paying at the same rate, for their momentum might increase as they got beyond the strongest German line.

Turning against the Roumanians, after advancing steadily in Eastern Transylvania, Austro-Hungarian and German troops by October 7 had distinctly defeated them. North of Fogaras, at the juncture of the Homorod and Altrimers near Reps, they were in retreat, pursued by Teutonic troops. This successful repulse was in the hands of Falkenhayn, who the week before had routed the Roumanians around Hermannstadt and driven them back to their own frontier. While the Roumanians were yielding before these blows, it was different in the Dobrudja, where, with Russian help, they appeared to be meeting with some success against Mackensen, and in Transylvania they took the offensive, south of Petroseny and Hermannstadt. Berlin then announced that "south of Hatszag the frontier height of Sigelu was wrested from the Roumanians," which threatened Roumania with invasion from a second point on her northwestern frontier, through the Vulcan pass. The Roumanian army, after being routed at Hermannstadt, was striking back desperately near Caineni, fifty miles northeast of the Vulcan pass, in order to regain Red Tower pass, through which Falkenhayn's invading army threatened to pour.

Transylvania and Macedonia continued well into October to be centers of great interest. According to Berlin, the Roumanians in Transylvania were retreating along the whole line. The Teutonic Allies had recaptured Toerzburg, fifteen miles southwest of Kronstadt, and within seven miles of the Roumanian border. In the Danube, north of Sistova, they had occupied an island, taking six guns and making prisoners of Roumanian troops. The recapture from the Roumanians of Kronstadt was regarded in Vienna as due largely to the generalship and strategy of Falkenhayn, ably supported by Austro-Hungarian generals. Falkenhayn had been able to execute what was regarded as one of the most brilliant open field maneuvers of the war. So alarming indeed had become the situation for Roumania, that on October 13 her king appealed to the Allies to save his country from the fate of Serbia and Belgium.

Germany had apparently seized upon Roumania as the scene for another victory over a small nation; first it had triumphed over Belgium, then over Serbia, and now it was to overcome Roumania. Victory elsewhere was hardly possible. There did not seem to be any opportunity for her to take the offensive in any other quarter, as the initiative had passed into the hands of her enemies. The offensive in Transylvania seemed largely inspired by the failure of Mackensen to come up to expectations in the Dobrudja. If his move there had been a success, and the bridge at Cernavoda had been taken, nothing could have prevented an invasion of Roumania from the east, and in such an event, the Teutons could well have afforded to permit the Roumanians to get as far as they wished into Transylvania. In fact, the further they penetrated the better the Teutons would have liked it, for the harder it would have been for them to get back. And the very minute the Teutons had begun to invade Roumania from the Dobrudja front, all the railroads in the rear of the Transylvania forces would have been threatened, and lines of communication and supply for the Roumanians would have been in serious danger. When the retreat came, the Roumanians would have been caught between the Teutonic forces in their front and forces in the rear which had crossed the Danube. This seemed the most logical explanation of the sudden shift in the offensive. The Teutons by October 16 had driven the Roumanians back to within a few miles of their border and had actually reached, if they had not crossed the border at at least one point. But there was no indication yet that Roumania had actually been invaded. It was clear that the Roumanian armies had suffered severe defeats. Their invasion of Transylvania had been flung back and an Austro-German force was on the point of entering Wallachia, as a Teuto-Turk-Bulgar army had already penetrated the Dobrudja.

First of all, there was general agreement that the Roumanians had made an error in attempting the invasion of Transylvania before Bulgaria was disposed of. Political considerations at home, the desire of Roumanians to seize the Transylvanian prize, had led them to embark on a sudden rush into undefended Austro-Hungarian territory. The results were immediately fatal. Apparently the whole Roumanian army, save for a division or two at Turtukan and

Silistria, had been sent across the Transylvanian Alps. Whether the army of Mackensen in the Dobrudja aimed for Bucharest, or the bridge, it had become necessary for the Roumanians to recall armies they intended for Transylvania, and so, after a few prosperous days, the invasion of Transylvania had come to an abrupt halt. It collapsed much as the French rush into Alsace-Lorraine collapsed in the first days of the war.

Ever since the beginning of the Russian drive in Galicia, the Germans had apparently been gathering up an army for a counter-attack from the Pripet Marshes to the Roumanian boundary. Germany was about ready to begin operations when the Roumanian declaration of war so changed the whole eastern situation that the new German force had to be turned against the Roumanians. Accordingly, the Roumanians suffered a punishment that originally was prepared for the Russians, an unhappy result for the Roumanians, but one which left the Russians in possession of all their summer's conquests, and enabled them to prepare for a counter-attack, if one should be directed against them, after Roumania had been sufficiently beaten. In other words, Roumania took from Russia's shoulders the whole Falkenhayn army and was well beaten in her effort. The net result of her intervention had thus far been to be compelled to meet the armies of Mackensen and Falkenhayn, which, had she stayed out of the war, would have been used against the Entente Allies in Galicia and Macedonia.

But the fact remained that, six weeks after the Roumanian declaration of war, virtually all the territory taken by the first drive of her armies into Transylvania had been wrested from her by Teuton forces under Falkenhayn, while powerful armies of Bulgars, Teutons, and Turks, commanded by Mackensen, held many square miles of the Dobrudja district, and menaced the vitally important railroad-bridge across the Danube at Cernavoda. Meanwhile her losses in men, according to German estimates, amounted to not less than 100,000. Until October 14 pressure of Austro-German forces was steadily compelling the Roumanian troops to fall back upon or toward their own frontier, altho the Roumanians were offering stubborn resistance. King Ferdinand personally took supreme command, Russian reinforcements were expected to arrive soon, and French officers, including General Berthelot, a well-known military strategist, were going to Bucharest.

Near Orsova, in one more brave effort, on the Danube the Roumanians gave battle, and at several points by violent counter-attacks gained some advantage. Bucharest admitted the retirement of Roumanian forces in the Kaliman Mountains, on the northwest front, but said that further south infantry of the Teutonic allies had been put to flight. Successes were also obtained by the Roumanians in the Oitzu and Jiul valleys, where violent attacks were repulsed. On both sides of the Szurduk pass the Roumanians continued on the offensive, but Berlin said their attacks were repelled. Apparently the Roumanians had been successful, for the time being at least, in stopping the advance of the Teutonic Allies along their border. At no point on the line was the claim made by either Berlin or Vienna of fresh successes, while Bucharest asserted that the troops of King Ferdinand at various points had repulsed attacks. The Roumanian Army, green in war as it was, was credited with having as good stuff as any in Europe, and was beginning to show that it had. Apparently it had for a time checked Mackensen, and now, perhaps, it had temporarily stopt Falkenhayn. Not only to the courage of the momentarily panic-stricken Roumanians, but to a certain amount of assistance from the Russians, was due this October check. The Russians would not have been the only troops to come to Roumania's aid, if it had not been for that fear of a deadly thrust in the rear which had been holding Sarrail's army motionless for months at Saloniki. That threat was Greece.

The first attack against Roumanian territory south of Kronstadt was delivered in the Torzburg pass. On October 8 the Teutons reached the town of Torzburg, and on the 10th the frontier ridge. By October 17 the widely extended tentacles of Falkenhayn's army, over a front of 200 miles in Transylvania, were tightening their grip on the mountain passes. His extreme right wing reached far to the southwest, where the advance guard of General von

Kraft's Bavarian Alpine Corps stood several miles into Roumania beyond Red Tower pass, south of Hermannstadt. His left wing, sixty miles northward of Kronstadt, threatened to cut off from Russian support the Roumanian Northern Army, then retreating beyond the Palanka passes, and thereby to endanger the Russian flank. Falkenhayn was advancing in three columns through Torzburg and Predeal passes, which led directly toward Bucharest, distant about eighty miles. The third column, forming the left wing of his center, was operating through the Altschan pass. The right column, which formed the right wing of the center, had gone about twenty miles southwest of Sinala. In the Predeal pass the center column had taken the northern summit of the heights of the pass, and possession of the pass up to the edge of the town of Predeal, which was under heavy fire.

The Germans and Hungarians had overcome many imposing obstacles in their rapid advance since the battle of Hermannstadt and Red Tower pass. No campaign in this war had demanded such tremendous physical endurance on the part of German troops. On the Somme it was with them largely a question of strong, steady nerves, but in these eastern mountains it was a matter of physical strength, an endurance of a degree that only relatively young and *élite* troops, such as Falkenhayn had, could furnish. At times Falkenhayn called on his troops for the well-nigh impossible. But good weather facilitated his whirlwind operations, and he made a spurt everywhere in order to get to the eastern and southern slopes of the mountains before heavy snows should render mountain-operations more difficult.[9] Already weather reports showed that the long winter snow was beginning to fall. In the Carpathians by the third week of October four feet of snow had fallen in some places.

By October 28, the Roumanians had won some success on the Moldavian frontier, where the Teuton invaders were endeavoring to force their way through the mountains, and appeared at the time to have put a definite check to these attempts. At the most northerly point of the Roumanian frontier, in the region of Dorna Watre, the Austro-German

[9] Karl H. von Wiegand in The *World* (New York).

forces had succeeded in driving the Russians from heights on the banks of Bystritsa, but elsewhere the advantage was clearly with the defenders. The Roumanians also scored a success in the Trotus Valley, where they recaptured Piscul, from the neighborhood of which the Teutonic troops were fleeing in disorder. In the Uzul Valley, the Roumanians, in a successful attack, captured over 900 prisoners and considerable war-material. For a time at least the Teutonic pressure in Transylvania appeared to have stopt. Roumanian military officials estimated the losses of the Austro-Germans in Transylvania as 80,000. Roumanians and Russians in the first week of November seemed at some points to be rolling the Teutons back, notably north of Campulung toward the Red Tower pass, and south of the Vulcan pass in the Juil valley. They were fighting over a front of about fifty miles south of the Bukowina border.

The ultimate success of the Germans was to become one of the impressive events of the war. Its military consequences might be large or small, and they were small—at least in comparison with their moral effect. But it was not the military but the moral result that counted immediately, and weighed heavily against the Allied harvest of accomplishments during the previous four or five months. The whole Balkan play had turned against the Allies; they had not been able to make use of the advantages that came into their hands when Roumania entered the conflict. With Falkenhayn's successful thrust in Transylvania and Roumania, and Mackensen's in the Dobrudja, the legend that the Germans had no remaining strategic reserve ended. Falkenhayn's army was a strategic reserve; it was assembled and flung at what was the critical gap in the German and Austrian lines, and it brought back a real triumph.

Pressing his attack in the Dobrudja Mackensen, late in October, assailed with the full strength of his army the entire Russo-Roumanian front which was falling back fighting hard to a prepared line that stretched from Hirsova, on the Danube, to Casapjeui on the Black Sea, where it was protected by swamp-land and a vast lagoon—the new line from forty to sixty miles north of the Cernavoda-Constanza railroad. About this time one hundred and twenty-eight

French aeroplanes arrived in Roumania for reconnaissance work, and four English aeroplanes from Imbros, an island of the Grecian Archipelago, making a flight of 312 miles in five hours. The Roumanians, having reformed their lines, were offering resistance on a line about fifty-five miles north of the railway, and Mackensen on November 2 halted his advance, apparently because of a shortage of men, in order to protect his line along the Danube, and to send several regiments to the Transylvania front to aid Falken-hayn. The withdrawal of these troops checked his offensive operations. Practically everywhere along the Transylvania front, excepting south of Red Tower pass, the Roumanians seemed to be holding their own. Southwest of Predeal and southeast of Red Tower pass, they made an advance.

The transfer by Russia of General Sakharoff to the Dobrudja was followed by a temporary rolling back of the line that had been thrown across the province by Mackensen. An official announcement from Bucharest said the Teutonic invaders had been driven not only from Orsova on the Danube, where the army was aided by a gunboat flotilla, but from Topal, twelve miles south of that town, and only thirteen miles north of the Cernavoda-Constanza railroad. The Teutons had been forced back to the narrowest diameter of the province, but they were expected to make a strong stand. Sakharoff's advance was described as brusque, just as that of his opponent had been. In one day Mackensen yielded more than twelve miles. Developments on this front depended on whether Mackensen had weakened his forces on behalf of Falkenhayn on the Transylvania Front, or whether Sakharoff's reinforcements would throw the balance in favor of the Roumanians. Russians and Roumanians continued for several days vigorously on the offensive. Keeping up operations north of the Cernovoda-Constanza railway, they pushed back Mackensen's men to a front running through Tropal, Inancesne, and Karanasuf.

Germany, suffering from inferiority of numbers, was apparently giving way before stronger opponents. The movements, however, were to a certain extent shrouded in mystery, so that it was difficult to follow the situation closely. But the outstanding feature was that Mackensen, whose spectacular advance had been hailed a short time before as the elimination of Roumania from the war, had been driven back with the same speed with which he had advanced. During eight days he retreated thirty-five miles, an average of over four miles a day. What had happened to cause this? Somehow the Roumanian and Russian forces seemed to have acquired sudden strength. The railroad between Constanza and Cernavoda, the key of all the Dobrudja fighting, was in imminent danger of recapture. When the Roumanians advanced to within a few miles of Cernavoda, Mackensen gave no indication that he was able to check their attacks.

On the Dobrudja front the situation for weeks remained confused and uncertain. Roumanians and Russians, with a line east and west through Topal across the province, were bombarding both of Mackensen's flanks with artillery. The Russians, operating from warships in the Black Sea, had apparently destroyed Constanza and undoubtedly caused the Germans considerable annoyance without directly threatening their line. Roumanians at this time gave as much as they received. The Germans were getting blow for blow, and securing few advantages. One other thing the Roumanian offensive in the Carpathian sector had accomplished; it protected the main railroad from Czernowitz to Bucharest, over which Russian reinforcements to Roumania were sent, for it was of the utmost importance to Roumania that this road be kept open. If it could be cut off, the Roumanian Army would practically be isolated from Russia and at the mercy of the Germans, who would in such a case be able to eliminate Roumania completely from the war.

The invasion of Roumania continued in November to make headway along the western half of the southern, or Wallachian, front. Falkenhayn's attack on this front was directed along three main lines; through Predeal pass and the valley of the Prahova, through the Rotenturm pass and along the valley of the Alt, and through the Vulcan pass along the valley of the Jiul. It was on the two latter lanes that the Teutons prest furthest into Roumania, the presumption being that these were furthest removed from Bucharest and the Russian frontier, and consequently easily reached by reinforcements from the capital or by troops which might be coming in from Russia. The river Alt bisects southern Roumania in almost a straight line from north to south, and it was in the region lying to the west of the river that the Teuton offensive was expected to develop most rapidly.

The forces of the Central Powers were endeavoring to make a drive on Bucharest, the Roumanian capital, from three directions. To the west, the troops of Falkenhayn had reached the Alt river; to the north, the Germans and Austro-Hungarians were pressing southward from the Predeal and Torzburg passes, and somewhere along the Danube, either to the south or southwest, the forces of Mackensen were crossing the river. By November 25 Western Wallachia, with the entire line of the Alt River, apparently was entirely in the hands of the Teutonic allies. In all directions the invaders were making progress with Bucharest their main objective, and they were daily coming nearer. When news reached Bucharest that the German-Bulgarian troops had successfully crossed the Danube at Zimnitza, it was decided to transfer the Roumanian diplomatic corps to Jassy, where a large number of refugees from the capital and from Western Wallachia had already congregated. After October 14, when the advance of the Germans to Predeal caused a sudden and lively scare, especially in diplomatic quarters, Bucharest had remained fairly tranquil, and the subsequent successes of the Roumanian troops in the Jiul valley had created a feeling of confidence and even of elation. Seven weeks went by, the latter portion of this period being marked by a recurrence of aeroplane attack, to which the population of the city had become more or less accustomed, altho the number of victims had increased to about a thousand killed, wounded, or injured. Public tranquillity, however, remained undisturbed. When on November 24 the authorities received news that the enemy had crossed the Danube, had established himself at Zimnitza, and was advancing on Rosiori, some six hours' journey by rail from the capital, no intimation of these tidings was conveyed to the population. As a consequence the train conveying the diplomatic corps, and a certain number of invited and uninvited persons, took its departure in comparative quiet, altho the station was already densely crowded with refugees.

The departure of the diplomatists took place on the night of November 25. When it was made known on the following day a state of panic ensued, which was increased by the arrival of several military officers, who at once took measures for the removal of their families. A *sauve qui peut* followed, and violent scenes occurred at the railway station, the doors of which were guarded by cordons of soldiers. Fabulous prices were paid for country-carts and other vehicles by those who despaired of reaching trains, but the bulk of the refugees set out on foot, carrying with them a portion of their household goods; many were compelled by fatigue to abandon their burdens, so that main roads leading east and north became strewn with objects which had been dropt or thrown away. One fugitive rented a peasant's cart, for which he paid fifty dollars. Another arrived at Jassy in a train composed of 60 carriages, only a few of which were fitted with air-brakes—a sudden stop occurred and the brakeless part of the train "telescoped" the other so that several persons were killed or injured.

The occupation of Giurgevo brought the line of Mackensen to within 37 miles of Bucharest on the south, while the capture of Curtea de Arges, 80 miles northeast of the capital, cleared the Topoiog sector of Roumanians and gave the invaders a railroad leading to the important town of Pitesci, the junction of the line running from Campulung to Bucharest. On December 1, the forces of Mackensen were almost within shelling distance of the southern forts which protected Bucharest. Desperately the Roumanians, aided by Russian troops, were defending the southern and western approaches to Bucharest, while the Teutonic advance continued to press forward more closely on the capital from the northwest. Exactly one hundred days after the declaration of war by Roumania, the Teutonic allies were in control of virtually one-half of the Roumanian territory—from the Transylvanian Alps northwest of the capital to the Danube south of it, and a large part of the Dobrudja.

By December 4, all hope of holding Bucharest had been

entirely abandoned, and the Roumanian troops were withdrawing toward the east through the whole width of Eastern Wallachia. There had never been any intention of holding Bucharest itself as a fortress. It is true the city was surrounded by an impressive girdle of detached works composed of eighteen large forts and an equal number of smaller forts and batteries, situated at distances from the center varying between three and seven miles and separated by intervals not exceeding three. The principal line of resistance, therefore, amounted to a length of about 50 miles, and it was calculated that at least 120,000 men would be required to hold the fortress. The most important of these defenses had been organized as far back as 1886, and were now completely obsolete. Even the experiences of the Austrians with Przemysl, where they had an immense superiority of artillery over the besieging Russian forces, could hardly have encouraged the Roumanians to try to hold Bucharest.

The evacuation of Bucharest began on the day when news arrived that the enemy had crossed the Danube at Sistovo. This news fell like a thunderbolt on the capital, and the authorities received an order to evacuate it as soon as possible. "The first few days which followed," wrote an eye-witness, "will remain deeply engraved in the memory of the inhabitants. The cry, 'the Germans are coming!' filled the population with terror, and everybody tried to escape." The word "overcrowded" only inadequately described the state of railway trains. Prices as high as four hundred dollars were offered for carriages to Ploeshti, distant only about 30 miles from Bucharest. By royal decree the meeting of the Roumanian Parliament was postponed and Parliament ordered to reassemble at Jassy. On December 1, when the last members of the Cabinet left Bucharest, the thunder of the invaders' guns could be distinctly heard, but the panic had then given place to a feeling of depression and resignation. To maintain order troops patrolled the streets, but this was not necessary, for life in the gay and busy city had become paralyzed. On December 4, a terrific report awoke the capital. The arsenal had been blown up by the authorities. With the destruction of this the last hopes of the Bucharest population fled. There could be no further doubt regarding the future.

On December 5, Mackensen sent an officer under a flag of truce into Bucharest, calling upon it to surrender. The Germans entered on the same day, Mackensen with his staff taking up headquarters in the Royal Palace. But the day on which they entered the capital was dark with smoke, and the night which followed was illuminated, the flames and the smoke rising from burning oil-tanks and wells in the district of Ploeshti. One of the richest regions of the world was being destroyed in order to prevent the Germans from getting oil. Simultaneously with the fall of Bucharest, came news of the capture of the important railroad-junction of Ploeshti, north of the capital, the conquest of which placed in the hands of the invaders the last railroad in the west and gave them the head of the line running north-ward to Jassy, the new capital of Roumania. The Central Powers were now in possession of four capitals of small Entente Allied States, the others being Brussels, Belgrade, and Cettinje. Beyond Bucharest they were able to press forward for weeks afterwards. So rapid and well conceived was this prolongation of the campaign that Russians and Roumanians were both taken by surprize. Counter-attacks on or near Mizil, on the Ploeshti-Buzen road, failed to make any impression. Even reinforcements of Russian cavalry, sent to stiffen the rear-guard, were unable to check the German pace. The weather, altho it mired the heavy Wallachian lowlands, opposed no effective barrier. The German system, with its combination of preparation, speed, and driving leadership, had reached its most formidable manifestation, exerted as it was against an inadequate resisting power. More than 1,000 persons were killed in Bucharest by German aircraft prior to the abandonment of the city. In a single day 300 persons were killed by Zeppelins and airplanes. A group of airplanes descended to a low altitude and spent several hours in seeking victims, killing workmen and work-women in fields and streets. Two airplanes which were pursuing a two-horse vehicle on the road had a race to see which could hit it first. The vehicle was going at a good pace, but the airplanes quickly overtook it. Driver, passenger, and horses, were all killed.

The capture of Bucharest led to no decisive military results, but the moral, political, and commercial consequences of its fall could not be ignored. Bucharest was to Roumania what Paris was to France, the whole life of the country being centered in the capital, where were many rich men who would now have to pay the same heavy contributions which had been extorted from the merchants of Brussels. When Mackensen entered the city he did so without firing a shot, its forts having all been dismantled since the fate of the Meuse fortress had proven Brialmont's work powerless against modern artillery.

It was suggested that the campaign in Roumania was only of subsidiary importance and, whichever way it went, whether for or against the Allies, could have no effect on the ultimate result of the war, which would be decided on the Western Front and on no other. It was hard to reconcile this opinion with the frantic appeals which had been made to Roumania a few months before to abandon neutrality and throw in her lot with the Allies. Those who had seen for themselves the cereal and mineral wealth of the country, relatively small as its territory was, knew what an accession of economic strength its conquest might bring to the Central Powers. Just when the Allied blockade was getting tighter and its pinch harder, some stores of corn and oil, which had been waiting over many months for export, fell into the hands of the German commander. As the Germans now held 50,000 square miles of the richest land in Europe, it was felt to be no exaggeration to say that the German conquest of Roumania had put back the hands of the war-clock. The whole Balkan Peninsula, from the Adriatic to the Black Sea, north of the front held by General Sarrail, was practically German territory. Even if Mackensen went further than the Sereth the Teuton front would have been shortened by 200 miles. The valley of the Danube, up which lies the easiest route into Hungary, was in secure possession of the Central Powers. The dividing zone between the Russians on the Sereth and the Allies in Macedonia, had been widened by more than 150 miles. A

THE KAISER WITH MEMBERS OF HIS STAFF VISITING ROUMANIAN OIL-WELLS

through line of railway had been opened between Germans and Turks. Submarines could now be sent in pieces to Constanza and launched on the Black Sea to prey on Russian commerce.

The Germans had still to undertake to crush Russia and eliminate the Czar's empire from the ranks of her enemies. The chief effort of the Allies was to break the German lines in the West and cut German communication with Constantinople in the Balkans, as the prelude to a new attack upon Constantinople. No sane observer could expect immediate peace, or peace within twelve months. In any consideration of peace, the German victory would increase the German demands, and the least that Germany now demanded was the right to settle the fate of Russian Poland, to control Serbia, and to dominate Asia Minor. The Roumanian army seemed as a whole to be still intact. It had suffered severe losses. Probably 75,000 men in all had been taken prisoners, but the others had made good their retreat, and were still a force with which sooner or later, Germany would have to deal. Roumania still existed, in many ways a danger and a menace to the German cause. This menace, in spite of the fall of Bucharest, could not be considered entirely removed until the Roumanian army had ceased to exist and all of Roumania—Moldavia, as well as Wallachia—had been completely conquered and occupied.

Roumania closed for the Germans the period of adventure which had opened with the attack on Liége, and for the Allies the period which began with the invasion of Gallipoli. To end the war quickly, and by way of Paris, was the Kaiser's purpose; it had failed within a month at the Marne. To end the war by way of Constantinople was the Allied purpose; this after nearly two years had now failed at Bucharest. To get at Paris the Kaiser had dared the crime of Belgium and brought down on himself the judgment of the world. To get at Constantinople the Allies had plunged into the quagmire of Balkan hatreds and ambitions. All that was now over. The Balkan possibilities were exhausted. Turkey, Bulgaria, Serbia and Roumania had disposed of themselves or been disposed of. Only Greece remained, and it was no longer possible to conceive that developments in Greece would change the military aspect in southern Europe. It was idle to speak of Constantinople, or of an invasion of Austria across the Danube. The great Allied problem now was the conservation of the army at Saloniki. Would that army be able to hold out against the enormous pressure which the Central Powers could bring to bear.

In two ways the Allies might draw advantage from the defeat of their Balkan hopes. There promised to be an end to divided councils, as between Western and Eastern offensives, which had undoubtedly hampered the conduct of the war both at London and Paris. There promised, therefore, to be in future an intense effort in the West. Shipping devoted to Mediterranean enterprise could largely be restored to the feeding of England and her Allies and to the munitioning of Russia, that inexhaustible reservoir of men, whose annual yield of recruits was a million and a half, and behind them an apparent determinaton to go on to the end. All doubts about a separate Russian peace with the Kaiser seemed now removed, which meant that the Allied Governments needed no longer to spend their energies on diplomacy. They could devote themselves with a single mind to the grim business of the simplified battlefield.[9a]

The temporary resurrection of the Roumanian Army which followed in the summer of 1917 was due not only to the qualities of resistance in the Roumanian peasant, but to the strenuous work of a French mission under General Berthelot. The Roumanian officers, altho they had learned much from the sad experiences of the 1916 campaign, were not really familiar with the modern art of war. Berthelot, accompanied by some 500 French officers, had arrived in Roumania late in 1916, when he could do little to avert disaster, but his services proved invaluable in reorganizing the army. During the whole winter the French lived with their Roumanian comrades, sharing all miseries with them and raising their deprest spirits. While the army was thus reorganized, working hard to get fit for another campaign, the Allies, who realized that one of the causes of the Roumanian disaster had been lack of ammunition and guns,

[9a] The *Tribune* (New York).

started to send out through Russia great quantities of munitions, guns of all calibers, trench-mortars and everything necessary for a modern army. The Air Service, which was practically non-existent at the outbreak of the war, was now in the hands of experienced French airmen, and had a fair number of French and British aeroplanes. Thus reorganized and prepared, the Roumanian army was ready by the beginning of July, 1917, to take the field again, and attempt to avenge the reverses suffered in 1916.

Roumanians suddenly crossed the Sereth on July 24, and, advancing astride the Susitza and Putna rivers, fell suddenly upon General Gerok's Austrian outposts, and drove them back on their supports to the slopes of the Vrancea mountains. A running fight went on till the 28th, resulting in the Teutons being pushed back toward the passes, the Roumanians following close on their heels to the village of Soveja and to Mont Casinlui. On their way back to the frontier the Austrians lost 4,500 prisoners, with 90 guns and a large quantity of war-material, which in their flight they were unable either to carry away or destroy. When Mackensen heard of the Roumanian movement he acted with his usual vigor. Leaving a containing force facing Galatz, he sent the bulk of his troops up the right bank of the lower Sereth to Focsani, and called up his reserves from Bucharest. Reinforcements were at the same time sent to Gerok. On August 6 he stormed the positions occupied by the Russian troops who were protecting the left flank of the Roumanian Second Army north of Focsani, and captured 1,300 prisoners with thirteen guns. This threat to their left flank caused the Roumanians to withdraw their center and left wing from the hills, to cover the approaches to the loop line between Marasesti and Tecuci, which connected the Sereth valley railway with the line running along the Berlandu to Jassy. On the 7th the Roumanian line extended on a semi-circular front from the west of Ocna in the Trotus valley through Soveja and thence between the Putna and Susita rivers to Sereth.

By this time Russian troops had been brought up in considerable force, and were supporting the Roumanians on both flanks and a stubbornly contested battle took place,

Mackensen endeavoring to throw the Roumanians behind the Sereth, while their object was to hold the loop-line and prevent the German commander from advancing up the river. While Mackensen attacked the Roumanians from the south on both sides of the Focsani-Adjulu railway, Gerok directed an enveloping movement against Ocna from the west with troops advancing down the numerous valleys between the Trotus and Casin rivers. On August 9 Mackensen forced a passage over the Susitza river and succeeded in holding the position against a Roumanian counter-attack on the following day. The battle extended to the Trotus valley, where the Austrians pushed the Roumanians back from the Casinlui heights and forced them to retire to a position west of the line Ocna-Gorozesti. On August 11 the battle was continued with the same intensity, the Roumanians withdrawing in the evening to the villages of Marasesti and Focsani on the left bank of the Sereth, while in the Trotus valley the Austrians gained ground west of the Ocna-Gorozesti position, the Roumanian right wing falling back on Ocna. On the 12th Russian and Roumanian counter-attacks resulted in the capture of 1,100 prisoners, but the Germans succeeded in occupying Panciu, the western terminus of the loop-line, for the possession of which there had been such prolonged fighting.

The battle continued along the whole line of the 13th and 14th with indecisive results, but on the latter day German troops captured the Baltavetu bridge-head, where the loop-line crosses the Sereth, and also stormed the village of Stracani, northwest of Panciu. On this day the Roumanian troops on the upper Susitza had to fall back from Soveja, which the enemy occupied, but on the 15th there was a rally, and after fighting a successful battle on the 16th the right wing of the Second Army retook the lost positions in the Susitza valley, and held them against a series of obstinate counter-attacks. On the same day Mackensen's further progress north of the loop-line in the Sereth valley met with a sharp check from the Russo-Roumanian forces concentrated at this point. Mackensen's object in invading Moldavia was doubtless to get possession of the harvest in that rich province. A letter dated August 8, found on the corpse of a Prussian officer, contained the following: "We are going to deliver a decisive blow here very soon. If we cross the Sereth, which I hope will not be difficult, Jassy and the whole of Moldavia will be ours. If we succeed, I believe we are going to be sent to Flanders, where things seem to be hot again."

The last Teutonic effort was made on the night of the 19th, when, after intense artillery-fire of all calibers, two German divisions and an Austrian brigade attacked the Roumanian positions northeast of Pancui. In the presence of their King, who, accompanied by Prince Carol, shared the risks of battle with his soldiers, the Roumanians fought with dash and bravery. The Germans were more desperate than ever, but when the last Roumanian reserves were brought forward and counter-attacked they fled in disorder. German soldiers, surprized by so violent an attack, threw away rifles and surrendered. Next day 600 Germans and Austrians were paraded before the King. On August 21 the battlefield was still covered with unburied corpses, piled up six deep, and a mile away the stench was unbearable. This German check on that front was the most serious they had had in the Near East. After a fortnight's fighting, with terrific losses, they had been stopt by a numerically inferior force. On the other hand the strategical advantage was with the Roumanians, who held the whole left bank of the Sereth, the very abrupt slopes of which dominated the right bank, which was partially in German hands.[10]

Only minor engagements took place afterward. The Germans had shifted their efforts to the north, where they had to deal with demoralized Russian troops, while the Roumanians could not continue an offensive alone, their losses having been too heavy, and there being no hope of further help from the Russian army. Strong local attacks made by the enemy from August 20 onward were intended to keep the Roumanian troops engaged on the whole front, and in the meantime to keep the initiative with the Austro-German troops, but from that date on the Austrians began to withdraw troops to the Italian front. On September 9 the Roumanians captured a few important positions, but

[10] London *Times'* correspondent.

the enemy, reinforced before the Roumanians could organize the captured ground, compelled them to abandon the temporary gain. This was the last effort made by the Roumanian army. The Russian revolution had rendered any further aid from the Northern ally unlikely.

From the second half of September the main effort of the Germans had been to demoralize the Roumanian soldiers in the same way as they had demoralized the Russians. A systematic propaganda was organized. Pamphlets, letters from relatives, proclamations from high clergy were spread among Roumanian peasant-soldiers, in order to break their faith in their chiefs and in their allies. The dissolution of the Russian armies that ensued was fatal to Roumania. At the end of December hardly 60,000 men were left in the trenches. A front which had been held by some 500,000 Russians and 250,000 Roumanians had to be held now by Roumanians alone, whose numbers had been considerably diminished through heavy losses in the July and August actions.

Such was the situation of the Roumanian army at the end of 1917, or only a few months before the conclusion of the so-called Roumanian "peace." When the Russian armistice was signed, Roumania was compelled by the joint threats of Germany and the Soviets to adhere to it. From that day Russian troops began to leave the trenches wholesale, and by the end of January only such Siberian forces and other troops remained as found it more convenient to spend their time in Roumania than to return to their own territory. Roumania, which suddenly drifted into a state of war with the Bolshevist Government of Russia, found herself completely cut off from the rest of the Allies. Of her desperate situation the Germans were not slow to take advantage. They determined to seize the immensely rich oil-fields of Roumania, and to secure for an unlimited period Roumanian corn for Germany at a price fixt by German authorities. Having secured these advantages, Germany caused eight Roumanian divisions to be demobilized under German Staff officers.

On February 23, 1918, Herr von Kühlmann and Count Czernin arrived at Bucharest, and, after presenting their peace terms to General Averescu, went to Jassy to see King Ferdinand. On March 2 the King held a Crown Council when it was decided to accept the terms offered and enter into negotiations in regard to details. On March 5 the preliminary treaty was signed at Buftea. Roumania ceded the Dobrudja up to the Danube to Bulgaria, and agreed to a rectification of her Transylvanian frontier, which included the territorial cession of the oil-fields of Campina to Hungary. She also agreed to allow a right of way for Austro-German troops through Moldavia to Odessa. The question of Bessarabia was not dealt with in the treaty, but according to reports the local government of the province favored incorporation with Austria-Hungary rather than with Roumania. This meant that Roumania would be cut off from access to the sea, the port of Constanza, which she had constructed at great expense, passing into Bulgarian hands.

Peace between Roumania and the Central Powers was finally brought about on May 6 by the signing of a formal treaty at Bucharest. Isolated from her Allies by the defection of Russia, nothing was left for Roumania but to accept from her relentless enemies the hard price they imposed. The treaty was signed in the same room of the castle where the entry of Roumania into the war had been decided. Men with a leaning toward pacifism had exprest a belief in the sincerity of Germany's profest desire for a just peace in the East, and ventured predictions that her lust for territory and greed for conquest were mere hostile estimates. They insisted that there yet remained in the empire a human element among the people and in legislative bodies. But to any one desirous of knowing what a German military peace meant, there was now an opportunity of learning from a careful reading of the treaty with Roumania which pointed straight to the impoverishment of the country by the appropriation of all its resources, to the seizing of some of its most valuable territory, the control of its army, and the reduction of the country to a state of vassalage to the Berlin Government.

Roumania was entirely cut off from the Black Sea and the port of Constanza lost, and the Austro-Hungarian border pushed down into the Wallachian and Moldavian plains. The Dual Monarchy secured control of all the mountain passes and strategic positions, much valuable mineral land and part of the petroleum fields. Possession was taken of all the oil-producing wells in the interior. The signatures of King Ferdinand and Queen Elizabeth were secured under threats that if they did not immediately accept the treaty they would be deposed and a new dynasty headed by a Prussian lordling substituted. Roumania, as a forced convert to the Alliance, was to become one of the chief connecting-links between Central Europe and Nearer Asia. In the darkest hours of their country's misfortune, Roumanian patriots were never weary of repeating their proud boast that Roumania had entered the war of her own free will, and that, notwithstanding losses in human life amounting to some 800,000 souls, and the crushing material losses involved by this enforced treaty, she had been true to her destiny in entering the war on the side of the Allies.[11]

[11] Principal Sources: *The Fortnightly Review* (London) ; The *Evening Sun, The Outlook,* the "Military Expert" of The *Times,* New York ; The *Times* (London), The *Sun* (New York), The *Herald* (Boston) ; The *Evening Post,* The *Times,* "Bulletins" of the National Geographic Society, New York ; The London *Times'* "History of the War," The *World* (New York).

IV

ALLIED SUCCESSES IN ALBANIA AND MACEDONIA AND BULGARIA'S SURRENDER—D'ESPEREZ IN COMMAND OF THE ALLIES

May, 1917—September, 1918

SINCE the abdication of King Constantine there had been in the spring of 1917 an occasional sign of military activity on the Saloniki front, but nothing of a major character. For example, in May British troops had struck out in blows that seemed almost like a spring offensive. Nearly three miles of trenches in the Bulgarian first-line system between Lake Doiran and the Vardar valley had been cut, the Bulgar left wing on the Struma front broken, and two positions captured. But after these operations the Saloniki front quieted down and so remained for weeks and months. It was known that the Greek army would be increased from three to ten divisions (approximately 200,000 men), the recruiting and complete equipment to be completed within four months. The army was then far below 200,000 men, but there was sufficient man-power, including the disorganized regulars, eventually to put a force of that size fully trained in the field. Activity on the front did not flare up again until the next year when, early in June, the Greeks made a successful attack on the Bulgarians at Sirka de Legan. These were the first Greek attempts on the Macedonian front since the autumn of 1916, when an Allied offensive culminated in the fall of Monastir. The Greeks in June captured first and second lines and improved the Allied position on a difficult sector and several Bulgarian counter-attacks were frustrated.

Then early in July the eyes of the whole Allied world were suddenly turned away from the absorbing battle-front in France, where Ludendorff was preparing in the Marne salient for his last and fatal great offensive, to Albania, where French and Italians were having marked success against the Austrians. The movement had possibilities which seemed interesting, since the Austro-Bulgar line, leading from the Adriatic eastward past Lake Ochrida, might be outflanked and an offensive launched along the Saloniki front with a view to drawing Austrian, and possibly German, troops from Italy and France. The Franco-Italians in a few days advanced fifteen miles in Albania and thoroughly defeated A u s t r o-Hungarian f or c e s . The battle - front stretched sixty miles or more from the Adriatic eastward to the Devoli River. The town of Fieri was taken and the Austrians retired hurriedly in disorder. Berat, an important interior town, was threatened and by July 10 had fallen. The Austrians recovered it afterward, but it was taken again early in October.

Leading an Albanian contingent was Essad Pasha, who had figured for many years as the Warwick of Albanian politics. After the Balkan Wars it was he who went to Germany at the head of a delegation which offered the

KING ALEXANDER OF GREECE

Alexander, 23 years old, succeeded his father, Constantine, whose second son he was. He had received a part of his education in England

crown of Albania to the unhappy Prince William of Wied. He remained the power behind the throne during the first months of that Prince's short-lived opera-bouffe tenure of a throne. Before the end came for the Wied prince, an Austrian coterie about the King conspired to eject Essad, and had him arrested, but finally allowed him to seek exile in Italy, where, when the Great War began, he became the recognized head of an anti-Teuton, pro-Italian faction among Albanians. When William afterward fled in panic from Durazzo, intimidated by a miniature revolution staged in the hills a little way back from the coast, Essad went back to Albania and became virtual dictator. He cultivated friendly relations with Serbia and, in the late autumn of 1915, helped the defeated Serbian armies to escape through his country to the Adriatic. Subsequently the Austrians recovered some of their supremacy in Albania, with Durazzo as their sea-base. Essad Pasha was a strong man among Albanians, not because he had the support of the whole country, but because he represented the Mohammedans, who were the most numerous religious body.

The Allied forces in 1918 had an advantage in Albania which they did not have on the Saloniki front, since they had Italy's base on the Adriatic at Valona, while the Austrians, except for Durazzo, had to depend on difficult communications through nearly roadless northern mountains. Could Durazzo be taken and an evacuation of southern Albania by the Austrians be secured, the Bulgarian right wing above Monastir would be left in the air. The position of the Austrians in this part of the Balkans had become precarious after April when the southern Slavs entered into the Pact of Rome, by which was reached an amicable political understanding with Italy that involved the creation of a united South Slav State after the war.

Italian forces, aided on land by French and Albanians, and from the sea by British naval units, now began to sweep northward across practically the entire width of Albania. Forces of Albanians under Essad rendered valuable assistance and soon grew to such importance that for a few days Albania held the center of the European war-stage. The Skumbi valley was the strategic objective of operations. Here ran an ancient route of travel from the Adriatic to Saloniki, the only practicable east and west highway across the Albanian mountains, a road the Romans had built, striking southeast from Durazzo, and still retaining its Roman name of Via Egnatia. In possession of the Allies this road opened a way to the Serbian boundary and thence around the head of Lake Ochrida to the flank of the Bulgarian positions north of Monastir. For a year the Allied army at Saloniki had been discharging a political rather than a military mission. With help from the re-

ATHENS FROM THE ACROPOLIS

On the extreme right is seen the Royal Palace; in the left center, the Cathedral. Between the hills in the right distance runs the road to Marathon, twenty-five miles away—the same road that was traveled two and one-half thousand years ago by messengers to Athens, saying the Persians had arrived in Greece. It is to Marathon that the first Marne battle has often been compared as a check to an invasion seeking to impose a lower type of civilization upon a higher

mobilized Greek army it had been defending Greece and at the same time keeping alive hopes of a partial redemption of Serbia. Military operations by 200,000 fresh Greek troops had seemed likely to follow in the near future, now that the right flank of the Bulgarian army was seriously threatened.

The great Roman road in Albania was still in a fair state of preservation in a land of steep mountains and rugged valleys. The Austrians were here fighting with their backs to the wall, for only bridle-paths lead from this road to the north. Secure in possession of the road the Italians could hold Elbasan, the most important town of interior Albania, and could command Durazzo, the Albanian capital and the Austrian army headquarters. The Via Egnatia over which Roman legions had marched to Thrace, Macedonia, and Thessalonica—the road of Julius Cæsar in his pursuit of Pompey to the field of Pharsalia and of Narses and Belisarius in the time of Justinian—thus once more became a strategic highway. The operation developed into one of the most hopeful phases of the war situation. It was in complete accord with the theory of military experts that the way to shorten the war was to make a flank or rear attack upon Germany. It also fell in with André Cheradame's insistent idea, in books and magazine articles, of stimulating to revolt the hostile elements of the population within the boundaries of the Central Powers. It was certain to put heart into Slavic disaffection in Austria and Hungary and into the Roumanians. Austria's defeat in Albania became by July 12 as proportionately overwhelming an Austrian reverse as the Piave rout had been in northern Italy in June. In a three days' advance of from twenty to twenty-five miles, the Italians and their Allies swept forward irresistibly, occupied the whole southern bank of the Semeni River, and entirely enveloped the city of Berat. Activity was developing along the whole Balkan front with indications that the fighting might spread over the 300-mile line from the Adriatic eastward. The right wing of the Austrians, retreating on a 60-mile front, was falling back so rapidly that the retirement in some places bordered on a

rout. Quantities of material fell into the hands of the
Italians and Albanians.

The operations which led to the capture of Berat was a
successful surprize attack. The Italians thrust forward at
night, taking the Austrians com-
pletely unawares. Near Fiere, at
dawn, cavalrymen captured an
Austrian a i r d r o m e, including
pilots, observers, mechanics and
machines. Horsemen swooped down
just as airmen and their helpers
were getting ready for a day's
work. A returning bomber, not
realizing that the place had
changed hands during his absence,
was about to alight when confronted by a squadron of Italian
horsemen who charged toward his
machine. Turning on his motor,
he attempted to rise again, firing
his machine-gun meanwhile at the
horsemen. The Italians answered
with a burst of fire from carbines,
one bullet striking him in the
mouth when he was about fifty feet
in the air. After this happened
the machine crashed to the ground.
On July 15 this small force worked
its way around several enemy
batteries. As soon as the attack
reached the town, the Austrian
officers, in panic, loaded their bag-

ESSAD PASHA

gage hurriedly onto the narrow gage railway-train which
was puffing away at its best when a handful of cavalrymen
riding at top speed overtook and forced it to stop. All the
Austrian officers, together with their baggage and much war
material, were taken prisoners. The first honors in the victory which yielded Berat to the Allies were due to cavalrymen who for twenty hours on one day and fourteen on
another had been without rest or food.[12]

[12] Cable dispatch from Ward Price to The *Sun* (New York)

A startling contrast was here offered between the big elder brother of the Slav, who lay prone and helpless in the far north under the heel of the Teuton, and the erstwhile weaker, younger brother who, thrown prostrate in 1915, was now standing erect and defiant before the mailed fist of the Central Powers. When paralysis suddenly overtook the Muscovite there had come a time which called for union and strength behind Slovenes, Croats, Serbs and Montenegrins—Slavs whose dominions in Central Europe had been split in two for hundreds of years by a Magyar wedge. Germans and Magyars alike had weighed heavily on Slav borders, and yet the Southern Slavs all by themselves had occupied a territory, and had a population so large, that they were absolutely capable of holding their own against outside aggression if only they could have been consolidated into a national whole and been wisely led. But it had been far beyond their powers to form a union which would hold together that great territory. Could they have secured a confederation that joined all Slav lands between Serbia's northwestern borders and the Isonzo River, in Bosnia, Dalmatia, Croatia, Slavonia, and the smaller provinces occupied by Slovene populations, it would have resulted, not merely in a dismemberment of Austria, but in the creation of a Slav commonwealth which in itself would

© PAUL THOMPSON.

WINTER SCENE IN ALBANIA

have been as powerful as Austria was and which, combined with the northern Slavs, the Czechs, and Slovaks, could have reduced Austria to the position of a German dependency.

What had seemed an insuperable barrier had been removed early in 1918 by the Pact of Rome. There were delegates to represent Poles, Roumanians, Czecho-Slovaks and Jugo-Slavs, while men of eminence were there to speak on behalf of Italy, France, Great Britain, and America. The resolutions adopted declared that, in the presence of a common danger, the difficulties which formerly had prevented an agreement between Italy and the Southern Slavs existed no longer, and that united and harmonious action henceforth would be firmly taken. The significance of the event was greatly enhanced when it was remembered that the agreement was entered into after Russia, under German intrigue and military force, had ceased to be a State or nation; and when Roumania, brought to her knees, had been stript of all she possest; when treason and hunger had broken the nerve of Italian detachments, so that the fruits of campaigns had been lost in a few days until the Italian army had fallen back in October before the Austro-German assault at Caporetto at a time when it was almost within sight of Trieste.

At this critical time the Southern Slavs held out the right hand of fellowship to the still undaunted sons of Italy, and in this league believed it had found a means of breaking the Austro-Hungarian yoke. Italy had become the ambassador of Europe to the Slav world and the Slavs had resolved to break their fetters by showing that Pan-Germanism could be dealt a mortal blow from the inside and at its very center. Events in Albania were now moving with a rapidity which presaged a complete transformation of the situation in the Balkans. Every success heartened the Southern Slavs and brought nearer to the Bulgarians the unwelcome necessity of abandoning the Morava valley which they had resolved to keep at any price. When Berat fell and a new line—Durazzo, Elbasan, Monastir—was fairly established, the Slav confederation with its close relationship with Italy began to take visible form. Few then thought that a year later these Southern Slavs and the Italians would be in bitter conflict over Fiume.

British troops at this time started an operation westward of Saloniki to aid the drive undertaken in Albania. West of Doiran they delivered a blow, while in Albania Italians, with French aid, continued to give the Austrians no rest, pressing them back daily and capturing strategic positions and villages. They took Narta and Gramashi which brought their eastern flank appreciably nearer Lake Ochrida. The strengthening of the Allied line meant not only a peril to the Austrians on all their fronts and to the Bulgar line in Macedonia, but the occupation of Albania, which was the western key to the Balkans, with the possible restoration of Serbia and Montenegro, and control of the Adriatic. The Albanians, one of the oldest races in Europe, have as dominant traits devotion to their mountain-land, their traditions, and their customs. They are born fighters and the law of the blood-feud, carrying a dispute through generations, had made their lives a continuous struggle for existence. There were no old men in those mountains; all had died fighting long before they were fifty. They never succeeded in ruling themselves after the time of their national hero, Scanderberg, largely because of irreconcileable differences in religion among Roman Catholics, Orthodox Greeks, and Mohammedans.

Italians and French were rapidly straightening out the Allied line from the sea to Monastir, with Greeks taking part in the fighting. Eventually the Entente forces, now under command of General Franchet d'Espérey, who had made a reputation on the Western Front, beginning in the battle of the Marne, and had now succeeded Sarrail, might begin a march up the Vardar valley, the most practical road into Serbia, but it would prove a difficult road because exposed on the east to attack by Bulgarians. Late in July Austrian preparations for an offensive in Albania were shattered by another drive, in which munition depots, stores of food, and war-materials were destroyed or captured and the Franco-Italian lines straightened at certain points over a front of twenty miles.

After some weeks of inactivity the reconstituted Serbian

GEN. FRANCHET D'ESPEREY, WHO DEFEATED THE
CENTRAL POWERS IN THE BALKANS

army, cooperating early in September with the French forces, stormed three strongly fortified Bulgarian positions and occupied Vetrenik, Dobropolje, and Sokal, the most important part of the Macedonian front. Further east, on the Doiran-Vardar front, the first- and second-line positions were taken over a ten-mile section. This operation was the prelude to an important offensive, in which British and Greek troops were to take part. In a highly mountainous country a Franco-Serbian army advanced nine miles into Bulgarian lines, altho for two years and a half Bulgarian, German and

DURAZZO, ON THE ALBANIAN COAST

Austrian troops had occupied the region and fortified it in a modern way.

The Near East as well as Foch's Western Front thus furnished sensational news. Its significance lay in the sign it gave of Allied confidence in its man-power. Since the Allies now had unity of command, it was assumed that Foch had felt sufficiently assured of his position on the main front in western Europe to indulge in distant and subsidiary operations. German man-power being at a stage where it needed Austrian troops to help out in the West,

Bulgaria and Austria could not expect Germany to give them any help in the Balkans. On this front the weather in summer was usually too warm to fight and in winter too cold, autumn being the favorite season for operations. Serbia had been overrun in the fall, and Monastir retaken in the fall. A campaign now might show results worth while, for Bulgaria was disheartened and on bad terms with Turkey and few Germans and Austrians were left on this front.

The Entente had maintained a large army in Saloniki for nearly three years, unable to help Serbia or Montenegro or cooperate with the Roumanians. It was able only to hold Greece in line and reconquer a little strip of Serbian Macedonia about Monastir, but now that Greece was ready in a military way, and the German and Austrian contingents had been largely withdrawn from the Balkans, the Allied investment in the Saloniki enterprise promised to show returns, for Bulgaria was compelled to defend Macedonia single-handed. Bulgarians and Turks had been quarreling over the disposition of spoils acquired through the Brest-Litovsk and Bucharest treaties and had become unfriendly allies, and Bulgaria faced a critical situation. Her front opposite Saloniki and Monastir had been so over-extended and was so undermanned that she might be compelled to retire north over the mountains, and possibly be driven out of southern Serbia altogether. In her extremity she would certainly call back any soldiers she had sent to the Italian and French fronts.

Two Allied offensives against the Bulgarians—one Franco-Serbian, the other Greek—had opened with striking successes, each on a front of about fifteen miles. The Franco-Serbians advanced more than five miles east of Monastir and took more than 3,000 prisoners. They were working down the valley of the Cerna, which flows northeast and empties into the Vardar south of Veles. An advance in this direction threatened Prilep, an important southern Serbian town forty miles north of Monastir. The Greeks were pushing up the east side of the Vardar, between the river and Lake Doiran. The Saloniki-Uskub railroad follows the Vardar valley, and control of that valley meant control of southern

Serbia. A Jugo-Slav division was fighting with the French and Serbians.

The Vienna peace overtures of September 17—an unmistakable sign of Teutonic defeat as appeared later—had scarcely been published when the Serbians swept over the mountainous region east of Monastir and occupied heights dominating the strongest position in that portion of the Macedonian line. The points gained offered advantages such as the Allies had not had since the beginning of the war. Serbians, whose spirit had not yet been crusht by Austrian

THE HARBOR OF ANTIVARI ON THE EASTERN ADRIATIC
IN MONTENEGRO, SOUTH OF CATTARO

oppression or by Bulgarian barbarity, thus had taken the first notable steps in a long-delayed restoration of their homes. The primary objective was to clear the Vardar valley and capture Prilep, the great enemy supply-base north of Monastir.

The Franco-Serbs, by September 20, were making an advance from Monastir to the Vardar, a distance of seventy miles, the Bulgars evacuating all front-line positions. The prisoners numbered upward of 10,000, of whom the Serbs captured half, besides sixty heavy guns. The Anglo-Greek attack east of Lake Doiran was thirty-eight miles distant from the flank of the Franco-Serbian forces. Serbian cavalry moved toward the Vardar with little opposition.

The Bulgars' chief concern was to escape capture. The east bank of the Cerna had to be held for more than ten miles. Over a country where mountains rise above 5,000 feet communications had been established altho maintained with great difficulty, and the defeat of the Bulgars began to assume the proportions of real disaster. Could d'Espérey's armies push up the Cerna a little further, they would compel an evacuation of all southern Serbia, and if they could reach the confluence of the Cerna and Vardar, would turn the formidable Vardar position at Demirkapu, and force Bulgars to abandon the whole region north of Lake Dorian. The Vardar was a corridor leading into middle Serbia. With the Bulgarian line shattered to a depth of twenty miles, and the army thoroughly beaten, Bulgaria's military establishment was getting to be more or less of a shell. It looked now as if a turn in the tide had really come in the Balkans, which for four years had been the scene of tragic Allied efforts and a grave of Allied hopes.

What had counted here, as in western Europe, was manpower exploiting the method of surprize. The Austrian defeat on the Piave and the German reverses in France had drawn upon Teuton resources in the Balkans and Foch had taken advantage of the weakening of enemy lines. In a new field the world again saw the inexorable pressure that was closing upon Germany from all sides. The drive rapidly developed into an operation of the first importance, the Allies advancing on a front of eighty miles. So sudden a success, after years of defeat, inspired the Serbian nation with new hope of redeeming their homes, and stirred anew the war spirit of the Greeks. It was not too much to hope that Bulgaria would now be conquered, that Turkey would be cut off from her Teutonic allies, and that a new Balkan front would be established from the Adriatic to the Black Sea, threatening Austria-Hungary once more with invasion.

Until the Teutonic hold on Serbia could be unloosed, Central Europe, made up of Germany, Austria-Hungary, Bulgaria, and Turkey, had to be recognized as an entity on the war-map, for it meant the preservation of economic and military lines of communication between Berlin, Vienna, Budapest, Sofia, and Constantinople. Possession of Serbia

THE BALKANS AND GREECE IN THE WAR

enabled Berlin to keep under restraint the Poles, Czechs, Jugo-Slavs and Roumanians, and, without changing names or frontiers, to make Austria-Hungary and Bulgaria her vassal states. No matter how long the war might last, the honor of Great Britain was pledged that Serbia should emerge from the conflict independent and completely restored. Nor was the matter merely one of honor; the safety of civilization was involved. As Belgium, in the west, had blocked Germany's way in 1917, so Serbia if recovered

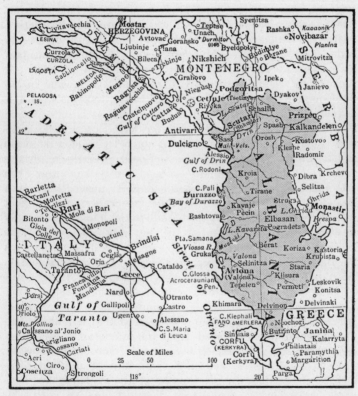

THE FRANCO-ITALIAN OPERATIONS IN ALBANIA

After the Allies had made their way into this country against the Austrians, taking Elbasan and Berat and threatening Durazzo, the Entente army from Saloniki, advancing beyond Monastir, overwhelmed the Bulgarians and forced an armistice

would become a check to the Central Powers in the east. Teutonic deeds of which Serbia had been the victim and the theater were no less atrocious than those from which Belgium suffered. The demand for reparation was as imperative in the one case as in the other.

On a front of more than ninety miles the Allied armies had broken through a mountain zone called impregnable, and were moving swiftly forward on the plains, where ran the vital railroad-system of southern Serbia. Italians were advancing on Prilep, north of Monastir. The Bulgarian army in this region, by September 23, had been cut off from communication with the Bulgarian army in the Doiran section. In the center, Serbian, French, and Greek forces had crossed the Drenska mountain and cut the German-built railroad from Prilep to Gradsko, where it joins the main line from Saloniki to Uskub; Allied cavalry were three miles from the Bulgarian frontier. Imperiled by the advance in the northwest, the Bulgarians evacuated their line from the Doiran to the Vardar. Bulgars and Teutons were in full flight toward the north. The Serbians alone had captured between 9,000 and 10,000 prisoners and 120 guns.

Germany's allies, Bulgaria and Turkey, were going down in defeat together. Turks in Palestine were falling before Allenby's brilliant stroke north of Jerusalem, and Ferdinand was losing his dividends on the Macedonian territory belonging to Serbia—the great prize he had lost at the end of the Balkan Wars, but which the Germans had delivered back into his hands. Turkey had expected to gain Egypt, the Crimea, and Persia, but had secured so far only three petty districts in Transcaucasia and meanwhile had lost Arabia, Mesopotamia, and Palestine, and was about to lose all Syria. The Bulgars, who were being chased out of Macedonia, might soon have to defend Sofia itself. The Bulgar defeat was already almost as crushing as the Turkish in Palestine.

General d'Esperey's reorganized armies had smashed the whole Bulgarian front, had dislocated the Bulgarian right and left wings as Foch's blow in 1917 dislocated Moltke's center at La Fère Champenoise. Astride the Vardar at Gradsko, French and Serbians cut the Saloniki-Uskub railroad, and the branch road to Prilep, forcing the Bulgarian First Army on the Monastir sector into a disorderly retreat north, pursued by Italians, holding the line above Monastir. The Second Bulgarian Army about Lake Doiran had also to retreat, and the difficulties in the way of their reunion were eneromous, with the wedge between them broad and deep. The Allies now held the sole northern artery into Serbia, which was the valley of the Vardar, and could drive up to Uskub through the mountains. On September 25 Allied cavalry, sweeping ahead of infantry on their east wing, reached Bulgarian soil and continued a sweeping advance against the beaten foe. New forces were thrown

© COMMITTEE ON PUBLIC INFORMATION.   FRENCH OFFICIAL PHOTO.

FRENCH OFFICERS TRAINING GREEKS TO USE THE "75"

across the Vardar and Cerna rivers in pursuit. Prilep was captured by French cavalry.

The drive gave promise of far-reaching consequences. Greco-British and Franco-Greek forces had effected a junction. The former had reached Smokvitsa, ten miles north of Lake Doiran. Strumitza, which had been called the Gibraltar of Bulgaria, was seriously menaced. The capture of Prilep not only opened up Serbia by removing conditions which deadlocked armies on this front, but placed Veles and Uskub in immediate peril. Uskub was the natural point of departure for an invasion of Bulgaria, and particularly for operations against Sofia, the Bulgarian capital. Serbian operations in the center were driving a wedge between the eastern and western Bulgarian armies, whose retreat was becoming disorderly, many of the troops deserting. So far 12,000 prisoners and 140 guns had been taken. On all sections from Lake Doiran to the Adriatic pressure was increasing. The Serbs had driven a wedge deep into the Bulgar line, the depth of which was about forty miles. It was spreading out at the apex east and west and gradually forcing a retirement on the entire front.

Bulgaria now accepted Baron Burian's abortive invitation from Austria for a peace conference with the Entente, saying she had sought neither conquests nor the establishment of hegemony over her neighbors. Bulgaria, however, as a matter of well-known fact, had joined the Central Powers for the express purpose of making "conquests." She had determined at all costs to get possession of Serbian Macedonia, as pledged to her at the beginning of the Balkan War, in the terms of the Bulgar-Serb-Greek alliance against Turkey, but she had lost all moral claim to it when she refused to revise those terms in accordance with the judgment of the Conference of London and treacherously attacked the Serbians and Greeks. Then, in 1915, as the price of her declaration of war, Germany had promised her Macedonia and had since delivered the goods to her.

One Bulgarian army had been nearly destroyed as a fighting force, and the Germanized Bulgarian High Command would be hard put either to extricate its remainder or replace it as an obstacle to a further Allied advance to Nish, the junction point of the Saloniki railroad with the main trunk line from Belgrade, to Sofia and Constantinople. Once Nish was reached Sofia would be in peril. This Belgrade-Sofia-Constantinople trunk-line had been Germany's sole connection with Turkey until Roumania was conquered, when the Germans acquired other lines to Constantinople through Bucharest and down the Black Sea coast. The loss of the Vardar valley line, however, would throw western Bulgaria open to invasion, and might start a Jugo-Slav uprising in Austria-Hungary.

VIII.

A GENERAL VIEW OF CONSTANTINOPLE

Bulgarians were retreating on a front estimated at 130 miles. A Greco-British invasion of Bulgaria seemed likely. A great movement had begun which would force a general retirement over the whole front of more than 300 miles from the Adriatic to the Ægean. The capture of Uskub, now imminent, would open the way to all northern Serbia and enable the Allies to advance eastward, flanking the powerful Strumitza position, which was the chief bulwark of Bulgaria against invasion from the west or south, and probably compelling its evacuation, leaving Sofia open to attack. The distance from Uskub to Sofia was about 100 miles and the road was not difficult. America received some credit for the victories in Palestine and Macedonia, altho no American troops were participating in those operations, because, without the American troops pouring into France at the rate of 10,000 a day, Entente forces could not have been supplied for the Balkans.

The Bulgarian army, estimated at one time at 300,000 men, was now retreating in confusion, leaving behind stores of material, and some thousands of prisoners. The downfall of Bulgaria would mean a separate peace and, should Bulgaria drop out, Turkey's strategic position would be ruined. Allenby's haul of prisoners had exceeded 45,000, and the number of guns he captured was over 265. Both victories in the Near East were the direct result of Foch's successes in the West. As an aggressive factor in the war Bulgaria had practically been snuffed out, and on September 25 King Ferdinand asked Mackensen, then in Bucharest, to take command of his armies, block the advance of the Allies into Old Serbia, and preserve Bulgaria from invasion. But Mackensen had something still to do in Roumania and two days later word came that Bulgaria had asked for an armistice of forty-eight hours with a view to making peace. Bulgaria's plea uncovered a state of panic in Sofia. She was in sore straits, and might be willing to capitulate. D'Esperey's army was nearing Uskub, and spreading east toward the Bulgarian border. Serbian troops had reached close to the Bulgarian line. Strumitza, the Bulgarian base above the Lake Doiran region, had been captured. Panic-stricken Sofia profest a willingness, if Teuton aid did not come, to break with Germany and Austria-Hungary and summarily get out of the war. Peace with Bulgaria could not come until she had restored her stolen goods, and so D'Esperey would grant no armistice that had not surrender for its object—military surrender, which meant the stacking of Bulgarian arms. Panic ensued in Berlin and panic ensued also in the German High Command, which informed the German Government that the war was lost and an armistice must be sought.

One of the extraordinary campaigns of the war, and one of the most extraordinary in history, was this Allied drive in Macedonia. The battle of the Cerna-Vardar had begun on September 14, and twelve days later the Bulgars had sued for peace. Tradition promised to enshrine Franchet D'Esperey as the thunderbolt of Macedonia. Prussia's Six Weeks' War of 1866 had been thrown into the shade. A war of weary deadlock, which at one time seemed destined to wear itself out in dreary exhaustion, had been hastened to its end by a lightning-stroke. That it should be the Serbs, the most sorely tried of all the Allies, her men at one time without a foot of national soil to stand on, driven upon a pitiful winter pilgrimage through trackless wastes and across the sea, now returning indomitably to the fight—that it should have been this small remnant of a people, the original target of Teuton ambition and hatred in July, 1914, who struck the blow that shook the Kaiser-power to its foundations was dramatic enough to suit any chronicler of great deeds.

What hurt the Bulgarians most was the fact that, in losing Prilep, their army became completely split, so that forces operating in the west, toward Albania, were cut away from army groups to the east, except for a roundabout road to Uskub, and this was a poor substitute for what the Bulgarians lost. The break spread panic everywhere, and the retreat became a disorderly flight. The entire military force opposed to the Allies entered a state of complete and unqualified collapse. Echoes of Foch's hammer-strokes in the west—victories in the Marne and Montdidier salients, the beginning of the break through on the Hindenburg line near St. Quentin—had become clearly audible in Sofia, where the German war game was seen to have ended. For Bulgarians it became a question of moving quickly in order to secure the best terms possible. Bulgaria now informed the world that, in her opinion, Germany had lost the war.

With Bulgaria hereafter neutral or on the side of the Allies, with Serbia recovered and direct communication be-

SOLDIERS OF THE GREEK ROYAL GUARD

tween Berlin and Constantinople cut off, with Allenby in Syria and Marshall in Mesopotamia swooping down upon remnants of Turkish armies, there was no longer any reason for Turkey to keep up a pretense of fighting. As for Austria, it was certain that her Government, defeated at the front and appalled at domestic dissensions, would jump at any kind of excuse for getting out of the war. The great crisis, and possibly the end of the war, was rising before our eyes. The iron ring that Germany burst out of when she murdered Serbia and hacked a corridor through the Balkan peninsula to Constantinople, had once more been closed. The keystone of the pan-German bridge into Asia was in ruins. Berlin to Bagdad, Berlin to Bokhara, Berlin to Cairo, even Berlin to the Bosporus, had become vanished dreams.

Whether Turkey yielded at once, or fought on hopelessly a few months more, Constantinople's fate was sealed. Allied navies would now enter the Black Sea. The more immediate effects would be a complete restoration of Serbia, an evacuation by the Austrians of Albania and Montenegro and a shifting of the Saloniki front to the Danube. Roumania, meanwhile, was to escape from German tyranny and reassert the claims which drew her into the war, while Mackensen, her conqueror, in a few weeks was to fret his soul in a Hungarian jail. The Jugo-Slavs of Bosnia, Herzegovina and other Austrian provinces, might now revolt and set up that new southern Slav state which Italy had formally recognized. In that event Austria-Hungary would have to recall her armies from northern Italy. Germany's had been a war of conquest, pure and simple, and it flourished so long as Germany was able to retain the offensive, but when it became defensive, as it had been since July 18, all the vitality had gone out of it. The Bulgarians had been smart enough to see that and simply rushed into the international court of bankruptcy ahead of other Central Powers. Bulgaria agreed to turn her railways over to the Allies, but German and Austrian troops still controlled vital links in the line. D'Esperey and his armies had to push northward from Uskub and seize Nish, a point vital to Teutonic-Turkish communications. Next was necessary an advance from Nish down the Morava valley to Belgrade. By October 4 the Austro-Hungarian forces in Albania were retiring before advancing Italians and blowing up their depots. Berat had been captured and Vienna admitted her armies had been recalled.

Italian, American, and British warships on October 3 destroyed the Austrian naval base at Durazzo and the warships anchored there. The attack took place at noon, when

THE BALKANS AND GREECE IN THE WAR

Italian and British cruisers, protected by Italian and Allied torpedo-boats and American submarines, made their way through mine-fields and, avoiding attacks by submarines, got into the harbor. No losses or damage, except a slight injury to a British cruiser, were suffered by the Allied squadron. For the first time in history, American ships had fought in the Adriatic. As Durazzo was founded by inhabitants of Corfu over 2,000 years before the discovery of America, antiquity and yesterday had come face to face.

There were twelve American submarine chasers in the engagement. After the engagement they escorted the British cruiser, which was hit by a torpedo, safely to the base from

GREEK TROOPS ON THE MARCH

which the expedition started. An enemy hospital ship was also taken in charge. During the bombardment, and when the big ships were approaching the harbor, the chasers circled swiftly around them. Heretofore the chasers had been patrolling the Adriatic, dropping depth-bombs, and firing on enemy submarines. The lower Adriatic and the railway which parallels it were now in Allied control. Elsewhere in a block of wild mountain-country more than twice as large as New Jersey, there were no railways except seventeen miles at Antivari and one or two spurs of temporary tracks extending a short distance inland from the coast.

D'Esperey's advance toward the Danube was as much a

detail in the campaign against the Germans as Sherman's march to the sea was a major circumstance in the destruction of the Confederacy. Allenby and d'Esperey were playing the part of Sherman and Thomas, while Entente armies in the West played the rôle of the Army of the Potomac.

King Ferdinand of Bulgaria followed the surrender by

GENERALS D'ESPEREY AND ALLENBY IN CONSTANTINOPLE
Their first meeting after the armistice with Turkey. The two are shaking hands, Allenby being the one wearing a **short coat**

abdication in favor of his son, who reigned for a few weeks and then retired before a revolutionary uprising. Ferdinand's career had been one of brutality and low cunning, his ambitions as boundless and full of greed as his abilities were limited. He cherished a grandiose scheme of restoring the ancient Eastern Empire and of controlling from Constantinople a powerful Balkan nation, in which Greece,

Serbia, and Roumania would be satellites of the Bulgarian sun. In pursuit of this ambition, he betrayed friend and foe alike, and sacrificed the true interests of his kingdom. Had he consented, after the victory over Turkey in 1912, to a just division of the conquered territory with other Balkan States, his country would have been spared the misfortune which afterward befell it. His treacherous attacks upon the Greeks and Serbians not only failed, but brought down upon him the Roumanians and the Turks. Bulgaria was defeated and her frontiers limited on all sides. Greater was his folly in bringing his country into the World War on the side of Germany.[13]

[13] Principal Sources: The *Sun*, William L. McPherson in The *Tribune*, The *Journal of Commerce*, The *Evening Sun*, The *Evening Post*, The *Times*, The *Tribune*, New York.

X